Women, Writing, and the Reproduction
of Culture in Tudor and Stuart Britain

Women, Writing, and the
Reproduction of Culture
in
Tudor and Stuart Britain

Edited by
Mary E. Burke, Jane Donawerth,
Linda L. Dove, and Karen Nelson

Syracuse University Press

41548268
DLC

5-3-01

Copyright © 2000 by Syracuse University Press
Syracuse, New York 13244-5160

First Edition 2000

00 01 02 03 04 05   6 5 4 3 2 1

The paper used in this publication meets the minimum requirements of American National Standard for Information Sciences—Permanence of Paper for Printed Library Materials, ANSI Z39.48-1984. ∞™

Library of Congress Cataloging-in-Publication Data

Women, writing, and the reproduction of culture in Tudor and Stuart
    Britain / edited by Mary Burke . . . [et al.]. — 1st ed.
        p.   cm.
        Includes bibliographical references (p.   ) and index.
        ISBN 0-8156-2815-3 (paper : alk. paper)
        1. English literature—Early modern, 1500–1700—History and
criticism.   2. Feminism and literature—Great Britain—History—16th
century.   3. Feminism and literature—Great Britain—History—17th
century.   4. Women and literature—Great Britain—History—16th
century.   5. Women and literature—Great Britain—History—17th
century.   6. English literature—Women authors—History and
criticisim.   7. Great Britain—Civilization—16th century.   8. Great
Britain—civilization—17th century.   I. Burke, Mary (Mary
Elizabeth)
    PR428.F45W66   1999
    820.9′9287′09031—dc21   99-16570

Manufactured in the United States of America

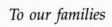

To our families

Contents

Acknowledgments   xi

Contributors   xiii

Introduction
Mary E. Burke, Jane Donawerth, Linda L. Dove,
and Karen Nelson   xvii

Part One: Women, Writing, and Material Culture

1. **Women's Poetry and the Tudor-Stuart System of Gift Exchange**
   Jane Donawerth   3

2. **"More Than Feminine Boldness"**
   The Gift Books of Esther Inglis
   Georgianna Ziegler   19

3. **Patronage and Class in Aemilia Lanyer's**
   Salve Deus Rex Judaeorum
   Mary Ellen Lamb   38

Part Two: Reproducing Cultural Roles

4. **The Education of a Prince(ss)**
   Tutoring the Tudors
   Kathi Vosevich   61

5. **"When Riches Growes"**
   Class Perspective in Pembroke's Psalmes
   Margaret P. Hannay   77

Part Three: Producing Gender Roles

6. **Queen, Lover, Poet**
   A Question of Balance in the Sonnets of Mary, Queen of Scots
   Mary E. Burke   101

7. **"Some Freely Spake Their Minde"**
   Resistance in Anne Dowriche's French Historie
   Elaine Beilin   119

8. **Mary Wroth and the Politics of the Household in "Pamphilia to Amphilanthus"**
   Linda L. Dove   141

9. **Elizabeth Cary's *Edward II***
   Advice to Women at the Court of Charles I
   Karen Nelson   157

Part Four: Popular Culture and Women's Pamphlets

10. **In Defense of Their Lawful Liberty**
    A Letter Sent by the Maydens of London
    Ilona Bell   177

11. **Eve's Dowry**
    Genesis and the Pamphlet Controversy about Women
    Barbara McManus   193

12. **Eleanor Davies and the Prophetic Office**
    Esther S. Cope   207

Part Five: Embodying Culture

13. **St. Frideswide and St. Uncumber**
    Changing Images of Female Saints in Renaissance England
    Carole Levin   223

14. **The Reproduction of Culture and the Culture of Reproduction in Elizabeth Clinton's *The Countesse of Lincolnes Nurserie***
    Marilyn Luecke   238

Works Cited   255

Index   289

ILLUSTRATIONS

1. Self-portrait of Esther Inglis   31
2. S. Wilgefortis or Saint Uncumber   224

Acknowledgments

This project was an experiment since one editor was a professor and three were graduate students. It evolved from a graduate seminar on early modern British women's writings. It was not the utopian feminist collective that we all longed for, but it came close enough to work. It started around dining room tables with lots of food and continued through the birth of three children. All four children of three of the editors were present at the historic printing of the final copy. We divided editorial responsibilities—Linda put together the final draft of the introduction from all our notes, Karen did the bibliography, and Mary and Jane managed data entry and computer foibles—but we all commented on each contributor's essay, and we collaboratively wrote the introduction.

We would like to thank several people—besides each other—who helped this project along. Jennifer Rush began the seminar and the project with us and helped formulate initial definitions of culture. The project would never have moved forward without the impetus and mailing lists of the several conferences at University of Maryland titled "Attending to Early Modern Women" sponsored by the Center for Renaissance and Baroque Studies under the directorship of Adele Seeff, and inspired initially by Virginia Beauchamp. The staff of the Department of English main office at the University of Maryland, especially Janet Duncan, Robin Evans, and Nancy Moore (who is sorely missed), were patient through all our questions and helped with equipment and back patting. Our families were great. We are also thankful to our contributors for their cheerful responses to requests and for their support and advice—especially Carole Levin. We are very grateful for the helpful suggestions from the reader for Syracuse University Press, Suzanne W. Hull, and we appreciate executive editor Cynthia Maude-Gembler's efficient guidance of the manuscript through the press.

Contributors

Elaine V. Beilin is professor of English at Framingham State College. She is the author of *Redeeming Eve: Women Writers of the English Renaissance* and various articles on early modern women writers. Most recently, she edited *The Examinations of Anne Askew* for the Oxford University Press series Women Writers in English 1350–1850. Her current project is *Constructing the Commonwealth: Early Modern Women Writers and History.*

Ilona Bell is professor of English at Williams College. She has published numerous articles on English Renaissance poetry and early modern women and a book *Elizabethan Women and the Poetry of Courtship* (1998). She is currently completing a book on Elizabeth I's politics of courtship.

Mary E. Burke recently received her doctorate in English literature from the University of Maryland at College Park. The American Association of University Women awarded her a fellowship for her dissertation, "Daughters of Debate: Literary Women in Early Modern Politics." She recently served as Project Manager for the W. K. Kellogg Foundation-sponsored project, "Postbaccalaureate Futures," which brought together leaders in higher education, government, and business to discuss innovative ways that universities can achieve the learning needs of workers in a knowledge economy. Her research interests include early modern women's participation in political discourse.

Esther S. Cope was a professor of history at the University of Nebraska–Lincoln prior to her retirement in May 1996. Her most recent publications are a study of Eleanor Davies, *Handmaid of the Holy Spirit* (1992), and an edition of thirty-eight of Davies's tracts, *Prophetic Writings of Lady Eleanor Davies* (1995).

Jane Donawerth is a professor of English and affiliate faculty in women's studies and comparative literature at the University of Maryland at College

Park. She teaches courses in Shakespeare, history of rhetorical theory, early modern women writers, and science fiction by women, and was named University of Maryland Distinguished Scholar-Teacher in 1995–96. Her first book was *Shakespeare and the Sixteenth-Century Study of Language* (1984). She has just finished editing *Rhetorical Theory by Women Before 1900: An Anthology* and coediting the proceedings for the 1997 Attending to Early Modern Women Conference. She has also published two books on science fiction by women and articles on renaissance literature, history of rhetorical theory, and pedagogy.

Linda L. Dove is an assistant professor of English literature at Hope College. She has published elsewhere on the topic of early modern English women sonneteers and is currently working on the use of the acrostic form in seventeenth-century religious verse.

Margaret P. Hannay, professor of English literature at Siena College, is the author of *Philip's Phoenix: Mary Sidney, Countess of Pembroke* (1990), and editor of *Silent But for the Word: Tudor Women as Patrons, Translators, and Writers of Religious Works* (1985). She edited *The Collected Works of Mary Sidney Herbert, Countess of Pembroke* (1998) with Noel J. Kinnamon and Michael Brennan for the Oxford English Texts series. Currently, she is editing *Teaching Tudor and Stuart Women Writers* with Susanne Woods for MLA, and writing a biography of *The Three Mary Sidneys: Lady Sidney, the Countess of Pembroke, and Lady Wroth.*

Mary Ellen Lamb is a professor of English at Southern Illinois University. She has published *Gender and Authorship in the Sidney Circle* (1990) as well as essays on Mary Sidney and Anne Clifford in *English Literary Renaissance.* She is currently working on a book about old wives' tales in Sidney, Spenser, and Shakespeare.

Carole Levin is a professor of history at the University of Nebraska, where she teaches English history and women's history. She is the recipient of the SUNY Chancellor's Award for Excellence in Teaching and has held fellowships at the Newberry Library and the Folger Shakespeare Library. She has published many articles and five books; the two most recent are *The Heart and Stomach of a King: Elizabeth I and the Politics of Sex and Power* (1994) and, coedited with Patricia A. Sullivan, a collection, *Political Rhetoric, Power, and Renaissance Women* (1995).

Marilyn Serraino Luecke is an assistant professor of English at the College of Mount Saint Joseph, Cincinnati, Ohio. Her article, "God hath made no difference such as men would': Margaret Fell and the Politics of Women's Speech," appeared in *Bunyan Studies* (1997). Her current project, *Crooked Ribs and Filthy Clay*, is a study of seventeenth-century women's reinterpretation of the story of Eve's fall as the basis of arguments for women's agency.

Barbara F. McManus is a professor of classics at the College of New Rochelle. She is author of *Classics and Feminism: Gendering the Classics* (1997) and coauthor, with Katherine Henderson, of *Half Humankind: Contexts and Texts of the Controversy about Women in England, 1540–1640* (1985). An interest in feminist theory, feminist cultural studies, and feminist pedagogy provides a unifying foundation for her work in apparently diverse areas, ranging from classical antiquity to Tudor-Stuart England to the humanistic potential of computers.

Karen Nelson is associate director of the Center for Renaissance and Baroque Studies at the University of Maryland. She received her doctorate from the University of Maryland at College Park with a dissertation entitled "Pastoral Literature and Religous Reform in England, 1570–1625." Her annotated bibliography of works by and about Aemilia Lanyer appears in *Gender, Genre, and the Canon* (1998), edited by Marshall Grossman.

Kathi Vosevich is currently manager of technical communications for a software development company focused on telecommunications markets. Before this, she was visiting assistant professor of English at Colorado College, where she taught Shakespeare and Chaucer. She received an NEH Fellowship and was named to *Outstanding People of the 20th Century* and *Who's Who*. Her publications include more than one hundred technical documents and several academic reviews and articles in such journals as *Journal of Popular Literature, Moreana, Sixteenth Century Review, and Rocky Mountain Review*. She is a contributing editor to the textbook *Language, Ideas, and American Culture* and a copyeditor for *War, Literature, and the Arts*. Her interview with Joseph Heller, author of *Catch 22*, appears in *Understanding the Literature of World War II*.

Georgianna Ziegler is the Louis B. Thalheimer Reference Librarian at the Folger Shakespeare Library in Washington, D.C. Her work focuses on early women as readers, writers, and subjects, and on the relation between literature and art. Recent publications include *Shakespeare's Unruly Women* (1997), an exhibition catalog; "Engendering the Subject: Florio's; Feminization of Montaigne's 'Moy-mesmes,' " in *Montaigne Studies* (1996) "Suppliant Women and Monumental Maidens: Shakespeare's Heroines in the Boydell Gallery," in *The Boydell Shakespeare Gallery*, edited by Walter Pape and Frederick Burwick (1996); and "Recent Studies in Women Writers of Tudor England, 1485–1603," in *English Literary Renaissance* (1994).

Introduction

And now I have a Nosegay got,
that would be passing rare:
Yf that to sort the same aright,
weare lotted to my share.
But in a bundle as they bee,
(good Reader) them accept:
It is the gever : not the guift,
thou oughtest to respect.

—Isabella Whitney, *A Sweet nosgay*
(1573), sig. A7ʳ

Isabella Whitney's metaphor of her text as a "nosegay"—a gathering together of various flowers into an agreeable whole—also works as an apt description of the writing process that she and other women of the early modern period undertook. Each writer surveyed in this collection borrowed from a variety of cultural sources to produce a "bundled" result: a text that reflects their process of cultural negotiation. Although fewer women than men wrote during this period,[1] and almost none of their writing survived the process of canonization for masculine literary education, those women who did write were not on the margins of cultural production. They took active roles in negotiating cultural ideologies and systems to gain power, in participating in politics through writing, in shaping the aesthetics and purposes of genre, and in fashioning feminine gender. Thus, in this collection, by studying texts by and about women through the theoretical lens of cultural studies, we explore the

1. One percent of the writings in print were by women—about 125 women appeared in print between 1475 and 1650. See Suzanne W. Hull, *Women According to Men*, 25; and Patricia Crawford, "Women's Published Writings," 211–82. But for a caution against taking printed matter for all of publishing by women, see Margaret Ezell on manuscript publication by women, *Patriarch's Wife*, chap. 3, 62–100.

ways in which "woman" was constructed in early modern British culture and the ways in which actual women worked to create culture(s).

Over the last two decades, scholars of the Renaissance have increasingly turned to newly emerging methodologies and theories to shed light on early modern texts. In particular, the practices of new historicism and feminist studies have yielded examples of groundbreaking research and critical inquiry into the early modern era. Here we adopt the methods of cultural studies, which cannot be summarized neatly; it is a crossover approach that seeks to bind together concepts of culture from Marxism and materialism, anthropology, popular-culture studies, and feminism, among others. As Lawrence Grossberg, Cary Nelson, and Paula Treichler have posited, this kind of approach allows a new kind of multilevel analysis: "Cultural studies is never merely a theoretical practice, even when that practice incorporates notions of politics, power, and context into its analysis. Indeed the sense that cultural studies offers a bridge between theory and material culture—and has done so throughout its tradition—is an important appeal to contemporary scholars."[2] In her essay in this collection, Elaine Beilin suggests that by identifying the multiple layers and references of a text, practitioners of cultural studies create a cultural "hypertext" that succeeds in recentering women writers as producers and reproducers of culture.

Because feminist voices have been strong in cultural studies since its beginning, and because feminists have developed techniques to analyze gender as a cultural practice, feminist cultural studies also offers a means to examine in complex ways the social processes that both inhibited and enabled women's writings. This approach has many advantages for feminists interested in expanding more traditional methods of reading early modern literature to include women. In the words of Judith Newton and Deborah Rosenfelt, feminist cultural analysis "is a way of seeing that prompts us to locate in the same situation the forces of oppression and the seeds of resistance; to construct women in a given moment in history simultaneously as victims and agents" (xxii). To study early modern women's marginalized positions to the exclusion of the very real and important contributions that they made to culture only continues their marginalization and masks divisions based on race, class, sexual orientation, and nationality. Although we recognize the real and terrible ways early modern women were oppressed by their culture, we do not want to overlook the ways that they worked to reproduce culture(s) that op-

---

2. Cary Nelson, Paula A. Treichler, and Lawrence Grossberg, "Cultural Studies: An Introduction," in Grossberg, Nelson, and Treichler, 6.

pressed them, nor can we ignore the ways women oppressed other women. Early modern women, moreover, resisted their cultural limitations and acted as agents of social change, if often only temporarily.

As a term under contention, *culture* is defined variously by the contributors to this collection and by scholars at large. For thirty years, Raymond Williams pursued the question of a definition of culture, and his texts have had a major influence on the definitions and methods of cultural studies. In *Culture and Society 1780–1950* (1958), he argued that a materialist "theory of culture will recognize diversity and complexity . . . [and] take account of continuity within change" but "will take the facts of the economic structure and the consequent social relations as the guiding string on which a culture is woven" (269).[3] He calls for "a complex argument" about culture in *Keywords: A Vocabulary of Culture and Society* (1976, rev. 1985) that links "human development" and "the works and practices of art and intelligence" (91). In *Marxism and Literature* (1977), he points out that it is essential to see "cultural production as social and material," not just economic (138). As a result, a literary tradition can be used to "ratify the present" in the interests of the dominant class (116). But a culture is always vulnerable, according to Williams, because it requires its participants either to identify with it or not; consequently, "negotiation" of culture always occurs at this point of response (118). However, the hegemony will seek "to control or transform or even incorporate" opposition (113). "The reality of cultural process," he suggests, "must then always include the efforts and contributions of those who are in one way or another outside or at the edge of the terms of the specific hegemony" (113). An analysis of such efforts and contributions by early-modern women is what we offer in this volume. In the twenty years since Williams wrote his texts, of course, feminists have accomplished a major feat of recovery of many early modern texts by women that were virtually unknown in 1960.[4] That process of recovery continues in this

3. See also Williams, "Analysis of Culture," in *The Long Revolution* (1960), rpt. in Storey, 56–64.

4. We are especially indebted to the recovery work of the editors of early anthologies of Tudor and Stuart women's texts: Betty S. Travitsky, ed., *Paradise of Women* (1981); Moira Ferguson, ed., *First Feminists* (1985); Katherine Usher Henderson and Barbara F. McManus, *Half Humankind* (1985); and Germaine Greer et al., eds. *Kissing the Rod* (1988). Recent editions of early modern women's texts include *Poems of Lady Mary Wroth*, ed. Josephine A. Roberts (1983), and Wroth's *The First Part of the Countess of Montgomery's Urania*, ed. Josephine A. Roberts (1995); *Poems of Aemilia Lanyer*, ed. Susanne Woods (1993); Randall Martin, "Autobiography of Grace, Lady Mildmay"; and *With Faith and Physic: The Life of a Tudor Gentlewoman, Lady Grace Mildmay, 1552–1620*, ed. Linda Pollock (1995); Elizabeth Cary's

volume with Elaine Beilin's discovery of biographical information about Anne Dowriche, for example, and with Esther Cope's analysis of Lucy Hastings's defense of her mother, Eleanor Davies (a multilayered recovery).

Feminist cultural studies scholars have argued that women, as participants in culture who remain resistant to the hegemony, must then negotiate their relationship with it, changing culture as a result. Christine Gledhill, writing about female spectatorship of film in "Pleasurable Negotiations" (1988), rejects the conclusion that women's opposition to hegemony is always "colonized, alienated or masochistic" (Storey, 242). Instead, she theorizes a negotiated position for female spectators where meaning "is neither imposed, nor passively imbibed, but arises out of a struggle or negotiation between competing frames of reference, motivation and experience" (244). Arguing that "female subcultural activity, resistance and pleasure" is in need of rescue, she suggests that the meanings of texts are negotiated by women and feminists at three junctures: at the site of institutional production, within the text itself, and through the text's reception. This concept of resistance at all points in the cultural process introduces "into the cultural exchange a range of determinations, potentially resistant or contradictory, arising from the different social and cultural constitution of readers or viewers" (244–46).

Transferring Gledhill's analysis to early modern Britain, we argue that women negotiated the meaning of a text at the point of its production because they needed to offset the ideology against women writing. For example, Jane Donawerth suggests in her essay that early modern women were enabled to write by treating poems as part of the gift-exchange system. Within the text, these women intervened to change culture by creating a positive ethos for a woman writer or by revising

---

Tragedy of Mariam, ed. Barry Weller and Margaret W. Ferguson (1994); *Letters of Lady Arbella Stuart,* ed. Sara Jayne Steen (1994); *Diary of Anne Clifford 1616–1619,* ed. Katherine O. Acheson (1995); *Prophetic Writings of Lady Eleanor Davies,* ed. Esther S. Cope (1995); *An Collins: Divine Songs and Meditacions,* ed. Sidney Gottlieb (1996); Anne Askew's *Examinations,* ed. Elaine Beilin (1997); and *Collected Works of Anne Vaughan Lock,* ed. Susan Felch (1999). Recent biographies of early modern women's lives include Margaret Hannay, *Philip's Phoenix: Mary Sidney* (1990), and Esther S. Cope, *Handmaid of the Holy Spirit: Dame Eleanor Davies* (1992). For recent feminist versions of literary "herstory," see *Silent But for the Word,* ed. Margaret P. Hannay (1985); Elaine Beilin, *Redeeming Eve* (1987); Barbara Lewalski, *Writing Women* (1993); and Karen Robertson and Susan Frye, eds. *Maids and Mistresses* (1998). Recent studies of Tudor and Stuart women writers that use cultural studies methodologies in particular include Ann Rosalind Jones, *Currency of Eros* (1990); Tina Krontiris, *Oppositional Voices* (1992); Wendy Wall, *Imprint of Gender* (1993); Louise Schleiner, *Tudor and Stuart Women Writers* (1994); *Political Rhetoric, Power, and Renaissance Women,* ed. Carole Levin and Patricia A. Sullivan (1995); and Naomi J. Miller, *Changing the Subject* (1996).

and revaluing women's roles. In her analysis of the sonnets of Mary, Queen of Scots, Mary Burke suggests that the queen used her political and class status to authorize her appropriation of this masculine genre. The Scottish queen thus redefined a potentially transgressive act as appropriate for her. Early modern women could also negotiate culture at the point they received it, such as when they read alone or in collaborative groups, resisting interpretations offered by the text or turning the text around to women's benefit. The essays included here on the pamphlet controversy show how the women pamphleteers considered themselves to be engaged in an ongoing conversation, reading and replying to earlier pamphlets and correcting men's misinterpretations of feminine roles. As Raymond Williams remarks, culture never gets reproduced wholly or accurately because the culture's participants reinterpret its forms in each and every encounter they have with it (*Marxism*, 116).

But *culture* is not the only term to be redefined in contemporary scholarship. In 1977, Joan Kelly asked the now famous question, "Did Women Have a Renaissance?" Scholarship over the past two decades has shown that the answers to this question are many and various—both "yes" and "no," with many gradations in between. Because of the complexity of those answers, we have chosen to use terms other than *Renaissance* in referring to the period we concentrate on in this collection. Our designation *Tudor and Stuart* offers a more focused period of time than the broader term *early modern*, and because of the extensive recovery of women's texts, we thus had no need to stretch historical boundaries in order to fill a volume. Our contributors survey a range of historical experience—beginning in the early sixteenth century with articles by Carole Levin on late-medieval female saints and by Kathi Vosevich on the education of the Tudor queens, and ending at the civil war with an essay by Esther Cope on Lady Eleanor Davies's visionary pamphlets.[5] We stop our study with the civil war because the war radically altered women's roles and because recent scholarship has increasingly conceded the centrality of women's voices during and after this social upheaval; however, it has yet to pay the women writers of the preceding generations similar consideration. Our collection begins to fill this gap.

Although recovery work is still weighted toward the upper end of the class hierarchy, we have selected women writers who would represent as many classes as possible. Thus, we include studies of the works

5. For studies of women writers beyond the Civil War, see Elaine Hobby, *Virtue of Necessity* (1988); Marilyn L. Williamson, *Raising Their Voices* (1990); Phyllis Mack, *Visionary Women* (1992); and Carol Barash, *English Women's Poetry, 1649–1714* (1996).

of the "Maydens of London" (a group of serving women), Anne Lok (a middle-class Marian exile), and Isabella Whitney (an unemployed serving woman from the gentry), as well as studies of the works of the countess of Pembroke, Lady Eleanor Davies, and Queen Elizabeth. Likewise, we incorporate those Tudor and Stuart women writers who have begun to represent a "canon," such as Aemilia Lanyer, Elizabeth Cary, and Lady Mary Wroth, as well as those who are studied less often, such as Esther Inglis, Anne Dowriche, and Queen Mary Tudor. We regret that we were unable to include an essay on the crucial topic of race in the discussions of this collection. Fortunately, in *Women, "Race," and Writing* (1994), Margo Hendricks and Patricia Parker have collected essays by scholars who use literary, historical, anthropological, and medical materials to examine women's writing in relation to racial imperialism and colonialism and to racial discourse on women in the period.[6] Finally, our study uses the term *Britain* to describe the cultures of both England and Scotland. We cannot call *English* a literature that was written in several languages—English, Latin, French, and Scots—so we use these terms cautiously, recognizing the contested nature of these words and the troubling connotations of English imperialism. As Roger Mason has noted, the Scottish "crown and court alike became identified—and identified themselves—as essentially English institutions" (10). It is this erasure of Scottish history that we wish to resist. Therefore, we acknowledge J. G. A. Pocock's observation in his essay "Postscript: Two Kingdoms and Three Histories?" that "there was, and still is, no 'British history' "; instead, this "term must be used to denote a multiplicity of histories" (Mason, 311).

A more conscious application of the methods of cultural studies to the study of early modern women and writing, then, allows us to explore with greater complexity such contexts as the material circumstances in which women's writings were embedded—the social relations, economic institutions, and gendered materials available to women. In the first section, "Women, Writing, and Material Culture," Jane Donawerth, Georgianna Ziegler, and Mary Ellen Lamb analyze the intersection of women's written texts and the material and financial modes of exchange in Tudor and Stuart culture. Circulated in the gift-exchange and patronage systems, these texts function as material objects in the formation of social networks. The women's works, constructed as gifts, served to cement social bonds, earn money for the authors, or influence major political decisions. Thus, these essays contribute to our understanding not

6. See also, Kim Hall, *Things of Darkness* (1995).

only of individual authors but also of authorship, publication, and the status of texts within Tudor and Stuart culture.

In "Women's Poetry and the Tudor-Stuart System of Gift Exchange," Jane Donawerth demonstrates that early modern women participated in a gift-exchange system that circulated such material goods as coins, jewelry, clothing, and embroidery, as well as original poems and other writings. Anne Lok, Isabella Whitney, and Mary Sidney, countess of Pembroke, all contributed poems to a gift-exchange process, situating themselves as integral members of their religious, literary, and social communities as a result. Moreover, Donawerth argues that these women were able to overcome social prohibitions against writing by seeing their poems as part of a gift exchange. They recorded this authorial negotiation in imagery of the poems themselves as herbal medicine or cloth gifts to readers. Thus, Donawerth adapts methods from anthropology, history of literature, and feminist literary criticism to construct women writers as negotiating cultural constraints. As a craft produced in the home, and as a vehicle for the reproduction of values other than those that were dominant, their poetry was associated with an older, "remnant" (to borrow Williams's term) cultural system. In this way, these women resisted the new hegemony of capitalism.

Georgianna Ziegler's essay, " 'More Than Feminine Boldness': The Gift Books of Esther Inglis," calls into question conventional notions of authorship and publication. She argues that because Inglis's texts do not fit traditional categories, we must expand our notions of author and publication to include not only the language of written texts but also the texts' forms. She notes that "Inglis asserts her 'author-ity' over each text by inscribing her 'self' into its form" through self-portraits, choice of material, design, illuminations, script, and embroidered covers. By defying expectations about published texts, Inglis redefined her books as "handiwork" suitable for women to undertake. Ziegler argues for these books as saleable merchandise, as works of art, as gifts in the patronage system, and as collectibles for display in a private cabinet, thus locating them in the contexts of larger cultural and economic institutions—market, court, gift exchange, patronage, and Protestant politics. By invoking the "conscious archaism" of illuminated manuscripts, Inglis resisted the dominant print culture and reproduced an alternative model.

In "Patronage and Class in Aemilia Lanyer's *Salve Deus Rex Judaeorum*," Mary Ellen Lamb identifies Lanyer's critique of the early modern patronage system, which Lanyer criticizes as hierarchical and mistakenly based on rank rather than on merit. Lanyer's awareness of the wider audience becoming available to her through the new capitalist marketplace allowed her to challenge the old patronage system; however, as Lamb further suggests, "[w]hile the printing press had provided Lanyer with an alternative way of thinking about patronage, it had not yet provided the financial means by which she could let it go." Lanyer thus exploited the fissure caused by a system on its way out clashing with a system on its way in and presented an appeal that encoded different ideological messages for two different classes of readers. Lamb's recovery of Lanyer as a professional writer depends on placing her within these economic and ideological institutions. As a result, she demonstrates how Lanyer resisted the dominant systems in which she participated and debunks the notion that Lanyer built a community based on the shared experience of all women.

Cultural studies brought to bear on early modern women's writings also complicates the questions we ask as we examine how women helped to reproduce the cultural roles they inherited. Although women in general were urged to be silent, women of the royal and aristocratic classes located the authority to speak in their high status. At the same time, these noblewomen were often more invested in the very hegemonic forms that sought to constrain them than women of lower social rank. In the second section of this collection, "Reproducing Cultural Roles," we offer two essays that discuss the ways that Mary and Elizabeth Tudor and Mary Sidney negotiated cultural systems—the masculine humanist educational system appropriated by the queens and the class system appropriated by the countess. Kathi Vosevich, in analyzing the queens' handlings of their royal titles, and Margaret Hannay, in exposing Mary Sidney's identification with the upper class, suggest that women's oral and written speech maintained some dominant cultural constructions but resisted others.

To recover the origins of their regnal styles, Kathi Vosevich investigates the educations given Mary and Elizabeth Tudor. In her essay, "The Education of a Prince(ss): Tutoring the Tudors," Vosevich stresses that these queens' different styles of rhetorical self-representation were influenced by the ideas of their tutors, which she traces through their educational manuals. Juan Luis Vives offered Mary cautious and discouraging pronouncements against female learning, whereas Roger Ascham encouraged Elizabeth's intellectual development. In addition, Vives advised Mary to master the feminine tasks of cooking and sewing, and emphasized silence as an appropriate feminine attribute, whereas Ascham promoted a more androgynous humanist program for Elizabeth and praised her public speaking. According to Vosevich, these "conflicting pedagogies" fostered queens who approached their position and wielded their authority in response to how they had been constructed as female rulers. Although Mary and Elizabeth to some degree reproduced their tutors' visions of the cultural roles appropriate to women, the queens also negotiated models of femininity for their culture as women in public roles. By interrelating cultural institutions and individual development, Vosevich shows how Mary and Elizabeth serve as markers of the cultural production and reproduction of "woman."

Margaret Hannay, in " 'When riches growes': Class Perspective in Pembroke's *Psalmes*," locates the *Psalmes* of Mary Sidney within early modern aristocratic anxieties about class. By altering her translation to reflect her personal experience of aristocratic life, Mary Sidney reveals an authorial bias in favor of wealth and privilege. On the other hand, she also describes the pitfalls accompanying this life, demonstrating, in Hannay's words, "an acute awareness of the dangers that come with high place." Because she identifies with the courtier and not with the poor supplicant, her God's heaven bears a striking resemblance to Elizabeth's court. Thus, in her reproduction of class, Mary Sidney also reproduces a cultural ideology. Although Sidney acknowledges her duty to help the poor, Hannay concludes that her text is far from a critique of the class system; rather, it exhibits "a strong sense of noblesse oblige, of the responsibility of those in high places to protect the poor, even while they disdained them." Sidney participated in and benefited from the class system, yet she simultaneously negotiated the dominant ideology against women who write.

In the collection's third section, "Producing Gender Roles," cultural studies provides the tools for examining how women, despite their circumscribed roles, negotiated power in the political systems in which they participated. Essays by Mary Burke, Elaine Beilin, Linda Dove, and Karen Nelson explore the strategies early modern women used to influence the political agendas of their countries. In order to intervene in the production of this political culture, some of these women writers set traditional feminine discourses against traditional masculine ones, and others set traditional masculine discourses against each other. Thus, their strategies for gaining power in the political realm were various—and variously successful.

In "Queen, Lover, Poet: A Question of Balance in the Sonnets of Mary, Queen of Scots," Mary Burke examines the strategies this queen adopted in order to exercise power in a country fitted for kings. Burke takes cross-dressing as a metaphor for Mary's attempt to use her political status both to occupy the masterful place of the Petrarchan speaker and to appear feminine enough to be attractive. As such, "Mary's poetic

cross-dressing . . . parallel[s] attempts in her own life to balance the demands of being a monarch and a woman." Burke argues that, like Elizabeth, Mary was adept at using androgynous codes to claim the authority
associated with masculinity. By negotiating the conflicting demands of
"woman" and "prince," and by rewriting her role of lover as "wife,"
Mary succeeded in producing an alternative gender role. Burke establishes Mary's engagement with these cultural forms by looking at the
sonnets as part of Scotland's social fabric.

In " 'Some freely spake their minde': Resistance in Anne Dowriche's
French Historie," Elaine Beilin suggests that although women were barred
from public office, "it does not necessarily follow that women writers
were on the margins of political discourse." By placing *The French Historie*
in its historical and cultural contexts, Beilin demonstrates that the poet
constructed a highly allusive text that includes general complaints about
the crackdown on nonconforming Protestants, as well as a specific reference to the censorship and imprisonment of Peter Wentworth, who challenged Elizabeth's authority in a speech to Parliament in 1576. Thus,
under the guises of history writing and poetry, Dowriche offers a Puritan
critique of English religious policy as well as a political critique of the
traditional relationship between subjects and monarchs. Beilin argues
that, as a result of these negotiations, Dowriche modeled an alternative
feminine role that is active, literate, religious, and therefore political.

In "Mary Wroth and the Politics of the Household in 'Pamphilia to
Amphilanthus,' " Linda Dove surveys the comparison of household to
state in Tudor and Stuart political theories in order to expose Lady Mary
Wroth's addition, through her appropriation of this comparison, of a
political valence to the otherwise romantic narrative of her sonnet sequence. According to Dove, Wroth sets the dominant cultural discourse
of the companionate marriage against the household-state analogy to
produce a critique of James's absolutist government. James rejected the
companionate model of marriage and instead disseminated a patriarchal
one, so Wroth's reversion to the discarded hegemonic form of a partnership represents a direct challenge to his rule. By staging this negotiation
within the confines of the sonnet sequence—another masculine form—
Wroth produces a feminine speaker who appears as likely as her masculine counterparts to resist the court's political culture.

In "Elizabeth Cary's *Edward II:* Advice to Women at the Court of
Charles I," Karen Nelson demonstrates how Cary drew on the strategies
of the mother's advice manual to identify Queen Isabel in her history as
a model for Henrietta Maria. Because she used her position as mother of
the future king to influence policy, Isabel represented the possibilities

available to Henrietta Maria for shaping the future of English politics. As Nelson argues, "Cary's version of the Edward II history is no passive retelling of a chronicle; it involves itself in political commentary and religious controversy, and it advocates an active role for women at court." In Cary's narrative, a queen gains power by bearing sons, by performing her role in public well, by employing rhetoric and tears, and by offering patronage. Thus, Cary conceptualized gender as other than "chaste, silent, and obedient," and revised the Elizabethan model of virgin queen. By appropriating the role of mother-as-advisor, she exploited a feminine discourse to produce a powerful role for her queen.

Cultural studies allows the contributors to our fourth section, "Popular Culture and Women's Pamphlets," to read pamphlets as sites of cultural negotiation. We understand *popular culture* not as culture confined to the lower classes but as culture that extended across classes in unexpected alignments and that enjoyed a broad audience, as pamphlets did.[7] Within these pamphlets (some of them written by women), women are portrayed as resisting normative gender roles and as carrying on a conversation with other pamphleteers regarding social mores. Ilona Bell, Barbara McManus, and Esther Cope provide essays that show how women pamphleteers appropriated various sources of cultural authority to reconceptualize women's social roles.

Ilona Bell, in her essay "In Defense of Their Lawful Liberty," considers the collectively authored text *A Letter sent by the Maydens of London* (1567) and its appeal for the rights of serving women in London. Bell shows that the authors use "precise accounts of serving women's daily chores and weekly schedules" to counteract masculine charges of idleness. As a result, the Maydens reproduce a cultural form—that of the defense of women—in order to correct a dominant ideology. Furthermore, they directed their appeal to the "Matrones & Mistresses" of London, who would have been their employers, in an attempt to take control of female readership and to construct all women's liberty as under a general attack. By presenting their defense in pamphlet form, the Maydens sought a broad urban audience of women from all levels of the class hierarchy, both mistresses and other serving women. Bell positions this treatise in relation to the experience of women and of servants and argues that the Maydens negotiated cultural forms in order to change them.

In "Eve's Dowry: Genesis and the Pamphlet Controversy about Women," Barbara McManus identifies an emerging female subject position in the

7. For a more thorough definition of early modern "popular culture," on which ours is based, see Lori Humphrey Newcomb, "'Social Things.'"

early modern "defense of women" genre. McManus argues that the pamphlets of such writers as Jane Anger, Ester Sowernam, Rachel Speght, and Constantia Munda, whether penned by "actual" women or not, present female subject positions and thus sponsored women as producers of culture, not just as products of it. In particular, McManus looks at the "master narrative of Adam and Eve" as a conflicted site that the female defenders could manipulate in order to alter the prevailing discourse of women as weaker and more sexual. Sowernam, for example, reproduces Eve's "dowrie" as her redemptive ability to bear children, even though "most writers of the time claimed that her dowry was rather the shrewish willfulness and unchastity that women ever after inherited from Eve." McManus also attests to the popularity of these defense pamphlets and notes that the "woman question" became part of literate, middle-class table talk.

In "Eleanor Davies and the Prophetic Office," Esther Cope suggests that Davies created a "prophetic idiom" based on traditional feminine virtues, which allowed her to enter public life despite the cultural prohibitions against autonomous women. By valuing her gender as part and parcel of her visionary identity, Davies succeeded in constructing an alternative role for women. Cope notes that "she had incorporated her personal identity in her prophetic persona" by using feminine markers, such as an anagram crafted from her name or the status of mother and virgin, to establish her authority. This consciously feminine self-image was passed on to her daughter, Lucy Hastings, who sought to vindicate Davies's reputation after her death by appearing as a "dutiful daughter and good Christian who is defending a mother who is equally virtuous." As Cope demonstrates, Davies used these feminine codes to negotiate new roles for women, such as when she claims to be God's "secretary," referring to her position as if it were a government office. Although Davies was aristocratic and frequently implied that her audience was likewise aristocratic, she also published more than sixty pamphlets for a public audience and saw herself as a national prophet.

The collection's fifth and final section, "Embodying Culture," displays its debt to cultural studies by relating women's material bodies to their social positions and by elucidating the ways women's material bodies factor into culture formation. The contributors' interpretations take into account the early modern texts written about women's bodies but also the women's bodies themselves as "texts" written on by their cultures. In essays by Carole Levin and Marilyn Luecke, we see the ways women designated female bodies as sites of resistance to dominant ideologies, as well as the ways that society used those bodies to control and ratify cultural norms.

In her essay "St. Frideswide and St. Uncumber: Changing Images of Female Saints in Renaissance England," Carole Levin considers sixteenth-century attitudes toward two female English saints—Uncumber, the saint of unmarried or ill-married women, and Frideswide, the saint of healing, especially by touch. Although these saints' shrines were despoiled during the Reformation and their followers ridiculed, Levin suggests that a synthesis occurred uniting the attributes of these female saints in Elizabeth's image. For Protestant women, Elizabeth was a female figure of authority in their culture who reproduced the saints' specialized functions—a powerful, unmarried woman like Uncumber and a healer of the king's evil, like Frideswide. Levin also relates a startling episode, culled from historical sources, about St. Frideswide's bones, which were exhumed and mixed with the exhumed remains of a Protestant woman, Catherine Martyr, during Elizabeth's reign. The early-modern confusion over women's roles is thus made literal in this mixing of the bones of a Catholic saint and a Protestant martyr. As Levin implies, all culture represents a mixture, with the remnant of the old in the new, and the comingling of these women's bodies represents the mixing of two religious traditions in the body of Elizabeth's church.

In "The Reproduction of Culture and the Culture of Reproduction in Elizabeth Clinton's *The Countesse of Lincolnes Nurserie*," Marilyn Luecke shows how Clinton negotiated systems of power by using the female culture of childbirth. Clinton urged women to nurse their own children instead of hiring wetnurses, which pitted her against the social pressures of husband and court. She based this advice on her own experience as a mother and on the fundamental right of all women to exercise their freedom of conscience. In the context of cultural theories about the dangers of maternal affection, Clinton's espousal of maternal affection as a reason for breastfeeding was a radical strategy of resistance to a husband's authority. Luecke further looks at "contradictory views of the female body" at the Stuart court, which opened up sites of resistance to cultural models of maternity. Because Clinton distrusted breastfeeding as an industry, she provided, in Luecke's words, "a materialist analysis of the impact of the emergent market economy on both women and children."

The essays in this volume, then, use a cultural studies approach to insist that women were not isolated on the margins of social discourse. As Barbara Jeanne Fields reminds us, in order for an ideology to be enforced, it must be continually reproduced and reiterated (112–13 and

117). Consequently, women as well as men can intervene in these ideologies to shape culture itself. This collection furthers the conversation that scholars continue to have concerning the nature and extent of the roles that women played in Tudor and Stuart Britain. In offering the nosegay to her readers, Isabella Whitney acknowledges her effort to "bundle" her flowers together, although she leaves their "sorting" out to others, observing that this activity is not "lotted to my share." Perhaps it should be the "share" or task of practitioners of cultural studies, who can position the texts of early modern women against other cultural forms, sorting out complex readings and multiple meanings in the process. Like Whitney, we, as editors of this "bundled" volume, hope to negotiate cultural systems and reproduce a culture in which women have a recorded history and broader roles.

Part One

Women, Writing, and Material Culture

1

Women's Poetry and the Tudor-Stuart System of Gift Exchange

Jane Donawerth

If women were constrained by early modern English culture to be "chaste, silent, and obedient," and if "silent" extended to writing, how did so many women come to circulate their writings in manuscript or print?[1] Drawing on early modern letters and documents, as well as on anthropological theory, I suggest that many women gained authority to write by envisioning their poems as part of the Tudor-Stuart gift-exchange system, which helped to weave the social fabric of court, community, and extended family.

Letters by sixteenth- and early-seventeenth-century English women show that women participated in and even managed a precapitalist gift-exchange system that was still a fundamental basis of English social life and economy. Centered on the family but extending across all classes to the family's political affiliations, the system circulated food, cloth and clothing, jewelry, animals, medicines, cash, prayers, relics, and favors.[2]

---

1. Many scholars have analyzed the early modern English ideal of the "chaste, silent, and obedient" woman: see Pearl Hogrefe, *Tudor Women*, 3–9; Suzanne W. Hull, *Chaste, Silent, and Obedient*; Lisa Jardine, *Still Harping on Daughters*, 103–40; Catherine Belsey, *The Subject of Tragedy*, 149–91; Peter Stallybrass, "Patriarchal Territories"; and Margaret W. Ferguson, "A Room Not Their Own." On women's publication despite the cultural prescription to be silent, see Margaret Hannay, introduction to *Silent But for the Word*, 1–14; Margaret Ezell, *Patriarch's Wife*, 62–100; Elaine Hobby, *Virtue of Necessity*, 1–23; Ann Rosalind Jones, *Currency of Eros*, 11–35; Mary Ellen Lamb, *Gender and Authorship*, 3–19; Betty Travitsky, introduction to *Renaissance Englishwoman in Print*, 19–20, 25–28; Wendy Wall, "Isabella Whitney"; and Tina Krontiris, *Oppositional Voices*, 1–23.

2. See Davis, "Beyond the Market," 69–88, who emphasizes the communal interchange; and Lisa Klein, "You Humble Handmaid," 459–93, who emphasizes the power and class politics of gift exchange. See also, Ronald Sharp, "Gift Exchange," 250–53; and Mark Burnett, "Giving and Receiving," 288–89, and 299–301.

For example, in the 1530s in France, the Lisle letters record exchanges between family members of money, cloth, clothing, and jewelry. In addition, gifts circulated between the Lisle family and the de Riou household, where the girls lived and learned French: the girls requested or the parents sent a "mastiff," "birds," "a needlecase," "a couple of lanners [falcons]," a "horn," "shoes and hosen," and "an English greyhound";[3] Mme. de Riou was not paid, for teaching French was also a gift.[4] The cover illustration is taken from an accouchement set—bowl and platter—that was designed to be a gift to the mother at a christening after childbirth; it depicts the bustling happy scene of attending on a new baby and mother. The exchanges recorded in the Lisle letters established the "reciprocal dependence" of gift exchange rather than the "reciprocal independence" of barter systems (to use the terms of anthropologist C. A. Gregory). The major purpose of exchanging gifts rather than payments was to establish social bonds.[5]

In a further exchange in the Lisle letters, Anthoinette de Saveuses, a nun who was cousin to Mme. de Riou, convinced Lady Lisle to offer her husband's intercession with the French king to restrain Mme. de Riou's husband from gambling away his wife's fortune; in gratitude the nun returned prayers, medicine, and a religious relic (Byrne, *Lisle Letters* [abridged], 121–24 [no. 99]). And in 1537, gifts of quails to the pregnant English queen, Jane Seymour, prompted her to invite one of the Lisles' daughters to live as a lady-in-waiting at court, giving the daughter an opportunity to make an aristocratic marriage (*Lisle Letters*, abridged, 205–7 [nos. 176-79]). Personal attention and signs of affection were part of the recognized value of a gift, which, as anthropologists Caroline Humphrey and Stephen Hugh-Jones explain, is a mode of "non-monetary exchange which derive[s] from, and create[s] relationships" (18).

In his classic treatise on gift exchange, Marcel Mauss analyzes the three principles of such a system of nonmarket exchange of goods and services: one must give gifts, one must receive gifts, and one must reciprocate (13, 39–42). A sixteenth-century humanist reader could have read these rules in Seneca's *De Beneficiis* (esp. sigs. Ai^r, Aiii^r, Bi^r, Eiv^v, and Gi^{r-v}). We can

---

3. See *Lisle Letters* (abridged) edited by Muriel St. Clare Byrne, 113 (no. 84), 115 (no. 88), 119 (no. 96), and 120 (no. 97).

4. See Fumerton, 36–43, who suggests that children, too, were circulated in the Tudor-Stuart gift-exchange system.

5. Gregory, 42. See also introduction to Humphrey and Hugh-Jones, 12. For the quotations from Marcel Mauss's classic treatise, see 5, 59, and 80. On gift exchange, see also, Pierre Bourdieu, "Selections from *The Logic of Practice*," 190–230, and "Marginalia," 231–41, in Schrift.

see the principle of reciprocity at work in Mary Stuart's 1587 letter to her brother-in-law Henry III of France: facing execution, she asks him to recompense her servants and to pay for masses for her soul, and obligates him with a gift of medicine—"two stones, rare for the health" (Travitsky, ed., *Paradise of Women*, 206–7). In an elaborate exchange recorded in a letter by Elizabeth More, Lady Wolley, to her father on 16 September 1595, Sir Robert Cecil gave Queen Elizabeth three partridges, and she gave them to Lady Wolley, "wth expresse charge that [she] should send them" to her sick father. But Lady Wolley instead returned them to Cecil at Cecil's request, writing her father to send thanks to the queen: in this case, the gift had gone through the hands of four people and, in a matter of minutes, returned to the original giver. Such a cycle is not unusual according to Mauss.[6] Lady Wolley managed this gift exchange for her family, standing in for her sick father and maintaining her family's political connections by giving the partridges back to one of Elizabeth's chief advisors. She follows both the requirement of receiving the gift by having her father pretend to receive the partridges and the principle of required giving by returning the partridges to Cecil. The episode further shows that gifts were not given once and consumed but were *circulated*, gathering value by the hands they had been through and establishing the bonds of community.[7]

In 1603, Arbella Stuart, cousin to King James, wrote Mary Talbot, Countess of Shrewsbury, that she would give the queen "2. paire of silk stockins lined with plush and 2. paire of gloves lined" and the king "a purse" "I am making" for New Year's presents. The letter demonstrates the English custom of gift giving on New Year's Day. It further illustrates that the value of a gift was linked to personal concern rather than cash equivalent, for Arbella criticizes the queen, who "neither liked gowne, nor peticoate so well, as somm little bunch of Rubies to hang in hir eare, or somm such dafte toy"—that is, who preferred jewelry to clothing embroidered by the woman who gave it. The letter also suggests that embroidery on New Year's gifts was done by the women who gave them, even among the aristocracy.[8] Many lists of the monarch's New

6. Elizabeth More, Lady Wolley, no. 130 in Kempe, 317–18. Elizabeth McCutcheon pointed out these letters at a 1990 conference; for a summary of her workshop, see Travitsky and Seeff, 103–5. Mauss discusses circular gift exchange or returning to the giver, 30.

7. In the Shakespeare Birthday Lecture at the Folger Shakespeare Library in 1993, Peter Stallybrass discussed the "magic" of cloth and clothing that had been circulated as gifts in Elizabethan England as appropriated for theatrical performance.

8. Letter no. 35, to Mary Talbot, countess of Shrewsbury, in Stuart, edited Sara Jayne Steen, 194–95. I learned of this letter at a 1990 conference; for a summary of Sara Jayne Steen's workshop, see Travitsky and Seeff, 103–5.

Year's gifts are extant, demonstrating "the affirmation of peaceful solidarity and the establishment of rank" ("Beyond the Market," 70) that
Natalie Zemon Davis assigns as the primary cause of early modern gift
giving.[9] Queen Elizabeth's New Year's donors, for example, are listed in
hierarchical and gendered order: earls and viscounts; marquesses, duchesses, and countesses; bishops; lords; baronesses; ladies; knights; gentlewomen; and (nonknighted) gentlemen.[10] Indeed, Mauss argues that
holiday gift exchanges are ceremonies of recognition of identity, compe-
titions for esteem (8 and 40). "The ritual exchange of gifts," maintains
Lisa Klein about Elizabeth's court, "fostered allegiances and affirmed
hierarchical relationships" (461).

The New Year's lists suggest that the gifts themselves were stratified
and gendered. To Elizabeth in 1598, all the earls gave gold coins except
for the earl of Northumberland, who gave a gown of pink taffeta; many
of the marquesses and countesses gave gold, but others gave pendants
(of gold, diamonds, and pearls), kirtles, petticoats, handkerchiefs, and
"loose gowns"; the bishops all gave gold coins; many lords gave gold,
but others gave gowns, pendants, mantles, and jewels; a few baronesses
gave gold, but others gave waistcoats, taffeta cloaks, loose gowns, embroidered accessories, and, in one case, a painted wooden gilt stool with
"stawberries in silkewoman's worke"; only two ladies gave gold, and the
rest gave bracelets, mantles, ruffs, kirtles, pendants, pettyrobes, smocks,

9. My thanks to Karen Robertson for the references to the lists of New Year's gifts.
Her responses to my paper on gift exchange at the Patristic, Medieval, and Renaissance
Conference at Villanova University, 1 October 1993, as well as those by Carole Levin,
Margaret Jaster, and Lori Newcomb, have helped me greatly. I have looked at the following
New Year's gift rolls: the 1556 list of gifts to Mary, in Nichols, *Illustrations,* no page num-
bering; the lists of gifts to Elizabeth I in John Nichols, *Progresses,* in vol. 1: 1561/2, 1571/
2, 1572/3, 1573/4 (and the 1574 list of gifts from Elizabeth's progress); and in vol. 2: 1576/
7, 1577/8, 1578/9, 1588/9, and 1599/1600. I have also looked at two gift rolls in vellum
manuscript (my thanks to the Folger Shakespeare Library in Washington, D.C.): Great
Britain, Sovereigns (Elizabeth), *Lists of New Year Gifts,* 1584/5 and Great Britain, Sovereigns,
Elizabeth, *List of New Year Gifts,* 1598–99. For lists of other extant New Year's rolls, see
A. Jefferies Collins, 247–53.

10. Based on the Folger manuscript lists under Great Britain, Sovereigns. In the Folger
manuscript for 1584/5, listing Elizabeth's gifts, there are no members of the royal family,
twenty-one earls and viscounts, eighteen marquesses and countesses, eighteen bishops,
fourteen lords, twenty baronesses, nineteen ladies, fifteen knights, thirty-four gentlewomen,
and thirty-four nonknighted gentlemen. In several of the lists recorded by Nichols, gifts
from members of the immediate royal family precede all others; in the list in Nichols's
Illustrations of Mary's New Year's gifts, bishops preceded all but earls and viscounts—
perhaps a difference in Mary's and Elizabeth's placing of the church in the hierarchy.

cloth, and "attire for the head"; only four knights gave gold, whereas the rest gave kirtles, pendants, and pettyrobes; no gentlewomen gave gold, but instead pendants, bracelets, handkerchiefs, gloves, smocks, ruffs, mantles, lawn (a kind of cloth), and a stool; nonknighted gentlemen gave gilt cups, a lump of silver, gloves, ruffs, ginger and other spices, and a book of arms.

Thus, it was more appropriate for lords and ladies to give gold coins and for gentlefolk to give spices or gloves or kirtles, but it was also more appropriate for men to give coins or gowns and for women to give feminine crafts—embroidered smocks or petticoats, looking glasses, worked combcases, and ruffs.[11] Indeed, in the lists of gifts from women, the most frequently recurring phrase is "embroidered all over" (Nichols, *Progresses*, 2:68). For example, in 1577–78, the current countess of Pembroke, Mary Sidney Herbert, gave the queen "A dublet of lawne embrowdred al ouer with gold, siluer, and sylke of divers collors, and lyned with yelow taphata." The ability to give gold was a good indication of status in sixteenth-century England: in the same class, women who gave gold usually gave smaller amounts than did their menfolk, and the value of the gold went down as one descended the hierarchy by class, until gentlemen and gentlewomen could not afford it. In the lists

11. In the list of gifts given to Mary in 1556, all the earls and viscounts gave gold coins, except for one, who gave a gilt cup; all the bishops gave gold coins (smaller amounts), except for one, who gave "Christophersen, a book written, couered with crymson vellat"; many of the duchesses, marquesses, and countesses gave gold coins, but others gave "a cushen-cloth, frenged and tasselled with golde," gilt salt and pepper sets, and "a smoke [smock], wrought all ou' with silke, and color [collar] and ruffes of damaske golde, purle, and siluer"; the viscountesses gave gold coins and handkerchiefs; most of the lords gave gold coins, but one gave crystal cruets and another embroidered handkerchiefs; many of the ladies gave gold coins, and the rest gave clothing, embroidered works, toiletries, and condiments—smocks, gloves, handkerchiefs, ruffs, waistcoats, cushion-cloths, a sacrament cloth, purses, combcases, "a faire christall glase [mirror]," and figs, orange water, and sugar loaves; most of the knights gave gold coins, and others gave a spice box, handkerchiefs, waistcoats, hose, a lute, a map of England, "a booke of Spanish, couered with blake vellat," and "a prymer, couerid with purple vellat"; the chaplains gave gold coins or religious items—a psalter, a book of prayers, a "table" embroidered with the passion; a few gentlewomen gave gold coins, but others gave partlets, ruffs, kerchiefs, smocks, silk bags, handkerchiefs, gloves, combcases, a picture of the Trinity, a gilt holy water sprinkler, a walnut stool, gilt spoons, turkey hens, geese, capons, swans, oranges, lemons, and pippins; some of the nonknighted gentlemen gave coins, while others gave cushions, handkerchiefs, fans, pots of conserves, oxen, cups, pomegranates, a cloak, a crossbow, rosewater, sugar loaves, ginger, nutmeg, a painting of "the Maundy," "a book in Laten, entitelid '*Vita Christ*,'" "an Exhortacion to younge men," and a book in French (Nichols, *Illustrations*, no page numbering).

I found, only men gave books, and only women gave smocks. But some women did give books, since Elizabeth gave her translation of Marguerite de Navarre's "The Mirror, or Glass, of the Sinful Soul" as a New Year's gift to Catherine Parr in 1544–45.[12] Gifts were given to the monarch in the morning, and the monarch reciprocated in the afternoon (Fumerton, 219–20 n. 41) by giving silver plate, the Tudor equivalent of savings bonds. As Arthur Marotti points out, New Year's was also an occasion for giving poems ("Transmission of Lyric Poetry" 22–24).

Thus, women of Tudor and Stuart times participated in this gift-exchange system and often even managed it. In this system, women who were subordinates could garner influence and trade power,[13] and despite the hierarchy, class boundaries could be crossed more freely than in the mainly masculine patronage system, where the purpose was to establish loyalty to a faction rather than more general social bonds.[14] Unlike market exchanges, this gift-exchange system figured into the value of the gifts the marks of caring, of personal concern, and of previous owners attached to them—Golding's translation of Seneca's *De Beneficiis* calls it the "goodwill" of the giver. As a result, the prayers and needlework of women were as important as cash or jewelled "toyes"; even if money

12. On Elizabeth's translation of Marguerite de Navarre's "The Mirror or Glass of a Sinful Soul" for Catherine Parr as a New Year's gift, see Travitsky, *Paradise of Women*, 76–77; and Lisa Klein, 476–81. On women giving books as gifts, see also Georgianna Ziegler's essay in this volume, "'More Than Feminine Boldness': the Gift Books of Esther Inglis."

13. See Barbara Harris, "Women and Politics," esp. 260 and 268, on the conflation of private and public in women's political actions; 265–67, on gift exchange; and 271 and 275 on New Year's gifts.

14. I am following the anthropologists in distinguishing between gift exchange, with its goal of unified community, and patronage, with its goal of political faction. See S. N. Eisenstadt and Louis Roniger, "Patron-Client Relations," 42–77, who argue that patronage differs from gift exchange in three ways—patronage is voluntary not obligatory, it is always hierarchical, and it establishes solidarity around the faction of the patron rather than solidarity with the more general society or community. See also Lewis Hyde on the differences between "commodity exchange" and gift exchange, *Gift*, 4. Frequently historians and literary critics of the early modern period do not distinguish between these different uses of gifts: see, for example, Robert Evans, *Ben Jonson*, 23–30, who subsumes all these relationships under the category of patriarchal, hierarchical patronage; or Krontiris, *Oppositional Voices*, 14, who writes, "Like the position of the courtier, that of the lady-in-waiting was part of the larger system of patronage, which was based on an exchange of favours." Clearly, gift exchange and patronage overlap, but it is useful in my essay to start with the distinction inasmuch as all women participated in gift exchange, but fewer women than men participated in the patronage systems in Tudor and Stuart Britain.

circulated, it was not in itself the standard of value.[15] Indeed, the letters recording these exchanges need to be considered part of the gifts. Arbella Stuart, for example, wished the countess of Shrewsbury to refrain from sending letters to others at court, for her letters were "a favour I desire onely may be reserved still for my selfe" (no. 35, 194).

This gift-exchange system also included other writings as gifts. The earliest poem by a woman in English that I know of is enclosed in a Valentine's Day letter from Margery Brews to John Paston III in 1477: Margery assures her fiancé in doggerel verse

> An yf ye commande me to kepe me true whereever I go,
> I wyse I will do all my myght yowe to love and never no mo.
> And yf my freendys say that I do amys, thei schal no me let so for
>   to do,
> Myn hearte me byddys ever more to love yowe.
>
> (Norman Davis, 1:106, no. 76)

As anthropologists argue about gifts in general, this poem as gift obligates the recipient by sending with it part of the donor's self (Mauss, 12). Because marriage negotiations between father and prospective son-in-law were foundering on the issue of money, this gift may also be a political move by the would-be bride to offer some of herself in order to lower the bridegroom's demands. Constance Aston Fowler's early-seventeenth-century commonplace book seems also to be a record of literary gift exchange, housing poems sent her by friends and especially by her brother: " 'Send me some verses,' " she writes in a letter to him, " 'I want some good ones to put in my booke.' "[16]

Much of English Renaissance poetry by women may fit into this system. Elizabeth Cary notes in her dedicatory poem that *The Tragedy of Mariam* (1603?)—presumably a manuscript book now lost—was a gift for her sister-in-law Elizabeth, which had been preceded by another play (also now lost) given to her brother-in-law (*Tragedy of Mariam*, 66). In Lady Mary Wroth's *Urania*, Pamphilia gives her poems to her cousin Amphilanthus before he goes off to battle, a reference to the sonnet sequence "Pamphilia to Amphilanthus" that closes the 1621 printed *Urania* and that perhaps was also a dedication and gift by Lady Mary Wroth to

15. In gift exchange, money may be circulated but cannot be the standard to determine value of other gifts (Strathern, 175). See Ralph Waldo Emerson, "Gifts," in Schrift, 26, on the value of a gift as resulting from giving part of oneself.

16. On Constance Fowler, see Ezell, *The Patriarch's Wife*, 72.

William Herbert, who was her lover (*Poems*, 24–27). In the rest of this essay, then, I read sixteenth-century poems by Englishwomen—Anne Lok, Isabella Whitney, and Mary Sidney—as gifts, asking what difference this context makes.

Anne Vaughan Lok, from the London merchant class, hosted and corresponded with John Knox, and spent several years with her children in exile in Geneva during the reign of Queen Mary.[17] Home in 1560, she published a translation, *Sermons of John Calvin, Vpon the Songe that Ezechias made after he had bene sicke*, with a sonnet sequence meditation on Psalm 51 to fill up the end pages of the book.[18] The book is dedicated as a New Year's gift to Catherine Willoughby Bertie, duchess of Suffolk, who had also been an exile in Geneva: "I wishe your grace continuall health of life and soule for your preseruation, not onely for this newe yeare, but also for the tyme that shall excede all extent of yeares, beschinge you to accepte bothe my worke and prayer" (sigs. A7^v–A8^r).[19] Thus, the first sonnet sequence in English, as Thomas Roche has pointed out, by a woman,[20] was also presented as a New Year's gift to another woman and so was part of the Tudor gift-exchange system.[21]

17. See Patrick Collinson, "The Role of Women," 258–72; my thanks to Virginia Beauchamp for remembering this essay from reading it fifteen years earlier! My thanks, too, to Carole Levin, for pointing out to me the letters by John Knox "To His Loving Sister, Mistres Anne Locke": see *The Works of John Knox*, Vol. 4, no. xxxii and xxxiii, 237–41.

18. The endpages containing the sonnet sequence are not paginated the way the other pages are. My thanks to Linda Dove, who introduced me to Anne Lok by bringing me a reference to Thomas Roche, *Petrarch and the English Sonnet Sequences*, 155. Because we have continued our discoveries about Anne Lok in conversation with each other, I will never properly sort out my great debt to her reading of Lok's poems, especially to her unpublished essay, "Anne Lok's 'poore basket of stones': Building a Reformed Church in Tudor England." On the question of the authorship of Lok's sonnets, see Hannay, "'Wisdome the Wordes,'" 79, n. 4; and Susan Felch.

19. See Collinson, 265; on the duchess of Suffolk, see Hogrefe, *Women of Action*, 86–103.

20. Roche, 155. As Davis notes, "printed books could be part of systems of gift and obligation in the sixteenth century, passing beyond the transactions of buying and selling ("Beyond the Market," 69); and "the world of gifts expanded as an alternative to the market and market values. . . . Books were dedicated or given for broad social purposes that went beyond strict reciprocity" (87).

21. In contrast, the second translation with accompanying poetry published by Anne Lok (now Anne Vaughan Lok Dering Prowse), *Of the Markes of the Children of God*, a sermon translated from Jean Taffin, seems much more in line with anthropologists' definitions of patronage systems than with the gift-exchange system. Prowse dedicates the work to the countess of Warwick, "a professour, but also a louer of the treueth" (sig. A3^v), apparently aiming to build a radical Protestant faction around the Sidney family and former Marian exiles, addressing an audience of English Protestants (sig. A3^{r-v}).

Designed to wish good health of body and soul to the duchess for the New Year, the book is presented by Anne Lok as both a prayer and a medicine, gifts regularly exchanged by women as we have seen in their letters. Lok distributes the making of the gift among a spiritual community: "This receipte God the heavenly Physitian hath taught, his most excellent Apothecaire Master John Calvine hath compounded, and I, your grace's most bounden and humble, have put into an Englishe box and do present unto you" (sig. A3^{r-v}). The book is a cure for the diseased mind, and just as we feel gratitude to a physician for curing our body, we must feel gratitude to God for curing our souls and to Calvin for making the medicine available to us. Anne Lok requires no thanks from the duchess because of the enormous duty she owes her; Calvin takes as recompense, Lok assures us, any Christian's profit from his medicine; and the duchess is a model of thankfulness to God, expressed through her "profession of his worde" and her "godly conuersation" (sig. A3^v). The epistle thus characterizes Lok's book as a medicine, a prayer, and a gift—"This medicine is in this litle boke brought from the plentifull shop & storehouse of Gods holye testament" (sig. A6^r). Lok invokes both the rule that a gift must be returned (the gratitude owed to God and Calvin) and the resulting community—not only God, Calvin, Lok, and the duchess, but also all "trewe beleiuyng Christians" (sig. A4^r).[22]

Extending the medicinal metaphor to the poetry, Lok uses the sonnet sequence as a meditation aimed at restoring spiritual health:

> With swete Hysope besprinkle thou my sprite:
> Not such hysope, nor so besprinkle me,
> As law unperfect shade of perfect lyght
> Did vse as an apointed signe to be
> Foreshewing figure of thy grace behight.
> With death and bloodshed of thine only sonne,
> The sweet hysope, cleanse me defyled wyght.
> Sprinkle my sould.

The fourteen-line sonnet in iambic pentameter from which I quote is written in plain style. It offers a meditation on verse 7 of Psalm 51, quoted in the poem's margin as "Sprinkle me, Lorde, with hisope and I

---

22. According to Lok's preface, however, this true-believing community cannot include papists (sig. A3^v), because they provide poisonous medicine, "the pangs wherof when the deceiued sick man feleth, he to late spieth the falshod of the murtherous phuysician" (sig. A4^r).

shalbe cleane: washe me and I shalbe whiter then snow." Anne Lok's psalm meditations were published in the same year as the Geneva Bible and typeset in similar but reversed fashion—biblical verse on the side, commentary in the middle. Indeed, the two works may be linked, although Lok does not quote from the Geneva translation; in the Geneva gloss to Isaiah 38, Hezekiah's penitential song, which is the text of the sermon by Calvin that Lok translated, the commentators recommend considering these two biblical poems together: "He left this song of his lamentacion and thankesgiuing to all posteritie, as a monument of his owne infirmitie & thankeful heart for Gods benefits, as Dauid did, Psal 51."[23]

Throughout her sonnet sequence Lok has heightened the metaphors of sickness of the soul and medicinal cleansing. The hyssop used to treat leprosy represents here the grace that cures sin.[24] Anachronistically placing Christ at the center of this psalm, Lok also provides an extremely reformed reading of David's lament: in the quoted poem she stresses Christ's mercy over the "law unperfect shade of perfect lyght," or faith over works fulfilling the law.[25] Throughout the sequence she emphasizes the healing powers of faith: translating the Geneva Bible's "God of my saluacion" as "God of my helth" and praying "my broosed bones . . . / Shall leape for ioy." Thus, this poem as a gift is also conceived as a medicine, something women in this culture made and exchanged among themselves.

Lok also uses the metaphor of a recipe for herbal medicine to link her own meditation on David's Psalm 51 to the sermons by Calvin on Isaiah 38 that she translates: Hezekiah's song, the subject of Calvin's sermons, ends with a recipe that heals him to show God's mercy (Isaiah 38:21). Several of Lok's wordings in her meditative elaboration of David's psalm recall Hezekiah's song: her Sonnet 6 (first line), like Isaiah 38:18–19, argues that the Lord needs to save the speaker so that s/he can praise him,

23. Thus Lok links herself as a poet to these two great biblical models, Hezekiah and David. Linda Dove first noticed this connection between these songs in the Geneva Bible.

24. See Hannay, "'Wisdome the Wordes,' " 65–82, esp. 72 on hyssop as treatment for leprosy. Hannay argues that Lok interprets negatively, as painful, in her translation of Psalm 51, the process of grace that the countess of Pembroke interprets positively, as gift, in her translation. I would suggest, instead, that Lok interprets as comfort the necessary, healing pain, whereas Sidney interprets as comforting God's erasure of pain—neither pictures a God who delights in punishment. See also Susanne Woods's more optimistic reading of Lok's poetry in "The Body Penitent," 137–40.

25. Contrast the verse translation by Mary Stuart, Queen of Scotland, of part of Psalm 51, "L'ire de Dieu par le sang ne s'appaise," which stresses works, in Travitsky, 260, and 200–201.

telling of his mercy; Lok's Sonnet 10, like Isaiah 38:13, emphasizes God's ability to break the speaker's bones; and Lok's Sonnet 16, like Isaiah 38:20, sees the singing of songs—by extension, the writing of poems—as an expression of gratitude for God's salvation. Lok thus places herself among poets who include Hezekiah and David, and she signs her poem with puns on her name—"look," "lock," and "bul-lock" (especially in Sonnet 11).

Dedicated to the duchess of Suffolk, Lok's book may be seen as a gift with political designs on its audiences, meant to build community, religious and social. The duchess was connected to many reformers in the new religion: Hugh Latimer dedicated a book of sermons to her and served as her chaplain; her sons studied with Martin Bucer at Oxford; and she supported both John Foxe and Miles Coverdale in her household (Hogrefe, *Women of Action*, 91–102). She was a popularizer of the word, supporting sermons, martyrology, and translations of the Bible and of continental reform treatises. At New Year's in 1560, she must have just returned from Geneva, and January 1 was also the anniversary of her exile from England in 1555 (Hogrefe, *Women of Action*, 86–103). As a gift to the duchess of Suffolk, Lok's book would further bind the duchess into the English Protestant community and would obligate her to help build the New Jerusalem.

Especially in the final four sonnets, Lok's meditations on David's psalm restate a principle of the reformed community: faith not works. Sonnet 18 suggests that a Christian must not count on an exchange of "cattel slayne and burnt . . . / On altars broylde" (5–8) but must instead rely on "thy swete sonne alone" (9), God's gift of grace. In return for God's gift ("The praise of that I yeld for sacrifice" [14]), one gives one's self, one's prayers, even a poem, all of which are more appropriate than going to mass. The true gift that God requires of his people is a "trobled sprite," a "broken and an humbled hart" (Sonnet 19, margin and 3–4, 11–12, and 14). In Sonnet 20 Lok suggests that, having given a gift, the speaker can then ask God to reciprocate with his grace for the New Jerusalem—"Defend thy chirch" (9). In Sonnet 21, I thus read "in thy walled towne" as London: reformed Christians in this new London under Elizabeth will offer God a new gift—"Many a yelden host of humbled hart" (6). Quoting from scripture in the margin of Sonnet 21, Lok lays her own name among the "bul-lockes" as a gift for God on the altar of her heart, asking other English Christians to do the same.

Isabella Whitney, a London poet of the gentry working class who left service because of illness, similarly uses the metaphor of herbal medicine to describe her poetry as gift. *A Sweet Nosgay of pleasant posye* (1573),[26] Whitney's second collection of poems, self-consciously employs gift exchange as a structural metaphor for a life well lived and well ended.[27] Echoing the diversity of popular miscellanies, the text organizes prose, verse, moral maxims or "flowers," a collection of verse letters to family members, and the "Auctors Testament" or will around the theme of the author's life-threatening illness. Demonstrating how to live and leave the good life through the unifying conceit of the exchange of gifts, these writings transform deathbed advice from sad to joyous. In her dedication to George Mainwaring, Whitney puts her writings in the context of gift exchange. Her poems are flowers, picked from Plat (a pun on the name of the author she used as source for her proverbs), made into a nosegay to prevent pestilence, and given to her friend as recompense for past benefits. "The Auctor to the Reader" figures the reader as recipient, too: "the Flowers are good, / Which I on thee bestow" (sig. A8ʳ).

Whitney begins and ends this section of maxims in *Nosgay* by presenting her poems as herbal medicine, the kind of gift frequently made and exchanged by women. In "The Auctor to the Reader," the speaker advises,

> But in a bundle as they bee,
>   (good reader them accept:)
> It is the gever: not the guift,
>   thou oughtest to respect,
> And for thy health, not for thy eye,
>   did I this Posye frame:
> Because my selfe dyd safety finde,
>   by smelling to the same. (sigs. A5–A6)

26. All quotations are from Isabella Whitney, *A Sweet Nosgay* (1573) from *Floures of Philosophie (1572) by Hugh Plat and a Sweet Nosgay (1573) . . . by Isabella Whitney*. On the few facts and speculations available on Whitney's life, see Travitsky, *Paradise of Women*, 117–18, and Jones, *Currency of Eros*, 37. My fellow editors tell me that the giving of "spiritual bouquets" is still practiced. Mary Burke's mother made them for her mother as a child, and Karen Nelson received one from the Phillipines as a wedding gift in 1990.

27. In *Currency of Eros* Jones suggests that *Nosgay* centers on the moral maxims, the epistles illustrating the Senecan themes of the maxims (37–43). In "Writing Public Poetry," 252–53, and 256–57, Elaine Beilin views Whitney as humanist who adapts the classical genre of the epistle to the purpose of social satire. In "Isabella Whitney and the Female Legacy" (35–58) Wall reads *Nosgay* in the tradition of the female legacy or mother's advice manual, and argues strongly that we must read all the writings together as a patterned whole; Wall also briefly places Whitney's work in the context of gift exchange: "By including letters sent between family members and friends and by referring to the text's place in a gift/patronage cycle, Whitney sets up a textual exchange system within the work" (47). See also Wendy Wall, *Imprint of Gender*, 297–98.

"Smelling" refers to the bouquets of herbs that Londoners smelled to ward off plague and other airborne diseases. This section concludes with "a soueraigne receypt": using the "Iuce of all these Flowers," the poet explains, make a "conserue" to "preserue" your health (sig. C5ʳ). Whitney's poems are thus a series of intertwined secular moral maxims—such sentences were often called "flowers"—put together for the moral health of her readers. As gifts, they are meant to create a bond of "respect" to the donor. Hovering behind these moral maxims drawn from the ancients are the many forms of Christian charity, here recast as obligations in the gift-exchange cycle. Advocating friendship, charity, and "the contented mind," and discouraging the dis-eases of love, Whitney's versified maxims also sketch the virtues expected of those involved in gift exchange: the requirement to give (no. 6, sig. B2ᵛ), especially to friends (no. 58, sig. B7ᵛ), the contented mind that doesn't "gape" after gifts (no. 81, sig. C2ʳ), charity to neighbors (no. 97, sig. C3ᵛ), and the capacity to reward those who ask least (no. 99, sig. C4ʳ).

Whitney extends this metaphor into the epistles to her siblings that are gathered after the "Nosgay." In "To Her Sister Misteris A. B.," for example, she reciprocates a gift already given from her sister: if she didn't write, her older sister might think she had "vainely . . . bestowed expence" on the younger. We see again the linking of family and binding of community through reciprocal exchange of letters and gifts: "for nature dyd you bynde: / To doo mee good: and to requight, / hath nature mee inclynde" (sigs. D1ʳ– D2ʳ). As her epistle to her two younger sisters shows, as well as later letters in the sequence from family members consoling her during her illness, moral advice counts as a gift, as well as material goods. The section of letters to the speaker's family thus defines charity as the family's provision of spiritual and material support; it depicts the family as an institution for facilitating gift exchange even when its members are separated from each other.

The benefit of family is linked to the *ars moriendi* theme of the next section in Whitney's sequence. The letters from and to family in this section constitute a conversation about the poet's ill health, her desire to die, and the proper attitude of a Christian humanist toward suffering— all within a supporting network of extended family. The letters are an enactment of an exchange of love expressed as advice, but this very human exchange of gifts is not enough. This section adds the divine—the speaker praying for God's gift of patience: "Wherfore (my God) geue me that gyfte, / As bedyd IOB vntyll: / That I may take with quietnesse, / What soeuer is his wyll" (sig. D6ʳ).

The fictional "I" of this set of poems does not recover but ends her sequence with her last will and testament, her last act in a joyous cycle of gift exchange that affirms her life and the leaving of it. In this last section, the speaker leaves to Londoners all the gifts of the streets of London.[28] Much like the New Year gift lists, Whitney's poem details the wealth that circulates in the gift-exchange cycle: "Linnen," "silke," "Juels," "Plate," "Siluer," "Golde," "Hoods, Bungraces ['bongrace,' veil or hat to protect from the sun], Hats or Caps," "French Ruffes," "Lawne," and "Purse or kniues . . . combe or Glasse" (sig. E4ʳ). Her death is not an ending because the abundance of gifts that constitute material life on earth continues—the giving and enjoyment go on without her. She uses her goods and moves on, leaving those goods to others—with joy.

Whitney's sequence of prose and verse writings is thus a joyful *ars moriendi*: the gift cycle works effectively as a symbol of preparing for death—through nourishing moral health and education, through establishing a community of kin and friends to support oneself in despair, through acknowledging the joy of the life one leaves to others—because the gift represents not only the humanist Christian's solace (God who freely gave his son), but also the thingness, the joyful materiality, of life.

Mary Sidney, countess of Pembroke, was a patron and poet, sister to the poets Sir Philip Sidney and Robert Sidney, whose mother had been lady-in-waiting and advisor to Queen Elizabeth.[29] The manuscript book of the Sidney translation of the *Psalms* includes Mary Sidney's dedicatory poem to Elizabeth (1599), "Even now that Care," in which she uses not the metaphor of herbal medicine, but the metaphor of cloth to describe the gift (24) that she and her brother have made:

> but hee did warpe, I weau'd this webb to end;
> the stuffe not ours, our worke no curious thing,
> . . . .
> And I the Cloth in both our names present,
> A liuerie robe to bee bestowed by thee. (27–36)

As editors have shown, Sir Philip Sidney translated the first 43 psalms, but the countess translated the remaining 106 and revised her brother's

28. "When she carefully details the streets of London," argues Wendy Wall, "describing the teeming activity and bounty they offer, Whitney casts this world as the object of her own generous bequeathing. She thus creates a myth of ownership to which she asks her reader to bear witness." ("Isabella Whitney," 50); see also Wall, *Imprint*, 301. I would argue, instead, that Whitney is creating a myth of community, where since gifts circulate abundantly, individual ownership is transient and unimportant.

29. On Mary Sidney's life, see Hogrefe, *Women of Action*, 105–27; Gary F. Waller, *Mary Sidney*; and Hannay, *Philip's Phoenix*.

work (*Psalms,* xi and xxv–xxvi). Mary Sidney presents his beginning and her ending the project as warp and woof of a piece of cloth, which they have made into a "liuerie robe" that Elizabeth may bestow on another: the poetry is like a piece of cloth in the gift-exchange system. But the poet also imagines the psalms as wearing this English translation as a livery. As in traditional gift-exchange cycles, the recipient has already given what is returned: Mary and Philip return to Elizabeth the English language that she already owns.

In this dedicatory poem Mary Sidney changes the tenor of the metaphor of cloth yet a third time, presenting David's prayers in the psalms as "holy garments" that "all sort to none but thee" (63–64)—clothing once worn by King David, put on in meditative exercises by every Christian, but fitting exactly only a similar holy monarch and poet, Queen Elizabeth. Mary Sidney also offers her translation of the psalms as a gift personally fitted to Elizabeth, and the personal concern is presented as part of that gift. As often happens in the gift-exchange system, then, this gift also represents an obligation: that Queen Elizabeth be like David, the king who originally wore these clothes, the king whom Protestants used to figure a militant Protestant intervention in European affairs.[30] The poem to Queen Elizabeth by Mary Sidney after her brother's death, like many of her brother's works before his death, thus attempts to garner influence over the queen's religious policies. Here the gift becomes explicitly political. As Margaret Hannay points out, "by reminding the Queen of Philip's death in the first half of the dedication, Mary Sidney was continuing the family tradition of seeking to influence Elizabeth toward a more radical Protestant stance. By comparing her to the Psalmist in the second half of the dedication, she was continuing the tradition of admonitory flattery, which was a standard element in the dedication of Scripture to sovereigns in both England and France" (*Philip's Phoenix,* 91). In the end, according to this poem, servant and monarch give each other the best gifts when they simply act the roles God gave them: the poet must "Sing what God doth," and the monarch must "doo What men may sing" (95).

Many women writers offered their poetry as a gift within the gift-exchange system. Seeing poetry as part of this system in which they had operated all their lives must have made it easier for them to write and to publish. Poetry, like herbal medicines and needlework, was a gift made by women in the household to give to family and friends, and to be

30. On the Protestant politics of the Sidney Psalm translations, see Waller, "'This Matching,' " 22–31; Hannay, " 'This Moses,' " 217–26, and " 'Princes you as men must dy,' " 22–41.

judged not only by the cash value or craftsmanship but also by the affectionate care intended. As Klein suggests, such gifts show "women as active participants in cultural exchange, using their material objects to forge alliances" (462). As a gift, however, poetry still might be a means to establish a larger political support community and even to influence political decisions. Also, like many gifts, once given, it could be given again.

In an essay that includes a pun in French, "Des marchandise entre elles"—the merchandise among themselves, among *her*selves—Luce Iragaray asks,

> *But what if the "goods" refused to go to market?* What if they maintained among themselves "another" kind of trade? Exchange without identifiable terms of trade, without accounts, without end. . . . Where use and exchange would mingle. . . . Utopia? Perhaps. Unless this mode of exchange has always undermined the order of trade and simply has not been recognized . . . [and we have been] forbidden a certain economy of abundance. (110)

In the Tudor-Stuart gift-exchange system, was it possible for the goods to get together among themselves—for women who were legally propertyless, who were sometimes themselves counted as merchandise—to circulate gifts? Certainly, in this system women could own and give many things: the nun's prayers, medicines, and relics mentioned in the *Lisle Letters*; the black velvet dress passed to Mary Sidney from her mother; recipes, medicines, spices, and embroidered "work" from women's hands on dresses, petticoats, and purses; and poems. The poems I have discussed were written by women and given to other women. Poems, especially, may circulate in an "economy of abundance," for they do not require much in the way of raw materials, and because given, they still are not spent.

2

"More Than Feminine Boldness"

THE GIFT BOOKS OF ESTHER INGLIS

Georgianna Ziegler

Sometime early in 1591, Queen Elizabeth received a small, pocket-size book entitled *Discours de la Foy*, written out neatly in a variety of scripts and presented to her by a twenty-year-old woman of French parentage who was living in Scotland. Bound in vellum, with plain pages unadorned by anything other than black ink, the book would have appeared but a modest token amid the splendid jewels and silks that formed the customary New Year's gifts to the queen. Yet, a youthful passion on its pages must have piqued the interest of a middle-aged queen, jaded by court life and political intrigue.

In her dedicatory epistle to Elizabeth, the author reminds her of the strong religious reform tradition in England, going back to John Wycliffe in 1372 and continuing in the reigns of Elizabeth's father, Henry VIII, and of her brother, Edward VI. England, she says, was the first country to which the Savior brought light, and it was the Savior who brought Elizabeth "from dangerous capitivity" to the throne in 1558, not only for her own safety but for that of "an infinite number of your best subjects," for England has become the sanctuary for those faithful who must flee their own countries. Although the author realizes that she is writing many things that the queen knows better than herself, she hopes that the telling of them will not be "desagreable" because it "magnifies the great goodness of the Lord towards your Realm," who chose England for the safety of His church.[1]

---

1. "D'autant qui'il tend à magnifiez la grande bonté de Dieu envers vostre Royaume." "Discourse de la Foy...M.D.XCI," Huntington Library, HM 26068; sigs. [4ʳ, 5ᵛ]. Translations from the French here and in the other manuscripts are my own. Many of Inglis's dedications are written in French, which was not only her family's first language, but that

After other reflections of a similar nature, the author concludes the epistle with a modest account of her own skills and her reasons for presenting this book to the queen. Because Elizabeth is charged with building the church, the author gives this little book ("livret"), which summarizes the discourse of Faith, "that I have written in diverse sorts of letters: and a portrait of the Christian Religion, that I have drawn with the pen, which I send to your Majesty to honor the small knowledge that God has given me in the art of writing and portraying. My small and base condition, the sex, the Religion, and especially the Royal clemency

---

of the court in Scotland. Later in her career, or when she is not sure the person knows French, she writes in English.

I have examined personally the manuscripts by Esther Inglis that are at the following libraries:

British Library: Add. MS. 19633, "Les Quatrains de Guy de Faur Sieur de Pybrac . . . 1615"; Add. MS. 22606, "Les six vingts et six quatrains de Guy de Faur, Sieur de Pybrac . . . 1617"; Add. MS. 27927, "Le Livre de l'Ecclesiaste, ensemble le Cantique de Salomon . . . 1599"; Harleian MS. 4324, "Les Quatrains de Guy de Faur, Sieur de Pybrac, Ensemble Les cinquante octonaires . . . 1614"; Royal MS 17.D.XVI, "Ce Livre contenant cinquante Emblemes Chrestiens premierement inventez par la noble damoiselle Georgette de Montenay en France . . . 1624"; Slane MS. 987, "Livret contenant diverses sortes de lettres . . . 1586" [Psalms 2 and 94].

Folger Library, Washington, D.C.: MS. V.a.91, "Octonaries upon the Vanitie and Inconstancie of the World . . . 1600"; MS. V.a.92, "Octonaries upon the vanitie and inconstancie of the world . . . 1607"; MS. V.a.93, "Les C.L. Pseaumes de David . . . 1599"; MS. V.a.94, "Argumenta Psalmorum Davidis per tetrasticha . . . 1608."

Houghton Library, Harvard University: MS. Typ.49, "Verbum Sempiternum . . . 1615"; MS. Typ. 212, "Argumenta in Librum Psalmorum Davidis . . . 1606"; MS. Typ.347, "Les six vingts et six quatrains de Guy de Faur Sieur de Pybrac . . . 1615"; MS. Type.428, "Argumenta singulorum capitum Geneseos per Tetrasticha . . . 1608"; MS. Typ. 428.1 [Quotations from Psalms and Proverbs, 1605].

Huntington Library, San Marino: HM 26068, "Discours de la Foy . . . M.D.XCI [microfilm].

National Library of Scotland: MS.2197, [Specimens of various styles of writing]; MS.8874, "Les Pseaumes de David . . . 1615"; MS.20498, "Le Livre de l'Ecclesiaste ensemble les Lamentations de Ieremie . . . 1602"; MS.25240, "Cinquant Octonaires sur la vanité et inconstance du monde . . . 1586."

Private Collections: National Library of Scotland, MS.361, Microfilm on deposit, "Argumenta Singulorum Capitum Evangelii Matthaei Apostoli . . . 1607"; Rome MS, Philadelphia, "Une Estreine pour tresillustre et vertueuse Dame la Contesse de Bedford . . . 1606."

University of Edinburgh Library: MS.La.III.75, "A Treatise of preparation to the Holy Supper of our only Saviour . . . [1608]"; MS.La.III.249, "Vincula Unionis sive scita Britannicae . . . Per Davidem Humium . . . [1605]"; MS.La.III.439, "Les Quatrains du Sieur de Pybrac . . . 1607"; MS.La.III.440, "Livret traittant de la Grandeur de Dieu . . . M.D.XCII"; MS.La.III.522, [Specimens of various styles of writing]; MS.La.III.525, "Album Amicorum," by George Craig, 1602–5, with inscriptions by Esther Inglis and Bernard Kello.

that makes you known as one of the most estimable Princesses of the earth, gave me courage to act on the great desire which I have had for so long to greet your Majesty with this present."[2]

One suspects that the naïve freshness of this appeal must have pleased Elizabeth, perhaps reminding her of the zeal with which she had met the trials of her own youth. Here was a young woman appealing to her on the basis of common gender and religion, with just enough modesty but without the usual groveling rhetoric of court poetry. Elizabeth did not like sermons, or as the bishop of Gloucester recalled, " 'Queen Elizabeth was wont to say she had rather speak to God herself, than to hear another speaking of God' " (quoted in Johnson, 54), but perhaps she didn't mind receiving religious instruction packaged thus attractively in rhymed sestets meant to be carried in a pocket and read at leisure. She was certainly willing to accept a second book from the same author eight years later, a collection of psalms, even more beautifully set forth.

The young woman with such passionate faith and desire to please the queen was Esther Inglis, or Langlois, as she still styled herself. The daughter of Huguenots who had escaped from France to London around 1569 and were then resettled in Scotland, Inglis knew in a very personal way how Elizabeth's accession to the throne had made England a sanctuary for the religiously persecuted. She was born in 1571, and when she was nine, her father, Nicholas Langlois, became master of the French School in Edinburgh, with a yearly pension from King James VI. Her mother, Marie Presot, was a skilled calligrapher, and Inglis acquired this art as she grew up in a household where learning was obviously respected and religious faith was central.[3] She was always to see her own talents as a

2. "J'ay appresté ce LIVRET contenant vn sommaire discours de la FOY, que J'ay escrit en diuerses sortes de lettres: et vn pourtraict de la RELIGION CHRESTIENNE, que J'ay tiré auec la plume, lequel i'enuoye à vostre Ma/té pour l'honorer de la petite cognoissance que, DIEV m'a donnée en l'art d'escrire et de pourtraire. Ma petite et basse condition, le sexe, la Religion, et sur tout la Clemance Royale, qui vous fait renomer l'vne des plus recommendables Princésses que soustienne la terre, m'ont enhardie d'effectuer le grand desir que J'ay eu, long temps y a, de saluëz vostre Ma/té de ce tel quel present" (Sigs. [7ʳ–7ᵛ]).

3. For biographical information on Inglis, see A. H. Scott-Elliott and Elspeth Yeo, 12–13. References to this bibliography are hereafter given as *Catalogue* or *Cat*. Since I wrote this essay in 1993, more work in Inglis has been published or is in progress. See Peter Beal; Frances Borzello; Susan Frye, "Esther Inglis"; Lisa Klein; Kim Walker; Henry R. Woudhuysen; and Georgianna Ziegler. According to Robert Williams, in an article on female calligraphers, "it is hard to deny that Marie Presot ranks among the leading scribes of her time" (90).

gift from God; as she says in the "Advertissement" at the end of her small volume, she dedicates to the queen "not only the exercise of my pen, but also all the industry that I have received from divine goodness."[4]

Like many Protestants, however, Inglis was more than religiously committed; she was also politically astute. How might it happen that a little book made by a relatively unknown woman in Scotland would reach the queen, and what accounts for the timing of this presentation of a book on the nature of faith? In the summer of 1589, the French King Henri III was assassinated by the Catholic League, leaving his Huguenot cousin, Henri de Navarre, to take over the struggle for his throne from the Catholic faction backed by Spain. As Henri IV he appealed to Elizabeth for help in the form of money and troops, and although the queen was more favorable to his cause than to that of the Protestants in the Netherlands because she saw a greater danger to her own interests in France, nevertheless she waivered during 1589–91 in the amount of support she was willing to commit (Somerset, *Elizabeth*, 480 ff.). I suggest that because of the ties of Nicholas Langlois with King James VI, Inglis's talents were called on at this particular time to help strengthen Elizabeth's resolve to aid the Protestant cause by reminding her of her own position as "savior" of the English church. That this theory is not far-fetched can be seen as we examine the circles of patronage in which Inglis presented her work over the years.

Some fifty-five manuscript books made by Esther Inglis have been identified by her bibliographers. Most were presentation copies of Protestant religious texts: the Psalms from the Geneva Bible and other versions, Proverbs, Ecclesiastes, the *Quatrains* of Guy du Faur de Pybrac, and the *Octonaires* of Antoine de la Roche Chandieu.[5] The books are often

4. "Non seulement l'exercice de ma plume, mais aussi toute l'industrie que J'ay receuë de la bonté diuine," (Sig. [50ᵛ]).

5. At least three other Inglis manuscripts have since surfaced. In 1993 the National Library of Scotland purchased a manuscript of the *Octonaires* dedicated to the earl of Shrewsbury (1607); in 1994 Sotheby's offered a manuscript of the *Quatrains* (see note 9 below); and in 1995 Thomas Lange reported the rediscovery at the Huntington Library of a sheet with an emblematical drawing of Mary, Queen of Scots, signed by Inglis and dated 1622 (See Lange in *PBSA*). Guy du Faur de Pybrac (1529–84) was a brilliant politician who became an influential member of the religious society founded by Henri III, the "Congrégation de l'Oratoire de Notre Dame de Vie Saine." His *Quatrains*, drawing on the Psalms and the Song of Songs, and first published in 1574, were very popular. See Michel Jeanneret, 352 ff; and *Catalogue*, 15–16. Antoine de la Roche Chandieu (1534–91) was a prominent Protestant theologian and pastor: "In 1584 he was appointed to the Chair of Hebrew at the University of Geneva." His *Octonaires* were not published under his name until 1601 after his death, but they appeared as early as 1586 in an anthology of religious verse (*Cat.* 16).

small enough to be held in the palm of a hand, and the text appears in a variety of calligraphic styles, usually on the recto only, and often decorated with flowers, birds, butterflies, or even little frogs at the top of the page. Later I consider questions of scribal publication and "authorship" of such texts, but first I want to focus on the aspects of patronage.

A list of the thirty-four dedicatees between 1591 and 1624 reveals a striking pattern of groups associated with the Scottish, English, and French courts and primarily involved in the Protestant cause. Between 1591 and 1599 there are no recorded manuscripts with dedications; then in 1599 there are four, dedicated to Queen Elizabeth, Prince Maurice of Nassau, the earl of Essex, and Sir Anthony Bacon, followed by one at the end of 1600 dedicated to the vicomte de Rohan, and three more in 1601 with dedications to the princesse de Rohan, to Catherine de Bourbon, and yet another to the vicomte de Rohan. The second Inglis manuscript made for Elizabeth was given to her (presumably at the end of March 1599 because that is the date of the dedication) along with a letter from King James of Scotland, recommending to her Bernard Kello, the Scots minister who was Esther Inglis's husband. Kello then sent a follow-up letter to the queen in July of that year, asking her permission to leave London, where he had apparently been languishing. This letter and another from Kello to Cecil suggest that the Scotsman was involved in the spy network whereby Robert Cecil, Elizabeth's secretary of state, maintained communication with King James VI.[6] Several of the other dedicatees in this group confirm such a supposition.

In the late 1590s James sought to intervene in "the factional struggle between the Cecils and the Earl of Essex," thinking such a move was in his best interest as regarded the succession. He engaged in secret negotiations with both groups, although he "mistrusted Cecil" and preferred

---

6. See *Cat.* 12 and 35 where the letter is reproduced. Looking at the three extant letters involving Kello, Cecil, and the Queen, Susan Frye has reached a similar conclusion "that Kello was part of the 'transition team' " at the end of Elizabeth's reign. She suggests further that "Kello's demands for payment for his wife's book in fact read as demands for payment for his covert activities." I am grateful to Frye for the opportunity to read her March 1994 work-in-progress, part of a larger project. Jonathan Goldberg, in *Writing Matter,* suggests that "Kello was in charge of passports, testimonials, and letters of commendation" (146). In addition to Goldberg's book, other recent published studies that consider Inglis are Robert Williams, 88–98 and Henry Woudhuysen, 34, 98–99. All place her within the context of Renaissance calligraphy and the circulation of manuscripts. Woudhuysen notes that there is some evidence for thinking that another contemporary master calligrapher, Peter Bales, worked for Walsingham; "his skill in shorthand, ciphers, and codes would have been useful to the government" (33). Kello's calligrapher wife must surely have been considered an asset to *his* career.

Essex; eventually he was persuaded that he ought to throw in his lot with Cecil, which was just as well given Essex's fall from grace beginning in late 1599 (Lee, 101). Before that fall, in April 1599, Inglis's books were presented to Essex and to Anthony Bacon, who was a diplomatic spy and Essex's close associate. In her dedications to Bacon and Essex, Inglis speaks of their "particular favor" to her husband, suggesting that Kello may have worked as a kind of double agent between James and both the Cecil and Essex factions.[7]

Of the other dedicatees, Henri, duc de Rohan (1579–1638), was a major military captain for the Protestant faction in France. He was also one of the key participants in James's secret correspondence with Cecil, smuggling letters from London to the earl of Mar in Scotland. Maurice, prince of Nassau, also a prominent Protestant figure, was a great favorite of young Prince Henry.[8] In her dedication to the duc de Rohan, Inglis hints at some assistance he had shown her both in Scotland and in France, a matter to be more fully discussed by her husband, who is to give him this book.[9]

The two French women, the princesse de Rohan and Catherine de Bourbon, initiated a period during the early 1600s, right before and after the death of Elizabeth, in which Inglis dedicated several books to prominent women who had either distinct Protestant leanings or husbands favored by the king. Catherine de Parthenay, vicomtesse de Rohan and mother of the duc de Rohan, was an ardent Calvinist who gave her fortune to the Protestant cause. An author in her own right, she is credited with several lost works, including a tragedy of *Holofernes* as well as the surviving satire *Apologie Pour le Roy Henri IV*, a family memoir, and a large correspondence.[10] Catherine de Bourbon or Navarre was the sister of Henri IV, with whom James was also strengthening his ties in the late 1590s. She was quite a scholar in her youth and did not revert to Catholicism with her brother in 1593, a fact that must have pleased Esther Inglis.[11]

During 1605–6, Inglis turned her attention to two women who were close to Queen Anna: Lucy, countess of Bedford—the queen's bosom

---

7. BL Add.MS.27927, sig. [3r]; and Bodleian Library MS.990, reproduced in *Cat.* 38.

8. See Akrigg, 1; Strong, *Henry*, 69 and 73. For a detailed discussion of the manuscripts dedicated to Maurice of Nassau and to the duchess of Rohan, see Ziegler, "Hand-Ma[i]de Books."

9. BN, Paris, MS.français 14849, reproduced in *Cat.* 45–46. An earlier manuscript dedicated to the Duc de Rohan has recently surfaced, offered in Sotheby's catalog, "English Literature and History," 13 December 1994, lot 21. It reproduces the *Quatrains* of the Sieur de Pybrac and is dated by Inglis 30 December 1600.

10. *Nouvelle Biographie Génénerale*, 42:258–59.

11. See Lee, 101; and M. M. Michaud, *Biographie Universelle*, 7:214.

friend—and Susan de Vere, Lady Herbert. The countess of Bedford's interest in fostering the arts is well known and has recently been detailed by Barbara Lewalski; she was also part of the Sidney/Harington circle of staunch Protestants.[12] Her kinswoman, Mary Sidney, had translated Philip de Mornay's *Discours de la Vie et de la Mort* in 1591 as "part of a series of translations undertaken by Sidney and his Continental friends to support Mornay and the Huguenot cause";[13] and the Sidney translation of the Psalms was circulating in manuscript by 1599. Susan de Vere, another member of the queen's inner circle, participated often in the court entertainments, including a performance of Ben Jonson's *Masque of Blackness* in 1605 during the season of festivities honoring her marriage with Philip Herbert (Lewalski, *Writing Women*, 31). Herbert, "the first of [James's] favorites in England," was promoted to earl of Montgomery in 1605 (Akrigg, 52). The third Englishwoman in this group of dedicatees, Elizabeth Norris, Lady Erskine, had as her third husband Thomas Erskine, first earl of Kellie, a man who had been educated with James and served as Gentleman of the Bedchamber, Captain of the Guard, and member of the Privy Council.[14]

The men to whom Esther Inglis presented copies of her books in the early 1600s were associated with Queen Anna—Christian Friis, chancellor of Denmark, who visited England—or with the Protestant faction at James's court—Sir Thomas Egerton, or Lord Ellesmere, the Lord Keeper,

12. Barbara Lewalski, *Writing Women*, chap. 4. In her dedication to the countess of Bedford, Inglis recognizes her virtues and beauty as well as her musical talent, particularly on the lute. Although unknown to the Countess, she presents this book to her "fait de ma main," "knowing how your noble nature is given to literature": "Sachant combien vostre noble nature / Est addonnee a la literature" ("Une estreine," Rome MS, f.2r).

13. Hannay, *Philip's Phoenix*, 61. The poet and calligrapher, John Davies of Hereford, made a fair copy of the countess of Pembroke's *Psalms*, probably intended as a gift for Queen Elizabeth (see Woudhuysen, 37, and Kinnamon). In the University of Edinburgh Library there is a commonplace book belonging to Esther Inglis containing, among other texts, a lengthy dedication to Philippe de Mornay by Jacob Dorsannus as a preface to his translation "of Cicero's *Scipionis somnium* into Greek" (see *Cat.* 33). It is likely that she was also familiar with works by Mornay. In 1577 and 1578, Mornay visited his friend, Sir Philip Sidney, at which time Mary Sidney probably entertained him. Hannay notes (61): "As a woman, she could not use the 'Pyke' for the Protestant cause, but she could use the pen, as her brother had done in his translation of Mornay," a statement that could apply equally to Esther Inglis.

14. In Franklin B. Williams's *Index of Dedications* there is a record of only one printed book dedicated to Lady Erskine, Joshua Sylvester's *The parliament of vertues royal* (1614–18), in which she is one of a number of dedicatees. As in the case of several others of her recipients, such as Prince Henry's friends Thomas Puckering and Thomas Wotton mentioned below, Esther Inglis did not necessarily choose them by their popularity as patrons.

and Sir Philip Sidney's brother, Robert, Baron Sidney, created Viscount Lisle by James in 1605, the year before Inglis presented her book.

Beginning in 1606, Inglis focused on the circle of Prince Henry, whose star was rising quickly and who also represented those with strong Protestant leanings. She gave books of quotations from Genesis and Ecclesiastes to the prince's young friends, Thomas Wotton and Thomas Puckering, and later in 1608 presented a work on the Holy Supper to Sir David Murray, Prince Henry's longtime companion and Gentleman of the Bedchamber.[15] In 1614, after the prince's death, which must have struck Murray hard, Inglis gave him a copy of the *Quatrains* of the sieur de Pybrac. This is an especially tiny book—2 by 3^1/$_4$ inches—and its simple dedication, "Pour Monsieur, Tresvertueux, et Mon Treshonore Mecoenas . . . Ester Inglis Souhaite Tont Bon Heur," suggests more the warmth of a personal friendship than a plea for patronage.[16]

To the prince himself Englis presented a copy of the *Octonaires* by la Roche Chandieu in 1607, followed by a book of selected Psalms in 1608 and *A Book of the Arms of England* in 1609. These gifts highlight two of the prince's main interests: the Protestant cause and the practice and study of arms. Roy Strong writes of "the strongly Protestant bias of Henry's household, where attendance at sermons was obligatory," and he quotes from a sermon by Daniel Price preached in 1613 in commemoration of the prince's death the year before: "'His *Magnetic* vertue drewe all the *eies*, and *hearts*, of the *Protestant* world'" (Strong, *Henry*, 54). Unlike his father, James I, Prince Henry also had a passionate interest in martial accomplishments, delighting in the arts of horsemanship and, according to a contemporary account, "'Now also delighting to confer, both with his own, and other strangers, and great Captains, of all Manner of Wars, Battle, Furniture, Arms by Sea and Land, . . . [etc.].'"[17]

Esther Inglis was obviously aware of and catered to these interests, suggesting that she had close contacts within the prince's household. Indeed, *A Book of Armes of England* represents a departure from the usual religious nature of her offerings. In a splendid volume, bound in green velvet with the Prince of Wales's feathers embroidered on front and back covers, she presents the coats-of-arms and crests of sixty-four members of the English nobility. The dedication, written within "a heart-shaped

15. Both Peter Bales and John Davies of Hereford were writing masters to Prince Henry, and Davies also tutored Thomas Puckering (see Woudhuysen, 35, 37, 38). These young courtiers obviously were familiar with and prized finely written books.

16. "Les Quatrains," BL.Harleian MS.4324, sig.[2r].

17. Quoted in Strong, *Henry*, 68; see also Akrigg, 129.

wreath of green leaves with red and gold flowers, surmounted by a hand holding a pen" (Scott-Elliot and Yeo, 65), emblematizes the frame in which it is placed: "'As your Highnes sees heir the figure of a heart and hand, even so the lively heart and hand of hir who formed it, so long as I breath ar vowed to your most Excellent Highnes service. Receave then, Sir, in good pairt this litle Mytte doone by Your most humble servand Esther Inglis.'"[18] After Prince Henry's death, Inglis dedicated a copy of the *Quatrains* to Joseph Hall, writer and one of the prince's chaplains "from a stoutly puritan background" (Strong, *Henry*, 53); the Psalms to King James; the *Quatrains* to his favorite, the ill-fated Robert Carr, earl of Somerset; and four books to Prince Charles: the *Quatrains* (1615), *Octonaires* (1615), *Psalms* (1624), and another of her masterpieces, the *Emblems* of Georgette de Montenay (1624), were reascribed to members of the English nobility.

All of these dedications indicate that through her own Huguenot background and later marriage to a Protestant minister who worked on James's behalf, Esther Inglis developed close ties with the court of James and especially with the more strictly Protestant circles of Queen Anna and Prince Henry.[19] Most of her works circulated at the English court were French versions of biblical texts and moral verses that were important in the Protestant tradition. Obviously there were religious and political as well as monetary reasons for such circulation, but the recycling or reprocessing of what were mostly already printed texts back through manuscript raises interesting questions about publication, authority, and the nature of these texts.

In his book on scribal publication, Harold Love defines publication broadly "as a social activity," occurring at that "moment at which a text passes from" the private to the public domain (39). Yet the biblical and poetic texts that Inglis transcribed in her large repertoire of calligraphic styles were *already* in the public domain. They were now being reinscribed

---

18. MS Private Collection, Norfolk; cited in *Catalogue*, 66. Inglis's reference here is to the widow who had nothing but two mites to put into the collection box at the Temple (see Mark 12:41–44).

19. Barbara Lewalski has noted that although Queen Anna herself seems to have had Catholic leanings, "she chose her closest associates from the Essex-Sidney faction of internationalist Protestants, whose hopes centered on her son Prince Henry. . . . Most of them were kin to her favorite and most influential courtier, the Countess of Bedford" (*Writing Women*, 23).

into a more private mode and recirculated to a more limited audience. Were they still being "published"? Two of Love's other criteria for defining a publication suggest that they were. One of these is profitability. As Love points out, "once the charges of copying and paper had been met, the presentation of a work in manuscript to a well-disposed patron could be expected to bring in a sum commensurate with that from the dedicating of a printed book." Furthermore, "the presentation could then be repeated to other patrons" (59). As we have seen, Inglis recycled the same texts to different patrons, and presumably this practice proved remunerative as well as politically useful. We have records of two payments to her, both from Prince Henry: on 20 April 1609 she was paid £5. from his household accounts "'for geving a booke of armes to his highnes'"; in 1612 a £22 payment was presumably for the book of Psalms she gave the prince not long before his death.[20]

One of Love's other criteria is what he calls "the dress of texts, in the sense of appearance as well as style"—in other words, the care with which a manuscript is written and the quality of the paper or vellum (42), to which I might add the quality of the binding and the presentation of the text on the page. There is no question that Inglis's manuscripts are "published" by her as gift objects. Not only are they showpieces of her technical skills with the pen, but many are beautifully bound, either in gold-tooled leather or in embroidered cloth bindings of velvet or silk, which she herself may have created. As Peter Beal has suggested, "Esther Inglis's calligraphic skills are basically an extension in the field of manuscripts of the traditional feminine handicraft of needlework." She *"literally* exchanges the needle for the pen" (Beal, 14, note 65, and private correspondence, 20 Dec. 1998).[21]

20. *Cat.* 12, 14, and 68. The Privy Purse records kept by David Murray for the prince reveal a number of payments for books, sometimes just to "a stranger" or "a frenchman" or "a poore man." The payments range from £2 to £4.10s; the £22 received by Inglis was a very large amount, compared, for example, with the £8.13s.4p paid to the man who cataloged the Lumley Library for the prince. Perhaps it represented a kind of terminal gift of patronage after the prince's death. See PRO SP 14/57/89.

21. See also *Cat.* 21. Upon recent examination of "Argumenta," Folger MS V.a.94, bound in red velvet with seed pearl, an embroidery specialist thought that the work was probably not that of a professional embroiderer. Like Beal, Susan Frye also suggests that "Inglis and other women calligraphers, embroiderers, translators, and poets who copied the work of males and also of one another, worked outward from approved domestic arts to the nonthreatening copying of others' texts through translation and calligraphy toward seeking recognition for their work in the public domain" (unpublished manuscript, March 1994). It might be noted, however, that a number of embroiderers were men who also copied patterns from printed books.

If we concede then that Inglis's books represent a special form of scribal publication, what were the results of reprocessing a printed text as a manuscript? In his calligraphic manual published in 1550, the Spaniard Juan de Yciar reminds the reader, "no print can quite compare with the work of the living hand" (8). Three years later in his dedication to a similar work, Wolfgang Fugger of Nuremberg explains how he sees writing as a gift from God that permits the existence of art and knowledge. Writing, he claims, is the means by which speech and thought can be made to affect "another man's understanding, opinion, mood and sense" (7). Modern critics such as Walter Ong and Martin Elsky see writing as moving "words from the sound world to a world of visual space," but still allowing for a recollection of the oral; print technology, on the other hand, "locks words into [visual] position" more relentlessly.[22] In the manuscript "world of visual space," Elsky argues, quoting Thomas Smith, "'letters are the pictures of spoken expression'"; they do not replace that expression, but they can serve as an "aide de memoire" for it.[23] Noting the difficulty of scripts, even in small books for private devotion, Elsky posits that they were not *meant* to be read through but to stand "as a memory aid for the spoken word" (130).

All of these characteristics of the manuscript format—its link with oral tradition, its spacial and pictorial qualities, its service as an intermediary between one person's thought and another's understanding, and its use as a memory aid—apply especially well to the biblical and moral texts chosen by Esther Inglis.

The lyric parts of the Bible—"Job, the Psalms, Proverbs, Ecclesiastes, and the Song of Solomon"—were of great importance to the Protestant literary tradition of early modern France and England (Lewalski, *Protestant Poetics*, 32). Of these, the Psalms formed the central text of Protestant faith and meditation. In France, the Huguenots read the perils of the Israelites as their own, memorializing the St. Bartholomew Massacre with the words of the Psalms, continuing to sing the Psalms publicly and privately in defiance of the prohibition under Henri II, and using Psalm texts to identify fellow Protestants (Diefendorf, 42–44). During the reign of Henri III, by contrast, translations of the Psalms were encouraged, and the king himself founded a religious group of courtiers, churchmen, and humanists for meditation and the study of the relationship among religion, morality, and the arts (Jeanneret, 35 ff.). The Psalms thus provided

---

22. Elsky, 115; Ong, *Orality and Literacy*, 121.

23. Thomas Smith, *De recta et emendata linguae Anglicae scriptione . . .* (Paris, 1568), quoted in Elsky, 117; see also Elsky, 115.

a bridge between French Catholics and Protestants, and the royal fellowship included the Catholic author of the *Quatrains* so frequently distributed by Inglis, Guy du Faur de Pybrac, as well as the Protestant commentator on the Psalms, Agrippa d'Aubigné (Jeanneret, 354–55). In England the Psalms were equally important both in their own right and as an inspiration for English poets. A large number of versions and translations were available: the French translations by Theodore de Bèze and Clément Marot, the ever-popular Sternhold-Hopkins metrical version circulated in more than five hundred editions by 1640, and the translation by Sir Philip Sidney and Mary Sidney, "written and widely circulated between 1589–1599."[24]

In the preface to his *Méditations sur les Psaumes*, Agrippa d'Aubigné says this to the reader about his chosen text: "the passages of Scripture are not only like enamel on gold, but like exquisite stones, and raise up the most elevated language, confirm by axioms, prove by Heavenly decree, illustrate by examples and revive those spirits who love God by ravishing light and perfect beauty."[25] One can add the more mundane observation from the title page of the Sternhold-Hopkins version that the Psalms are "'Very mete to be used of all sortes of people privately for their solace and comfort'" (quoted in Lewalski, *Protestant Poetics*, 40). Taken together, these two passages provide a defining context for the religious texts Inglis produced. Each of her books based on the Bible gives only a selection from Psalms, Ecclesiastes, Proverbs, or Genesis; the point was not to be comprehensive but to present the texts—jewels themselves, as d'Aubigné suggests—in a beautiful framework that would encourage the recipient to return to them again and again for private meditation. The intricately drawn title pages, ornamental designs, and calligraphic bravura that inform each of them give delight while drawing the reader into the spiritual and moral content. Because the texts themselves are often incomplete or are difficult to decipher through their ornamentation, the reader is also called upon to recollect her or his memory of the oral tradition to which the lyrics properly belong.

Inglis understood perfectly how her little books should be used. In her dedication of Psalms to Prince Maurice of Nassau in 1599, she writes: "While the variety of handwriting delights the sight the spirit may similarly be raised towards the great Creator, by the diversity of prayers and

24. See Blayney, "The Numbers Game," 399, who revises the number given by Lewalski, *Protestant Poetics*, 39–40.

25. Agrippa d'Aubigné (1969 ed.), 493; translation mine.

Self-portrait of Esther Inglis from Folger MS.v.a.93, *Les Psaumes de David* (1599). By permission of the Folger Shakespeare Library.

Royal songs sung by the great Prophet [David]."[26] In a version of the *Octonaires* presented in 1607 to her friend and landlord, William Jeffrey, Inglis recalls the story of Alcides who chose Lady Virtue over Vice, for Virtue persuaded "him with gifts and graces of the soule" that led him to the Castle of Felicity. An obvious parallel is suggested with her own gift of virtuous verses, a "singular work of my pen and pensill for recreation of your mynd," designed to make him "persist in Virtue to the end."[27]

The small size of many of Inglis's books also points to the very personal nature of their use. She asks Maurice of Nassau to accept "this little booklet ['petit LIVRET'] written by my hand in a little volume to be more easily carried"; the prince, then serving as governor and captain general of the United Provinces of the Low Countries, would have had little space for books in his baggage and little time for reflection, but a volume of such small size could be slipped easily into a pocket and perused in odd moments. She imagines him "leafing through it often" in order "to draw from it council and courage against the enemies of God and his Religion."[28] Similarly, when dedicating verses from Ecclesiastes to Anthony Bacon in the same year (1599), Inglis believes that he will delight in the smallness of the volume and the writing "non vulgaire," and that perhaps he will even favor it with a place in his cabinet, not for the merit of her work but for the "dignity of the material joined with the good will of her who only desires a part in your good graces."[29] Such works were thus designed to be kept in the cabinet or place where objects of beauty and value were collected to be enjoyed, but they were also meant to be kept in the cabinet of the heart as incitements to a life of virtue.

26. "A fin que la varieté de l'escriture delectuant la veuë l'esprit soit pareillement eslevé envers le grand Createur, par la diversité des prieres et chansons Royales chantez p[ar] ce grand Prophete." "Les C.L. Pseaumes," MS Folger V.a.93 [5]; translation mine.

27. "Octonaires," MS Folger V.a.92, [f.3 r].

28. "ce petit LIVRET escrit de ma main en petit volume pour estre plus aisement porté . . . et q[ue] le fueilletant souve[n]t puissiez tirer du conseil et courage d'i celui contre les ennemis de Dieu et sa Religion . . . ." "Les C.L. Pseaumes," MS Folger V.a.93 [5–6]; translation mine.

29. "La petitesse de volume et l'escriture non vulgaire vous fourniront de la delectation, et encore que mon travail ne merite pas tant de faveur que d'avoir place en vostre cabinet touteffois la dignité de la matiere iointe a la bonne volonté de celle qui ne desire qu'avoir part en vos bonnes graces. . . ." "Le Livre," BL MS Add.27927, sigs. [3r, 3v]: translation mine. As Patricia Fumerton notes, the fact that an enthusiasm for sonnets "coincided with the miniature craze suggests that the last years of the sixteenth century were ripe for 'personal' arts generally." She discusses the developing sense of the "private" as miniatures were kept in cases in the personal closet or chamber where their viewing could be controlled. See *Cultural Aesthetics*, 104 and chap. 3 generally.

It was also appropriate that such objects of spiritual value and aesthetic beauty be given as gifts. In her study "Beyond the Market: Books as Gifts in Sixteenth-Century France," Natalie Zemon Davis points to the long tradition in which "copying manuscripts was a meritorious and godly act" (72). Even after the introduction of printing, it was still considered wrong to view the book "only as a source of profit" (87). The rationale behind this thinking dates back to the early middle ages when knowledge was considered " 'a Gift of God [that] cannot be sold' " (71). By Esther Inglis's time, printing had produced a much greater variety of religious as well as secular books, but biblical text was still associated with the word of God meant to be freely given. Thus, a biblical translator in 1535 dedicates his book to the church, saying his gift is different: " 'it is made only to be given and communicated . . . it enriches those to whom it is given, but does not impoverish in any way those who give it.' "[30] Although Inglis's gift books were meant for the moral and spiritual enrichment of those who received them, there are, as we have seen, monetary and political intentions as well, which her recipients would implicitly have understood.

These intentions were an inherent part of the patronage system in which Inglis worked, an elaborate variation on the gift-exchange system that encoded obligations between donors and recipients on both sides. The giver of a book, who might be its "author" or just as likely its translator, printer, or publisher, expected to be rewarded for his or her gift; in other words, the original recipient in turn became a giver, providing money, lodging, or political protection to the presenter of the book.[31] Because Inglis gave manuscripts and not printed books, she had much more control over her audience, which was narrowly private rather than generally public. She also assumed in her audience the skills to appreciate a gift that was a conscious archaism: illuminated manuscript in the age of the black-and-white printed book.

Inglis's audience was expected to appreciate the handmade over the manufactured. Again and again in her volumes she points to her personal skill in creating these books. In at least eight of them she reproduces the motif of gold pens crossed through a crowned wreath with the

30. Robert Olivétan, Protestant translation, *La Bible . . .* (Neuchâtel, 1535), quoted in Davis, 80.

31. On reciprocity as a part of gift-giving, see Davis; see also Mauss, *Gift*. In her study of the relationship between needle and pen, Lisa Klein observes that "a personal gift such as an embroidered dress or book is particularly appropriate for fostering the mutual obligation that was the aim of the gift exchange. A hand-wrought gift has a particular intimacy, authority, and efficacy that other gifts, like money or plate, lack" (Klein, 471).

motto "Vive la Plume" or "Nil Penna Sed Usus" ("not the pen but skill").[32]
In her dedication to Prince Maurice she mentions that the book was
"escrit de ma main," a point that she often reiterates: to Lucy, countess
of Bedford, knowing how her noble nature is given to literature, Inglis
presents this work "fait de ma main"; to Anthony Bacon, this little book
"escrit de ma main"; to Sir Thomas Egerton, this work "escrit et trace par
ma plume et pinceau"; to Queen Elizabeth, this little book "which I wrote
in diverse sorts of letters"; and finally, in her old age, to Prince Charles,
"to offer to your Highnesse this two yeeres labours of the small cunning,
that my totering right [drawing of pointing hand], now being in the age
of fiftie three yeeres, might affoord."[33]

A similar focus on the importance of the hand occurs in the several
laudatory poems in Latin by her father and by the Protestant Scotsmen
Andrew Melville, John Johnston, and Robert Rollock that Inglis frequently
included in her manuscripts. Thus, in one poem Melville writes:

> One *hand*, emulous of nature, expresses a thousand figures, animating
> feeble signs with painted figures, creating animated signs, signs that are
> redolent of heaven. The elaborate edge of the page surrounds these
> signs. It's a wonderful work, but more wonderful is the *hand*. As the
> *hand* presses on with its task, the mind which governs the *hand* sur-
> passes all wonders.

In another poem, he notes:

> If I had the same mind as you have *hand*, then I would try to depict my
> mind this work which your *hand* has painted. If I had the same *hand* as
> you have mind, then I could try to depict by my *hand* the work which
> your mind has delineated. But I have neither such a *hand* nor such a
> mind. Your *hand* alone can depict your mind, and your mind alone can
> depict your *hand*.

Similarly, John Johnston writes: "By what better *hand* could those things
have been depicted, those things sent down from heaven and revealed

---

32. The Golden Quill was the prize given in a number of writing contests on the Continent and in England. The crowned crossed-quills with the motto "Nil Penna Sed Vsvs"
appears in Jacobus Houthusius *Exemplaria sive formulae scripturae ornatoris xxxvi* (Aquisgrani,
1591) and may have been copied from there by Inglis. See Croiset Van Uchelen, 324, plate 1a.

33. "Les C.L. Pseaumes," Folger MS V.a.93 [5]; "Une Estreine," Rome MS, sig. [2r]; "Le
Livre," BL Add. MS 27927, sig. [3r]; "Argumenta," Houghton Library MS.Type 212, sig. [2r];
"que J'ay escrit en diuerses sortes de lettres," "Discours," Huntington Library MS HM
26068, sig. [7v]; "Ce Livre . . . Emblemes" BL Royal MS 17D.XVI, f.[4r].

with a mind and *hand* that were heaven-borne? All things here are divine: and we wonder at all things. Thus mind and *hand*, material and arts, contend at the same time."[34]

The process described here sees Inglis's hand as mediating instrument between divine nature and human understanding, or as Fugger said, handwriting is a gift from God. It is this skill that causes wonder for the audience or recipient of such handmade gifts. The gifts maintain and hand over a part of the body that created them along with a spark of the divine; they are handbooks for a good life, made by a handmaid of the Lord.[35] As Michael Neill suggests, "In writing itself the hand writes the self" (29). Though Inglis was not, in the strict sense of the word, the "author" of the texts she wrote, yet she asserted her "author-ity" over each text by inscribing her "self" into its form through her choice of text (how much and what to use), her choice of design (title page, introductory matter, page layout, styles of handwriting, choice of decoration [see Chartier, 53]), her selection of patrons, her dedicatory epistles and poems, her inclusion of valorization by other writers, and, most literally, the insertion of her self in author portraits. A. H. Scott-Elliot and Elspeth Yeo have identified four different types of three-quarter length portraits in eighteen of the volumes, as well as portraits of heads in four volumes (18–19). In the larger portraits, Inglis faces out toward the viewer from behind a table, usually with a pen in her hand, and some combination of inkwell, book, paper, music score, and musical instrument on the table. Often the bit of paper in front of her is inscribed in small letters, "De l'Eternel le bien, de Moi le mal ou rien," reiterating the Protestant notion that all good gifts come from God and that we are worthy only through

34. All of these Latin poems appear on f.[7] of "Ce Livre . . . Emblemes," BL Royal MS.17.D.XVI. Inglis also uses them in a number of her other volumes. I am indebted to Professor James Binns of the Center for Medieval Studies, University of York, for his prose translations of this rather thorny late Latin.

35. On the "hand" in handwriting, see Goldberg, *Writing Matter*. See 150 for his comments on Melville's poem (Goldberg calls him "Melvin"). In a provocative essay, "'Amphitheaters in the Body,'" Michael Neill speaks of the significance of the "hand" in early modern Europe. He points out that "the very act of writing indeed may seem to involve an uncanny mimesis; for if scripture routinely represents 'the hand of God' as the instrument of divine power, it also expresses destiny as a kind of script—like the fatal handwriting of Belshazzar's Feast (Daniel 5:5, 24–28)." He goes on to say that the hand is the "symbolic guarantor of individual difference, privacy, and possession against the mechanical usurpations of print" (28). "The hand writes the self [and] also speaks it"; it is (quoting John Bulwer, the author of the *Chirologia*) "'the Spokesman of the body,'" "second only to the tongue" (29–30).

God.[36] The format of such portraits is both ancient and modern. On the one hand, it harkens back to manuscript portraits of the four Evangelists or of King David receiving divine inspiration for their writing; on the other hand, it "reinforce[s] the notion that the writing is the expression of an individuality that gives authenticity to the work" (Chartier, 52). Though Inglis often borrows her authority, as medieval writers did, from the biblical texts she uses, nevertheless, as we have seen, she inscribes her self in her work in a number of ways. The frequent use of the portrait is a form of self-assertion, of self-authorization, as are the laudatory verses and the "I" of the dedications.[37]

Rather than hiding her gender, she calls attention to it. In her dedication to Prince Maurice, she says she has taken on the spirit of "une roine des Amazones," and though she later calls herself "une pauvre Dame," she has also just called the prince her Alexander and expressed the hope that her little book will serve as his *Iliad* of Homer, thus implying a parallel between herself and the classical poet! She frequently talks about transcending the usual timidity of women: she addresses the earl of Essex with "a boldness more than feminine"; she asks the earl of Argyle to excuse "the rash boldness of a simple Lady"; she trusts that Lady Erskine shall not "esteme me impudent or that I have transcendit the limites of shamefastnes (wherewith our sexe is commonly adornd)"; and she says that she hopes the countess of Montgomery will accept her gift, "rather becaus it is the work of a woman" who, like the bee, has not spent years gathering honey for itself, "no more haue I payned my self mony yearis to burie the talent God hes geuen me in obliuion," thus echoing the biblical parable of the talents (Matt. 25:14–30).[38]

---

36. Goldberg says of this motto and the use of the golden pens: "If she is not her hand—or hands—they are in the service of the transcendental, God, and the golden pen. These are the contradictions that found the instrumental hand" (150). Frances Borzello notes that beginning with Sofonisba Anguissola in the mid sixteenth century, women artists painted their self-portraits with music or a musical instrument. It was also common for painters to identify their sitters by putting their name on a book or piece of paper held by the sitter (Borzello, 46–47, 49; see also her discussion of Inglis, 47). Here, Inglis inscribes her personal identity through the religious motto.

37. See Dunn, 8 and 11.

38. "Les C.L. Pseaumes," Folger Library MS V.a.93, fols.[4r, 6r]; "hardiesse plus que feminine," Bodleian Library MS 990, xi [quoted in *Catalogue* 38]; "l'hardiesse temeraire d'une simple Dame," "Le Livre," National Library of Scotland, MS 20498, f.2ᵛ; Newberry Library, Wing MS—ZW 645.K292, f.2ʳ [quoted in *Catalogue* 52]; and "Argumenta," Houghton Library, MS Type.428.1, f.1ʳ.

Though not immune to the usual language of obsequiousness and flattery, Inglis shows a marked sense of self-worth and of pride in the gifts of her hands. It may be that because the texts she dealt with as well as the handiwork with which she produced them were deemed "acceptable" for women, she felt herself more secure than someone such as Margaret Tyler or Lady Mary Wroth who was attempting to publish secular fiction.[39] It is also likely, however, that Inglis received a sense of self-worth from her parents, her husband, and the circle of humanist men who were her friends. This respect is evident, as we have seen, not only in their laudatory poems, but also in the pride with which her husband spoke to Queen Elizabeth about his wife's work, in the way in which Inglis presented *her* work to those who helped her husband in *his,* and in her association with a scholar such as David Hume, who asked her to make a copy of the unpublished second volume of his treatise, *Vincula Unionis.* . . . Inglis was an educated woman who worked with three languages, had access to a variety of Continental books, and used her maiden name professionally throughout her career. She was, indeed, "Rarissima Foeminam," as John Johnston styled her: "Most rare of Women."

39. Goldberg notes that "Inglis transcribes just the sorts of texts that Vives thought appropriate for a woman; she is a copyist of religious texts." On the gender of her hand he writes: "The contradictions of the woman's hand expose the strains in the social construction of the hand: regulatory governance, on the one hand, and the opening of difference, on the other" (*Writing Matter,* 147 and 153). For a discussion of the "biblical sanction" given to women as writers, see Wendy Wall, *Imprint,* chap. 5. Lisa Klein writes: "A hand-made gift embodied a unique contradiction that surely enhanced its efficacy: a skillful needlework or a neatly penned manuscript, though presented with a conventional plea to forgive its defects, paradoxically proclaimed its worth and that of the giver" (Klein, 483). Placing Inglis within the context of contemporary writers such as Isabella Whitney and Mary Fage, Kim Walker writes that "it is in Esther Inglis's productive combination of self-effacement and self-aggrandizement that I suggest we find an emerging sense of professionalism, a legitimation of writing for money" (Walker, 151).

3

Patronage and Class in Aemilia Lanyer's

SALVE DEUS REX JUDAEORUM

Mary Ellen Lamb

Aemilia Lanyer's *Salve Deus Rex Judaeorum* shows evident, even blatant, signs of its production under a patronage system: eleven prefatory dedications, the tailoring of various states of the text as presentation copies, explicit allusions to Lanyer's fall from former status, lengthy addresses to the countess of Cumberland.[1] Yet, although various critics note Lanyer's transparent bids for patronage, until recently, most discussions of the *Salve Deus Rex Judaeorum* have bracketed off financial motives as somehow extraneous to the work.[2] The notion of compensation seems to sit uncomfortably with what Robert C. Evans has called "a modern urge to enshrine the poet as a creative culture-hero, somehow set apart from and above ambition" (36).

1. All citations are taken from *Poems of Aemilia Lanyer: Salve Deus Rex Judaeorum*, ed. Susanne Woods. For individual versions see Woods's "Textual Introduction" (xlii–li) discussed further in Tina Krontiris, *Oppositional Voices*, 120. Lanyer alludes to her fall from status under Elizabeth in her dedication to Queen Anne (8). I regret that the excellent essays in *Aemilia Lanyer: Gender, Genre and the Canon*, ed. Marshall Grossman, appeared too late to shape my argument; I can only acknowledge some of them in my notes.

2. Krontiris engages most directly with Lanyer's use of the dedications and the *Salve* as a way of making money (*Oppositional Voices*, 102–20). Various critics dismiss Lanyer's poem for its financial motive: see Muriel Bradbrook's review of *Paradise of Women*, ed. Betty Travitsky, 92; and A. L. Rowse, Introduction to *Poems of Shakespeare's Dark Lady*, 33, who explains the supposedly "stony silence" with which her dedicatees greeted Lanyer's book as caused by the "too obviously sycophantic poems." Betty Travitsky, in *Paradise of Women*, notes that Lanyer's "obsequiousness is obvious" for "she had to flatter for favors" (92). More recently, critics have begun to consider her patronage more seriously as a topic. Recent essays contrast the discursive positions of Lanyer and Ben Jonson in a patriarchal patronage system: Ann Baynes Coiro, 357–76; and Susanne Woods, "Aemilia Lanyer and Ben Jonson," 15–20, and also "Vocation and Authority: Born to Write," 83–98; Leeds Barroll. See also a discussion of Lanyer's use of religion to undercut the class status of the patronage system in McBride, 60–82.

This natural and generous impulse to idealize beloved poets is especially intense regarding women writers, whose works have been devalued and relegated to obscurity for centuries by a masculinist system. To account for Lanyer's "fulsome, self-serving flattery of potential patrons," Elaine V. Beilin explains that the virtue Lanyer describes for them is actually designed to reveal "the ultimate reality behind the virtuous life" (*Redeeming Eve,* 183 and 200). Beilin and Barbara Lewalski both respond to Lanyer's flattery of women patrons by discussing a religious sincerity that is surely difficult to ascertain from the text.[3] Alternatively, critics advance Lanyer's feminist principles. Susanne Woods, for example, interprets her flattery of women patrons as a feminist celebration of a "community of good women" (xxxi), and Lewalski represents her as rewriting the institution of patronage "in female terms" (*Writing Women,* 241). But the language of Lanyer's dedications to women was not unusually celebratory by early modern conventions, and by the early seventeenth century women patrons were a standard feature of the patriarchal system of patronage.[4]

To pass over the various self-announcements of the *Salve Deus Rex Judaeorum* as merely standard motions toward patronage or to read them narrowly as protofeminist celebrations is to discount a central feature of the work. As numerous materialist critics have pointed out, a failure to analyze literary works in terms of the historical moment of their production risks the anachronistic tendency of liberal humanism to dissolve historical difference by projecting generalized meanings upon texts.[5] Scholars of early modern women writers are not exempt from these universalizing tendencies. The feminist project of recuperating women's texts lends itself to attributing modern feminist values to early modern women, to depict them as bonding together across class boundaries to resist an

---

3. Beilin, *Redeeming Eve,* 188; Barbara Lewalski assures readers that Lanyer "appears to have been sincerely, if not very profoundly, religious" (*Writing Women,* 219).

4. Strains especially from class difference within this "community of women" are, however, ably discussed by Coiro and Schnell. Krontiris describes the language of Lanyer's dedications as an "institutionalized language shaped by and for men" (*Oppositional Voices,* 108). For dedications addressed to women, see Franklin Williams, *Index,* 5, 94 and 211. Edwin Haviland Miller points out that beginning with the countess of Pembroke, both major and minor poets were commonly "mothered" by female patrons (45); see also Brennan, *Literary Patronage,* 7.

5. John Barrell, 1–7; Jonathan Dollimore and Alan Sinfield, foreword to *Political Shakespeare;* Catherine Belsey, *Subject of Tragedy,* 1–10; Judith Newton and Deborah Rosenfelt, Introduction to *Feminist Criticism,* xv–xxxix; Valerie Wayne, Introduction to *Matter of Difference,* 1–27. See also Herz for Lanyer's nonconformance with dominant feminist narratives of women writers.

oppressive patriarchy. These projections are particularly tempting for the *Salve*, which includes a thoroughgoing critique of gender ideology in its "Eve's Apology," but the *Salve* is equally thoroughgoing in its critique of class. Unlike her women dedicatees, Aemilia Lanyer was a working poet. She needed money.[6] This asymmetrical power relationship between writer and patron emerges as a primary preoccupation of the text so that, far from erasing disparities in class, the *Salve* is predicated upon them.

Lanyer's expressions of ambivalence toward the wealth and power of patrons make the *Salve* a particularly valuable text for the study of patronage. Lanyer's work provides a timely alternative to the conservatism described by M. D. Jardine for models of patronage in both the old and new historicisms. The *Salve* enacts neither the "willing, idyllic sharing of values and culture . . . in a conflict-free society" depicted by the old historicism, nor the "power circuit, with art reduced to a 'cash for propaganda' level" depicted by the new historicism (287 and 290). Instead, stresses and strains in Lanyer's work expose the complexities of early modern patronage, whose origin in a feudal society set it at odds with a protocapitalistic economics.[7] Neither patronage nor the newer market exchange system were working very well for authors in the early seventeenth century. The feudal form of patronage was fast becoming obsolete because upper-class consumption patterns were changing in the shift from a "lineage society" based on a network of kin and clients to a "civil society" based on ties to a centralized government (Stone, 100). Although some poets such as Samuel Daniel had been able to find temporary positions as tutors, aristocratic households were increasingly divesting themselves of retainers, clients, and other extrafamilial ties to retire "from the great hall to the private dining-room," as Stone demonstrates (95). But the emerging capitalist alternative of selling books to a consumer public had not yet matured enough to support its writers. As Elizabeth Eisenstein notes, writers would remain in a "quasi-amateur status" until the copyright laws were enacted in the eighteenth century

6. Lewalski, among others, discusses Lanyer's visit to the astrologer Simon Forman, in which she expresses anger at her reduced circumstances (*Writing Women*, 215); her husband had apparently squandered the money she had received from Hunsdon. Later, in 1620, a chancery suit mentions that "she . . . for her maynetaynaunce and releefe was compelled to teach and educate the children of divers persons of worth and understandinge" (Lewalski, *Writing Women*, 217). After the composition of the *Salve*, she kept a school from 1616 to 1619 (Lewalski, 218).

7. Arthur Marotti, "Patronage, Poetry," 1–26, discusses this change; Edwin Miller claims that "by 1600 patronage like many other medieval institutions was obsolescent, but this fact was not to be widely recognized for almost another century and a half" (94).

(101). Until then, authors sold their works to stationers for a onetime payment no matter how many copies were sold; sometimes unauthorized publications evaded payment of even that fee. Edwin Miller has described how both systems were strained yet further by the increasing number of authors attempting to make money from their work at this time (95–96 and 137–40).

The frustrations of appealing to both systems, neither of which were effective, provided for the *Salve* precisely that oppositional voice notably unremarked in both old and new historical treatments of the topic.[8] Such oppositions to dominant discourses do not happen spontaneously. According to a theorist of culture such as Paul Smith, spaces for resistance emerge from the gaps and discrepancies existing between competing ideologies (xxxiv–xxxv). In Lanyer's case, the contradictions between feudal and protocapitalist discourses of patronage enabled her opposition to dominant class ideologies. Although Lanyer's numerous dedications to noblewomen, beginning with the queen, advertise the *Salve* as a book appropriate for upper-class readers, passages within these dedications point out the injustice of an economic system in which wealth is distributed by rank rather than by merit. Lanyer creates a multiple female audience in the dedications, which contradicts the meditation's depiction of the countess dowager of Cumberland as its sole reader.

Lanyer's long addresses to the countess dowager evoke the feudal role of family poet writing a work for and even about an aristocratic patron. The countess dowager is not only her sole reader, but her sole subject of writing:

> And knowe, when first into this world I came,
> This charge was giu'n me by th'Eternall powres,
> Th'everlasting Trophie of thy fame,
> To build and decke it with the sweetest flowres
> That virtue yeelds. (113)

The sheer excessiveness of Lanyer's assertion that God Himself charged the author, at her birth, to devote her life to representing the countess's virtue moves beyond traditional bonds of service to verge on parody of the inflated rhetoric of patronage. This assertion of a lifetime commitment, however unlikely, suggests that Lanyer was soliciting a position within the household either of the countess dowager or of her daughter Anne. This bid for employment was not necessarily confined to writing,

8. M. D. Jardine, 298; see also Krontiris, 105.

for sustained patronage often took the form of household service rather than long-term hospitality. From medieval estates to the countess of Pembroke's country house, writers were often employed in other capacities—as tutors, as chaplains, as personal attendants.[9] Allusions within the text reveal that Lanyer had already served in the countess dowager's household, possibly as an attendant or caregiver for the young Anne, in whose sports she "did alwaies beare a part" (135). The grief Lanyer expresses that she can no longer "dayly see" the countess's daughter Anne, recently married to the wealthy earl of Dorset, implies a specific desire to become a member of this newly formed household:[10]

> Unconstant Fortune, thou are most too blame,
> Who casts us downe into so lowe a frame:
> Where our great friends we cannot dayly see,
> So great a difference there is in degree. (134)

The resolution of Lanyer's grief is obvious, and Anne has the power to confer it.

The prefatory dedications operated according to a less feudal system of patronage newly made possible by the availability of printed copies that Lanyer could present to a number of dedicatees, any or all of whom might remunerate the author with a onetime stipend.[11] The "Authors Dreame to the Ladie *Marie,* the Countesse Dowager of *Pembrooke*" explicitly sets the scene for such an act: waking from an elaborate dream glorifying the countess for her translation of the Psalms, the author is moved to present to her "the fruits of idle hours" (30). Although Lanyer was well acquainted with the countess dowager of Kent, "the mistress of my youth" (18), others she had never met, as she confesses freely in her dedication to the countess of Suffolke: "It may seem right strange, / That I a stranger should presume thus farre, / To write to you" (36). Dedicating works to strangers was a new phenomenon in the early modern period. According to Edwin Miller, "The medieval lord had never found on his threshold an unknown man with a recently printed book replete with effusive dedications—and a hand outstretched" (95). This common

---

9. K. J. Holzknecht, 179–86; Mary Ellen Lamb, "Countess of Pembroke's Patronage," 207–26.

10. The *Salve* was entered in the Stationers' Register on October 2, 1610 (Lanyer, ed. Woods, xxv); Anne Clifford married the earl of Dorset in 1609 (Lewalski, *Writing Women,* 127–28).

11. Miller discusses presentation copies and their abuses and effects (110–29); according to the records of one Richard Robinson, the average remuneration was £2 (126).

practice of multiple presentation copies shows how the printing press worked to loosen bonds between writer and patron. In some cases, authors never intended to present their works to specific patrons at all because dedications served to advertise the worth of a book to the general public (Miller, 130).

Lanyer's multiple dedications to aristocratic women thus not only functioned according to a loosened form of patronage, but also provided an early modern form of celebrity endorsement to sell books to anonymous consumers within the capitalistic system of market exchange. The opportunities and difficulties posed by this faceless audience for Lanyer's work appear in the contradictory representations of that audience in her two dedications to it. Her verse epistle "To all vertuous Ladies in generall" appeals to a consumer mentality invested in advancing or affirming its high location in class. Her much less conventional prose letter "To the Vertuous Reader" appeals to a feminist or protofeminist consciousness that does not rely on class consciousness. Thus, the very anonymity of these women consumers of printed books empowered Lanyer to imagine them in varying terms according to her own predictions or desires. Although buyers and readers were not yet numerous enough to support writers, the fact that they existed at all created a site of resistance that enabled Lanyer's critique of the class hierarchy underlying patronage.[12]

Lanyer's verse epistle "To all vertuous Ladies in generall" constructs the reading of the *Salve* as enacting high worldly, intellectual, and spiritual class or status. First, by reading (and presumably buying) the *Salve*, anyone could become the personal companion of Queen Anne: "Let this faire Queene not unattended bee" (12). This allusion to the immediately preceding dedications to Queen Anne and her daughter creates an additional function for prefatory dedications as a form of advertising by placing typically middle-class readers vicariously within the glittering social register of the time. The epistle then constructs reading the *Salve* as a sign of intellectual status, also depicted in terms of class, by inviting readers to "let muses your companions be, those sacred sisters that on Pallas wait." Finally, by seeking out Christ, readers become "in the eie of heaven so highly placed, / That others by your virtues may be graced" (15). With this high rank, readers have attained the power to patronize or "grace this little Booke" of Lanyer's. Employing such terms as "so highly placed" and "grace" to represent rank in heaven, the poem appeals to a

12. Patricia Thomson, "The Literature of Patronage," 267–84, describes how the "desire to be free from patronage arose before the public could be relied on" (282). See also Marotti, "Patronage, Poetry," 2 and 25.

language of class that simultaneously reifies worldly status (for those who have it) and subverts it (for those who don't).

The prose letter to "To the Vertuous Reader" constructs an alternative audience for the printed book and an alternative representation of the *Salve* itself. Mentioned only in the dedication to Queen Anne, the defense of women in "Eve's Apology" now becomes the central point of the *Salve*. In this dedication, rather than high birth, successful aggression toward men creates status for women. Angered by the wrongs done by men to women, God has sent "wise and virtuous women" to bring men down—women such as Deborah, Jael, Hester, Judith, and Susanna. Status is also conferred by a relationship with Jesus, who was born of a woman, who healed women, who appeared to a woman after his death. The striking absence of almost all allusions to patronage, to class, to Lanyer's financial need, or to the possible "gracing" of her book by its readers creates an egalitarian relationship with her buyer-reader, constructed as believing feminist principles. This buyer-reader was not apparently compatible with the usual aristocratic woman patron. As Tina Krontiris has pointed out, this prose letter and four dedications were removed when the book was reissued, apparently because its feminist statements offended its aristocratic dedicatees (120). The letter's construction of a feminist audience for the *Salve* suggests that the radical interrogation of gender in "Eve's Apology" was enabled by the buyer-reader of a protocapitalist print culture.

Although buyers and readers were not yet numerous enough to support writers, their very existence created a site of resistance that enabled Lanyer's critique of the class hierarchy in her prefatory dedications to individual patrons. This resistance was waged primarily by means of a religious discourse able to level social distinctions. Lanyer's devotional constructions of reading engage in what Evans has called a series of "micropolitical performances" (29), struggles for personal mastery that often play upon the insecurities of prospective patrons. As Wendy Wall has noted, the dedication's plea to Arbella Stuart only to "spare one looke / Upon this humbled King" constructs the *Salve* as the body of Christ: to refuse to accept and read this work would be to refuse Christ himself.[13] Similarly, the dedication to the countess of Bedford constructs the reading of the *Salve* as letting Christ into her heart, to "entertaine this dying lover" (33). Who would dare to shut Him out? For "vertuous Ladies" and the countess of Dorset, reading the *Salve* would mean filling

13. Wendy Wall, *Imprint of Gender,* 324; Krontiris has also made this point (*Oppositional Voices,* 110), and it is well discussed in McBride.

their lamps with oil to be ready, like the wise virgins, for the Bridegroom (12 and 41). Who would risk being a foolish virgin, arriving at the marriage feast only to find the door of the kingdom of heaven shut? These representations of the act of reading imply a spiritual threat to those who do not read the *Salve* intensely, participating fully in its meditation on Christ's passion.

These devotional constructions of reading unsettle the asymmetrical relationship between needy author and wealthy patron. There is also perhaps something in the act of reading itself that unsettles this power relationship inherent in patronage. In the actual experience of reading, an author's words typically assume an authority, even if only a temporary one, over a reader's thoughts, ordering and directing them to the author's will. This relationship of intellectual authority is diametrically opposed to the author's social experience of patronage—as enacted, for example, in the act of kneeling before a patron to present a book.[14] Lanyer's justification of her authorship in terms of the temporary and acceptable authority of a hostess encompasses the radically unstable nature of the author's role. As Lanyer welcomes several of her readers—Queen Anne, Princess Elizabeth, the countess dowagers of Kent and Pembroke, and the countess of Dorset—to her feast (book), she offers them wholesome heavenly food. But what is her role as she invites the queen to feed upon the "paschal Lamb" she has prepared as a "pretious Passeover" (7)? Is she a lowly cook, or does her invitation assume the authority of a priest's officiation at a holy communion or mass?[15] This oscillation between divergent roles reflects the complexities of the author-reader relationship.

In this context, it is striking that one of Lanyer's first critiques of class occurs in the imagined scene of the presentation of the *Salve* to Queen Anne. As her dedication explicitly states, such a scene never in fact occurred, for Lanyer had been barred by "meannesse" from Queen Anne's throne. As her proxy, then, Virtue performs the actions of a poor presenter of a book to the queen:

> This holy worke, Virtue presents to you,
> In poore apparell, shaming to be seene,
> Or once t'appeare in you[r] judiciall view:
> But that fair Virtue, though in meane attire,
> All Princes of the world doe most desire. (6)

14. Werner Gundersheimer, "Patronage in the Renaissance," 15–16. The frontispiece of the Huntington Library copy of Caxton's *Hystoryes of Troye* portrays the author kneeling before his patron, the duchess of Burgundy.

15. McGrath, 104, assumes the latter, as does McBride.

In this version of a Cinderella story, Virtue's "meane attire" does not prevent "all Princes of the world" from perceiving her worth. Why then could not Queen Anne perceive the author's worth, similarly obscured by the "meanness" of her position in class? Within this depiction of the deference of Virtue, "shaming to be seene," lurks a protest against the queen's evidently shabby treatment of the author, whose value, like Virtue's, cannot be measured by her clothes.

Lanyer extends this disparity between social class and "true" worth by drawing on conservative devotional discourse to destabilize wealth as a reliable signifier of class. In the reference to the "Monarch whose dayes were spent in poverty and sorrow / And yet all Kings their Wealth of him do borrow," the implied threat in the term "borrow" darkens the representation of the queen's own wealth. Whereas monarchs, presumably including Queen Anne, may someday have to pay back the monies they have borrowed, Lanyer is debt free, and her heavenly finances remain sound. Her "real" rank is much higher than her worldly one:

> Yea in his kingdome onely rests my lands,
> Of honour there I hope I shall not misse:
> Though I on earth doe live unfortunate. (6)

Within the discourse of patronage, an author's assertions of need are never without point. It is up to the queen, this passage implies, to narrow the discrepancy.

Lanyer's most radical challenge to the class system comes, however, in her dedication to the countess of Dorset, to whom she writes "as God's Steward" (43), inverting the traditional assertion that class reveals the innate *virtu* of aristocrats, whose illustrious ancestors bequeathed them worth as well as rank (Whigham, *Ambition*, 73–82). She thus asserts, on the contrary, that class is not innate at all, but must be newly constructed in each generation. She thus moves beyond a traditional emphasis upon external show as the enactment of class to align herself with popular protest by claiming the common ancestry of all people.[16] As Woods notes in her introduction to Lanyer's poems, this claim echoes the rhyme "When Adam delved and Eve span, Who was then the gentleman?" (40) chanted in popular uprisings:[17] "All sprang but from one woman and one man, / Then how doth Gentry come to rise and fall?"

---

16. Elias, *Court Society*; see also Howard Kaminsky, "Estate, Nobility," 684–709.

17. Lewalski discusses these "radical egalitarian conclusions" in terms of a female succession grounded on "virtue and holiness" (*Writing Women*, 225).

(42). Even more radically, Lanyer suggests that unworthy descendants may in fact be illegitimate somewhere along the line:

> Whose successors, although they beare his name,
> Possessing not the riches of his minde,
> Howe doe we know they spring out of the same
> True stocke of honour, beeing not of that kind? (43)

Lanyer's personal situation gave this argument special point. Her own son, the illegitimate child of Lord Hundson, did not receive riches or honors from his noble blood but was instead reared as the ordinary child of a musician, Alphonso Lanyer. From this perspective, class hierarchy became highly contingent not on blood lineage but on social convention.[18]

Lanyer uses this issue to appeal for patronage by proposing that worth (and therefore legitimacy) may best be proven by good stewardship that "must for all the poore provide." Moreover, she addresses Anne specifically as a steward: "To you, as to Gods Steward I doe write," as she advises her to "shew from whence you are descended" by bestowing her wealth worthily: "Succour the poore, comfort the comfortlesse, / Cherish faire plants, suppresse unwholsom weeds" (44).

Pleading for patronage was a tricky rhetorical task; outright requests were demeaning for patron and supplicant alike. But Lanyer comes perhaps as close as possible to such a request when she states the significance of Anne's demonstration of her worth (and legitimacy) through her stewardship, presumably especially for Lanyer's *Salve*: "So shal you shew from whence you are descended, / And leave to all posterities your fame" (44).

Why did Lanyer choose this dedication to the countess of Dorset in which to voice these radical ideas? What possible reading strategies did she assume? Did she have reason to believe that the countess, embroiled in her own suits to inherit lands, would agree with her? The hierarchical and extremely class-conscious view of the world that emerges from the countess's later diaries suggest the unlikelihood of such sympathy.[19] Lewalski's supposition that Lanyer behaved as if "privileged to do so by former familiarity" (*Women Writing*, 224) seems more probable. As Lewalski notes (239), Lanyer was twenty years older than Anne Clifford

---

18. Lewalski, *Writing Women*, 214–15; Rowse also relates this passage to the illegitimacy of Lanyer's own son, calling it "sour grapes" (23).

19. Lewalski, *Writing Women*, 130–40; the later diaries are discussed in Mary Ellen Lamb, "Agency of the Split Subject," 347–68.

when she "did alwaies beare a part" in *"Dorset's former sports."* Did Lanyer assume for her authorship the authority she may have exercised over Anne Clifford as her tutor or caregiver? Did Lanyer's early contact with Clifford as a very young girl decrease her sense of the deference owed to her? If Lanyer were in fact bidding for employment in Dorset's household, as the "Description of Cooke-ham" would suggest, then she took some significant risks in her placement of this critique of class.

The religious discourse that unsettles class ideology in the dedicatory epistles also surfaces within the meditation itself. Lanyer first seems to endorse this class structure in her claim that Jesus suffered even more than others because of his aristocratic nature:

> Yet, had he beene but of a meane degree,
> His sufferings had beene small to what they were;
> Meane minds will shew of what meane mouldes they bee;
> Small griefes seeme great, yet Use doth make them beare. (104)

Yet Christ was "A seeming Trades-mans sonne, of none attended, / Save of a few in poverty and need; / Poore Fishermen" (124). Lanyer portrays the countess's love as superceding apparent class difference when her "heart doth rise" at Christ's appearance as a "good old man" in a "Shepherds weed" (109). She depicts the countess's ministrations to Christ as "sometime imprison'd, naked, poore, and bare / Full of diseases, impotent, and lame" (109). Krontiris's insight that this passage allowed Lanyer to solicit "economic support for herself" (110) gains further force through the allusion to Christ's promise of a heavenly reward for those who fed him when he was hungry, clothed him when he was naked, and visited him when he was sick or in prison. In Matthew 25, a threat accompanies this promise: those who do not tend to the needs of the poor (the latter perhaps including Lanyer) depart into "everlasting fire" (Geneva Bible, Matt. 25:40–41).

Passages such as this one render Lanyer's relationship of authority to her patron-reader deeply ambiguous. On the one hand, Lanyer continually defers to the countess as her sole reader. Her choice of genre itself apparently represents a response to the countess's habit of meditating on the grounds of her estate, "placing his holy writ in some faire tree, / To meditate" (133). On the other hand, her authorship of a meditation creates her as a kind of a spiritual advisor, for the meditation, perhaps more than any other genre, is designed to order the thoughts of readers toward specific ends, to attain specific spiritual fruits (Martz, 14 and 32).

As was traditional for meditations on the passion (Martz, 33), the *Salve* is meant to enliven religious devotion by eliciting sorrow for Christ's suffering from the time of his capture at Gethsemene to his crucifixion. For this meditation to work, the countess must engage in an especially intense practice of reading specific to techniques of meditation. The goal, finally, of this text is nothing less than absolute absorption—the internalization of Christ's image in the countess's heart so that she herself becomes a shrine:

> Therefore (good Madame) in your heart I leave
> His perfect picture, where it shall stand,
> Deeply engraved in that holy shrine,
> Environed with Love and Thoughts divine. (108)

To achieve this purpose, Lanyer relies heavily on a common meditative technique of composition in which the reader is made to be imaginatively present at scriptural scenes (Martz, 30). She addresses various characters—by empathizing with Jesus as he is arrested ("But greater horror to thy Soule must rise, / Than Heart can thinke, or any Wit devise" [71]) or by mourning with the Virgin Mary at the crucifixion ("How canst thou choose [faire Virgin] then but mourne" [99]). The narrator models appropriate responses herself by crying out, "Oh hatefull houre! oh blest! oh cursed day!" (72) as the soldiers arrive to capture Jesus at Gethsemene. The daughters of Jerusalem also provide a pattern for practitioners. Watching Christ stagger past as he bears His cross, they weep and cry out, and He turns His head to comfort them. The narrator addresses them as "most blessed daughters of Jerusalem / Who found such favour in your Saviors sight, / To turne his face when you did pitie him" (93). The blessing achieved by these women spectators is the blessing offered by this meditation to any readers who achieve an intense feeling of compassion. A receptive reading confers grace.

The disruptive nature of "Eve's Apology" within this conventional English meditation must not be underestimated. It both critiques gender relations and also validates women's anger. Making herself imaginatively present at Christ's trials, the narrator feels such grief at Christ's pain that she is led to inveigh against his persecutors. She accuses Caiphas, for example, in this way: "Thou rend'st thy cloathes, in stead of thy false heart" (82). Usually presented as a narrative of the redemption of sinners of both sexes through Christ's love, *Salve* rereads the passion as a narrative of gender relations—of continuing and characteristic male cruelty to

Christ and other innocent victims, especially women.[20] Lanyer's new version of the passion is a static narrative; there is no change or redemption. In its gender arrangements, the present day remains frozen in the events of Christ's passion. The cruelty of men is unredeemed because male tyranny continues to dominate women in Lanyer's time. Because women did not participate in the crucifixion of Christ, they were not implicated in its sin. They require no redemption because, in their grief, they attempted to prevent it from occurring at all.

Lanyer's retelling of Christ's passion justifies not only women's anger, but also their words. Pilate's sin of condemning Jesus was part of another sin—that of not listening to his wife. The narrator pleads, "But heare the words of thy most worthy wife" (84). This blame represents a powerful counterargument to a prominent reading of the Eve story—by William Whateley's *Bride-Bush,* for example—as a narrative of the disastrous consequences of endowing women's words with authority (sig. CC4^v). Lanyer retells the Pilate incident to argue that, on the contrary, Pilate's refusal to listen to his wife was a primary cause of the crucifixion. Like Whateley, Lanyer generalizes this domestic incident to refer to all men and women: "(Poore soules) we [women] never gave consent" to the crucifixion: "Witnesse thy wife (O *Pilate*) speakes for all" (87). Addressed in its entirety to Pilate who stands for all tyrannical men, this apology for Eve—deceived by cunning and moved by "too much love" (86) for her husband—culminates in an argument for marital equality: "Your fault beeing greater, why should you disdaine / Our beeing your equals, free from tyranny?" (87).

This radical retelling of the passion story as a tale of domestic tyranny is not limited to the few pages labeled "Eve's Apology." It also plays an important part in Lanyer's construction of the countess of Cumberland as a reader. Beneath the devotional meditative role offered the countess emerges the subtext of her own domestic martyrdom to a dashing husband who had deserted her for various and notorious affairs at court. The countess's withdrawal into the country revealed her rejection of worldly pleasures (58) but also signified her unhappy separation from her husband.[21] Lanyer's comparison of the countess with Matilda,

20. This point has been made by various critics, such as Wall, *Imprint,* 320; Krontiris, *Oppositional Voices,* 116–18; Mueller, "Feminist Poetics," 101; and Miller, "(M)other tongues," 159.

21. Lewalski points out that Cookeham was a royal manor owned by the countess of Cumberland's brother (*Writing Women,* 396); and that she probably retired there when she separated from her husband. For his notorious affairs, see 127.

who served Christ as the true spouse of her soul (61), in turn evokes another comparison with the countess's flagrantly untrue spouse of her body. Lanyer's praise of the countess as even more heroic than Deborah and Judith in her battle against sin everyday (114–15) sanctifies her emotional duress. According to Lanyer's narrator, the countess approaches martyrdom in her innocent suffering: "Loe Madame, heere you take a view of those [martyrs], / Whose worthy steps you desire to tread" (128). Most relevent to the countess's domestic difficulties are the excoriations of Antony's mistress Cleopatra as she is informed in three stanzas of personal address that her inner beauty cannot compare to the countess's (112–13). A natural analogue for the Other Women who attracted the countess's unfaithful husband, Cleopatra also appears prominently near the beginning of the *Salve* in "An Invective against outward beuty unaccompanied with virtue" (59–60). These passages offer "equipment for living"[22] to a countess whose "perfit features" resided in "a fading face" (59).

By superimposing a narrative of domestic martyrdom on a meditation of Christ's passion, Lanyer enacts the feudal role of a family poet, addressing the family issues of her patron. This role exists in tension with the authorial power as spiritual guide produced for her in the act of writing a meditation. Writing in the role of family poet, Lanyer inevitably permitted the countess's anticipated reading of the *Salve* to shape her treatment of the topic. A brief apology near the beginning of the *Salve* suggests that even as she complied with the countess's wishes, she contested her patron's power over her authorship. Ruffling the smooth surface of deference, this apology presents the meditation as a substitute for what the countess dowager of Cumberland had already requested:

> And pardon (Madame) though I do not write
> Those praisefull lines of that delightful place,
> As you commaunded me in that faire night,
> When shining *Phoebe* gave so great a grace. (51–52)

If Cookeham was indeed this "delightful place," then the *Salve* demonstrates its eventual conformity to the countess's desires with the "Description of Cooke-ham" appended to the meditation. The earlier apology

22. The phrase is Kenneth Burke's, from "Literature as Equipment for Living," in *Philosophy of Literary Form*, 293. The prominence of these allusions to Cleopatra has been noted by Beilin, who supposes that she represented a fantasy of worldly power (*Redeeming Eve*, 200); and by Rowse, who supposes that Lanyer imagined herself a type of Cleopatra (29).

is then rendered oddly unnecessary when, in the appended poem, the meditation is represented as having been written specifically at the countess's request: "from whose desires did spring this worke of Grace" (130). The only function of this apology seems to be to record Lanyer's power to resist the countess's commands even as she obeys them. This assertion of an independent subjectivity, however lightly sketched in, signals Lanyer's resistance to the feudal ideology forming the basis for the traditional patron-author relationship.

Alluding to her resistance to the countess's initial request would not seem to be in the best interests of a poet bidding for patronage. Other passages, especially her discussion of illegitimacy in the dedication to the countess of Dorset, suggest that her search for patronage was not consistently rational. Competing issues of class and dominance apparently got in the way. Patronage was, in the early seventeenth century, an emotionally fraught topic. Although many twentieth-century discussions tend to treat patronage as a form of compensation, to early modern writers it was much more. As Evans has noted, this system was built "on expectation and apprehension, on the deepest hopes and fears," and involved "more than how writers were paid; it involved ... how they lived their lives" (23, 25). Most writers remained unsuccessful in finding sustained literary patronage, but patronage somehow remained a central social construct arranging relations of power throughout early modern culture.[23] Central to this construct was the ideal of service, according to which subordinates—servants, wives, suppliants of any kind—voluntarily offered their labor to the figures of authority to whom it was naturally owed. This model of interaction moved into emotional spaces seemingly removed from public power. As John Barrell has astutely pointed out, relations of patronage, including literary patronage, were commonly represented in terms of love (25). More than representations may be at stake. Coppélia Kahn's analysis of patronage in terms of the "infantile dependence on the mother who, it seems to the child, can give or take all away" invests this interaction with deeply psychological roots.[24]

Lanyer's "Description of Cooke-ham" appeared at a liminal point. Although patronage remained a widespread and powerful model of negotiating hierarchical relationships, it was also experiencing considerable strain: in thirty years, a civil war would renounce this ideal of natu-

---

23. For the centrality of patronage as a social and psychological construct, see, for example, Gundersheimer; Frank Whigham, "Rhetoric," 864–82; M. D. Jardine; and Evans, 23–30.

24. Kahn, "'Magic of Bounty,'" 57.

ral service by cutting off the king's head. A contributing cause to this event, according to M. D. Jardine, was the rising capitalistic economy, through which labor was bought and sold according to a perceived motive of self-interest rather than of service (301–2). The inconsistencies within and between the *Salve* and its dedications point to the ideological contradictions fissuring the text at a time when writing, like other forms of labor, was also positioned between these competing social formations. "The Description of Cooke-ham" explores the emotional contradictions of patronage as a system that extended far beyond mere compensation to a mode of feeling. In the process, it provides insights into the "discrepancies between the celebrated service ideal . . . and the conditions of servility which it concealed," as Jardine has noted, at a time when divergent concepts of the service ideal and patronage system were most apparent (295). Recapitulating the language and gestures as well as the frustrations and anxieties of service, this "last farewell" to Cooke-ham (138) not only expresses the emotional contradictions inherent in patronage, but also mourns its loss.

As part of her bid for patronage in the household of either the countess dowager of Cumberland or her daughter, Lanyer projects the experience of service onto the landscape and creatures of Cooke-ham so that her pleasure in the company of the young Anne Clifford and her expressed pain at its subsequent loss structures the "Description" as a whole. This projection is most explicit in the treatment of the nightingale Philomela, whose identification with the poet is made most evident in the similarity of their literary tasks, which are even described in the same words: "*Philomela* with her sundry leyes, / Both you and that delightfull Place did praise" (131) echoes Lanyer's description of the countess's demand to write "those praisefull lines of that delightfull place" (51).[25] Once the countesses (and their patronage) depart, Philomela's song is silenced—"Faire *Philomela* leaves her mournefull Ditty, / Drownd in dead sleepe, yet can procure no pittie" (137–38)—and so, it is implied, will be Lanyer's poetry, unless she procures the "pittie" of a countess. The other creatures of Cookeham experience the same heightened emotions conventional to representations of patronage. The birds, flowers, trees, streams, and hills—all express in their own ways Lanyer's "reverend Love" in the joy they experience in the company of the countess dowager and her daughter; they, too, are inconsolable when the countesses depart.

25. For a discussion of nightingales as a common figure for early modern women poets, see Mary Ellen Lamb, "Singing with the (Tongue) of the Nightingale," in *Gender and Authorship*, 194–230.

The emotionally overwrought flowers and trees of Cookeham represent a literalization of the gardening metaphor in Lanyer's prefatory dedication to Anne, advising her to show her stewardship (or patronage) by cherishing "faire plants" and suppressing "unwholsom weeds" (44). This metaphor was implicitly tied to patronage by the early modern usage of the word "plant" to mean "to set up a person or thing in some person or estate" (OED). Like the streams and the birds, the flowers and the trees share a goal: to please the countess of Cumberland and her daughter. Explicitly described as servants, the "walkes put on their summer Liveries" (131). The trees turn themselves into canopies to shade the eyes of the countess dowager. The hills imitate the gallant gesture attributed to Raleigh, who supposedly spread his cloak in the mud for the queen to step on:

> The very Hills right humbly did descend,
> When you to treat upon them did intend.
> And as you set your feete, they still did rise,
> Glad that they could receive so rich a prise. (131)

These same hills strike the humble posture of a suitor as they kneel before the countess of Cumberland:

> Where beeing seated, you might plainely see,
> Hills, vales, and woods, as if on bended knee
> They had appeared, your honour to salute,
> Or to preferre some strange unlook'd for sute. (133)

None of these actions can be dismissed as simple flattery, empty gestures, or even poetic whimsy. Instead, they represent, in Frank Whigham's terms, "repeatable assertions of relation," necessary to maintain the "class-stratified patronage system" that organized power and privilege in early modern England ("Rhetoric," 864 and 867). These small gestures of deference from plants enact the large gesture of deference that is the "Description of Cooke-ham" and even the *Salve* itself. Such gracefully humble demeanor both confirms the class status of its recipient and provides for suitors and writers alike a rhetorical power that attests to their gentility and therefore to their suitability for employment. Drawing from a "feudal vocabulary of personal service" (Whigham, "Rhetoric," 873), these exaggerated assertions of a desire to please were designed to assure noble employers that interactions in the limited space of a country estate would be easy and pleasant.

Not all of the creatures at Cookeham experience unmitigated joy in the presence of the countess dowager and her daughter, however, and these exceptions hint at a dark side of patronage. With the word "attend" invoking the language of service, the especially anxious need of the birds to gain the countesses' approval suggests the asymmetries of a patronage relationship: "The pretty Birds would oft come to attend thee, / Yet flie away for feare they should offend thee" (132). The patron's power is not merely imaginary. Small animals first wish to display themselves by playing in her sight, but then they cease their games in fear as the countess wields a bow, ready to inflict real damage:

> The little creatures in the Burrough by
> Would come abroad to sport them in your eye;
> Yet fearfull of the Bowe in your faire Hand,
> Would run away when you did make a stand. (132)

Lanyer describes herself as taking part in Anne Clifford's "sports"; they no doubt also "sported" under the countess dowager's eye. The echo of this word and of the activity it represents perhaps suggests a fear that such games were in some sense dangerous, possibly because they might incur the countess's disapproval.

Perhaps the worst aspect of patronage, however, was its undependability. Patrons could let employers (and writers) go, and as in the case of the countess dowager and her daughter, they could go themselves. As they depart, the "Description" depicts the countess of Cumberland and her daughter as treating the creatures, both vegetable and animal, as soon-to-be unemployed servants,

> requiting each according to their kind,
> Forgetting not to turne and take your leave
> Of these sad creatures, powreless to receive
> Your favour when with griefe you did depart. (136)

The mourning of the plants produces winterlike effects. Trees lose their leaves, and they also weep, "letting their teares in your faire bosoms fall / As if they said, Why will ye leave us all?" (136). The briers and brambles "caught fast your clothes, thinking to make you stay" (138). Although these operatic excesses cannot be taken at face value, their implications for the experience of patronage cannot be ignored. Like plants, poets in service are not invested with the rights to make explicit demands; they can only weep or gesture. Like plants, they are powerless to affect the actions of their patrons, even when these actions have devastating effects on them. Barrell's observation that the discourse of patronage often uses relations of love to "purify and idealise what was always of course an economic transaction" (25) may be only partly true. As anyone unemployed for a length of time can witness, a lack of work can *feel* like an absence of love; this irrational conflation of love and employment was all the more likely to occur in a feudal system, in which service was depicted as voluntary.

The odd resonances given to the word "chaines" by its placement at the very end of the "Description" gathers together the ambivalences of this complicated poem in a complicated work. Making her own farewell to Cookeham, the author presents her work as commissioned by the countess of Cumberland and then expresses her never-dying devotion to both countesses:

> This last farewell to *Cooke-ham* here I give,
> When I have perform'd her noble hest,
> Whose virtues lodge in my unworthy breast,
> And ever shall, so long as life remains,
> Tying my heart to her by those rich chaines.

On one level, "chaines" certainly can be read, according to editor Susanne Woods's gloss, as chains of the countess's virtues. But "tying" can also modify "I" instead of "virtues." This grammatical construction releases other possible meanings for "chaines." Its meaning as a "bond of union or sympathy" *(OED)* is consistent with representations of patronage in terms of love. Its meaning as a sign of office is supported by the discourse of service: the poet has been and hopes to be invested with such a "rich" chain.

All three meanings are simultaneously possible, but a fourth meaning for "chaines" as "bond or fetter" is most evocative of the *Salve's* oppositions to the power relationships structuring patronage.[26] The adjective "rich" suggests that these fetters are based on money so that "rich chaines" thus devalues the ideal of voluntary service by constructing the poet's bond with the countess dowager as based on remuneration or on hopes for remuneration. This image describes the countess's dominance,

---

26. Coiro discusses how women were "bound by rich chains of marriage, or service" (373); Holmes reads them as "Platonic love" (183); Berry asks if it is necessary to choose whether these chains are motivated by heaven or profit (224). Mary Sidney uses chains to signify pride in her translation of Psalm 73, ll. 16–18, as discussed in Margaret Hannay's essay in this collection.

based on money, as a constraining fetter rather than as a basis of union. The agency ascribed to the poet "I" in tying her own heart to the countess presents her entry into a patronage relationship as freely chosen rather than as "natural" or ordained by God. This perspective on the patronage relationship was possible for Lanyer because she lived at a time when she could move outside the ideology of service to a capitalistic mode of construing the connection between patron and writer. Yet she may not have been able to abandon the ideology entirely. Although the printing press had provided Lanyer with an alternative way of thinking about patronage, it had not yet provided the financial means by which she could let it go. The sense of loss conveyed by the "Description of Cooke-ham" over the departure of her two women patrons suggests that even if Lanyer could have supported herself through selling her books, the feudal model for interactions, however constraining, still possessed emotional power for her. She might struggle to subvert her power, but she would remain tied to a patron "so long as life remains."

Part Two

Reproducing Cultural Roles

4

The Education of a Prince(ss)

TUTORING THE TUDORS

Kathi Vosevich

E ven as a child, Elizabeth Tudor seems to have been conscious of
the significance of a title. When her father Henry VIII proclaimed
that she would be called "Lady" but her older sister "Lady Princess,"
Elizabeth (then only three years old) perceptively asked, " 'How happs
it yesterday Lady Princess and to-day but Lady Elizabeth?' "[1] Although
the facts of this story may not be entirely correct—Mary was never called
"Lady Princess"—it is accurate in portraying Elizabeth's precocious sen-
sitivity to titles. Like her younger sister, Mary was protective of her title
because of the issue of her illegitimacy. When Elizabeth made her redun-
dant, Mary refused to give up the title of princess until she was twenty
years old and then only after her father finally wore her down.[2] Even
after she became queen, she often referred to herself as "princess." Elizabeth, however, recognized the political efficacy of degendering or cross-
gendering her title by calling herself "king," something Mary never did.

Their choices of title significantly reflect the contradictory pedagogies
of their tutors. Juan Luis Vives's education plan for Mary was primarily
moral rather than academic. He focused on training a good Christian
woman—in other words, a silent and submissive woman. Roger Ascham
was not quite so interested in his pupil's Christian virtues, but rather
encouraged her scholarly abilities, both written and oral.[3] These oppos-

---

1. This story dates from the reconciliation of Henry VIII with Mary orchestrated by
Queen Jane Seymour and is retold in Milton Waldman, *Lady Mary*, 122.

2. Her mother, similarly stubborn, called herself "queen" until her death.

3. Before Ascham, Elizabeth's education began with Katherine (Kat) Champernowne
in 1536. Her masters in Latin and Greek were Dr. Richard Coxe, Sir John Cheke, and
William Grindal. For a fuller discussion of these instructors, see Somerset, *Elizabeth*, 11, and
Hibbert, 26. It is interesting to note that Henry VIII had never been taught Greek as a boy
(Somerset, *Elizabeth*, 11).

ing pedagogies produced very different Tudor rulers: Mary, who fashioned herself a "princess" or "queen," and Elizabeth, who preferred "prince" or "king."

Mary's education was promoted by her mother, Katherine of Aragon. As queen of England, Katherine came to be praised more for her extraordinary skills in oratory than for her womanly skills in sewing, and early in her marriage, Henry would often seek her advice in political matters.[4] In 1513, Henry appointed Katherine to act as regent while he warred in France. With Henry away, the Scots took the opportunity to attack England's northern border, but they underestimated Katherine: the queen traveled north to make a speech urging the reserve forces to victory. Although these reserves did not fight at the Battle of Flodden, her speech is still noteworthy, for she took command of the situation. She was indeed, as Erasmus noted, *"egregie docta"* and more than just a "miracle of her sex."[5]

Katherine continued her mother Isabella's active support of education.[6] Unlike Katherine, Mary had no brother (yet) to inherit the crown and was next in line for the throne. Consequently, Katherine asked Vives, the noted humanist scholar, to develop an education plan for the princess, but such a plan posed some problems because of her gender. What should a princess study and should this curriculum differ from what a prince studies?

4. Although Katherine could read, write, and even extemporize Latin in her childhood, she was also taught the more useful feminine tools of spinning, sewing, and painting—tools that her brother, the future King Juan, would not need to master to be an effective ruler. See Foster Watson, ed., *Vives*, 8–9.

5. As cited in Watson, 10, Erasmus also called Katherine *"unicum pietatis exemplar"* (the only or highest example of piety). If Shakespeare can be used as a meter of popular opinion about the queen's abilities, we see his Katherine in *Henry VIII*, Act 1, scene 2, deliver an ahistorical oration that seems plausible because of her education and scholarly reputation. She is Henry's rhetorical adversary throughout the play. In fact, most of the speeches that Shakespeare gives her are merely Holinshed versified.

6. In Watson's words, Isabella's "own early education had not been profound," so she found herself "deficient in Latin" when dictating "despatches to her secretaries" (6). Eventually she achieved what might be termed a "critical accuracy" in Latin and soon came to celebrate both the classics and classical education (Watson, 6)—highly unusual for a woman of fifteenth-century Spain (or anywhere for that matter). She became the "most learned Princess in Europe" and personally taught her four daughters (Watson, 8). But despite her exceptional promotion of the classical education of her daughters and other female nobility, she still, in Garrett Mattingly's telling words, "differentiated between the training of her *girls* and that of the son who was to wear the crown." See Mattingly, 187, emphasis mine.

Although he probably never taught Mary himself, Vives responded to Katherine's concerns with *De Institutione Feminae Christianae* (1523), *De Ratione Studii Puerilis* (1523), and "Satellitium" (sometimes titled "Symbola") (1524) to guide Mary's education.[7] *De Institutione Feminae Christianae* is usually hailed for its radical advocacy of the education of women, yet in it Vives maintains:

> I give no license to a woman to be a teacher, nor to have authority of the man but to be in silence.... [A] Woman is a frail thing, and of weak discretion, and that may be lightly deceived: which thing our first mother Eve sheweth, whom the Devil caught with a light argument. Therefore a woman should not teach, lest when she hath taken a false opinion ... she spread it unto the hearers, by the authority of mastership. (56)

Not very practical advice for a possible ruler of England. Looking to the Bible to validate his view that women should be subordinate and silent, Vives cites St. Paul on Eve's inferiority: "Let a woman learn in silence with all submissiveness. I permit no woman to ... have authority over men; she is to keep silent. For Adam was formed first, then Eve" (1 Tim. 2:11–13). A female ruler, hence, is an oxymoron.[8] Mary would be violating Christian doctrine by her very existence as a sovereign.

Despite his purpose to design an education plan for a princess, and despite his patron queen's distinguished rhetorical abilities, Vives consistently insists that "eloquence" is an unnecessary skill: "for maids to be eloquent of speech, that is to say great babblers, is a token of a light mind and shrewd conditions" (113). Moreover, he states: "though the precepts for men be innumerable: women yet may be informed with few words. For men must be occupied both at home and abroad, both in their own matters and for the common weal" (34). He clearly does not envision Mary as concerned with the "common weal." Even in his preface, he

7. See Juan Luis Vives, *Instruction of a Christian Woman* [*De Institutione Feminae Christianae*], trans. Richard Hyrde, in Watson, 29–136; *Plan of Studies for Girls* [*De Ratione Studii Puerilis*], trans. Foster Watson, in Watson, 137–50; "Satellitium," trans. Foster Watson, in Watson, 241–50.

8. John Knox's *First Blast of the Trumpet* (1558) made clear that he thought a female was incapable of rule and thus deserving of hatred rather than obedience. Knox is also responsible for giving Mary the prefix of "Bloody" (Waldman, 191). The Italian Francesco Barbaro would agree with Knox: "It is proper ... that ... the speech of women never be made public; for the speech of a noble woman can be no less dangerous than the nakedness of her limbs." See Barbaro, *On Wifely Duties*, trans. B. G. Kohl, in *Earthly Republic*, ed. Kohl, Witt, and Welles, 205.

stresses the young princess's developing the proper feminine virtues of chastity, modesty, and morality.[9] He feels that a woman need only concern herself with her honesty and chastity, "Wherefore when she is informed of that, she is sufficiently appointed" (34), adding that Mary cannot help but be "good and holy" if she takes after her parents and, of course, follows his instruction (37–38).

Vives urges that a maid should have proper instruction, even "from the teat" because "I wot not how, but so it is, that we suck out of our mother's teat, together with the milk, not only love, but also conditions and dispositions" (40). The mother and the nurse should be good women, wise and chaste. However, he is not so concerned about who nurses a baby boy: "Neither I will so great diligence to be given in seeking a nurse for a boy" (40). Apparently, the weaker female needs moral strengthening from birth, whereas a male can somehow compensate for a less than virtuous wet nurse.

As the maid grows, she should be taught necessary skills such as needlework, housecrafts, and cookery.[10] Vives specifically mandates that even a "Princess or a Queen" know how to "handle wool and flax" (43–44). After all, he later claims, she will most often be in the company of women (and what should women talk about?). He digresses to make other gender assumptions, this time about teachers: it does not "becometh a woman to rule a school" because it is better if "none at all hear her" (55). It apparently did not occur to him that Mary might someday rule a country.

Vives also prohibits maids from reading books of war and love, both types being antithetical to chastity. However, he is not so prohibitive about a boy's reading.[11] Because of these differences in reading material,

---

9. In Richard Hyrde's dedicatory preface to his translation of Vives (printed in 1540), he recognizes the earlier educator's emphasis: "surely for the planting and nursing of good virtues in every kind of women, virgins, wives and widows, I verily believe there was never any treatise made, either furnished with more goodly counsels, or set out with more effectual reasons, . . . than Master Vives hath done in his book" (30). For the complete text of this preface, see Hyrde, in Watson, 29–32.

10. These were also Isabella's ideas of necessary skills.

11. See Vives's reading list for boys in his study plan for Charles Mountjoy in *Plan of Studies for a Boy* [*De Ratione Studii Puerilis ad Carolum Montjoium Guilielmi filium*], trans. Foster Watson, in Watson, 245–50. According to Barbara McManus in *Classics and Feminism*, 21–22, "in the Renaissance the male aristocracy made classical learning the core of an education specifically designed to prepare men of rank and social standing (and only such men) for political and civic roles."

he does not advocate coeducation.[12] He is also prohibitive about a maid's clothes and makeup, forbidding the use of velvet and silk—recommending wool and coarse linen (83) instead—and the application of ceruse (the white lead face paint that Elizabeth came to be so fond of) because it makes maids "lose all the honour of beauty" (72). Although he gives "precepts for all women in general" (86), his restrictions on attire particularly do not suit a princess who customarily dressed her rank.

Books II and III of *De Institutione Feminae Christianae* deal with wives and widows, and they have much the same moral emphasis that continues through *De Ratione Studii Puerilis*. In this plan, Vives allows the princess to speak with her tutor and fellow (female) pupils in Latin but to learn only by imitation. He is definitely not training an orator. However, in his education plan for William Mountjoy's son Charles, likewise written in 1523, he encourages both a wider range of subjects to prepare for conversation and the (male) pupil's active questioning of the teacher.[13]

Vives apparently felt that Mary merited an education befitting her station—that of a silent, submissive woman and not of a vocal, aggressive ruler. Like her grandmother and mother, Mary had great academic abilities (certainly learning Latin as a child is no small feat), yet Vives stifles her potential by delineating a less aggressive plan of study for her than he does for a mere lord's son.[14]

However, Catherine Parr, Henry VIII's last wife and Mary's last stepmother, encouraged her in her studies, urging her to publish her translation of Erasmus's *Paraphrase of the Gospel of St. John*[15] under her own name: "you will, in my opinion, do a real injury, if you refuse to let it go down to posterity under the auspices of your own name, since you have undertaken so much labor in accurately translating it for the great good of the public."[16] Mary refused, as befitted her instruction from Vives, who had trained her to be silent, and she did not take credit for Erasmus's voice.

12. Needless to say, Vives would not have approved of Edward VI and Elizabeth's studying together. See Alison Weir, *Life of Elizabeth I*, 7.

13. Vives is not primarily concerned with inculcating morality in Charles. See the full discussion in Watson, 244–45.

14. There is strong psychological evidence that backs up my statement. Brown and Gilligan's recent *Meeting at the Crossroads* emphasizes how the "muting of female vigor and trenchancy . . . occurs at adolescence," in the words of reviewer Carolyn G. Heilbrun, "How Girls Become Wimps," 14.

15. This translation is in *The first tome or volume of the Paraphrase of Erasmus vpon the new testamente*, ed. Nicholas Udall (London, 1548).

16. Catherine Parr's 1544 letter to Mary is quoted in Travitsky, ed., *Paradise of Women*, 78.

After Mary gained the Crown in 1553, perhaps it was not so surprising that her official proclamations often began "the Queen our sovereign Lady," an obvious and explicit reference to her sex.[17] She was acutely conscious of herself as a gendered queen, just as Vives had been conscious of her as a princess and not as a future king. In fact, her regnal style ran: "Of the most high, most puissant, and most excellent Princess Mary the First, by the grace of God Queen of England."[18]

Mary continued to cast herself in feminine terms when Wyatt's Rebellion threatened in 1554. In her address to the men awaiting her enemy, she stresses the maternal aspects of her queenship:

> I am come to you in mine own person to tell you . . . how traitorously and rebelliously a number of Kentishmen have assembled themselves against both us and you. Their pretence . . . was for a marriage determined for us . . . [but] the marriage seemed to be but a Spanish cloak to cover their pretended purpose against our religion. . . . What I am ye right well know—I am your Queen. . . . And I say to you, on the word of a prince, I cannot tell how naturally the mother loveth the child, for I was never the mother of any, but certainly if a prince and governor may as naturally and earnestly love her subjects as the mother doth love the child, then assure yourselves that I, being your lady and mistress, do as earnestly and tenderly love and favour you.[19]

Even though Mary calls herself a "prince," she does not see the title as cross-gendered in relation to herself, the way Elizabeth certainly did. Moreover, she does not appropriate the title of king with its patriarchally authoritative connotations. Rather, she compares a prince's love to that of a mother, a role she would like to relate to, a role that can be only female. Perhaps Vives's lavish praise of her mother Katherine as "holy" and "good," "excellent" and "gracious" (32, 37), prompted Mary to revere and use this maternal imagery to elicit her subjects' affections and support.[20] She stresses that she is a "lady and mistress" who loves her sub-

17. Leah S. Marcus has an enlightening discussion of a monarch's self-references in "Shakespeare's Comic Heroines," 140–41.

18. Quoted in Paul L. Hughes and James F. Larkin, eds., *Tudor Royal Proclamations*, II:12. As David Loades succinctly puts it in *Mary Tudor*, Vives "did not encourage [Mary] to believe that she possessed the intellectual resources of a man"(33). For she would someday be the wife of a king, not the king.

19. This speech is reproduced in H. F. M. Prescott, *Spanish Tudor*, 303–4.

20. Her choice of imagery may also be ascribed to the fact that after her father bastardized her, her mother fought for her. This maternal imagery thus becomes highly and positively charged.

jects (H. F. M. Prescott, 304), then goes on to ask the men to defend her. Her loyal subjects repelled the rebels for their maternal queen, who clearly voiced herself as a female—one who needed to be defended by men. (Elizabeth would cast herself differently when an enemy threatened, as seen in her Tilbury speech.)

In addition to educating a specifically gendered pupil in Mary, Vives also wanted her to develop a proper conscience. Gloria Kaufman points out that his texts are more like conduct books than educational treatises (894). His education plan was not so much academic or rhetorical as ethical in its underpinning. He wanted to develop Mary's conscience, but as Anne Somerset states, "it was [Mary's] conscience that was the lodestar that guided all her actions, and . . . this sometimes disadvantaged her as a ruler" (*Elizabeth*, 32). Her decision to marry the Catholic Philip of Spain was based in part on this conscience. The concept of wifely duty created great political difficulties for her, especially after it was made clear that the man she doted on would never be allowed to claim the throne, even after her death. During her lifetime, so that she would not have to be politically submissive to her foreign husband, Parliament refused his coronation, and they insisted that he follow all English laws.[21] However, she was submissive to her ministers. As the Venetian ambassador Giovanni Michieli pointed out, the councillors were "the lords of the kingdom. . . . Respecting the government and public business she is compelled (being of a sex which cannot becomingly take more than a moderate part in them), . . . to refer many matters to her councillors and ministers."[22]

Her proclamations also usually began with deference to Philip as king, despite the fact that he held that title only in name and only through her.[23] She definitely perceived Philip to be her lord, as detailed in a 1556

21. Parliament was suspicious when Philip proposed his coronation and also feared that it would bring England into the Franco-Habsburg War. Moreover, Parliament wanted to ensure through the marriage treaty provision that Philip would have no claim to the throne of England should Mary die first without heirs. See Loades, 210 and 257–59, for the details of Parliament's concerns. A text of the marriage treaty can be found in Hughes and Larkin, II:21–26.

22. This quotation from Michieli, cited in Loades, 316, seems to confirm Loades's assessment of Mary's education, the result of which was "uncertainty rather than emancipation" in that it gave her "no practical guidance whatsoever"; thus, "she continued to accept the 'natural' opinion that many matters were not amenable to a woman's judgment"(6).

23. Her proclamations most typically begin either "Philip and Mary by the grace of God King and Queen of England" or "The King and Queen's most excellent majesties." See Hughes and Larkin, II, for Mary's proclamations.

letter to him concerning a marriage for Elizabeth. Mary wanted to get her own way and to refuse her sister's union (Elizabeth likewise refused the match with Don Carlos), but instead of simply informing Philip of her decision, in the letter she begs him to see things her way:

> Wherefore, my lord, in as humble sort as I may, I, your most true and obedient wife—(which indeed I confess that I ought to be, and to my thinking more than all other wives, having such a husband as Your Highness—not that I am speaking of the multitude of kingdoms, for that is not the chief thing in my eye), I beg Your Majesty.[24]

Even in her will, she styles herself as "Marye by the grace of God Quene of Englond, . . . and lawful wife to the most noble and virtuous Prince Philippe, by the same Grace of God Kynge."[25] The title that she gives herself is not merely a matter of formality; her priorities are the conventional ones stressed by Vives and her society. She then mistakenly and pathetically claims to be with child and writes only "with the full consent, agreement and good contentment of my sayd most Dere L^d and Husband" (Loades, 370). She is a wife who acts only with her husband's permission. In *De Officio Mariti* (1529), Vives quotes Socrates as saying that "men should be ruled by public and common laws, and women by their own husbands."[26] Mary apparently agreed, for she did not challenge the status quo.

Her successor and sister, however, did. Elizabeth's education was similar in many ways to Mary's. Foster Watson concludes that Elizabeth must have mastered Vives's "Satellitium" because her brother had in 1546, and at that time both she and Edward shared the same tutor, Richard Coxe (1–2). Moreover, Roger Ascham, who became Elizabeth's tutor in 1548, often appropriated Vives's techniques (particularly that of double translation) and otherwise often had similar attitudes about education (for example, the abhorrence of romances as suitable reading material). However, if we accept the accuracy and veracity of Ascham's retrospective in *The Scholemaster* (1570),[27] there is a great discrepancy between his attitude toward his pupil and Vives's attitude toward Mary. By teaching and encouraging his student seemingly without regard for her sex,

---

24. For the complete text of the letter, see Prescott, 492–93.

25. Mary's will is reproduced in Loades, 370–83. The original will does not survive.

26. See Vives, *Duty of Husbands* [*De Officio Mariti*], trans. Thomas Paynell, in Watson, 202.

27. I follow the 1570 version of *The Scholemaster* in *Roger Ascham*, ed. William Aldis Wright.

Ascham, unlike Vives, unwittingly may have prepared her to formulate her subsequent self-fashioning as prince and king of England rather than as queen.[28]

In fact, Ascham holds Elizabeth up as the model that "the yong Ientlemen of England" should emulate because she goes beyond them all "in excellencie of learnyng and knowledge of diuers tonges" (219). She has "perfit readines" in Latin, Italian, French, Spanish, and even Greek (219). He concludes, "that which is most praise worthie of all, within the walles of her priuie chamber, she hath obteyned that excellencie of learnyng, to vnderstand, *speake*, & write, both wittely with head, and faire with hand, as scarse one or two rare wittes in both the Vniuersities haue in many yeares reached vnto" (219, emphasis mine). Here, the gap between the two tutors is clear. Ascham praised Elizabeth for her *speaking* ability, whereas Vives emphasized submissive silence for Mary. When Elizabeth studied Demosthenes and Cicero, she studied their oratorical skills rather than primarily focusing on their ethics as Mary had been instructed to do. Elizabeth could speak rhetorically and not risk being considered a "babbler," to use Vives's terminology for "eloquent woman."[29]

Ascham modestly accounts himself "one poore minister in settyng forward these excellent giftes of learnyng in this most excellent Prince" (220). In calling Elizabeth by her preferred title "prince," he seems to acknowledge her successful rhetorical strategy of "building the myth of her own androgyny in order to palliate the political anxieties aroused by her presence on the throne" (Marcus, 137). Whenever she was addressed as "princess," she would respond by referring to herself as "prince" unless she was cultivating a more maternal aspect.[30] Besides Ascham, others

28. Somerset states that Elizabeth's instructors were "to the left-of-centre in religious outlook" (*Elizabeth*, 10), unlike the Catholic Vives. This difference is reflected in their translation exercises: eleven-year-old Mary translated a Latin prayer of St. Thomas Aquinas into English, while Elizabeth at thirteen chose a work by the Protestant theologian Jean Calvin (*Elizabeth*, 10).

29. Elizabeth's education may have earned her this very qualified praise from Bishop Aylmer in a sermon delivered before her: "Women are of two sorts: some of them are wiser, better learned, discreeter, and more constant than a number of men; but another and worse sort of them are fond, foolish, wanton, flibbergibs, tattlers, triflers, wavering, witless, without counsel, feeble, careless, rash, proud, dainty, tale-bearers, eavesdroppers, rumour-raisers, evil-tongued, worse-minded, and in everyway doltified with the dregs of the devil's dunghill." See C. L. Powell, 161.

30. See Marcus's discussion of titles (140). As a sidenote, Elizabeth's father was painfully aware that his child was a "Princes" [*sic*], for he hurriedly had the final "s" added to the birth announcement of his much-awaited "Prince," Anne Boleyn's first-born.

were aware of her vocabulary of rule to the point that her ministers considered her "bossy" (Hibbert, 115). Her regnal style early in her rule read: "Of the most high and mighty princess, our dread sovereign" (Hughes and Larkin, 2:103). "Dread" seems to negate the feminizing effect of "princess." She preferred fear to femininity. By contrast, when she referred to her late sister in a proclamation about licensing shipping and suppressing piracy, she diminished Mary by calling her the "princess Queen Mary."[31]

Unwittingly, then (for I am not implying that this was his conscious motive), Ascham prepared Elizabeth for her entrance into the masculine arena of kingship by allowing and encouraging her to speak instead of inhibiting her orality. Although both Tudor sisters learned Latin, it was a rite of passage into the male world of princely authority only for Elizabeth because she was the one who focused on speaking it. In *Rhetoric, Romance, and Technology,* Walter J. Ong discusses Latin as a Renaissance puberty rite. Learning Latin prepared the schoolboy "for adult life by communicating to him the heritage of a past in a setting which toughened him and thus guaranteed his guarding the heritage for the future" in the extrafamilial world (140). By extension, learning Latin prepared Elizabeth for the same thing. Ong distinguishes Elizabeth as one of a handful of learned Renaissance women. The learned world was a "Latin-writing, Latin-speaking, and even Latin-thinking world" (120), into which Elizabeth successfully passed, initiated by Ascham. And she made use of her learning.

In *The Scholemaster,* Ascham details his "plaine and perfite way of teachyng children, to vnderstand, write, and speake, the Latin tong" (171). He focuses on "youth in Ientlemen and Noble mens houses" (171), and his choices of the nongendered terms "children" and "youth" rather than "boys" is telling. In his book, he praises not only his outstanding pupil, Elizabeth, but also Lady Jane Grey.[32] In his "Preface to the Reader," he says that on 10 December 1563 his writing of the book was occasioned after he "read with the Queenes Maiestie . . . in the Greke tongue . . . that noble Oration of *Demosthenes* against *Aeschines,* for his false dealing in his Ambassage to king *Philip* of Macedonie" (177). He thus begins his study plan with a success story about his most accomplished pupil, whom he says Sir Richard Sackville also praises as the "best Scholer, that euer were in our tyme" (178). As the best schoolmaster, Ascham must impart his knowledge to others, Sackville suggests.

31. For the complete text of this proclamation, see Hughes and Larkin, II:100.
32. Ascham cites Lady Jane as evidence that a gentle tutor produces a pupil who takes pleasure in learning, in this case, *Phaedon Platonis* in Greek (*Scholemaster,* 201–2).

Asham's "first booke for the youth" emphasizes that children learn by praise, not punishment (183). He asserts that the scholar should never be afraid to "aske you any dout" in order to attain, among other academic benefits, "a readines to speake" (183–84) which he stresses as fundamentally important:

> I wish to haue them speake so, as it may well appeare, that the braine doth gouerne the tonge, and that reason leadeth forth the taulke. *Socrates* doctrine is true in *Plato*, and well marked, and truely vttered by *Horace* in *Arte Poetica*, that, where so euer knowledge doth accompanie the witte, there best vtterance doth alwaies awaite vpon the tonge: For, good vnderstanding must first be bred in the childe, which, being nurished with skill, and vse of writing (as I will teach more largelie hereafter) is the onelie waie to bring him [or her] to iudgement and readinesse in speaking. (185-86, addition mine)

Ascham concludes Book I by emphasizing "honestie of liuing," which is "wholie within the compasse of learning and good maners" (237). Like Vives, he deems a Christian education important, but the English educator's views are not as limiting. He does not hold silence as a virtue for Elizabeth or for any youth because speaking is central to his pedagogy. Vives, however, did not "license" Mary for speech.

Book II teaches "the ready way to the Latin tong" (239). Ascham agrees with Vives that double translation or *translatio linguarum* is the best exercise for youths to begin with, but he then deviates from the earlier humanist's methodology by advocating *paraphrasis* for the more advanced student "to translate the best latin authors, into other latin wordes" (246) and *metaphrasis* to translate verse into prose or prose into verse. He cites *epitome* or the use of commonplaces as something to be deployed sparingly to achieve maximum effectiveness and *imitatio* as a skill not for "yong beginners" (268). In his ascending hierarchy, the last way to teach and learn Latin is *declamatio*, and he concludes this section and his book by naming Caesar as the finest example of eloquence "for the tong," in whose writings "could neuer yet fault be found" (301–2).

Ascham himself gives evidence that Elizabeth adhered to his methodology:

> And a better, and nerer example herein, may be, our most noble Queene *Elizabeth*, who neuer toke yet, Greeke nor Latin Grammer in her hand, after the first declining of a nowne and a verbe, but onely by this double translating of *Demosthenes* and *Isocrates* dailie without missing euerie

forenone, and likewise som part of Tullie euery afternone, for the space
of a yeare or two, hath atteyned to soch a perfite vnderstanding in both
the tonges, and to soch a readie vtterance of the latin, and that wyth
soch a iudgement, as they be fewe in nomber in both the vniuersities,
or els where in England, that be, in both tonges, comparable with her
Maiestie. (245–46)

That she benefited from Ascham's other five points is apparent in her
speeches and letters, and that benefit is described in a letter that Ascham
wrote to John Sturm:

She talks French and Italian as well as English: she has often talked to
me readily and well in Latin, and moderately so in Greek. . . . She reads
with me almost all Cicero, and great parts of Titus Livius; for she drew
all her knowledge of Latin from those two authors. She used to give the
morning of the day to the Greek Testament, and afterwards read select
orations of Isocrates and the tragedies of Sophocles. For I thought that
from those sources she might gain purity of style, and her mind derive
instruction that would be of value to her to meet every contingency of
life. To these I added Saint Cyprian and Melanchthon's common places,
&c., as best suited, after the Holy Scriptures to teach her the foundation
of religion, together with elegant language and sound doctrine. Whatever she reads she at once perceives any word that has a doubtful or
curious meaning. She cannot endure those foolish imitators of Erasmus
who have tied up the Latin tongue in those wretched fetters of proverbs.
She likes a style that grows out of the subject; chaste because it is suitable, and beautiful because it is clear.[33]

Unlike Vives, Ascham allows political reading for his royal pupil,[34]
and Elizabeth uses her knowledge of Isocrates[35] in a letter to James VI of
Scotland, dated 7 August 1583:

33. Letter from Ascham to Sturm (or Sturmius), reproduced in Baldwin, *William
Shakspere's small Latine*, 259. Lisa Jardine reads this passage as Ascham's stressing the "'chas-
tening' effect of [Elizabeth's] accomplishment on her personality and ability" in *Still Harping on Daughters*, 53. However, as I show, Ascham is not solely interested in producing a
Christian woman as Vives had been.

34. Katherine Usher Henderson and Barbara F. McManus point out in *Half Humankind*, 84–85, that Elizabeth "ignored Vives' injunction against the study of government for
women" by reading Xenophon, Aeschines, Demosthenes, and even Machiavelli.

35. Her letters also include various allusions to Ulysses, Scylla and Charybdis, and
Prometheus.

Among your many studies, my dear Brother and cousin, I would Isocrates' noble lesson were not forgotten, that wills the Emperor his sovereign to make his words of more account than other men their oaths, as meetest ensigns to show the truest badge of a Prince's arms. . . . You deal not with one whose experience can take dross for good payments; nor one that easily will be beguiled. No, no, I mind to set to school your craftiest Councillor. (*Letters*, 159)

Elizabeth not only remembers her lessons years later, but also takes on the male role of "schoolmaster reminding James of his" (Frye, 5). As she did with her tutor, she still perceives words that have "doubtful or curious" meanings, particularly those of James's councillors, but she is no longer the student; she turns the tables in becoming the teacher who will do the schooling. Moreover, she is clearly conscious of how a king should behave, and she reminds James that his word should not be dross but mean more than other men's oaths. Clearly, Ascham's idea of education did not limit Elizabeth as Vives's had limited Mary.

Elizabeth, then, was better prepared for the throne than her sister had been. In addition to her better (oral) academic training, she also had the experience of watching Mary make mistakes.[36] Mary herself had obviously been no stranger to adversity, but her experiences alone were not enough to prepare her to rule when her education had given her conflicting underpinnings that a "good Christian woman" was to be silent and submissive, and her councillors had shared these views.

These were the same views that Elizabeth had to struggle against as sovereign, but she made use of her strong academic background to help her win this struggle by means of her rhetoric. For example, in a 1563 speech written by Elizabeth but read to the Commons by Lord Keeper Bacon, she states that she has not resolved the issue of succession. She buries this simple message under an impressive and daunting display of rhetoric, however. She begins by saying that she will keep her "Prince's word" and name a successor—eventually—but not "without I see some glimpse of your following surety after my graved bones."[37] She also claims

---

36. Although Jennifer Loach tries to rectify what she calls "misperceptions" of Mary's reign as a failure, she uses suspect reasoning. Saying that the parliaments of Mary's reign were "highly successful" compared to those of Henry VI and Charles I is not saying much. See Loach, *Parliament and the Crown*, 234–35.

37. Quoted in J. E. Neale, *Elizabeth I*, 127.

that she still may marry out of duty, though it takes some time to work out her meaning. Anne Somerset points out about this speech that "Once again, she was reminding the men about her that they were dealing with no mere woman, but an extraordinary being, endowed with gifts that bordered on the sublime" (159). In other words, Elizabeth was making it plain that she was not a woman to be manipulated like her sister Mary, but a powerful prince. Elizabeth would ultimately be married only to England, a fact she often stressed, and would remain in control of herself and her country.

In her speech at Tilbury to rally her troops against the invading Spanish Armada in 1588, Elizabeth, not content to be only a "prince," now terms herself "king." She also forestalls attempts to question her supposed frailty because of her sex by appropriating typical and denigrating beliefs about women to use against any detractors:

> I know I have the body of a weak and feeble woman, but I have the heart and stomach of a king—and a king of England too—and think foul scorn that Parma, or Spain, or any prince of Europe should dare to invade the borders of my realm. To which, rather than dishonor shall grow by me, I myself will be your general, judge, and rewarder of every one of your virtues in the field.[38]

Here, Elizabeth is clear and concise to encourage her subjects. Unlike Mary in her speech against the Wyatt rebels, she does not ask to be defended. She will fight the other princes on her own terms, as a king. Ascham wished to have pupils speak as if reason led forth the talk; Elizabeth certainly would not have disappointed him in this speech. She reasons that if she goes on the offensive and quells the misgivings and fears of her subjects, not only about her gender but also about the impending invasion, they will more likely be on the defensive against the Spanish and fight alongside her, their general (another traditionally male role that she appropriates). In a rousing speech, she maneuvers and inspires her subjects by making her gender no longer a weakness. Despite her physical body, she reminds her subjects that she has a body politic that is far from feeble. As Anne Somerset states, "The creative energies which had been released by her education . . . found an outlet in her artful manipulation of her own tongue" (12).

---

38. Frances Teague summarizes the problems associated with the text of this speech in "Queen Elizabeth in Her Speeches," 63–78. I have used Teague's text of the speech as it appears in Katharina Wilson, ed., *Women Writers*, 542–43.

Any discussion of Elizabeth's rhetorical abilities needs to address her 1601 "Golden Speech" delivered to an audience grateful that she had repealed many monopolies.[39] It was her privilege to grant these monopolies in the first place; she issued the repeal only when faced with the possibility that the Commons would make a bill against them and in effect against her. But she keeps her detractors off balance by variously calling herself "prince," "queen," or "king."

She first affirms that "there is no prince that loves his subjects better," thus placing herself by her choice of pronoun in and above the male arena of sovereignty. She then suggests her more feminine (perhaps motherly) side by rejoicing that God made her "a Queen over so thankful a people." She continues to focus on this same aspect of her nature when she says, "My heart was never set on any worldly goods, but only for my subjects' good" (Teague, "Elizabeth I," 543). Yet she does not fashion herself this way for too long, soon shifting to emphasize her kingly side and insisting that her motives in regards to the monopolies must not be misunderstood: "That my grants should be grievous to my people and oppressions privileged under color of our patents, our kingly dignity shall not suffer it" (Teague, "Elizabeth I," 544). She does not let her audience forget that she is the one in charge. Moreover, they should not attribute any failing to her person: "if my kingly bounties have been abused, and my grants turned to the hurt of my people, contrary to my will and meaning, and if any in authority under me have neglected or perverted what I have committed to them, I hope God will not lay their culps and offenses to my charge" (Teague, "Elizabeth I, 544). Elizabeth then pointedly asks, "Shall I ascribe anything to myself and my sexly weakness?" (Teague, "Elizabeth I," 545). She by no means undercuts herself by asking this question, for she immediately states, "I were not worthy to live then" (Teague, "Elizabeth I," 545). By crediting God with making her "His instrument to maintain His truth and glory" (Teague, "Elizabeth I," 545), she ensures that no one will gainsay her authority, for if they do, then they are gainsaying God's. Her gender thus becomes irrelevant. Her academic training and her experience have served her well. In his work, Ascham states that she liked a style that grows out of the subject. In this speech, she genders herself to fit the sentence and the meaning—unlike Mary, who restricted her gender.

Thus, although both Mary and Elizabeth received humanist educations, their tutors placed a distinctly different emphases on speaking.

39. There are various versions of this speech. I follow Teague's text in Wilson, 543–45.

Even though Vives stressed ethics over academics, Mary is no more re-membered for her ethics than for her learning.[40] In fact, she does not usually make the list of learned Renaissance women that includes Lady Jane Grey, Margaret Roper, and of course her sister. Elizabeth, on the other hand, is remembered for her learning and her impressive reign. She did not see herself as a silent, submissive female, and Ascham, with his glowing praise of her speaking ability, among other things, did not treat her as such.[41] Yet she owed her success as ruler to more than her academic education; she certainly had a practical education as well. Eliza-beth watched her sister's authority debilitated by her unfortunate and ineffectual casting as Philip's barren wife, and perhaps she determined not to make the same mistakes.[42] Instead, she took her cues from her father and cultivated a sense of kingly presence and authority, calling herself "prince" and "king." Unlike Mary, Elizabeth did not have an education manual dedicated to her, but she did have at least one tutor who was dedicated to her education and from whom she may very well have learned how to be a prince.[43]

40. Elizabeth certainly was not spotless, yet Mary remains the more notorious of the Tudor sisters in popular memory. Even Walker, in *Dissing Elizabeth: Negative Representations of Gloriana*, admits the "massive amount of positive material" to support Elizabeth's "pe-rennial popularity" (1–2).

41. Susan Bassnett calls Elizabeth "a model of an independent woman" in *Elizabeth I*, 3.

42. In addition, Constance Jordan states in "Woman's Rule," 440, "The political ar-rangements devised for Mary's marriage had not proved workable in practice, and this failure must have been significant to her half-sister." Weir calls Mary's example to her sister "calamitous" (11).

43. The feminism of the Tudor queens is relative (in more ways than one), but Eliza-beth clearly voiced herself more effectively.

5

"When Riches Growes"

CLASS PERSPECTIVE IN PEMBROKE'S *PSALMES*

Margaret P. Hannay

Mary Sidney, countess of Pembroke, understood social decorum, demonstrating what she would have seen as appropriate humility before the few who were above her in the social scale and demanding a similar humility from those men and women below her. This sense of social class is reflected in her correspondence, in her translations, and particularly in her *Psalmes*, where she demonstrates an acute awareness of the dangers that come with high place, expresses considerable disdain for the "meaner people," and yet articulates a strong sense of noblesse oblige. That social obligation is purely charitable, however, and implies no threat to the power structure. Pembroke's class consciousness produces some striking differences in wording from her biblical sources, for she identifies with the courtier, not with the poor, and she describes God's heavenly court in terms reminiscent of Elizabeth's.

Ignoring social class, Renaissance polemicists often refer to women as though they were an undifferentiated mass, placing them in "an ontological category, a category that implies . . . manual domestic work" for all ranks, as Constance Jordan demonstrates.[1] Giovanni Michele Bruto, for example, argues that even noblewomen should be deprived of an education that would make them discontent with domestic chores, and Lodovico Dolce claims that even royal women should spend their time "spinning and weaving."[2] Early feminists, in contrast, argue that rank

---

1. Constance Jordan, "Renaissance Women," 93. See also Jordan, *Renaissance Feminism*, particularly the concluding section on seventeenth-century England, 286–307. For the additional factor of race, see, for example, the essays in *Women, "Race," and Writing in the Early Modern Period*, edited by Margo Hendricks and Patricia Parker; and Kim Hall, *Things of Darkness*.

2. Lodovico Dolce, *Dialogo della alogo della institutione delle donne* (Venice, 1545), sig. B5, cited in Jordan, "Renaissance Women," 93.

could supersede gender, thereby enabling a queen to govern. Domenico Bruni da Pistoia more specifically ties a woman's tasks not only to gender but also to class: "Each woman in her rank does as well as a man in taking care of her affairs and in organizing her tasks, however modest or imposing they may be; she behaves according to her station in life."[3] Like Bruni, we have come to realize that it is impossible to make valid generalizations about Renaissance women without taking social class into account. Chastity was a requirement that did transcend class boundaries, encompassing even Elizabeth herself—who brilliantly turned that stricture into the cult of the Virgin Queen—but the requirements of silence and obedience were based on class. Although all *women* were instructed to be silent and obedient before their husbands, all *persons* were instructed to obey their social superiors.

Within the family, any wife occupied dual positions, as "An Homily on the State of Matrimony" from *The Second Tome of Homilies* (1563) explains: "To obey is another thing then to control or command, which yet [wives] may do to their children and to their family, but as for their husbands, them must they obey and cease from commanding and perform subjection."[4] The duality of subject positions was most extreme in the case of a regnant queen, as John Aylmer, Bishop of London, argues: "I graunte that, so farre as perteineth to the bandes of mariage, and the office of a wife, she muste be a subjecte: but as a Magistrate she maye be her husbands head."[5]   Although a reigning queen was an exceptional case, a married woman of high rank, like Pembroke, also occupied dual subject positions. Any woman "must of dutie be unto hir husband in all things obedient," as Edmund Tilney phrases the commonplace, but an aristocratic woman would also be entitled to immediate obedience from the men and women who served her ("Flower of Friendship" 135). This

3. Domenico Bruni da Pistoia, *Difese delle donne* (Milan, 1559), sig. C3, cited in Jordan, "Renaissance Women," 99. On "exceptional women" at the top and bottom of the social scale, in contrast to the ordinary woman, see Amussen, "Elizabeth I and Alice Balstone," 219–40. See also the voluminous studies on Queen Elizabeth, particularly such recent work as Jordan, *Renaissance Feminism*, 116–33; Benson, 231–50; Frye; and Levin.

4. "An Homily on the State of Matrimony" from *The Second Tome of Homilies* (1563), reprinted in *Daughters, Wives, and Widows*, ed. Joan Larsen Klein, 17.

5. John Aylmer, *An harborowe for faithfull and trewe subjects* (1559), sigs. C4ᵛ–D, cited in the introduction to Tilney, *The Flower of Friendship*, ed. Valerie Wayne, 45. Aylmer was writing in response to John Knox, *First Blast of the Trumpet against the Monstrous Regiment of Women* (1558). For an overview of women's position in the family, which involved negotiating between contradictory ideals of obedience and of companionship, see Susan Amussen, *Ordered Society*, 34–66; and Margaret L. King, 1–80.

dual position of a high-placed woman is dramatized in Pembroke's rendition of Psalm 45, with its admonitions to the king's young bride. She must obey the king, but only the king, for he is her only superior: "for onlie hee on thee hath lordlie right / him onlie thou with awe must entertaine" (45.43–44). If she obeys her lord and king, then her position as queen consort will give her power over all his empire:

> then unto thee both Tirus shall bee faine
>   presents present, and richest nations moe,
> with humble sute thie Roiall grace to gaine,
>   to thee shall doe such homage as they owe. (45.45–48)[6]

Like the queen described in Psalm 45, Pembroke was required to submit to an arranged marriage, to produce heirs for her husband's family, and to obey her husband; however, her deference to her wealthy husband raised her social and economic position, as such obedience had done for the young queen in the Psalm.

Because of the dissonance between the Sidneys' status and their rank, young Mary Sidney would have been particularly class conscious.[7] Her mother, Mary Dudley Sidney, was the daughter of a duke, John Dudley, duke of Northumberland, who had virtually ruled England during King Edward's reign. She was permitted to marry the rising young courtier, Henry Sidney, despite his lack of an aristocratic title, because he was a dear friend of King Edward and seemed destined for greatness. But Edward died in Henry Sidney's arms—and with Edward died the Sidneys' hopes for advancement. Under Queen Mary they managed to maintain their estate of Penshurst, despite the attainder against the Dudley men and despite the execution of Lady Sidney's brother Guildford along with his wife, Lady Jane Grey. When Elizabeth came to the throne, the Sidneys' fortunes rose with those of Lady Sidney's brother, Robert Dudley, eventually earl of Leicester. Yet after Lady Sidney lost her beauty to the smallpox she caught while nursing the queen, she was rarely at court; "[my] wonted lodginge" was "taken from me," she complained, and she

---

6. All Pembroke quotations are taken from the *Collected Works of Mary Sidney Herbert*, ed. Margaret P. Hannay, Noel J. Kinnamon, and Michael G. Brennan. The Penshurst *Psalmes* manuscript is quoted with the kind permission of the Viscount de L'Isle, MBE, from his collection at Penshurst Place. On the literary influence of the Sidney *Psalmes*, see Freer, 73; Lewalski, *Protestant Poetics*, 33–52, 241–45, 275–76, 301–2; Woods, *Natural Emphasis*, 175; Fisken, 166–83; Richard Todd, 74–93; Zim, 185–210; and Rienstra.

7. For biographical details, see Hannay, *Philip's Phoenix*.

was reduced to begging for any suitable room.[8] To this daughter of a duke came the bitter task of turning down a barony for her husband because of "our ill abylyty . . . to maintaine a hier tytle then now we posses": without additional revenue, even that lowest of aristocratic ranks would cause the family "utter ruwin."[9]

In these years when the family perceived itself as slighted by Elizabeth and as impoverished by her service, young Mary Sidney nevertheless grew up seeing her father honored as the virtual ruler of Wales and Ireland, her uncle Leicester courted as the most powerful man in England, and her brother Philip honored on the Continent as the hope of the Protestant alliance. Celebrated as "Proregis Hibernici filius" and "Baron de Sidenay" on the Continent, titles that enabled him to negotiate with princes, Philip Sidney was reminded at home of his (relatively) low status at court by the queen herself.[10] If Fulke Greville's account of Sidney's tennis court quarrel with the earl of Essex is accurate, the queen undertook to prevent a duel by reminding Sidney of "the difference in degree between earls and gentlemen; the respect inferiors owe to their superiors . . . and how the gentleman's neglect of the nobility taught the peasant to insult upon both."[11] Such a resolution must have been bitter indeed for Sidney, once heir to the earldoms of both Leicester and Warwick, but now merely a "gentleman."

The complexities of the countess of Pembroke's social position are reflected in her holograph correspondence. Her humility to those above her can best be demonstrated through two letters, one to her uncle Leicester and one to Queen Elizabeth. Leicester served as Mary Sidney's patron at court, gave her rooms in the private block when the queen visited Kenilworth, and, when she was just fifteen, arranged her marriage with his enormously wealthy friend and contemporary, Henry Herbert, earl of Pembroke, thereby giving her the rank that her family would have seen as her due. (Leicester took evident pleasure in terming his contemporary, Henry Herbert, his son after Herbert's marriage to Mary Sidney, whom Leicester called his daughter.) A letter written when she was a new bride demonstrates the subservience she showed to Leicester: "My most honorid Lord, ~~your sone~~ I perceive by your lordships

8. Mary Dudley Sidney to Sussex, 1 February 1574, Cotton MS, Vespasian, F.xii, f. 179, and Mary Dudley Sidney to Sussex, no date, Cotton MS, Titus, B.ii, f. 302.

9. Mary Dudley Sidney to Sir William Cordell, Master of the Rolls, 2 May 1572, PRO SP 12/86, f. 33.

10. On the significance of his Continental titles, see van Dorsten, 49.

11. "A Dedication to Sir Philip Sidney," in Fulke Greville, 40.

leteres your a~~r~~ ofendid with me for not sending you worde of your sones a mendment, from agreter Siknes then I thanke god ther was cause, it shuld be reportid so." She goes on to explain that Pembroke had a trifling illness, "sume payne in his hede" as she had written earlier, but he had recovered even before the physician arrived. Her problem is not her husband's headache, but rumor. Someone who wanted to make trouble between Pembroke and Leicester had apparently accused the young countess of not showing adequate respect to her uncle by sending word of Pembroke's recovery:

> truly my lord if ther had bine any such caus you shuld have hard of it
> by me tho I know it would have bine ~~ve~~ most unwellcome, and Nues
> that I would very unwillingly writ to your lordship, yet much rather
> then ~~if~~ you shuld here of it after this maner. I trust your anger will be
> at anend when you here how littell I ame in faute.[12]

The worried tone is reinforced by the physical appearance of the letter. It was indeed "Cribled in hast," full of blots and deletions. Pembroke must have been furious at her because of Leicester's anger. Caught between these two powerful, irascible earls, it is no wonder that she hopes his "anger will be at anend when you here how littell I ame in faute." Already, at age sixteen, she has learned to beware of envy and slander, which she and others saw as the bane of the honest courtier.

Similar abasement is demonstrated later in her life by her letter to Queen Elizabeth, thanking the queen for accepting her son William at court. The importance of this letter is also demonstrated by its physical appearance, for it was clearly not "Cribled in hast." It is the one extant letter in the countess of Pembroke's own hand that has no deletions, no blots, and no corrections; undoubtedly copied time and time again, it is symmetrical on the page, with her signature in the lower right-hand corner, signifying the utmost humility. She reminisces about her own early days in Elizabeth's court, and then, knowing that flattery is usually more effective when presented in person, she attempts to turn her current absence from court into a rhetorical ploy: "blessed indeed ar they that may behold yow. My pen hath now hitt uppon my parte of torment, I that doo not, and yet still doo behold yow with the humblest eies of my

---

12. Mary Sidney, countess of Pembroke, to Robert Dudley, earl of Leicester, undated, probably 15 August 1578. Addressed "Very good Lord and the Earle of Leycester geve these." (The left margin of the address is worn off.) Holograph. Manuscript of the Marquess of Bath, Longleat House, Warminster. Dudley Papers II/ 187. *Collected Works* 1:285.

mynds love, and admiration." Ending with a prayer for the queen, she signs her letter, "Yowr hyghnes / most bound / the humblest of yowr Creturs / M. Pembroke."[13]

Pembroke was "the humblest of . . . Creturs" only when addressing her few superiors, for she knew her own social rank and her position as sister of the legendary Sir Philip Sidney. For example, a business letter transcribed by her secretary has an impassioned postscript in her own hand, declaring, "It is the Sister of Sir Philip Sidney who yow ar to right and who will worthely deserve the same."[14] The poets who sought her patronage groveled before her and complained of envy at Wilton (the principle estate of the earl of Pembroke), echoing the courtiers around Elizabeth. Pembroke became adept at using connections at court and refused to accept injustice meekly, even later in her relatively powerless position as a widow. Although she was repeatedly brushed aside by King James and his ministers, she finally brought to trial servants who abused her trust, as well as jewel thieves, pirates, and murderers. One tenant, Peter Samyn, complained that she had been "incensed against [him] by the reports of some malicious person," even as she herself had been the victim of rumor.[15] If the letters printed as hers by John Donne the younger are authentic, then she flaunted her own "brave choler, as some of them know, who are near me, and must have a part of that humour, whether they will or no."[16]

Pembroke's awareness of her own rank is evident, not only in her business correspondence, but also throughout her works and particularly in her *Psalmes*. Her aristocratic milieu is revealed even in such details

---

13. Mary Sidney, countess of Pembroke, to Queen Elizabeth, dated 1601, using the new style. Addressed "To the Queenes most Excellent Majesty." Endorsed "1601, Countesse of Pembroke to her Majesty." Sealed twice with the Sidney pheon. Holograph manuscript of the Marquess of Salisbury. Cecil Papers 90, f. 147. *Collected Works* 1:291–92.

14. Mary Sidney, dowager countess of Pembroke to Sir Julius Caesar, BL Add. MS 12, 503, ff. 151–52. The letter is sealed with the Sidney pheon. *Collected Works* 1:295.

15. Chancery Proceeding, Bundle 324, No. 56 (1617–1621) in *Cardiff Records*, ed. John Hobson Matthews, 95–96.

16. John Donne the younger published three letters said to be from the Countess of Pembroke in his edition, *A Collection of Letters Made by Sir Tobie Matthew, Knight* (London: Henry Herringman, 1660) 85–92. Her temper would pale beside that of Sir Philip Sidney, who threatened a devoted servant he thought was reading his letters, and of young Robert Sidney, who stabbed his tutor with a penknife. Her husband, earl of Pembroke, was infamous for his rages. "Of what temper the man is your honor knows sufficiently," Sir Edward Winter wrote to Sir Robert Cecil and Charles Howard, Lord High Admiral, November 1595, *HMC Salisbury* 5:79–80. Katherine Duncan-Jones discusses Sir Philip Sidney's choleric nature, 22–23.

as the falconry imagery in Psalm 83 and her interpretation of the "mighty man" of Psalm 78 as a "knight" (197). God's establishment of the temple on Mt. Syon is described as "there he his house did Castle-like enclose" (78.206). Allusion is made to aristocratic travel with the "lords conduct" in Psalm 126.2 and the "pasport" in 72.60. Psalm 50 adds the "pursevant" (3)—a "messenger" or "warrant-officer" *(OED)*—as well as the courtly "garde" and "usshers" (6). To the biblical phrase that "he counteth the nomber of the starres and calleth them all by their names" (Geneva, 147:4), Pembroke adds a courtly metaphor, describing the stars as "the torches of his heav'nly hall" (147.11–12). Psalm 135 refers to God choosing "Israel his own Domain to be" (l. 9) in the original sense of a lord's lands or possessions, and speaks of God punishing "Pharos court" (l. 28), whereas the Psalter speaks of "Pharaoh, and all his servants" (also in Geneva 135:9).[17]

In the *Psalmes*, Pembroke devotes particular attention to the precarious lot of the courtier, a theme also emphasized in her 1590 translation of *A Discourse of Life and Death* by Philippe de Mornay.[18] The central section of the *Discourse* focuses on Ambition, presenting an extended discussion of the life of the courtier from one who knew its dangers. Using the ventriloquism of translation, Pembroke could safely present her own judgment of the English court. One courtier, like her brother Philip, wins favor by offering up his body as a soldier, "hazarding his life upon every occasion, with losse ofttimes of a legge or an arme, and that at the pleasure of a Prince, that more regards a hundred perches of ground on his neighbours frontiers, then the lives of a hundred thousand such as he." Others gain place by giving up their conscience, "flattering a Prince, and long submitting . . . to say and doe . . . whatsoever they will have them: whereunto a good minde can never commaund it selfe." Like a "Lions keeper," courtiers have "made a fierce Lion familiar," but they still live in constant danger. Princes enjoy toying with them, raising them "to great height" only "to cast [them] downe at an instant." Thinking themselves surrounded by friends, courtiers are deceived, for "their inferiors salute them because they have need of them," and their equals are consumed with envy. If we believe that they enjoy their high place, we are misled by outward appearances: others think them high, but so long

17. For additional examples see May, 208.

18. See also Beilin, *Redeeming Eve*, 128–29. *Antonius* also presents the aristocracy as the champion of the people, through Philostratus, the wise aristocrat who can foresee ruin; see particularly ll. 279–83. Samuel Daniel, in his play *The Tragedie of Cleopatra*, written because the countess's Antony "Requir'd his Cleopatras company," includes a similar emphasis, perhaps at Pembroke's request; see particularly the chorus at the end of Act I, sig. H5.

as anyone is above them, "they think themselves very lowe." Referring to the gold chains of office, the *Discourse* states that the only difference between courtiers and the "most hardly intreated prisoners" is that the one has fetters of iron and the other of gold, one is chained in the body and the other in the mind, "the prisoner drawes his fetters after him, the courtier weareth his upon him" (l. 231–308, *Collected Works* 1:235–37).

Pembroke uses this same image effectively in her paraphrase of Psalm 73:5–6, wherein the psalmist considers the "prosperitie of the wicked," declaring that because "They are not in trouble as other men . . . Therefore pride is as a chaine unto them and crueltie covereth them as a garment" (Geneva).[19] She may have derived the idea of the chains of office from the Geneva note to verse six, "They glorie in their pride as some do in their chaines: and in crueltie, as some do in apparel." The emphasis on the presumption of the wicked may have been inspired by the familiar Sternhold-Hopkins version:

> Therefore presumption doth embrace,
> their necks as doth a chaine:
> And are even wrapt, as in a robe,
> with rapine and disdayne. (*The Whole Booke of Psalmes*, Psalm 73:6)

Pembroke's version refers specifically to the chain and robes of office worn by the wicked:

> therefore with pride, as with a gorgious chaine,
>   their swelling necks encompassed they beare:
>   all cloth'd in wrong, as if a Robe it were. (73, ll. 16–18)

As one might expect in the 1590s, clothing metaphors, which Pembroke uses so effectively in her dedicatory poem to Queen Elizabeth, "Even Now that Care," are expanded in the *Psalmes* to describe social status (ll. 27–35, 63–64). As in satires on the upwardly mobile, the wicked in the *Psalmes* inappropriately adopt aristocratic dress, even if it is allegorical.[20] For example, when Thomas Nashe mocks the pretensions of Gabriel Harvey, a professor at Cambridge but the son of a rope maker, he accuses

---

19. Noel J. Kinnamon (10–29) suggests a comparison between these chains and George Herbert's "The Collar." See also Schleiner, 72–73.

20. Elizabeth's 1597 sumptuary law is reproduced in Lisa Jardine, "'Make thy doublet of changeable taffeta': Dress Codes, Sumptuary Law and 'Natural' Order," in *Still Harping on Daughters*, 142–45.

him of "ruffling it out huffty tuffty in his suite of velvet."[21] Philip Stubbes rails against the sin of "pryde of apparell," defining it as "wearyng of Apparell more gorgeous, sumptuous & precious than our state, callyng or condition of lyfe requireth."[22] Pembroke herself was careful to dress according to her own rank, as evidenced by the Simon van de Passe engraving that portrays her wearing ropes of pearls, a gown of embroidered silk trimmed with exquisite lace, and a velvet robe edged with ermine. She no doubt shared the antagonism of members of her class toward upstarts who would imitate them by wearing similar apparel.[23]

As in Psalm 73, the enemies of God may be described in terms of their presumptuous clothing.[24] In contrast, Psalm 109 prays that the wicked be clothed more appropriately, that "wretchednesse [may be] his cloake" and "woe . . . his garment," that they will wear worse disgrace "then ever clothed me, / trailing in trayne a synnfull shamefull gowne" (ll. 45, 49, 77–78). More original is Pembroke's version of Psalm 55:28–30, wherein she expands the biblical personification of "iniquity" and "mischief" who are in the streets of the city, adding the image of the costume from the masque:

> These walk their cittie walles both night and day,
> oppressions, tumults, guiles of ev'ry kind
>   are burgesses and dwell the midle neere,
>   about their streetes his masking robes doth weare
> Mischeif cloth'd in deceit, with treason lin'd. (25–29)

The deceit inherent in any masque (in both senses) links the dissemblance of corrupt courtiers with "Mischeif" and with treason.[25]

21. Thomas Nashe, *Have with you to Saffron Walden, or Gabriell Harveys Hunt is Up* (1596), cited in Jardine, *Still Harping*, 147. Jardine suggests that this was appropriate dress for his academic rank. On the quarrel between Nashe and Harvey, and its connection with Pembroke, see *Philip's Phoenix*, 139–42.

22. Philip Stubbes, *The Anatomie of Abuses* (1583), cited in Jardine, *Still Harping*, 147.

23. Their accounts demonstrate that Sir Henry and Lady Mary Sidney also dressed in aristocratic silk, satin, and velvet, with gold and silver embroidery and laces, and many jewels. See, for example, Lady Sidney's jewels for 1568–50, De L'Isle MS U1500 A9/5, 6, 7, 12; clothing accounts for the Sidneys in 1568, U1474 A36; and dress accounts for 1571 in U1474 A53/3. See also the accounts for the children in the early 1570s, including MS U1475 A4/5, A50, A56.

24. In the *Psalmes* the metaphor is frequently used in connection with Nature, as in 74, ll. 85–88, 85, ll. 32, or 102, ll. 82–84.

25. Deceit, or hypocrisy, as a robe lined with treason is reminiscent of Dante's *Inferno*, Canto XXIII, wherein the hypocrites are punished by being forced to walk endless circles wearing golden robes lined with lead, clothing that looks sumptuous but causes anguish.

As the hypocrisy and the punishment of the wicked can be shown in terms of their clothing, so can God's power. Many of the Hebrew Psalms celebrate the kingship of God, a theme that Pembroke often presents through imagery that reflects Elizabeth's court. "Cloth'd with state and girt with might, / Monark-like Jehova raignes" (93.1–2), an idea developed in the courtly imagery of Psalm 104, wherein Pembroke follows John Calvin in rendering the curtain of the heavens as a canopy of state:

> th'eternall lord: ô lord, ô god of might,
> to thee, to thee, all roiall pompes belonge,
> clothed art thou in state and glory bright:
> for what is els this Eye-delighting light;
> but unto thee a garment wide and long?
> the vauted heaven but a Curtaine right,
> a Canopy, thou over thee hast hunge? (2–8)

God is represented as the monarch, wearing robes of light (perhaps the cloth of gold restricted to the rank of countess or above) and sitting under his canopy of state. Even so, the godly are represented as God's retainers, wearing God's livery. In Psalm 106.8–14, for example, the speaker asks that God will grant him the safety of wearing his livery that he may join God's people: "make me with them thy safeties liv'ry weare." The speaker also asks to wear God's badge, a device that would identify the followers of a lord, such as the Sidney porcupine or the Dudley bear with a ragged staff. In the earlier Variant Psalm 105.45, for example, God leads forth his joyous people, those "Who his choyces badg had worn." (Compare the variant phrase, "deaths badg," in Psalm 49.17 as recorded by Samuel Woodforde.) The imagery of Nature in Psalm 74 also includes such metaphors: "the summers corny crowne, / the winters frosty gowne, / nought but thy badge, thy lyvery are" (96–97). Similarly, in Psalm 65. 7–12 the Psalmist recounts the joy of those on God's "checkrole," or the court payroll—in other words, those who have been received into God's court and feast at his table.

In Psalm 84, the psalmist longs for God's presence, again described as God's court. The Geneva Bible renders the passage without regard to present rank: "a daie in thy courtes is better then a thousand other where: I had rather be a dorekeper in the House of my God, then to dwell in the tabernacles of wickednes" (84:10). A note explains God's courts as "Gods Church," a word never used in Pembroke's *Psalmes*, although it is used by Philip Sidney (Psalm 29.24). Pembroke's version does emphasize rank, as the speaker longs "to view thy Courtes farre" (84.3) Happy is he, the psalmist says, "who remaineth / thy houshold-man" (84.17–18). Happier would he be "to spend my ages treasure / waiting a porter at thy gates: / then dwell a lord with wicke'd mates" (84.38–40). This does not imply a lower-class perspective, as it may first appear. Rather, in Pembroke's interpretation the aristocratic speaker would be willing to give up even his rank to serve in God's house (May, 208).

In Pembroke's *Psalmes* it is often the courtier, rather than the poor, who cries for justice, as throughout Psalm 86. For example, the Geneva Bible reads "incline thine eare, o Lord, and heare me: for I am poore and needie," and the Psalter also emphasizes the poverty of the speaker, "for I am poor, and in misery" (86:1). Pembroke's speaker may be "oppressed," even "helplesse" because of the machinations of the ungodly, but she is not poor.

Matthew Parker also uses courtly imagery in Psalm 86 and in Psalm 143, wherein his phrase "heare my sute" (1) seems to inspire Pembroke's courtly context.[26]

> Æternall lord, thine eare incline:
>   heare me most helplesse, most oppressed:
> this Client save, this servant thine,
>   whose hope is whole to thee addressed. (86.1–4)

Using the language of the courtier, Pembroke's speaker asks that God will hear her "carefull suites of my commending" and "advance" her from "saddnes" to "gladdnes." The prayer is that of a servant not in the literal sense, but in the metaphorical sense—a courtier who, like Pembroke, had a mother who served the monarch and who has also served at court herself: "who in thy service have attended, / and of thy handmaid am descended" (86.39–40).[27] The courtier pleads to be rein-

26. But note *Psalmes* 66, l. 63, where Pembroke misses an opportunity to add courtly imagery, as Matthew Parker's phrase, "no tyme my sute reject" (v. 20), *The Whole Psalter*.

27. Because the voice of the *Psalmes* is David's as well Pembroke's, I have followed convention in using the male pronoun. Pembroke's speaker is carefully nongendered, however, not one who is the "son of thy handmaid," as in the bible, but "of thy handmaid am descended." Cf. Ps 144.13, where the phrases "this child" and "whose neerest kinn is nought" replace the biblical phrase "the sonne of man" (Geneva v. 3). One gendered reference is the "young man" of Psalm 119:2, but he is not necessarily identified with the speaker. On gender in Pembroke's *Psalmes*, see Hannay, "'House-confined maids,'" 20–35.

stated, to be given some mark of favor that will demonstrate the lord's grace and embarrass his enemies:

> O lett some token of thy love
>   be eminently on me placed;
> some Cognisance, to teach and prove,
>   that thine I am, that by thee graced.
>   to dye their cheekes in shamefull hue
>   that now with spite my soule pursue (86.41–46).

A similar presentation is given of the courtier making "hott and harty sute" to God in Psalm 119.H4. Here, the image apparently comes from Calvin, "made sute untoo thy face" (119:58). In Pembroke's rendition, the speaker makes "entreaty" by sending a "suite" and asking that the Lord will "yeeld audience to me" and hear her case (119.H4.1–6).

Pembroke's own experience at court is evident in her depiction of the queen and her maids of honor in Psalm 45, a royal epithalamion traditionally ascribed to the wedding of Solomon. The queen is dressed in fine embroidery and in the cloth of gold that identifies members of the highest social ranks:

> On thie right side thie dearest queene doth stand
>   richlie araid in cloth of Ophir gold. . . . (45, ll. 35–36)
> This Queene that can a king hir father call,
>   doth only shee in upper garment shine?
> Naie under clothes, and what shee weareth all,
>   golde is the stuffe the fasshion arte divine,
>   brought to the king in robe imbrodred fine. (ll. 49–53)

Beth Wynne Fisken reads this paraphrase as "a rich tapestry of interwoven privilege and obligation, as the rights and duties of the king, the noblewomen of the court, and the maids-of-honor are carefully outlined," with primary emphasis, however, on explaining to the new queen "her position, the homage due her by the court and other nations, as well as her corresponding duty to leave behind memories of her family and home to concentrate on producing an heir to guarantee the perpetuation of the hierarchy," a duty that, as we have noted, reflects Pembroke's own experience as an aristocratic bride (172–75).

Pembroke also emphasizes the role of the queen's attendants. The women who surround the queen are not, in her version, the other wives of the notoriously polygamous King Solomon, but rather the queen's "courtlie band," her "maides of honor."[28] "Daughters of kings among thie courtlie band, / by honoring thee of thee doe honor hold (Psalm 45, ll. 33–34). As Fisken notes, these aristocratic women are completely dependent "on the monarch's good will," for only by honoring the queen will they receive honor (173). Pembroke specifically points to degrees of favor, for these "maides of honor" attend the queen "with such, to whome more favoure shall assigne / in neerer place their happie daies to spend" (Psalm 45.55–56). This is the sole indication of the complexities and dangers that surround the waiting women, dangers that must have been all too evident to the daughter of Mary Dudley Sidney.

Many other Psalms more explicitly address the perilous position of the courtier, particularly the dangers of envy and slander, as David experienced in the court of Saul. Commentators such as Martin Bucer, John Calvin, and Franciscus Vatablus were drawn to "what they took to be the prevalence of bad-mouthing and slander in the political world they thought David described in his poetry," according to Anne Prescott (164). Pembroke typically emphasizes or even expands such slanderous references. For example, in Psalm 71:32 Pembroke adds to the biblical "enemies" (71:10) the concept of "Spies" who had been watching the Psalmist and who then debate how best to destroy him.

Pembroke's translation of the *Discourse* also refers to the dangers of court life. Meditating on the possibility of offering valuable service to the state, the *Discourse* pessimistically concludes that perhaps in "former ages" a good courtier could accomplish much, but as things are now, if you do ill, "you have God for your enemy, and your owne conscience for a perpetually tormenting executioner." But if you do well, "you have men for your enemies . . . whose envie and malice will spie you out, and whose crueltie and tyrannie will evermore threaten you" (435–44). The theme of envy gains resonance in Pembroke's works because the Sidneys believed that Sir Philip was slain by envy. He died in the Netherlands in a campaign doomed by inadequate troops and supplies. Sidney's family and friends attributed the queen's lack of support to envy and slander at court, a recurring theme in elegies for Sir Philip in *Astrophel* and also in Book VI of Edmund Spenser's *The Faerie Queene*, wherein Sir Calidore is traditionally believed to represent Philip Sidney.

28. The Geneva Bible renders the phrase more accurately as "honourable wives" (v. 9), whereas the Psalter reads, "honourable women" (v. 10). Théodore de Bèze avoids the reference to polygamy. Calvin acknowledges the polygamy but says that Solomon's indulgence is contrary to the law of God (comment on Psalm 45:10).

Pembroke accentuates the corrosive power of envy when she dedicates the *Psalms* to Sidney's "Angell spirit," now safely in heaven "where never Envie bites" ("To the Angell spirit," line 63, *Collected Works* 1:111). In her use of the Psalms to portray the sufferings of those who have been brought down by envy and court factions, she had been anticipated by two of her uncles. When John and Robert Dudley were imprisoned in the Tower for their efforts to put their sister-in-law Lady Jane Grey on the throne of England, each translated a Psalm to speak of his own experience as a fallen courtier. John Dudley used Psalm 55 to cry out against those who betrayed him; Robert Dudley used Psalm 94 to identify his own cause with God's.[29] Such usage of the Psalms was an integral part of the Protestant tradition, wherein the persecuted cry out for justice, adapting the words of the psalmist as their own.[30] Although present both in the original Hebrew and in the Protestant Psalms and commentaries that were Pembroke's primary sources, their bitterness and desire for retribution are also noticeable aspects of her paraphrases. Her rendering of Psalm 55:39 is equally fierce in its prayer against "my soule, my other self, my inward frend" who betrayed the speaker; her prayer goes even beyond the vehemence of the Geneva version, which asks that the enemies be sent "quick to their grave." In Pembroke's version, God is asked to "lett a soddaine death work their decay, / Who speaking faire, such canckred malice mind," and to have them buried alive, still "breathing in theyr beare" (55.43–45). Her rendition of Psalm 94 opens with a prayer addressed to the "God of revenge" that the wicked, who "crush" the godly, will be punished. Pembroke, like other members of the Dudley/ Sidney/Herbert Protestant alliance, had no doubt that she was among the godly.

Dozens of other Psalms cry out to God for justice against slanderers, because slander and envy, as Mornay said, are the chief dangers to the courtier. For example, in Psalm 52.5–7 the speaker prays for protection from tyrants who contrive "lewd lies . . . sharper then sharpest knives" and Psalm 140.4–5 rails against those "whose tongues are sharper things / then Adders stings." As the tyrant contrives lies (indeed is defined as a tyrant *because* of his lies), so the just ruler in Psalm 101 promises to overthrow the malicious and the "whisp'ring biters" or slanderers. Em-

---

29. *The Arundel Harington Manuscript of Tudor Poetry*, ed. Ruth Hughey, 289–90. Writing metric Psalms was almost *de rigeur* for prisoners in the Tower. See John N. King, *Tudor Reformation Literature*, 232–35.

30. See, for example, the oft-reprinted direction of Athanasius for readers to apply the Psalms to their own condition because "It is easy . . . for every man to finde out in the Psalmes, the motion and state of his owne soule," *The Whole Booke of Psalmes*, sig. *7ᵛ.

phasizing the tongue imagery implicit in the original, the king promises
that he will "for truth-tellers seeke and search the land." Calvin's commentary on this passage uses slander as a synecdoche for all evil that a
person can do, for "Backbiting is a noysome plague above all others. For
it is all one as if a man should kill a body by treason: nay rather, a
backbiter dispatcheth menne unwares no lesse than a poysoner" (*Psalms*,
n.p.).

Psalm 69 contains another cry for justice from one who has been cast
down from high estate, whose very weeping is mocked by his enemies.
In her paraphrase, Pembroke adapts verse 12 ("They that sate in the gate,
spake of me, and the drunkards sang of me" [Geneva]) and dramatizes
the situation:

> If I weepe, and weeping fast,
>   if in sackcloth sadd I mourn,
> in my teeth the first they cast,
>   all to Jeast the last they turn.
>   now in streetes with publique prating
>   powring out their inward hating:
>   private now at banquetts plac't,
>   singing songs of wyny tast. (69, ll. 33–40)

Protesting his own innocence, the speaker claims that his suffering is
only because of his "zeal," that particularly Protestant term for godly
service. When the wicked are angry at God, they turn on the speaker:
"while the shott of piercing spight / bent at thee, on me doth light"
(69.31–2). Because of his innocent suffering, the Psalmist prays for God's
fierce retribution against his enemies, asking God to rain His fury upon
them and to "lighten [lightening] indignation downe" until He has

> turne to wast, and desert plaine,
>   house, and pallace, field and towne.
>   lett not one be left abiding
>   where such rancor had residing. (69, ll. 75–78)

Changing the metaphor, the Psalmist prays that as their sins grow, ciphers be added to their sum (zeroes that would change one hundred sins
to one thousand or ten thousand), and then that they be completely
crossed out of God's book.

Pembroke's *Psalmes* not only fulminate against the ungodly in general, but point out class distinctions among them. For example, by expanding on the biblical phrase that God sent judgment "upon Pharoh,

and upon all his servants" (135:9), Pembroke emphasizes that all social classes suffered when God punished Egypt:

> not only meaner men had cause to rue,
>   but ev'n the best
> of Pharos court, the king among the rest. (135, ll. 26–28)

In her *Psalmes,* such distinctions of rank are apparently present even within the elect. Psalm 45, line 19, is particularly striking in its discussion of the "meaner people" who must be controlled by force. The Geneva Bible translates the passage, "Thine arrowes are sharpe to perce the heart of the Kings enemies: therefore the people shal fall under thee" (45:5). That is, the people who will be controlled by God's force are God's enemies. Yet in Pembroke's translation, the people appear to be the poorer subjects of the king:

> Sharpe are thie shaftes to clive their hartes in twaine
>   whose heads doe cast thie Conquestes to withstand:
> good cause to make the meaner people faine
>   with willing hartes to undergoe thie hand. (45, ll. 17–20)

The passage is nominally about God's justice, but it is difficult to read it without remembering that the words were written by the daughter of Sir Henry Sidney, the English governor of Ireland and Wales. Force is acclaimed as an effective way to govern these "meaner people."[31]

The Sidneys clearly classified themselves among "the best," not among the "meaner people." Their class consciousness nevertheless seems to have included a strong sense of noblesse oblige—of the responsibility of those in high places to protect the poor, even though they disdained them. Although he may have shared the pervasive Elizabethan belief that the Irish were barbarians, Sir Henry Sidney did seem concerned for the peasants who were oppressed by their great lords. For example, he reported to Queen Elizabeth that in Ireland he heard the "lamentable Cryes and dolefull Complayntes, made by that small Remayne of poor People which yet are lefte." He was evidently moved to compassion by "the View of the Bones and Sculles of the ded Subjectes, who partelie by Murder, partelie by Famyn, have died in the Feelds; as, in Troth, hardelie

31. Such dismissal of the lower classes appears to echo Philip Sidney's harsh comedy in the *Arcadia*, as in the witty wordplay used to trivialize Musidorus's slaughter of the people who came to rescue Pamela from him (*The Countess of Pembrokes Arcadia*, 308).

any Christian with drie Eies could beholde."[32] Whether this concern was prompted by genuine or politic or a confused combination of motives, Philip Sidney uses similar language in "Discourse on Irish Affairs" to defend his father against accusations of mismanagement by lords such as the Irish earl of Ormonde. His father's decision to tax the "rich men of the Pale" was just, he argues, for otherwise "the burden only [lies] upon the poor, who may groan, for their cry cannot be heard" (*Miscellaneous Prose*, 8). *Nobilis*, an account of Philip Sidney's life written by Thomas Moffet as a model for Pembroke's son William, praises him for serving as the "agent and pleader" for the poor (80); similarly, Nicholas Breton praises Pembroke's generosity at Wilton, where "the poore [are] blessedly relieved" (*Wits Trenchmour*, in *Works*, 2:19). This may be merely encomium, but the terms of praise themselves establish a norm; if the Sidneys did not always demonstrate concern for the poor, the encomia imply, they should have. Pembroke's own consciousness had undoubtedly been raised by her chaplain, Gervase Babington. In 1583 he had dedicated to Pembroke a sermon on the responsibility of those who have "riches, treasure, and honour" to use them for "others helpe." Feeling compassion for the poor is not an adequate response to God, for "both feeling and faith" are necessary, "the one to conceive, the other to applie." Pembroke is urged to continue in "the studie of his worde, and all other good learning" and also in "the practise of duty to your God," a duty that clearly includes generosity to the poor. In the dialogue between Frailtie and Faith, Frailtie worries about facing poverty, but Faith advocates reliance on God and, by implication, reliance on the countess herself (*A Brief Conference*, sigs. A2–A5). Lest the Pembrokes take pride in their riches, Babington later reminds them that "Gayne is not godlinesse . . . but godlinesse is great gayne."[33]

Following Babington's admonitions, Pembroke chose to emphasize in her works the responsibility of the aristocracy to their people. In her *Psalmes* she expands those verses that recount the duties of magistrates and rulers. Although the cry for justice against corrupt officials is present in the Hebrew original, Pembroke frequently stresses the theme through her use of parallel construction, her expansion of metaphors, and her use

32. Sir Henry Sidney to William Cecil, 25 February 1569, printed in Arthur Collins, I:43. See also Sidney's own account of his tenure in Ireland, Sir Henry Sidney to Sir Francis Walsingham, 1 March 1583, PRO SP 12/159.

33. Babington, "To the Right Honorable . . . Henry Earle of Pembrooke," in *A Profitable Exposition of the Lords Prayer*, sig. A3. This particular admonition is addressed specifically to both the earl and the countess.

of political terminology. For example, in Psalm 72, traditionally read as David's prayer that his son Solomon will rule justly ("Deus Judicium"), she expands the section on the king's duties to the poor:

> Teach the kings sonne, who king hym self shalbe,
>   Thy judgmentes Lord, thy justice make hym learn:
> To rule thy realme as justice shall decree,
>   And poore mens right in judgment to discern. . . .
> Make him the weake support, th'opprest relieve,
>   Supply the poore. (72, ll. 1–12)

If he protects the poor, then the kingdom will have peace and prosperity. If he will "heare the poore when they complain, / And lend them help, who helplesse are opprest," using "his force" to "free their lyves that lyve distrest," then he will have a long and happy life, with the blessings of health, wealth, and international respect, as he is held "of perfect blise / A patterne to the rest" (72.41–45, 79–80).

Psalm 101, traditionally read as David's vow to rule with justice and mercy when God gives him the throne ("Misericordiam et judicium"), combines Pembroke's interests in both social classes—protection against slanderers for the aristocracy and protection against unjust magistrates for the poor. As Calvin states in his commentary, "although the Prince be never so good, yet shal his subjects hardly be parttakers of his uncorruptnesse, except his officers be according to himself," a reading the countess emphasizes by changing the usual English translation of "those within his house" to the more explicitly political terms "Counsailors" and "Officers," terms that are closer to the original Hebrew, as Theodore Steinberg has demonstrated.[34] Psalm 82 speaks specifically to those officers, warning magistrates that over their court, God "hathe his tribunall pight, / adjudging right / both to the judg, and judged wight" (3–5). That is, even as the magistrates pervert justice, the true Judge is condemning them for oppressing the poor. In a series of parallel imperatives, Pembroke gives directions to magistrates:

> you should his owne unto the helplesse give,
> the poore releeve,
> ease him with right, whom wrong doth greeve.

---

34. *Philip's Phoenix*, 105; Steinberg, 1–17. On Philip Sidney's possible knowledge of Hebrew sources see also Weiner, 157–62.

> You should the fatherlesse defend:
> you should unto the weake extend
> your hand. (82, ll. 8–13)

This is the ideal: "This should you doe: but what doe ye?" Rather than defend the poor, false magistrates pervert the very ground of judgment, confounding right and wrong. They may sit high now, God says, but they will "fall, and low, as others ly." The Psalm ends with a prayer to God as the just judge, "of all the earth king, judg, disposer be; / since to decree / of all the earth belongs to thee" (82.28–30).

The promised day of the Lord will bring true justice as corrupt earthly magistrates are replaced by God Himself. In Psalm 98, for example, the earth rejoices, for the Lord will "with upright justice judg the lands / and equall lawes among the dwellers make" (98.23–24). Similarly, in Psalm 103,

> the lord hys right
> unto the wronged wight
>   doth ever yeld:
>   and never cease to shield
> with Justice them, whome guile and fraude pursue. (ll. 20–24)

As the magistrates are to dispense justice to all, so the duty of princes is to shield the godly, which Pembroke asks Queen Elizabeth to do in her dedicatory poem, "Even Now that Care," when she pointedly refers to the queen's responsibility in "theise most active times," using a Protestant code for intervention in the religious wars on the Continent.[35] In her rendition of Psalm 47, Pembroke also emphasizes this duty. Whereas the Psalter translates the passage (v. 9), "The princes of the people are joined unto the people of the God of Abraham," Pembroke's interpretation develops the Geneva note for verse 9—"He praiseth Gods highnes, for that he joyneth the great princes of the worlde, whome he calleth shields to the felowship of his Church":

> On sacred throne, not knowing end,
>   for god the king of kingdomes raignes
> the folk of Abrahams god to frend
>   hee, greatest prince, greate princes gaines;
> Princes, the shields that earth defend. (47, ll.16–20)

---

35. See, for example, Fulke Greville's nostalgic use of the term "active" to apply to Queen Elizabeth's foreign policy, "A Dedication to Sir Philip Sidney," in *Prose Works*, 7 and 85.

That is, God, the greatest prince, uses great princes to defend the church, "the folk of Abrahams god." Pembroke has a similar usage in Psalm 89. 49–50, wherein the sacred king that God gave to Israel is conflated with "Jehovas shield" that protects his people. Babington urges the earl of Pembroke to fulfill a similar role, to be "an honorable maintainer and furtherer of his truth," "A shield and defence to all the godly,"[36] a "sword of holy Justice" (sig. A5).

Although these issues are present in the Hebrew Psalms and in her usual sources, Pembroke chooses to accentuate the aristocratic role. For example, in Psalm 104 she adds an apparently original allegorical interpretation of the cedars that tower over other plants as princes who should demonstrate noblesse oblige to "the rest."

> thence, lord, thy leaved people bud and blow:
> whose Princes thou, thy Cedars, dost not spare,
>   a fuller draught of thy cupp to allow,
> that highly rais'd above the rest they are.
>
> Yet highly rais'd they doe not proudly scorne
>   to give small birdes an humble entertaine,
> whose brickle neastes are on their branches borne,
>   while in the Firrs the Storks a lodging gaine. (104.53–60)

She suggests that it is the responsibility of the cedars to help the "small birdes," thus following Calvin in interpreting the Psalm as a comment on the responsibility of the rich to "releeve the want of their brethren" (v. 15). Her presentation of the cedars and the birds is reminiscent of Sidney's fable, which he attributes to his mentor Hubert Languet, Huguenot writer and diplomat, "As I my little flock on Ister bank." In the fable, the king destroys the power of the "nobler beasts," which allows him to prey upon "the meaner cattle." Deprived of the aristocracy, the poor are without protectors, and the "worst [fate] fell to smallest birds, and meanest herd" (Philip Sidney, *Poems*, 98–103).

It is always difficult to separate the translator's own voice from her source, a problem that is even more severe in the Psalms with their nested authors and voluminous commentaries; nevertheless, we can see how Pembroke emphasizes the concern for the people inherent in her

---

36. Babington, "To the Right Honorable . . . Henry Earle of Pembrooke," in *A Profitable Exposition*, sig. A4. Babington is careful to cloak his admonitions in terms of praise, negotiating the difficult position of spiritual advisor to the one on whom he is dependent for his living.

originals. In her *Psalmes* she frequently speaks of the dangers of power misused—to the rulers themselves, to the aristocracy, and to the people. Proud as she is of her own position as a Sidney and as countess of Pembroke, arrogant as she may sometimes be to those beneath her on the social scale, she nonetheless calls on those in power to consider those on the margins, to "heare the poore." Yet, although Pembroke frequently speaks of the duty of the rich to protect and to relieve the poor, she never identifies with the poor and never questions the social structure that produced their poverty.[37]

Most striking is her rendition of Psalm 62:10, "*if* riches increase, set not your heart thereon" (Geneva), which she renders: "and take good heed, *when* riches growes / let not your hart on riches dwell" (62.35–36) (emphasis mine). Her paraphrase here reflects not her biblical sources, but her own experience, for she had left behind the financial problems of the Sidneys to share the wealth of the earls of Pembroke. Class perspective could hardly be clearer.

37. So evident is the upper-class perspective throughout Pembroke's work that the alteration of Psalm 123 from an aristocratic to a lower-class perspective suggests that the revision is not authorial. See "Relationship of the Texts of the Psalmes," in *Collected Works* 2:337–57.

Part Three

Producing Gender Roles

6

Queen, Lover, Poet

A QUESTION OF BALANCE IN THE SONNETS OF MARY, QUEEN OF SCOTS

Mary E. Burke

> To promote a woman to bear rule, superiority, dominion, or
> empire above any realm, nation, or city is repugnant to nature,
> contumely to God, a thing most contrarious to his revealed will
> and approved ordinance, and, finally, it is the subversion of
> good order, of all equity and justice.
>
> —John Knox, *First Blast* (1558)

John Knox's virulent attack on the "monstrous regiment" of women ruling Scotland and England reveals the difficulties Mary, Queen of Scots, faced in ruling a country whose customs and political institutions were established for kings.[1] In the face of the common disapproval of a ruling woman, how did she negotiate the contradictions inherent between the categories "prince" (dominant, authoritative) and "woman" (passive, obedient)? With her sonnets, critics have a rare opportunity to explore how Mary negotiated these contradictory demands within the context of a romantic relationship.[2]

1. It is important to note that for Elizabeth, Knox was only an impudent commentator on royal authority. For Mary, however, Knox was the leader of the established church and a preacher with significant following and political contacts. Thus, Knox's works posed an immediate threat to Mary that they did not for Elizabeth.

2. There exists a controversy over the authenticity of the sonnets. Produced as part of the "Casket Letters" at her first trial in England, the English court decided that these writings did not prove that Mary was involved in murder. Scholars have debated since then whether or not Mary actually wrote the sonnets. Those who argue against Mary's authorship include Antonia Fraser, who claims "these long rather turgid verses" do not resemble any of Mary's known poetry (*Mary*, 403). Also, she argues that Brantôme and

In his analysis of the sonnet convention, Arthur Marotti notes that the sonnet form was used to metamorphize the courtly ambition of the author. The sequences thus become "mini-utopias, imaginative heterocosms within which ambitious men could fantasize a kind of mastery they lacked in their actual experience" ("Love Is Not Love," 398). Mary, unlike a poet such as Philip Sidney, did experience mastery outside the poetic realm, so she transformed the sonnet form into a fantasy of mastery within a romantic relationship. As the speaker in a sonnet sequence, Mary adopts a dominant role, constructing her (silent) male beloved and their relationship as the inverse of traditional gender roles in the sonnet. Like the traditional male sonneteer, she adopts a submissive attitude toward her beloved; however, gender roles cannot be so neatly reversed because of early modern cultural expectations of female submission and male dominance. Despite her rank, Mary can occupy the position of the active lover only by maintaining a delicate balance between overt claims of submission and covert expressions of dominance— a balancing act Laurie Finke has noted in her study of another politically powerful poet, the countess of Dia, a medieval *troubador*. Finke argues that in her poetry Dia needed to "remain at the same time both sexually available and chaste. She must act without appearing to act. She must be aggressive while appearing passive" (61). Likewise, Mary's poetic cross-dressing results in an uneasy conjunction of expressions of domi-

---

Ronsard, who had "intimate knowledge of Mary's earlier verses" denied these were hers (403). Fraser also notes that aside from stylistic problems, the contents of the poems indicate they were written by another woman: "This unhappy poetess has abandoned all her relatives and friends for her lover, unlike Mary who neither did nor was asked to do any such thing. There are references to Bothwell's wealth, which were unthinkable for Mary to make. To her Bothwell was a comparatively poor man, who had to be subsidized with grants of money. . . . It was she who encouraged the profitable Gordon marriage on his behalf, and finally she gave him grants of money after their marriage" (*Mary,* 404). Fraser's argument that the poetic content does not match the historical situation, however, does not disqualify Mary from authorship, only Bothwell as the recipient of the poems. The attribution of the sonnets to Bothwell comes from the nobles whose own agenda makes them suspect. Gordon Donaldson and M. H. Armstrong argue that the Casket documents were made out of an "amalgam of letters, some by Mary to Bothwell, some by Mary but not to Bothwell, some to Bothwell but not by Mary" (Donaldson, *First Trial,* 73; Armstrong). Betty Travitsky argues that the sonnets were written by Mary: citing Mrs. P. Stewart-MacKenzie-Arbuthnot, "a partisan of the queen's and the compiler of the most complete anthology of her poetry yet published," Travitsky argues that the meter and spelling of the poems match those of the proven poetry of Mary (Travitsky, *Paradise of Women,* 188). Although this evidence does not guarantee their authenticity, coupled with the resemblance of the *Sonnets* to the poetry of Du Bellay, a favorite poet of Mary, the evidence makes her authorship highly likely.

nance and extreme passivity, which parallel attempts in her own life to balance the demands of being a monarch and woman. By manipulating gender conventions, both in her sonnets and her political actions, Mary could act aggressively while appearing passive. Also, as a poet expressing love for a married man, she presents herself as sexually available only to him in an attempt to present herself as chaste—a crucial requirement for ruling women. Finally, her poetry results in a critique of the institution of marriage, which makes commodities of women.

The humanist education Mary received at the sophisticated Valois court may have helped her articulate this combination of passivity and aggression. In addition to training in rhetoric, she was exposed to the best poetry of France. She was the subject of poetry by Du Bellay and Pierre de Ronsard, enjoyed the work of the Pléiade, and acted as a patron of poets. According to courtier Pierre de Brantôme: "Above all she delighted in poetry and poets, and most of all in M. de Ronsard, M. du Bellay and M. de Maisonfleur, who made such fine poems and elegies for her, which I have often seen her to read to herself in France and Scotland, with tears in her eyes and sighs in her heart" (Fraser, *Mary*, 79). John Durkan notes that Mary's library contained the largest collection of vernacular poetry, mostly French, in Scotland (78–79), and Michael Lynch points out that the Scottish court during Mary's personal reign was a "focal point for a literary renaissance," part of which was a court of chivalry that arose in conjunction with her marriage to Henry Stuart, Lord Darnley ("Queen Mary's Triumph," 3 and 14). Out of this courtly, poetic milieu comes Mary's sonnets.

Mary's sonnet sequence chronicles a love triangle in which the female speaker alternately despairs of convincing her married beloved of her fidelity, complains of the wife's coldness to her husband, and claims she excels the wife in duty. She fears the wife's renewed interest in her husband and protests that her sole reason for writing is to complain that the beloved has broken his promise to join her. Expressing an almost fanatical desire to prove her submissiveness and, therefore, her love, the speaker appears to have internalized at least one part of early modern culture's demand that the "perfect" woman be chaste, silent, and obedient.[3]

---

3. Extensive work has been done on the early modern demand that women be chaste, silent, and obedient, and on how women negotiated this demand. These works include Belsey, *Subject of Tragedy*, 149–91; Ezell, *Patriarch's Wife*, 62–100; Ferguson, 93–116; Hannay, *Silent But for the Word*, 1–14; Hogrefe, *Tudor Women*, 3–24 and 118–43; Hull, *Chaste, Silent and Obedient*; Lisa Jardine, 103–40; Ann Rosalind Jones, *Currency of Eros*, 1–35; Jordan, *Renaissance Feminism*, 1–246; Krontiris, *Oppositional Voices*, 1–23; Lamb, *Gender and Authorship*, 3–19; Sankovitch, "Inventing Authority of Origin," 227–43; Stallybrass, "Patriarchal Territories," 123–42; Travitsky and Haselkorn, 1–41; Woodbridge, 13–136.

The speaker falls short of this ideal by composing a sonnet sequence, and this lapse severely undercuts her claims of submission. In the traditional Petrarchan sonnet, a male speaker languishes from unrequited love, speaking about the beauty, superiority, excellence, and cruelty of his beloved. The poet thus sets himself up as the single, dominant subject, despite oft claimed assertions of servitude to the woman he has constructed as the object of his desire. Mary also transforms her beloved into an object and offers him servile devotion; however, her poetry often makes modern readers uncomfortable because she seems to sanction early modern views on women's proper place. Yet her ability to occupy the rhetorical position of the male sonneteer may be a result of her dominant position as queen. Like the male poets who can play with submission to sonnet mistresses while enjoying real power over their wives, Mary can play with submission to a male beloved while exercising mastery within the political realm. In order to present herself as attractive to her lover or to the reader, however, the female sonnet speaker must adhere to certain conventions of feminine behavior. In her analysis of early modern women writers, Ann Rosalind Jones argues that women enacted certain strategies in order to write in the face of overwhelming pressure to remain silent. She asserts that these women "carried out a sort of *bricolage* with social dictates, enacted a partial obedience toward them, earned the right to fame through a series of subtle approaches and reshufflings of prevailing notions of feminine virtue" ("Surprising Fame," 80).

In Sonnets I and II we see Mary engage in this sort of bricolage. Here, the male beloved, like the "Cruel Fair" of the Petrarchan convention, occupies the passive position of object while the speaker asserts her submission to him. In Sonnet I she prays:

> O dieux ayes de mon compassion
> & m'enseignes quelle preuue certane
> ie donner qui ne luy semble vain
> de mon amour et ferme affection"

> [Oh you High Gods, have pity, and let me find
> Somehow some incontestable way to prove
> (So that he *must* believe in it) my love
> And this unwavering constancy of mind!] (1–4).[4]

4. Mary, Queen of Scots, in Travitsky, 193–98. Although the French text is not divided into individual sonnets, I have maintained Clifford Bax's divisions of the sonnets and used the line numbers as given in the French text. Robin Bell has recently come out with a new edition of Mary's poetry. Although in many ways his translation is better than Bax's, Bell

Here the speaker focuses exclusively on herself, her own steps to prove her love to the beloved. His wishes do not seem to matter. In Sonnet II, she again focuses on her own independent actions and transforms her beloved into a passive recipient of her desires: "mon ame assubiectie / et toute a luy, et nay autre vouloir / pour mon object que sens le disseuoir" [My all-surrendered soul hath no intent / But despite any trouble which may ensue / Make him see that my great love is true] (19–21). She again is the single actor in these poems, and the male object occupies the traditional position of the passive lady waiting for the poet to prove his love.

In Sonnets VI and XII, the speaker addresses the issue of female authorship directly. In Sonnet VI the wife, fearing the loss of her husband, turns to sending her husband plagiarized love poetry:

> et [elle] vouldroit bien mon anydesseuior
> par les escripts tout fard es de scauior
> qui pour quelque auteur eluissant. . . .
> ont tant guagne que par vous sont guardes
> ses lettres escripts.
>
> [she tries to wheedle, flatter, and deceive my friend
> With writings that are so astutely done
> That never in *her* brain were they conceived
> But, rather, from some splendid writer thieved,
> Thus hiring eloquence though having none. . . .
> And (you) hold her letters under lock and key.] (VI.74–78, 83)

The effect of the speaker's statements is to draw attention to her own eloquence in the poems. Her poems gain sincerity because of her authorship and the specificity of subject. However, what she gains in sincerity, she loses in submission to the ideal of silence. After all, men did not require eloquence in women. In the discussion of her writing, the speaker

---

rearranges the order of the poems to interpret the events of the Bothwell-Mary "romance." With a portrait of a naked woman on the cover (some argue that Mary was the inspiration for the portrait), Bell's book is the most recent contribution to a long line of books that construct Mary in terms of her sexuality (Robin Bell, 31–57). In recent years, however, there have been some notable exceptions to this trend of romanticizing Mary, including Donaldson, *All the Queen's Men*; Donaldson, *The First Trial of Mary Queen of Scots*; Donaldson, *Mary Queen of Scots*; I. B. Cowen, *The Enigma of Mary Stuart*; Lynch, *Mary Stewart*; J. E. Phillips, *Images of a Queen*; Alison Plowden, *Two Queens in One Isle*; Jenny Wormald, *Mary Stewart, a Study in Failure*. Although at times Antonia Fraser's biography does figure Mary as a romantic heroine, it is a thorough and very useful study of Mary. See Fraser, *Mary Queen of Scots*.

implies that the beloved himself is at fault for her transgression of the patriarchal rules that bind most women. If the beloved married her—that is, kept her under lock and key—then she would have no need to compose. By Sonnet XI, we see the speaker abandoned, despite the beloved's promises, and afraid she will lose him. Presumably, if the beloved were with her, then she would have nothing to write about and no opportunity to write. In Sonnet XII, the accusation becomes more glaring in her description of the act of writing:

> Ne vous voyant selon qu'aues promis
> iay mis la main au papier pour escrire
> d'un different que ie voulou transcrire
>
> [Not seeing you, despite your word to me,
> I take up pen and paper, and indite,
> Concerning a hard case of wrong and right.] (155–57)

In blaming the beloved for her act of writing, the speaker can reconcile her resistance to her society's patriarchal discourse of feminine silence. Her language implies that if the beloved had kept his word, then she would happily drop the pen.

Mary's balancing act is more subtle in Sonnet II, which seems to exemplify the kind of submissiveness early modern culture demanded of women:

> Entre ses mains et en son plein pouvoir
> le metz mon filz mon honneur at ma vie
> mon pais mes subjets, mon assubiectie
> et toute a luy . . .
>
> [Into his hands, utterly into his power,
> I place my son, my life, my honour and all
> My subjects and my country, being in thrall
> To him so fast . . .] (1–18)

Although the speaker says she gives all, she also subtly undercuts such claims of womanly submission by stressing her rank and the magnificence of her gift to the less-powerful male. She gives a country to the beloved, as if a dowry, yet the beloved will always be subordinate to her because, as we see in the speaker's possessive language ("mon pais mes subjets" and "mon assubiectie"), the Scots remain the *speaker's* subjects, not the beloved's.

The ambiguity of a queen regnant's status—particularly if she were also a wife—caused great anxiety because Christian doctrine taught that women were subject to their husbands as the church is subject to Christ. Paul writes: "But I would have you know, that the head of every man is Christ; and the head of every woman is the man" (King James Version [KJV], 1 Cor. 11:3). Could a queen defy scripture and become the head of her husband as she was head of her subjects? In an attempt to circumvent scriptural prohibitions, John Aylmer divides a queen's public and private duties: "God hath apoynted her to be subject to her husband. . . . [T]herefore she maye not be the heade. I graunte that, so farre as perteineth to the bandes of mariage, and the office of a wife, she muste be a subjecte: but as a Magistrate she maye be her husbands heade. . . . Whie may not the woman be the husbandes inferiour in matters of wedlock, and his head in the guiding of the commonwealth" (sig. Cvi).

In early modern Scotland, however, there was no division between the queen's private marital relationship and the public weal as Alymer posits.[5] Contemporary accounts of Mary's marriage negotiations reveal the Scots took for granted that her husband would rule as king of Scotland; therefore, the private aspect of her marriage was of immense public concern. For example, a powerful Catholic prince might end the Reformation and introduce foreign troops into the country. During marriage negotiations with Henry, Lord Darnley, the chief nobles of Scotland met to consider whether Mary should wed him: "Muche disputation there was among men about her mariage. Some thought after the death of her first husband, she ought have the libertie that weomen of low degree have. Others said, the case was not like, becaus in choosing herself a husband she choosed also a king to the realme; and that it was more equitable that the people should choose a husband to one woman, than one woman a king to all subjects" (Calderwood, 2:291). The fact that her marriage was publicly debated with the understanding that her spouse would be king renders Alymer's argument theoretical. Even if the queen's husband were not invested with a king's power, the line between the queen's public authority and her private wifely submission would remain unclear. For example, in filling certain powerful (and lucrative) court positions, such as that of the prince's guardian, should Mary act as a monarch or defer to Darnley as the head of the household?

5. In her recent book on Elizabeth, Carole Levin notes that in England Aylmer's division between public and private was not as easy to maintain as he suggests ("The Heart and Stomach of a King," 42).

For Mary, a queen-subject marriage destabilized gender hierarchy by subsuming gender to class. English ambassador Thomas Randolphe dolefully spells out the fate of a man who would gain a crown by marrying Mary: "[A] man that shalbe broughte from all quietness of lyf, from honour inoughe, from lyving sufficiente, to dwell in a straynge countrie, with an unknowne people, to lyve in daynger and subjection (as whoe so ever that is not a kinge and mariethe a Quene, musted and shall submyt hym self to a thousande adventeurs and parels, which no friend that loved him could advise him to do)" (Great Britain, *Calendar of State Papers, Scotland,* 2:131).[6]

Randolphe's description accurately illustrates the fate of Darnley, who, although Mary's husband, was dependent upon her for power and position. In an attempt to narrow the gap between their ranks, Mary acted as his patron, rewarding him with the three chief honors of her patrimony. He was created the Lord Aramenacke, duke of Rothsay, and earl of Ross two months before their marriage (Great Britain, *Calendar of State Papers, Scotland,* 2:157). On the eve of their wedding, she had him proclaimed king, ordering that documents be in the names of the "Prince, our future husband, and us as King and Quene of Scotland conjunctle" (Burton, 345). The proclamation posits a mutual governorship, but with her name given last, Mary appears to have accepted a secondary role in the government, behind her "head." However, as Randolphe notes, her submission did not last long: "A while there was nothing but 'Kynge and Quene, his majestie and hers'; now, the 'Quene's howsbonde' is most common. He was wont to be first named in all writings, but now is placed second. . . . There are also private disorders among themselves" (Great Britain, *Calendar of State Papers, Scotland,* 2:248). The private, disordered relationship had consequences in the public arena of governance. The shift in Darnley's identification from the independent "king" to the status of Mary's appendage as the "queen's husband" signaled the diminution of his importance in the commonweal, and Mary's passive response—a change in Darnley's appellation—masked an aggressive suppression of his hopes. Although Darnley pressed for the crown matrimonial, Mary refused him because he was grossly inadequate, concerned more with pleasure than rule. Despite marriage, Scotland remained Mary's, not Darnley's.

In Sonnet XI, Mary similarly undermines traditional gender relations by effacing the beloved's individual self through poetic convention. She

---

6. Randolphe does not appear aware of the irony that what he would not condemn a friend to endure was common practice for royal women at that time.

describes the beloved in a blazon, which should celebrate his physical qualities but in effect dissolves his own subjectivity within hers: "Mon coeur, mon sang, mon ame" [My Heart, my Blood, my Soul] (141). This fantasy inverts Paul's interpretation of the second Genesis creation story: "For the man is not of the woman; but the woman of the man" (KJV, 1 Cor. 11:8). In Mary's sonnet, the male beloved gains status from his relationship to the female speaker. Interestingly, as the speaker attempts to incorporate him within herself, she simultaneously dissects her own body as if she were the object of the desiring male poet.[7] Unlike male poets who concentrate on the visible body they "celebrate," Mary concentrates on the inner, invisible, and crucial aspects of herself. In doing so, she reworks a poetic form designed to render the female body bare to the voyeuristic gaze of the male reader and simply removes her body from examination.

As the speaker masks her aggression by appearing passive, she also masks her actions by using the language of service to a lord. In Sonnet VIII, she asserts:

> pour luy ie veux rechercher la grandeure
> et faira tant qu'en vray connoistra
> que ie n'ay bien heur ni contentement
> qu'a l'obeyr et seruir loyamment
> pour luy iattendz tout bon fortune
> pour luy ie veux guarder sante et vie
> pour luy tout vertue de suiure i'ay enuie
> et sens changer me trouuer tout une

> [For him would I . . .
> seek out high honours to advance his state,
> And do for him so much that he will know
> How all my hopes of true content or wealth
> Do in obedience and in service lie.
> For him I covet fortune and bright fame;
> For him I value mine own life and health;
> For him it is that I do shoot so high;
> And he will find me evermore the same.] (104–8)

Unlike in Sonnet II, the speaker does not talk of *her* country or *her* subjects in Sonnet VIII; she is no longer the powerful patron bestowing

---

7. For an excellent discussion of the dissection of women in early modern European poetry, see Nancy Vickers's important essay "Diana Described," 265–79.

honors on the weaker beloved-client. Although, as queen, she possesses the power to advance her beloved, she denies that power and constructs herself as a (valuable) servant to a lord. Interestingly, the speaker, who earlier claims to have risked dishonor (I.7) and public censure (III.35) for her illicit love, now, in a poem about her active goals, asserts that for her beloved she will covet *"vertue."* In his *Dictionarie of the French and English Tongues* (1611), Randle Cotgrave defines *"vertue"* in both traditional feminine ideals of "goodness, honestie" and masculine traits of "valour, prowess, manhood . . . force, power" (sig. Lllliv). Such multiple, gendered definitions of *"vertue"* allow Mary to claim the active masculine virtues while appearing to remain a virtuous woman. She can thus challenge the gendered definitions.

In seeking economic and political advancement for the beloved, the speaker also cloaks her own ambitions. Instead of seeking fame and fortune for herself, she disguises her ambition as service for a man. As a woman, Mary was not supposed to covet political or economic power, but as a monarch she needed such power to function. Humanist tutor Juan Luis Vives's instructions to Mary Tudor, however, show that even the women born into powerful families were actively discouraged from meddling in politics: "All this same meaneth that you shall nat medle with matters of realmes or cities. Your owne house is a cite great inoughe for you" (Jordan, *Renaissance Feminism,* 119). In transferring her own ambition to the beloved, however, the speaker disguises her ambition by claiming society's definition of a woman's proper place. Also, unlike the male sonneteers who regularly go into decline for their beloveds, this speaker makes it a point to mention how well she takes care of herself— again only for the sake of the beloved: "pour luy ie veux guarder sante et vie" [For him I value mine own life and health] (VIII.110). In camouflaging her own goals as service, Mary successfully maintains the balance between action and passivity.

In her life as well as in her poetry Mary played with social dictates to diffuse anxiety over her rank. For example, she used conventional notions of women's weakness to gain support from the Vatican for her religious policies (or lack thereof). In a memorial recognizing the Scottish queen's claim to the English throne, the Vatican recommended that she be married to a Catholic prince in order to promote the Counter Reformation in England: "If [Mary] were a man she would, perhaps, need no other aid than that of her party in that kingdom" (Hungerford, 176). In letters she is described as alone, destitute of help, and too frightened to oppose the Protestant congregation (Hungerford, 338). By utilizing stereotypes of feminine weakness, Mary thus maintained good relations with Catholic powers, receiving financial support while, in effect, doing nothing to squelch Protestantism in Scotland.

From the beginning of her personal reign, Mary also used traditional feminine occupations to dispel anxiety over the sight of a woman exercising power. Randolphe notes that while at council meetings, she "ordinarily sits most part of the time, 'sowinge some worke or other'" (Great Britain, *Calendar of State Papers, Scotland*, 2:651). Thus, Mary could both govern and appear demure, as if concerned only with a feminine and harmless occupation.[8]

In addition to manipulating notions of feminine weakness, at times Mary appropriated masculine characteristics. As a result, she displaced the aggression unsuitable to her gender and eased anxieties over her actions. While subduing her most powerful noble, Huntly, Mary appeared relaxed, undismayed by battle, and "merrie" to her soldiers. Randolphe writes: "She repented nothynge but . . . that she was not a man to knowe what lyf yt was to lye all nyghte in the feeldes, or to walke upon the cawsaye with a jacke and knapschall, a Glascowe buckeler and a broode swerde" (Great Britain, *Calendar of State Papers, Scotland*, 1:651). This fantasy of masculine power serves to connect Mary's spirit with those of her male subjects. She may not be a king, but she has the heart of a king. While emphasizing her masculine disposition, this speech also emphasizes her feminine vulnerability: Mary is relying on her soldiers's valor to protect her. Elizabeth's famous speech to her troops at Tilbury served similar purposes. Although possessing the "body but of a weak and feeble woman," she claimed to have the spirit, "the heart and stomach of a king" (quoted in Teague, "Elizabeth I," 542). As the legend goes, Elizabeth appeared at Tilbury with armor and sword to stress her military leadership; however, her skirts reminded her troops that she would not take part in the actual battle.

Although Mary did not often use the term "prince" to describe herself, she used her body to signify the androgyny Elizabeth expressed in words. Leah Marcus argues that Queen Elizabeth encouraged her subjects to identify her with a "set of symbolic male identities. . . . [She] presented herself to the nation as both man and woman, queen and king, mother and firstborn son. . . . [She built] a myth of her own androgyny in order to palliate the political anxieties aroused by her presence as a 'frail' woman on the throne" (137). However, Mary's visual display of androgyny

---

8. Mary's ruse was brilliant because the sight of her exercising the traditional role of the monarch caused Knox to remark: "Such styncken pryde of wemen as was sein at that Parliament, was never seen befoir in Scotland" (Knox, *Works*, vol. 2, 381).

seemed designed not to ease her subject's uneasiness over female rule but rather to assert her own power—to claim the privileges of masculinity signified by male clothing—without seeming to take action. In a masque celebrating Darnley's investiture with the French order of St. Michael, Mary's cross-dressing was politically very significant. Julian Goodare notes that Mary refused to allow Darnley to use the royal arms at the investiture, which was "taken as a signal that the forthcoming parliament . . . would refuse him the coveted crown matrimonial" (165). Goodare claims that this night was the genesis of Darnley's plot to overthrow Mary. In a masque before Darnley, the French ambassador, and the court, Mary and her ladies "wer all cled in men's apperrell" (Thomson, *Diurnal,* 87). Mary's pregnancy, five months along, may have been visible through her doublet and hose, and even if it were not, her condition was known to all parties. In essence, Mary presented herself as the self-sufficient, male-female monarch, who also held within her the heir and who no longer needed Darnley. By allowing Darnley to use only his own arms and not the royal arms, Mary denied him power without taking definitive action. By appropriating the sartorial signifier of "male," the pregnant Mary laid claim to the power and privilege of men within the domestic sphere. Her actions fulfilled Vives's warning that wearing men's clothing will "lette [a woman] thinke she hath the man's stomacke" (quoted in Garber, 28). She embodies Knox's conflation of the cross-dressed woman and the monstrous queen whom he calls "a woman clad in the habit of a man, yea, a woman against nature reigning of above man."[9]

In her analysis of Elizabeth's Tilbury appearance, Marjorie Garber emphasizes that Elizabeth's rank enabled her to cross-dress with impunity (28). Similarly, Mary's rank was the key to the importance of her cross-dressing: her royalty allowed her to hold the masculine privileges in marriage as well as in the lines of a sonnet sequence. After the investiture, Darnley was reported to be "so violently indignent" that he avoided Mary (Hungerford, 308). Almost a month later to the day, he attacked Mary through the most visual signifier of her gender: he attempted to kill her by trying to provoke a miscarriage.[10]

9. Knox, *First Blast,* 75. Cross-dressing was considered sinful because it violated scripture: "The woman shall not wear that which pertaineth unto a man, neither shall a man put on a woman's garment" (*KJV* Deuteronomy 22:5).

10. Mary thought the attack was an attempt to make her miscarry and perhaps lose her life. Fraser notes that miscarriages late in the pregnancy usually resulted in the mother's death (Fraser, 253).

Because Mary was a woman ruler, her reputation for chastity became as important as her ability to negotiate expectations of feminine passivity with the activity required of a ruler. Although a ruler, she was not exempted from the prohibitions against sexual license imposed on early modern women. Quite the inverse, Mary's ability as a ruler was directly connected to her sexual continence; impugning her chastity became a way to attack her rule. In 1562, one year into her personal reign, a Captain Heiborne sought to discredit her by shaming her in front of the English envoys:

> The daye before Sir Harrie Sydneis departeur, he walkinge with the Quene . . . [Captain] Heiborne presenteth her grace a byll . . . there wrytten iiij as shamfull verses . . . [as] anye dyvleshe wytite coulde invent, and under them drawne with a penne the secreat members both of men and women in as monstrous a sorte as nothynge could be more shamfullye dyvisede. This offends her grace greatly, the more also that it was done at a time to give Sir Harrie Sydney and the other gentlemen with him to muse mych at his boldness, or otherwise judge of herself than any occasion given by her or hers. (Great Britain, *Calendar of State Papers, Scotland*, 2:646)

As Mary realized, the note was specifically designed to weaken her position in the eyes of the English with whom she was negotiating her status as Elizabeth's heir. This attack on her honor served to remind all concerned that despite her rank, she was still a woman and therefore defined by and open to attack through her sexuality.

The attacks on Mary's honor became even more serious in the following year with Chartellat's attempt to compromise her:

> Chartellat, Monsieur Danville trustie servant, hath by violence attempted thys Quens dyshonour in the moste shamfull sorte that ever the same was donne unto anye lyke personage. . . . [Y]ester nyghte . . . the Quene . . . goynge to her bedde, Chartelet retired hym self to a secret corner, and onlye two of her gentlewomen present, commethe forthe, and ther settethe uppon her with suche force, and in suche impudent sort, that the Quene herself was fayne to crie for helpe, and the matter so manifeste that no couller coulde be founde to hyde the shame and dyshonour. (Great Britain, *Calendar of State Papers, Scotland*, 2:684)

Although Mary wanted Chartellat executed for his actions, he was considered mentally unbalanced and excused with only a warning. One week later he was found hiding in Mary's privy—this time with a dagger. According to Randolphe, his purpose was "to have tried her constancie, and by force to have attempted that which by no perswations he coulde attayne unto."[11] If Chartellat had been successful in raping Mary, he would have stained her honor because of the suspicion in early modern culture that rape was a woman's fault.[12] With her honor ruined, she would have been effectively finished as a ruler. Vatican letters reveal that the papacy saw Chartellat's attack as part of a plot to replace Catholic rulers with Protestants: "As for the Queen of Scots, who is a Catholic, they determined not to kill her, but to dishonor her, in order to prevent her from marrying" (Hungerford, 167). Mary could be rendered dead as a ruler merely by destroying her honor.

Throughout Mary's personal reign, her gender made her uniquely susceptible to attack, particularly rape and forced marriage. Almost from the beginning of that reign, various nobles, including her third husband Bothwell, saw marriage (forced or otherwise) to her as the best path to power. In Sonnet IX, Mary describes the consequence of her vulnerability:

> Pour luy aussi ie iete maint larme
> premier quant il se fit de ce corps possesseur
> du quel alors il n'auoyt pas le coeur

> [For him what countless tears I must have shed:
> First when he made himself my body's lord
> Before he had my heart.] (114–15)

In these lines, the speaker talks *about* the beloved rather than *to* him in order to distance both him and herself from a traumatic event: his rape of her. With the use of the first person there is an accusation rather than a description of events, as there would be in the third person. The violated body is described as a separate entity ("ce corps") from the speaker's own body; therefore, the self who is speaking can potentially *love* the

11. *Calendar of State Papers Scotland*, II, 685. In this same dispatch Randolphe resembles Chartellat in his outrage at the arrogance of a woman who declines to grant her sexual favors to a man. He wonders how Chartellat could think to "come by that which she herself (I beleeve) judgithe verie fewe in the worlde worthie of."

12. Knox asserts that Mary was quite the hypocrite in objecting to Chartellat's visits. He argues that she flirted shamefully with the young man, leading him on: "All this wynter Chattelatt was so familiare in the Quenis cabinett, ayre and laitt, that scarslye could any of the Nobilitie have access unto hir. The Quene wold ly upon Chattelatis shoulder, and sometymes prively she wold steall a kyss of his neck" (Calderwood, 368).

man who raped the separated body. The speaker also distances herself from her own emotions in her description of her feelings. By expressing her love in negative terms ("il n'auoyt pas le coeur"), the speaker's love appears very ambivalent, undercutting her other expressions of love and devotion.[13] In effect, this poem also denies the speaker's responsibility for the first sexual encounter because she claims to have been ravished. At the end of the sonnet, Mary switches to a direct address to the beloved when the danger of falling into an accusatory tone recedes and the speaker desires to persuade the beloved to enter into an alliance with her ("de vous seul ie cherche l'alliance"). The speaker's legalistic (and rather unromantic) language obscures the extramarital nature of their relationship. She wants to formalize their relationship and, in fact, uses the same term, *alliance*, that she used in Sonnet IV to describe the beloved's marriage vow to his wife. Furthermore, in other sonnets the speaker continually asserts to the beloved that she is faithful within this relationship: "vous m'estimes legier ie voy / et si n'auez en moy nul asseurence / et soubconnes mon coeur sans apparence [You think me light, as far too well I see / And watch me with suspicion all day long / Though without cause] (VII.89–91). Thus, she can claim to be chaste within an irregular relationship that she hopes to legalize. Despite the speaker's attempts to assert her chastity, the very fact that she writes at all, however, renders her open to charges of wantonness. Peter Stallybrass observes that the early modern injunction to silence was connected to the woman's body and her enclosure within the private sphere of the home. He cites R. Toste, who writes:

> Maides must be seene, not heard, or selde or never,
> O may I such one wed, if I wed ever.
> A Maide that hath a lewd Tongue in her head,
> Worse than if she were found with a Man in bed. (126)

Thus, speaking was equated with a lack of chastity because, as Ann Rosalind Jones points out, speaking was presumed to be an action in the public world among men. Jones argues that the woman love poet was especially transgressive because she publicly expressed desire for a man not her husband (*Currency of Eros*, 7). Mary's expression of desire for a *married* man made her need to appear chaste even greater.

The sonnets lay bare the sexual double standard in early modern culture by drawing attention to the disgrace the speaker incurs when she

---

13. I am grateful to Linda Dove for pointing out Mary's use of the negative in this poem.

participates in an illicit love affair against the advice of friends, but there is no mention of the beloved experiencing disgrace. She asserts:

> pour luys depuis i'ay mesprise lhonneur
> ce qui nous peut seul prouoir de bonheur
> pour luy tous mess parens iay quiste et amys
> et tous aultres respects son a part mis
>
> [For him I turned my honour to disgrace,
> Though honour is our one sure joy and pride
> For him bade Conscience find a humbler place
> Chilled my most-trusted friends, and set aside
> Every consideration.] (IX.121–25)

The speaker has made the ultimate sacrifice in allowing her honor to be stained. As she poignantly expresses in the last line of the sequence, however, the beloved gains much from the connection: "vous diries bien qui plus y guagnera" [easily may you measure which gains most] (XII.160).

One reason adulterous relationships existed was that aristocratic marriages in early modern Scotland were used to cement political and economic ties among clans. In Mary's poetry, we see her implicitly criticize a system that used people in this way.[14] Throughout the sonnet sequence, the speaker constructs love and marriage in monetary terms. For example, she calls the beloved "mon seul bien" (VII.87), which can be translated as "my sole wealth, riches, possessions." Furthermore, the wife profits ("pour son profit") by her fidelity, yet she "n'a prise ni jamais estime un si grand heur" [never prized (her great fortune) at its own just rate] (III.33, V.70).

Sonnet IV reveals the emotional costs individuals pay in marriages based on family economics rather than personal choice. The speaker describes the social and material gains that the wife and her family receive from her marriage to the beloved:

14. The Gordon family's achievements are an excellent example of the kind of power possible in this system of political marriages: "The Gordon earls of Huntly had established themselves in the northeast in the fifteenth century, building up their patrimony through the cultivation of royal favor and the pursuit of a judicious policy of advantageous marriage and prudent family alliances." One of their marriages took place between the earl's daughter Jane and the earl of Bothwell (White, 55).

Par vous (mon coeur) et par vostre alliance
elle a remis sa maison en honneur
elle a iouy par vous de la grandeur
dont tous le siens n'auoyent nul asseurance
de vous mon bien elle a eu lacointance

[. . . [B]y winning you for mate,
Once more the fortune of her House ascends:
By you she has enjoyed a high estate
Beyond all expectation of her friends.] (IV.43–46)

Early modern aristocratic families used their daughters' marriages as ways to enhance their economic and social positions, but Mary exposes the underlying cost of making women family commodities: "Nor did she [the wife] suffer any loss beyond / A dull fool's joy of whom she once was fond" (IV.51–52). Although the speaker does trivialize the wife and her suitor's loss, this translation obscures the extent of her loss and the similarity between the speaker and the wife. The French text reads, "[elle] n'a perdu sinon la jouissance d'un fascheux sot qu'elle aymoit cherement," which can be translated as (and I want to bring out the multiple meanings of *jouissance*) "she lost nothing but an enjoyment (orgasm) or absolute possession of a foolish sot whom she loved dearly." Both the wife and the speaker lose in this relationship because neither has the full enjoyment of the man she loves. The beloved, on the other hand, enjoys the services of a wife and a mistress. By examining the different positions of the speaker, the wife, and the beloved, the text exposes the victimization of women in a society that uses them as commerce among men.

In the fragment of the last sonnet we see an emblem of women's writing in the Renaissance. We see the speaker alone, with pen and paper, her voice abruptly silenced. The story of her love is broken off, and she disappears into historical oblivion; from our historical vantage we even question her authorship. We are left with a jagged edge, a yawning gap in the story of the speaker's attempts to construct an erotic relationship in the face of the contrary demands of being a queen and a woman. Does she finally renounce the beloved for his swinish behavior, or does she work harder to win him? If she renounces him, does she seek another man? Does she drop the pen because she finds that she cannot maintain the balance between aggression and passivity, action and inaction, sexual availability and chastity? The questions left unanswered in the Mary's sonnets, like the innumerable questions we have about Renaissance women's lives, may never be answered. In those sonnets we have a mirror of the psyche of a woman battling to reconcile the contrary positions of ruler and woman.

In Mary's poetic and physical cross-dressing she attempts to bring into harmony what society tells her a woman is (chaste, submissive, silent, inferior to men) and the demands placed upon her as queen regnant. In her poetry, her attempt at balance fails because of the very nature of the sonnet form: the "naturally" passive woman and traditional sonnet mistress becomes a speaking subject rather than a silent object. The speaker's assumption of a subject position and her reduction of the male beloved to an object subverts the language of feminine submission that she uses to convince the beloved of her love. The speaker is also doomed to failure because of her superior position as queen. To be a ruler requires action, not passivity; furthermore, she cannot be completely submissive to the beloved because she outranks him. Her most strenuous attempt at reconciling her authoritative position as queen with the submissiveness demanded of women leads to a challenge of the institution of marriage and of the costs to individuals, in particular women, of economically arranged marriages.

7

"Some Freely Spake Their Minde"

RESISTANCE IN ANNE DOWRICHE'S *FRENCH HISTORIE*

Elaine Beilin

> I conclude that in this House which is tearmed a place of free
> speech there is nothing soe necessary for the preservacion of the
> prince and state as free speech, and without it it is a scorne and
> mockery to call it a parliament house for in truth it is none, but
> a very schoole of flattery and dissimulacion and soe a fitt place
> to serve the Devill and his angells in and not to glorifye God
> and benefitt the comonwealth.
>
> —from Peter Wentworth's speech in
> Parliament, 8 February 1576
> (Trinterud, 173)

> We may no longer then dissemble in this case:
> But what we thinke must plainlie showe (o King) before your face.
> We cannot (as you would) the certain *Truth* denie;
> But that defend: though for the same we wer condemnd to die.
>
> —from Annas Burgeus's speech
> in Anne Dowriche's *The French
> Historie*, 1589

Anne Dowriche's commitment to the spiritual and political ideology of the puritan movement emerges from every page of her
long narrative poem, *The French Historie*. Because she was a woman,
Dowriche could not, however, pursue her religious and political agenda
in a public office; it was her brother, Piers Edgcumbe, who sat in six
Elizabethan Parliaments. Unlike such radical puritans as Peter Wentworth
or Job Throkmorton, she could make no stirring speeches in the House
of Commons on topics of particular concern to nonconformists—the threat
from Catholic Europe, the royal succession, the continued reformation of

119

the church, and the freedom to debate these topics in Parliament. Yet Dowriche's zeal to discuss these very matters and her championing of parliamentary free speech are strongly evident in her poem, which narrates the persecution of French Protestants by three successive French kings. She tells her brother in the Epistle, "You shall finde here manie things for comfort worthie the considering, and for policie the observing," thus proposing her poem as serious religious and political discourse perhaps addressed to policymakers, but perhaps also to a wider national audience of possible converts to the "truth."[1] Dowriche's political mission is clear in the central section of the poem, where she narrates the conflict between the "godly" counselor, Annas Burgeus (Anne du Bourg), and his king, Henri II, for she represents parliamentary conflict in the admonitory and apocalyptic terms often favored in the oppositional discourses of the Elizabethan House of Commons. Although a woman's exclusion from public office may imply that she was on the political margins, reading Dowriche's poem along with parliamentary texts from the 1570s and 1580s clarifies that she was not on the margins of political discourse.[2]

The religious fervor that so profoundly shapes the politics of *The French Historie* may be one reason why Dowriche has not been popular in the recent revival of work by early modern women writers. Perhaps another reason is that the poem is written in the often scorned poulter's measure— alternating hexameter and heptameter couplets. As Margaret Ezell has convincingly argued in *Writing Women's Literary History*, the achievements of many early women writers are effectively erased by an "evolutionary" model of women's writing that places women writers along a continuum, a model influenced by later practices of genre and publication.[3] Thus, at first glance, Dowriche's self-deprecating remark to her brother, "If you finde anie thing

---

1. Anne Dowriche, *French Historie* (1589), sig. A2[r-v]. The *OED* defines "policy" as "political sagacity; prudence, skill, or consideration of expediency in the conduct of public affairs; statecraft; diplomacy; in bad sense, political cunning." Each of these meanings is relevant to the unfolding episodes of *French Historie*.

2. In "Cunning in Controversies," Micheline White discusses Dowriche's contributions to current religious-political debate, arguing persuasively that the final section of *The French Historie* on the St. Bartholomew's Day Massacre should be read in the context of English anxiety about Catholic invasion.

3. See particularly chap. 1 of *Writing Women's Literary History*, in which Ezell argues that "anthologies and literary histories strongly stress the repressive nature of being defined as 'different,' and of society's power to silence women through culturally maintained inhibitions, trapping the creative woman in a web of repressive definitions of 'femininity'" (25); and chap. 2, in which she exposes the similarities between patriarchally constructed canons and the canon of women's literature, which thus "owes much to the institution it sets out to redefine, sharing certain assumptions about literary genre, value, and the format of presentation" (63).

that fits not your liking, remember I pray, that it is a womans doing" (sig. A2ᵛ), and her brief characterizations of female figures might simply suggest an early stage of development. But to open up Dowriche's text more fully to her cultural moment requires different approaches and assumptions. Aiming to bring together current historical criticism and French feminist theory, Ezell calls for the development of a "feminist historicism" because "we wish to preserve our ability to hear multiple voices of women writing in the past, not simply a universal female voice, and not to insist on continuity where diversity flourishes" (13). Agreeing with the spirit of such a resolution and mindful of the illuminating rereading of Quaker women's writings that Ezell produces, I want to define further the nature of the historicism required for reading Dowriche's poem.

I begin with the rather obvious points that women's texts are interpreting and reporting multiple facets of their culture even as they appear to be articulating only a "feminine" discourse—piety or domestic affairs, for instance—and that the extent of their referencing is most likely to be discernible if their texts are read in multiple historical contexts. These contexts can be supplied by the narratives of local history relating to a particular family, town, or county; by texts that debate dominant national issues of politics and religion; and by generically related texts. To borrow a term from current computer discourse, the text might be conceived as part of a "hypertext"— a multilayered and multireferenced text—and the reader's task is to identify and assess the many aspects of the culture on which the writer draws.[4] Certainly, such historical "hypertextuality" is applicable to many writers, but for the study of women writers it has the particular value of minimizing—or removing—the concept of marginality from the discussion.

The construction of a cultural hypertext for Dowriche's *French Historie* clarifies the discursive parallels between the poem of a Puritan woman living in Devon and the speeches of such Puritan members of Parliament as Peter Wentworth and Job Throkmorton.[5] Linking Dowriche's family

4. In this regard, Randall Martin places *The French Historie* in the context of English Machiavellian discourse, arguing that Dowriche's representation of the Machiavellian Queen Catherine de Medici is a breakthrough critique of Machiavellian patriarchy; see Martin, "Anne Dowriche's *The French History*," 69–88.

5. *Puritan* is the most familiar term for dissenting Protestants, although Puritans included both moderates and radical separatists. In *Drama of Dissent* Ritchie D. Kendall suggests "nonconformist" as a more accurate term to describe dissenters who "self-consciously viewed themselves as opposition figures" and who "regarded their dissent as a means of reforming existing institutions" (6); and see particularly chap. 4. Kendall's argument that nonconformists from John Bale to Martin Marprelate define themselves through ritual dialogues and confrontations is directly relevant to Dowriche's poem, particularly the narrative of Annas Burgeus discussed below. Nonconformists themselves favored the term "godly."

history, some aspects of local, political, and religious history, and the texts and genres she appropriated permits a tentative reconstruction of her material presence in the Puritan movement. Like the texts of many Puritan writers, her poem offers an inexhaustible supply of anti-Catholic propaganda along with an inextinguishable longing for a "purified" church and state and for a completed Reformation. The pointed dedication to her brother, accompanied by a cautionary acrostic of his name, suggests the poem may specifically address Piers Edgcumbe as a member of Parliament actually sitting in the current session for 1588–89.[6] In her characterization of the senator, Anne du Bourg, Dowriche also creates a leader whose scriptural rhetoric and constitutional theory provide a model for the leadership of the Puritan political movement at a moment when its existence was profoundly threatened.[7]

If we ask how Anne Edgcumbe Dowriche reached the point in July 1589 when she dedicated to Piers a historical poem that "hath beene my ordinarie exercise for recreation at times of leasure for a long space together" (sig. A2^v), we discover that an answer based on life records will be brief. Specific details of her upbringing are sparse, although some family papers and records make possible a biographical context, if not a life.[8] The date of Dowriche's birth is uncertain, but it was before 1560, when she is mentioned in her father's will. Both parents came from prominent west country families; her mother, Elizabeth Tregian, was from

---

6. Suggesting that Dowriche was addressing some conflict that Piers experienced are the words on his monument: "Lief Tenant to my Queen long Time, / And often for my Shire a Knight; / My Merit did to Creddit clime, / Still biddinge in my Calling righte; / By Loyalty my Faith was tryede, / Peacefull I liv'd, hopeful I diede."

7. In *The Elizabethan Puritan Movement*, Patrick Collinson remarks that although 1588 saw the defeat of the Armada and a victory for Protestantism, it also "marked the beginning of a definite decline in the fortune of the Puritan movement. Not of the Puritan religion: that was something now widely dispersed and year by year growing roots which were not to be easily torn out. But Puritanism as an organized force . . . was now under sentence" (385).

8. The entry for Anne Dowriche in the *Dictionary of National Biography* incorrectly identifies a second husband as Richard Trefusis. There were actually two Anne Edgcumbes— the poet who married Hugh Dowriche, and her brother Piers's daughter, Anne Edgcumbe Trefusis Manaton. In the Mount Edgcumbe papers at the Cornwall Record Office, Truro, a letter of obligation (ME 869) signed by Ambrose Manyngton (Manaton) clarifies the two separate identities: if Manaton married and survived the widow Anne Trefusis, he would pay one hundred marks to Piers Edgcumbe, a hundred marks to Richard Edgcumbe, and twenty marks to Anne Dowriche. See also the "Key Pedigree" in W. H. Edgcumbe, *Records of the Edgcumbe Family*; and Elaine V. Beilin, "Anne Dowriche" in *Dictionary of Literary Biography*, 172.

a Catholic family and married Sir Richard Edgcumbe in 1535.[9] Their
grandson, the poet and historian Richard Carew of Antony, later composed a portrait of his grandfather as a "fine old English gentleman,"
famous for his hospitality and generosity. In *The Survey of Cornwall* (1602),
Carew also praises Edgcumbe's great house, Mount Edgcumbe, superbly
located overlooking Plymouth Sound, noting its deer park, rounded tur-
rets, and great hall, and ranking the house "for health, pleasure, and
commodities, with any subjects house of his degree in England." Carew
also notes that Sir Richard had a "very good grace in making English
verses" (fol. 99[v]). Another mention of literary activity in Dowriche's family concerns her brother Piers, born in 1537, who wrote a copy of the
letters of Pelagius to Libanus Gallus in 1559 (Edgcumbe, 114). When Sir
Richard died in 1561, he provided in his will for the education of his two
young daughters, Anne and Honor (Edgcumbe, 91). Even if Anne
Edgcumbe was very young when her father died, it is possible that she
grew up in a home that contained books of poetry and theology, and in
a family who supported the education of girls. At some point Dowriche
became interested in writing poetry, for in the preface to *The French Historie*
she declares her intention to "restore againe some credit if I can unto
Poetrie, haveing been defaced of late so many waies by wanton vani-
ties." The desire to regenerate poetry along with religion and government links her to numerous Reformation writers, and her adoption of
poulter's measure may be an allusion to its use in a handful of psalms
in the Sternhold-Hopkins Psalter and in verse chronicles. She did not
choose the more popular fourteeners of the Psalter, however, suggesting
that she wanted not only decorous but unmistakeably weighty and so-
norous couplets.[10]

In 1580 Anne Edgcumbe married Hugh Dowriche, the rector of Lapford,
fifteen miles northwest of Exeter.[11] Their writings indicate that both Anne
and Hugh Dowriche were committed to Puritan doctrine and perhaps also
to active nonconformist circles in Devon.[12] As progressive Protestants, they
advocated the further reformation of the English church, an educated clergy,
scripturalism, and the essential importance of preaching. This agenda

9. Their marriage settlement is recorded in the Mount Edgcumbe papers (ME 826).
10. C. S. Lewis once unkindly compared poulter's measure to "labouring up a steep
hill in bottom gear for the first line, and then running down the other side of the hill, out
of control, for the second" (*English Literature*, 233).
11. See G. E. Trease, "Dowrich and the Dowrich Family of Sandford," 210–11.
12. In his study of early seventeenth-century Puritan families, *Puritan Gentry*, J. T.
Cliffe calls Devon "one of the most Puritan counties in England" (92). See Micheline White,
chap. 2, for evidence of Dowriche's noncomformist connections.

reflects basic reformation ideology—but, as Patrick Collinson suggests in distinguishing Puritans from the mainstream church, with "differences of degree, of theological temperature so to speak, rather than of fundamental principle." He cites a contemporary pamphlet: "The hotter sort of Protestants are called puritans" (*Elizabethan Puritan Movement*, 26–27). Such heat is discernible in the Dowriches' language, for Anne writes in order to "edifie, comfort and stirre up the godlie mindes unto care, watchfulnesse, zeale, and firventnesse in the cause of Gods truth," and Hugh writes an impassioned call to heed good preaching so that the people will "joyne in one godly unitie to worship and serve the Lord in the mount of Jersalem."[13] Even these brief quotations suggest how this fervency is inseparable from politics, particularly the sense that godly people form a "unitie," a movement dedicated to the supremacy of God's law and to the duty to resist rulers who are perceived not to honor it. Here, Collinson concludes, is "the political potency of puritanism" (*Elizabethan Puritan Movement*, 27).

Hugh Dowriche was licensed to preach in 1583 and became rector of Honiton, about fifteen miles east of Exeter, in 1587. Some evidence that the Dowriches may have been part of an active Puritan circle comes from the preface to his book, *The Jaylors Conversion* (1596), where he warmly addresses his longtime friend, Valentine Knightley, "the Worshipfull, and my approved good Friende," specifically mentioning that his first published work goes to "the first friend, that ever was truely possessed of my hart," someone he has known since youth and still deeply admires. The Knightleys were a prominent Puritan family of Fawsley, Northamptonshire. Sir Richard Knightley, Valentine Knightley's father, was a friend of the earl of Leicester and a recipient of his patronage; he hid the printing press used to publish the "Martin Marprelate" tracts—the first of which were probably written by Job Throkmorton—and was brought before the Star Chamber in February 1588–89 "for maintaining seditious persons, books, and libels." In 1584, Valentine Knightley was the member of Parliament for Tavistock in Devon, one of the Puritan earl of Bedford's boroughs; he was also the dedicatee of one of William Perkins's treatises, "both for the profession of the faith which you make as also for that Christian friendship you have shewed me."[14]

In *The Jaylors Conversion*, a work apparently based on a sermon he had preached, Hugh Dowriche contrasts English recalcitrance with the

---

13. Anne Dowriche, "To the Reader," *French Historie*; Hugh Dowriche, *Jaylors Conversion*, sig. A3ᵛ.

14. Collinson, *Elizabethan Puritan Movement*, 278 and 394; *Dictionary of National Biography*; J. T. Cliffe, 36.

zeal of his exemplum, St. Paul's jailor of Acts 16, whose "conversion" begins with an earthquake that prompts him to ask, "what must I doe, to be saved?" Dowriche declares, "If we consider this, we may lament, that the Lord in 38. yeares peace and preaching of the Gospel, hath not by his grace given unto us so perfect harts" (sigs. C3^{r-v}). In the thirty-eighth year of Elizabeth's reign, Dowriche expresses the common lament of the Puritan movement that the English church was so far from purification that apocalyptic punishments immediately threatened. His indictments span all "offices" of society and religious persuasion. Exploiting the biblical context, he deplores the sinful deeds of soldiers, kings, princes, noblemen, gentlemen, justices, lawyers, physicians, and finally "Protestants and professours of the Gospell" who have fallen short of complete devotion (sigs. B2^{v}–B3^{r}). From his biblical text, Dowriche instructs his readers how "blind potentates . . . doe persecute the truth" (sig. B5^{r}), and he includes a prayer for Queen Elizabeth that her sins be forgiven along with those of her subjects.

Anne Dowriche's poem, published earlier, may have influenced her husband's sermon, or his sermon may have been written years before publication and influenced her work; in either case, there is a marked similarity in their depiction of England's profound need for further reformation. A defining difference between them, however, is that *The French Historie* is fundamentally concerned with the relations of ruler and people—vividly representing both the breakdown of the ruler's responsibility to the people and to the "truth"—and with the duties of subjects in furthering the Reformation by resistance to rulers. Like Hugh Dowriche's sermon, Anne Dowriche's poem derives authority for its politics from scriptural examples. The sermon, rooted in the story of Paul's persecution and imprisonment in Acts 16, emphasizes providential deliverance through earthquake and internal conversion. The poem develops its political text by drawing on historical commentary as well as on Huguenot constitutional and anti-absolutist ideology circulating in England in texts such as Dowriche's immediate source, which she designates only as "the French Commentaries." Direct borrowings and close textual similarities indicate that she wrote the poem from material in Thomas Tymme's *The Three Partes of Commentaries, Containing the whole and perfect discourse of the Civill warres of Fraunce* (1574), a prose translation from Latin.[15] Examining Tymme's multivolume prose translation and

---

15. Tymme thought he was translating Petrus Ramus's Latin *Commentaries*, whereas he was actually translating *Commentariorum de statu religionis & reipublicae in regno Galliae libri* (1572–75) by Jean de Serres; however, the first part of de Serres's text is an abridged

Dowriche's 2,400-line poem together suggests that Dowriche saw herself as a popularizer of a political-religious movement. Indeed, she declares that one of her reasons for reproducing this history in verse was "for the more noveltie of the thing, and apt facilitie in disposing the matter framed to the better liking of some mens fantasies, because the same Storie in effect is alreadie translated into English prose" ("To the Reader"). Selecting three episodes from Tymme's collection of orations, letters, manifestos, and chronicles—the attack on the reformers in the rue St. Jacques, the martyrdom of Anne du Bourg, and the Massacre of St. Bartholomew—Dowriche juxtaposes and recontextualizes three politically potent narratives, each with a specific resonance for her English audience.

The point remains, however, that the poem is a *French* history and so bears examining as a text that "by indirections finds directions out" (*Hamlet* 2.1.63). A considerable and varied body of historicist work has shown that resistance to Tudor and Stuart absolutism and censorship resulted in a pervasive political "encoding" of sixteenth- and seventeenth-century texts. Long the advocate of "reading between the lines," Annabel Patterson, for example, has shown the importance of recovering the "conventions of oblique discourse" in texts possessing ideologies opposed to official policy on matters of rule and religion.[16] Recently, Patterson has argued that the 1587 edition of Raphael Holinshed's *Chronicles*, "for all its descriptive or antiquarian format, was probably recognizable as the vehicle of a clear and ideologically potent theory, a theory of Parliament's role as the emblem (if not the guarantor) of limited monarchy, government by the consent of the governed, and the freedom of speech necessary to arrive at that consent."[17] If Dowriche's history, published two years later, is not so obvious or voluminous a constitutional landmark, it is nevertheless a history of France that explicitly comments on the religion and politics of late-sixteenth-century England, with an agenda for the rights of the Commons freely to respond to the monarch on the subjects of religion and national security.

---

translation of Pierre de la Place's *Commentaires de l'estat de la religion* (1565). See *STC* 22241–22243. For convenience, I use "Tymme" and "*Commentaries*" to designate the text Dowriche refers to as "the French Commentaries."

16. Annabel Patterson, *Censorship and Interpretation*, 15; see particularly chaps. 1 and 2. See also Patterson's "The Small Cat Massacre: Popular Culture in the 1587 'Holinshed,'" 117–59.

17. Annabel Patterson, *Reading Holinshed's Chronicles*, 99–100. For another example, see *Virgil and the Tempest*, in which Donna Hamilton argues that *The Tempest* revises the *Aeneid* in order to represent and to supplant Jacobean absolutism with the opposing "constitutional principles of consent and reciprocity" (xi).

All the preceding contexts for *The French Historie* clarify the value of reading the poem along with Puritan parliamentary texts of the 1570s and 1580s. It is quite conceivable—although at present simply speculation—that Dowriche discussed parliamentary sessions with her brother, Piers Edgcumbe, or with her husband's friend, Valentine Knightley, or that she obtained copies of parliamentary speeches from an extended nonconformist network that actually included members of Parliament such as Peter Wentworth and Job Throkmorton.[18] The significance of the similarities between the discourses of her poem and of parliamentary speeches is not that Dowriche had access to a copy of these speeches, but that she was part of the discussion itself. A brief look at some excerpts from speeches by Peter Wentworth and Job Throkmorton indicates the substance and the "temperature" of their zealous discourse and provides a clarifying frame of reference for the fervent discourse of Dowriche's leading heroes.

The heat of Peter Wentworth's speech to the House of Commons in 1576 was incendiary; he was stopped in the middle of it by the House. The portion of the speech that he did deliver concerned the principles of free speech and the hindrances to free speech from "rumours and messages" originating with the queen or her servants, which intimidated members from speaking: "I would to God, Mr. Speaker, that these two were buried in hell. I mean rumours and messages; for wicked undoubtedly they are. The reason is, the Devil was the first author of them." The Commons' task, he said, was to make "good laws that do set forth God's glory," and so "to avoid everlasting death and condemnation with the high and mighty God, we ought to proceed in every cause according to the matter, and not according to the Prince's mind."[19] Wentworth took particular offence at a message sent from the queen in the previous session of 1572 "that we should not deal in any matters of religion, but first to receive [it] from the bishops." But if Parliament cannot deal with "God's causes," he argued, it cannot pass laws to protect the sovereign against Catholic conspiracies, nor can it continue to restore "true religion"; thus, "the accepting of such messages, and taking them in good part, doth highly offend God, and is the acceptation of the breach of the liberties of

---

18. Peter Wentworth sat for Barnstaple in north Devon (1571) and Tregony (1575–76 and 1581); and then Northampton (1586). Job Throkmorton sat for Warwick (1586–87). Perhaps the Dowriches knew Wentworth and Throkmorton through the Knightleys or through Piers Edgcumbe, who also sat in the Parliament of 1586, as well as the sessions of 1562–63, 1572, 1584, 1588, and 1592.

19. "Peter Wentworth" in *Elizabethan Puritanism*, ed. Trinterud, 174–75.

this honourable Council" (Wentworth in Trinterud, 177–80). Parliamentary records reveal that just as Wentworth was attacking the queen's abrogation of frank debate on two bills concerning Mary Stuart, he was silenced by his peers in the House and called before a Commons committee that very afternoon. In his own account of his examination, he explains that he decided to deliver the speech even though he feared trouble because his duty as a subject required him "to warne my prince from walking in a dangerouse course. . . . Yet when I uttered these words in the House, that there was none without fault, noe, not our noble Queen, I pawsed and beheld all your countenances and sawe plainlye that those words did amaze yow all."[20] Wentworth's self-presentation highlights the moment when, in his own eyes, his bold attack on the queen's errors stuns his listeners. But despite this dramatic claim for his own singular resistance to Elizabeth's prohibiting debate on the interrelated issues of Mary Stuart, religion, and the safety of the realm, Wentworth was more likely reflecting an institutional culture of opposition. As T. E. Hartley has convincingly argued, "political criticism of the Queen permeated the Commons," and the roles of sovereign and subjects were a constant subtext of parliamentary business; thus, although Wentworth was outspoken, he was "never a lone voice."[21] In 1587, Wentworth further risked his career by drawing up a list of ten questions to be presented to the House, again raising issues of free speech and censuring any parliamentary "tale-carrier" who ought to be "reputed as an enemy unto God, the Prince, and State" for reporting any matter to the prince "that is here in hand to the hurt of the House" (Wentworth in Trinterud, 189–90). Once more Wentworth was silenced both when the Speaker of the House "pocketed" the questions and when shortly afterwards he was imprisoned in the Tower, apparently on the charge that he discussed parliamentary affairs outside the House, an act forbidden by law (Hartley, *Elizabeth's Parliaments*, 138). Although Wentworth was excluded from Parliament, his texts continued to be circulated in manuscript.

20. *Proceedings in the Parliaments of Elizabeth*, ed. T. E. Hartley, I: 439.

21. T. E. Hartley, *Elizabeth's Parliaments*, 11–13. In his chapter "Peter Wentworth Revisited," Hartley challenges earlier readings, including J. E. Neale's claim that a Puritan and revolutionary Wentworth was advocating "for freedom of speech a fundamental, entrenched place in the constitution, entirely removed from its historical status as a privilege resting on the grant of the monarch and subject to definition by him [sic]," in *Elizabeth I and her Parliaments*, 1: 324–25; and G. R. Elton's revisionist—and cynical—view that Wentworth was an isolated ideologue whose every word "reeks of a selfsatisfied conceit," in *Parliament of England*, 346–47.

Job Throkmorton also spoke in the Parliament of 1586–87. Although the execution of Mary, Queen of Scots, on 8 February 1587 had stilled some fears of a Catholic conspiracy, open war with Spain loomed. Militant Protestants believed that the independence of the Protestant Netherlands from Spain was crucial for English security. In his speech of 23 February 1587, Throkmorton supported this foreign policy, beginning his address by vilifying all of Catholic Europe. Pointedly reviewing the Catholic conspiracy widely thought to be conducted by Catherine de Medici, her son, Charles IX of France, and the Spanish, and reminding his auditors of the slaughter of French Protestants in 1572, he congratulated the Commons for the execution of Mary: "The kings and princes of the earth assembled themselves and laid their heads together against the Lord and His anointed; but He that sits on high, even our Jehovah, hath laughed their devices to scorn." He continued his invective against Catherine, whose sons delighted only in "nothing almost but in hypocrisy, filthiness of life, and persecuting of the church of God" (quoted in Neale, 2:169–70). He imagined God addressing the English: "Though your sins do swarm in abundance . . . if ye will reform your church and lives in time, I will here offer you a means whereby ye shall be able to stand alone, yea, and to withstand all the foreign invasions of your ungodly enemies" (quoted in Neale, 2:171). Throkmorton also addressed the issue of free speech on 27 February, rising to support the radical Puritan agenda of Anthony Cope's Bill and Book—a proposal to terminate all existing church government and forms of worship, and to substitute a Presbyterian structure and a version of the Genevan Prayer Book. The queen sent for and suppressed this legislative item the day it appeared. With irony, Throkmorton remarked: "Ye shall speak in the Parliament House freely, provided always that ye meddle neither with the reformation of religion nor the establishment of [the] succession (quoted in Neale, 2:150). For both Wentworth and Throkmorton, free speech on religion was clearly the linchpin of foreign policy, domestic security, and church reform.

But again in 1587, the queen repeated her prohibition in a message addressed to Parliament headed, "Why you ought not to deal with matters of religion," in which she stated:

> Her Majesty thinketh it very inconvenient and dangerous, whilst our enemies are labouring to overthrow the religion established, as false and erroneous, that we by new disputations should seem ourselves to doubt thereof. . . . Her Majesty taketh your petition herein to be against the prerogative of her crown: for by your full consents it hath been confirmed

and enacted (as the truth therein requireth) that the full power, authority, jurisdiction and supremacy in church causes . . . should be united
and annexed to the Imperial Crown of this Realm. (quoted in Neale,
2:163–64)

To oppose such unequivocal assertion of the queen's privilege was dangerous. Both Peter Wentworth and Job Throkmorton spent time in the
Tower for their outspokenness, so we may conclude that Dowriche wisely
chose to represent resistance to the royal prerogative in a poem about
French history.[22] It was printed in London for booksellers in both London
and Exeter, near Dowriche's home, making available a cheap, popular
version of what Wentworth could not publicly complete: an extended
critique of the relations between the monarch and her subjects on topics
such as Mary Stuart, the safety of the realm, and the continued reformation of the church.[23]

The French Historie opens with a symbolic prologue when the English
narrator, walking in the woods, is paralyzed with fear at the sound of a
"shrilling voyce, and mournfull tunes"; he worries that thieves are at
work or perhaps "savage beasts," but finally "casting feare apart," he
runs toward the sound to offer help (sig. 1ʳ). He then overhears a French
"pilgrim" lamenting the "popish ignorance," tyranny, and resulting destruction of all parts of the commonwealth of France. By contrast, the
pilgrim praises "happie England . . . Which hast the truth established with
peace and perfect rest" (sig. 2ᵛ). However, this Edenic vision of England
is considerably destabilized by the Englishman's already expressed fear
of thieves and wild beasts in the English woods, and as the French pilgrim unfolds his narrative of tyranny and persecution, the initial distinction between the two countries is completely compromised, even erased,
when clear historical analogies are signaled in the text.

The meeting of the English and French narrators at the beginning of
the poem symbolically represents contemporary links between the Huguenot exiles and English Protestants, particularly those in godly circles.
Huguenot refugees were a presence in Dowriche's home county of Devon, and in the second half of the sixteenth century, many settled in East

22. John Stubbs's *Discoverie of a Gaping Gulf, whereinunto England is like to be swallowed by another French marriage, if the Lord forbid not the banes* (1579) was a publication on another forbidden subject, the projected marriage between Elizabeth and the duc d'Alencon; for his seditious act, Stubbs's hand was publicly cut off. See Robert P. Adams, "Opposed Tudor Myths," 67–90.

23. John Guy notes "that the size of an average print run had climbed to roughly 1,250 copies" between 1580 and 1603 (416).

Devon (Coxhead, 23). The Huguenots seemed to be natural English allies, but to the great concern of Puritan leaders, Elizabethan policy focused on placating the French monarchy just enough to keep France and Spain apart so that the French Protestants never had Elizabeth's unequivocal support. On a more local level, the status of the "strangers" who came to England after the French persecutions, including the Massacre of St. Bartholomew (represented in the third part of Dowriche's poem), varied according to where they settled and how integrated they were into the English economy and culture. Collinson has suggested that for English nonconformists, the foreign reformed churches may have been continuing "living models" of the further Reformation in terms of their forms of worship and presbyterian organization; at least in the case of Puritan and French churches in London in the 1580s, there is evidence of parallel developments in Puritan synods and foreign congregations as well as of Puritan financial support for hard-pressed French congregations.[24] For the Puritans, France itself could be an example of both tyrannical persecution of the true church and the heroic resistance of the godly. In his dedication, Thomas Tymme, Dowriche's source, praises the original *Commentaries* for their "godly lessons both concerning doctrine and manners" and for their "notable examples of Gods great mercyes, in defending and preserving the Christian professors of his name in Fraunce," particularly "in overthrowing the cruel tyrants."[25]

The second section of Dowriche's poem focuses on the "notable, famous, and constant Martirdome of Annas Burgeus." Always using the Latin form of his name as she found it in the *Commentaries*, Dowriche retells the story of Anne du Bourg, a counselor in the Parlement of Paris who was burned for heresy in 1559. The representational principles that Dowriche articulates earlier in "To the Reader" clearly shape her creation of this moment in French history and reveal her way of constructing the history of England. In describing her method of composition, she indicates how she read and revised her historical source, Tymme's *Commentaries:* "of purpose the nature both of the person that speaks and also of

24. Patrick Collinson, "The Foreign Reformed Churches," 247 and 265–72. Collinson names John Bodley as an elder in the French refugee church in London (267–68); Hugh Dowriche's sister, Ann, married William Bodley of the same Devonshire family.

25. Tymme, *Three Partes of Commentaires, Containing the whole and perfect discourse of the Civill warres of Fraunce,* sig. aii[r]. Tymme was a minister, probably with Puritan affinities; he appears to have been helped by Bishop Edmund Grindal, an early patron of English Puritans. Addressing Grindal in the Epistle to his translation of Calvin's *Commentarie upon S. Paules Epistles to the Corinthians* (1577), Tymme noted "the benefites, which long ago in Cambridge and els where since, I have receyved by your Graces preferment."

the matter that is spoken, are lively set downe: so that here are not bare examples of vertue and vice, but also the nature and qualities of those vertues or villanies are manifestly depainted to them that will seeke for it" [A4]. Clearly informed about contemporary literary discussions, Dowriche draws attention to her reproduction of the speaker as well as of the speech, and suggesting that readers must "seek" as they read, she promises to "amplify" the orations that were "onely in substance lightly touched" in the French *Commentaries.* In other words, she calls upon her readers to recognize the significance of individual speakers and to examine how they display virtues and vices in their particular persons. They are not "bare examples" in that they are clothed in the specificity of an unrepeatable historical—and political—moment; yet the implication is that within a providential framework, this moment is exchangeable for other historical moments, that examples of virtue and vice are continuously relevant and reapplicable.[26] Dowriche's text thus confronts the problems of coordinating providential history, which interprets scriptural exempla as eternal paradigms of events and actions, with political history, which interprets the specific moment, drawn from "Commentaries" or from contemporary events.[27] Both kinds of history are constructed from texts capable of multiple interpretations—even among a community of Protestant readers—and Dowriche exploits this multiplicity by developing both the scriptural and historical exemplarity of her poem. Describing herself as an amplifier of the French *Commentaries,* she models her own reader's task as actively hermeneutic, always ready to extend and multiply the meanings of the text. As Timothy Hampton has argued for humanist historical examples, "the exemplar can be seen as a kind of textual node or point of juncture, where a given author's interpretation of the past overlaps with the desire to form and fashion readers," and the process of decoding these examples is one of historicizing and interpreting the rhetoric of that historical moment (3).

From the beginning of the section on Annas Burgeus, Dowriche selects material from Tymme, recontextualizes it within a scriptural setting,

---

26. For a useful discussion of the rhetoric of Edwardian and Marian Protestant resistance, see Donald R. Kelley, "Ideas of Resistance," 48–76. Kelley emphasizes the "'topical' method" of Protestant political language: "the basis of this method, ideal for preaching and propaganda, was argument from concrete but more or less indiscriminate examples, whether classical, biblical, or historical" (53). My reading of Anne Dowriche's poem argues that the ideas and rhetoric of early Protestant resistance were still evident during Elizabeth's reign and that her exempla were discriminate.

27. See Beilin, "Writing Public Poetry," 258–67, for a discussion of Dowriche's providential and political conceptions of history.

and carries out the amplification she promised. Examining her developments and revisions of Tymme's text clarifies her historical vision: in its textual layering, her poem represents the struggle of the Huguenot counselors against Henri II in the Parlement of Paris as a paradigm of the struggle of the godly against tyranny as far back as the Old Testament and as far forward as Elizabeth's Parliaments from 1572 to 1589. The rulers vary in the extent of their oppression, but the resistance to kings is constant, and if not always politically successful, the resisters are always morally and spiritually dominant. Taking as her starting point Henri II's peace with Philip II of Spain in 1559, Dowriche found in Tymme that "It was reported among the common sort of people, that the Kings made a peace to this ende, that they might joyne in force togither to warre against the *Lutheranes*."[28] Clearly agreeing with the voice of the people, Dowriche develops their perception of the pact between the Catholic kings with a popular scriptural amplification: "But *Herode* to agree with *Pilate* was content, / And for to murder *Jesus Christ* they both doo joyne consent" (9). In the Parisian "Senate"—Dowriche adopts Tymme's term for the Parlement—there has been much debate on how severely to punish the Lutherans.[29] Although acknowledging the differences between France and England and particularly drawing on post-Armada discourse that praises Protestant England and Elizabeth's rule as superior to that of foreign tyrants, Dowriche also raises the possibility of an assembly where religion may be officially debated. However, the dangers to the parliamentarians are evident. In Tymme's *Commentaries*, the king's Solicitor tells the Parlement that its policies on heresy are inconsistent and ought to conform instead to the death penalty prescribed in the king's edict. The chronicler cynically remarks that asking for public debate was simply "the most speedie and readie way to detect those Judges that were suspected of religion"; nevertheless, the debate proceeds and "when every man freely uttered his mind and opinion, as the custome is," there was clear resistance to the king's plan. Dowriche paraphrases and consigns Tymme's judgment to a marginal gloss: *"This was Sathans subtiltie to bewray such of the Judges, as were suspected for Religion"* (sig. 9ᵛ). Fulfilling her goal

28. Thomas Tymme, *First Booke of Commentaries*, 24. At the beginning of the *Commentaries*, the chronicler notes that when the Reformation came to France, reformers were "banished, burnt, and with all maner of torments vexed, they were also called *Lutheranes*, which name then was made a common reproch to the godly" (4).

29. According to the *Dictionnaire des Institutions de la France aux XVIIe et XVIIIe Siècles*, the term *Senate* for the French Parlement was sometimes used in the context of praising the institution, or sometimes with irony. There are also instances when "Senate" is used to refer to the English Parliament.

to characterize the person who speaks, she brings the king to life as an aggressive ruler who "doth thirst / To have them all agree in matters touching faith." She develops the chronicler's remark that sentencing all Lutherans to death was a political move to make the godly betray their conscience: "yet among the rest some freely spake their minde; / That reason for so cruell act as yet they could not finde" (sig. 9^v). Here, she depicts the godly senators considering the *reason* for the king's edict, one that they judge to be "cruell" and one that many of them resist. They argue that the king wants to execute Lutherans as heretics, but they challenge his very assumptions of what constitutes heresy, redefining heretics as "they . . . as dare the Scriptures to denie," a definition they claim does not apply to "the godlie" for whom Scripture is "the Author of our faith." More important, they claim that if the godly are executed, "God would revenge their blood" (sig. 9^v).

Not only does Dowriche represent the necessity for free speech on religious issues, but she also raises the issue of parliamentary independence so crucial to Wentworth and Throkmorton. She includes Tymme's account of the role played by two counsellors who report the parliamentary debate to the king "before the court had concluded what should be done (against both lawe and auncient custome)," warning him that senators were deriding the Catholic religion and ignoring his edicts. Hearing this "newes," the king is "inflamed" and comes to the Senate in person the next day. In *The French Historie*, the tale carriers are two "hounds" who bring the king not "news" but a "message" about those who ignore "his Lawes and Edictes past" (sig. 10^r), and they urge the king to recognize the political danger from "these rebels" who might deprive him of his crown. The choice of "message" links the poem to the Commons' concern about royal monitoring of their debates, perhaps even alluding to the text of Wentworth's 1576 oration against "rumours and messages" or to his 1587 questions. The "inflamed" king's rage lends an ironic cast to the "high and princelie stile" (sig. 10^r) in which he is then said to address the Senate.

In Tymme's text, the king's desire is to set "matters concerning religion, in a good and uniforme order," and the keeper of the seals tells the senators to continue "shewing their opinions" (26); in Dowriche's text, the monarch himself speaks a much more chilling couplet: "Yet one thing there remaines to perfect this my State, / That in Religion one consent might banish all debate." Nevertheless, the king invites everyone to "shew his minde" (sig. 10^r). In both texts, many senators fear to speak in the presence of the king, but some do, especially Annas Burgeus, "as the chiefe this doubtfull silence brake" (sig. 10^v). Tymme provides an eleven-line summary of Burgeus's speech in which the counsellor "very boldly and freely uttered his mind," agreeing that a special session should be called to discuss religion and proposing that persecution of Lutherans should cease. At this point, Dowriche leaves her precursor text far behind, developing Burgeus's oration into a speech 121 lines long.[30] Certainly she continues to amplify what is "signified" in Tymme's text, but she also constructs another text that articulates Puritan religious and political ideology, allegorizes English parliamentary debate, and creates a parliamentary hero. Through Burgeus's oration, she reconstitutes a language and an ideology clearly in opposition to official policy, which by 1589 had quelled the Puritan movement, although not, of course, the godly faith. Would it have escaped the notice of Dowriche's immediate circle that this impassioned oration is delivered in parliament before the king by "Annas Burgeus"—that is, by a man named "Anne"?

The first six lines of Burgeus's oration essentially paraphrase Tymme's summation of the speech, but the following eighteen lines strongly establish Dowriche's own direction by clarifying the scriptural basis of Burgeus's thought. The marginal gloss provided at this point emphasizes that *"He setteth out the power and vertue of the word of god, and what a blessing it bringeth to them that so fullie receive it"* (sig. 10ᵛ). Dowriche gives Burgeus a rapid-fire succession of fourteen scriptural loci, all containing symbols of "the word of God" and all introduced by an anaphoric "This is the . . . ,"—for example, "This is the dustie booke which good *Hilkiah* found: / Which read before the King, did give a sweet and silver sound." It is probably safe to assume that the long list of marginal references are authorial and meant for active readers to use—so that these "seeking" readers could look up all of Burgeus's scriptural allusions and ponder their relevance to the present. None of the scriptural allusions was likely to be unfamiliar to Dowriche's immediate circle, but her wider audience (like her twentieth-century readers) probably benefited from the marginal documentation. If those readers used a bible with a gloss, such as the Geneva Bible, they would develop an even richer appreciation of Dowriche's religious and political thinking. A number of the allusions were standard Protestant allegory for the struggle against Catholic conspiracy and persecution and for the return of the "Israelites" and the

30. Although it is possible that Dowriche found other sources for the content of Du Bourg's speech to the king, it was apparently du Bourg's later speech to the Senate that was copied and circulated. Tymme's *Commentaries* include this second oration and du Bourg's long confession of faith. Later in this section of her poem, Dowriche includes the second oration to the Senate.

"true faith" to England. Thus, David's returning the ark to Jerusalem, the reign of good king Josiah, and Gideon's defeat of the Midianites and Amalekites were familiar religious-political texts. Still, if we take seriously the process of Dowriche's scriptural selection and interpret such references as the one to Hilkiah cited above, we encounter further textual layers. Her marginal reference to 2 Kings 22:8 in the Geneva Bible leads the reader to the story of the high priest Hilkiah, to the recovery of the book of God's word (v. 8–12), to good king Josiah's grief "that our fathers have not hearkened unto the words of this book" (v. 13), and to the prophetess, Huldah. When Hilkiah visited her "in Jerusalem in the colledge" and "communed with her," she prophesied dire destruction for Israel for forsaking God, except for Josiah, whose humility and grief over evildoing wins him a peaceful grave (v. 14–20).[31] Huldah's voice articulates God's punishments and rewards—as do the voice of Annas Burgeus and the voice of his creator, Anne Dowriche. In her preface to the reader, she invests *The French Historie* with a prophetic role: "I have also, for the more terror unto the wicked, diligentlie collected the great plagues and just judgements of God shewed against the persecutors in every severall History . . . that everie proud persecutor may plainly see what punishment remaineth due unto their wicked tyrannie" [A4]. All of Burgeus's other citations direct the reader to scriptural texts concerning the role of prophets when the people commit evil and to the power of God's word both to sustain and to destroy. The Old Testament prophet, speaking in a political context and from a religious position, is indeed the acknowledged precursor and example of much Puritan self-representation.[32]

In the climactic final position after these fourteen citations is a scriptural allusion that Dowriche gives its own extended marginal gloss and an eye-stopping choice of language. Burgeus concludes that God blesses the land that loves scripture and punishes "the contemners of his truth. . . . For why came *Ashur* up Gods chosen to molest, / And led the King with Commons all in *Babel* for to rest?" (sig. 10ᵛ). The marginal gloss reads, *"Hoshea the King and al Israel were carried captive to Babylon by the King of the Assyrians for dispising the Woord and Commandements of the*

---

31. "Colledge" is glossed in the *Geneva Bible* as "the house of doctrine which was nere to the Temple, and where the learned assembled to intreat the Scriptures and the doctrine of the Prophetes."

32. For example, the gloss in the *Geneva Bible* for the verse du Bourg cites from Jeremiah 20:9 reads, "He sheweth that he did his office in that he reproved the people of their vices and threatened them with Gods judgements: but because he was derided and persecuted for this, he was discouraged and thought to have ceased to preache, save that Gods Spirit did force him thereunto."

Lord. 2 Kings 17.4, 5, 6."[33] In case the reader missed the word "Commons" the first time, six lines later Dowriche repeats it during Burgeus's sharp warning to Henri II: "And if he doo not spare a King; ô King take heed: / If people all to thraldome goe; this land, ô Lord had neede / To weigh the cursed cause of this their finall fall; / Least for the like, the like consume our King and Commons all" (sig. 11ʳ). In these two instances, "Commons" would certainly mean "the common people," but it also recalls the House of Commons at a moment when Dowriche articulates her direst warning. Later, in Burgeus's second oration to the Senate, where Dowriche follows Tymme more closely, she rewrites Tymme's language concerning the "destruction of the King and the whole kingdome" to "Such as wil Prince and Commons all to deadlie ruine bring." In the first couplet cited above, the gloss for Babylon indicates that the punishment for abjuring scripture is political subjugation. More, "Babylon" is written "Babel," as it habitually was in the Geneva Bible, fortuitously providing another allusion to the confusion of voices that Parliament is doomed to become without the clarity of scripture to guide it.

But Burgeus has hardly begun to speak freely, and in subsequent lines he launches an attack on the king's powerlessness to subdue "Truth." Although Dowriche certainly positions the attack safely within the framework of the Protestant counselor correcting the Catholic king, once readers substitute "England" for "France" and "queen" for "king," the words may be taken to resonate boldly against Elizabeth's prohibitions on free speech:

> Now sith we have the seale from feare
> that makes us free,
> And shining light from popish shades
> the Lord hath made us see,
> We may no longer then dissemble in
> this case:
> But what we thinke must plainlie showe
> (ô King) before your face.

33. Dowriche conflates the victory of "King Asshur" who "caryed Israel away into Asshur" and dispersed the Israelites (*Geneva Bible*, 2 Kings 17:6) with the Babylonian captivity and Nebuchadnezzar's destruction of Jerusalem in 2 Kings 24 and 25. Dowriche's frequent references to Kings might derive from the ideology expressed in the Argument to "The Seconde Boke of the Kings" in the *Geneva Bible*: "In this boke are notable examples of Gods favour towardes those rulers and people which obey his Prophetes and imbrace his worde: and contrary wise of his plagues towardes those commune weales which neglect his ministers and do not obey his commandements."

> We cannot (as you would) the certain
>   *Truth* denie;
> But that defend: though for the same we
>   wer condemnd to die. (sig. 11ᵛ)

Burgeus decries the king's hatred and persecution of "godlie men, the best in all your land. / Whose faith you doo not see, whose life you doo not know," and warns him against creating a dangerous situation for himself, for "God will not long maintein their raign that shal his truth denie" (sigs. 11ᵛ–12ʳ). But Burgeus's threats modify into a prayer for the king's continuance, largely deconstructed by the hope that Henri will survive only to establish the true religion: "The lord preserve your noble grace, and shield ye with his hand, / That long in perfect peace your Grace may rule and raigne; / That in your time Gods knowen truth may once revive again" (sig. 12ʳ). Notably, these words echo at the very end of *The French Historie,* where the French pilgrim concludes his narration with a prayer for England:

> The Lord grant *England* peace and mercie
>   from above,
> That from the *Truth* no trouble may their
>   fixed heart remove.
> With wished life and health Lord long
>   preserve and keepe
> That Noble Queene *Elizabeth* chiefe Pastor
>   of thy sheepe.
> And that she maie finde out, and hunt
>   with perfect hate
> The Popish hearts of fained frends before
>   it be too late.[34]

The lines might easily derive from the often repeated expression of relief that so benign a Protestant ruler guards England, and yet if read with Burgeus's attack on Henri, the repetition of six key words—"Lord," "peace," "truth," "preserve," "noble," and "perfect"—reproduces the French moment with English allusiveness. Burgeus's earlier prayer for Henri revises the reader's interpretation of the French pilgrim's conventionally pious wishes for the queen, making it an extension of Burgeus's

---

34. Anne Dowriche, sig. 37ᵛ. The *Geneva Bible* gloss on Jeremiah 23:1, "Wo be unto the Pastors that destroie and scatter the shepe of my pasture, saith the Lord," is "Meaning the princes, governors and false prophetes."

irony: Elizabeth's longevity gives her a particular responsibility to establish the "true" religion, for the poem continually foregrounds the fate of those kings not fully committed to scriptural supremacy. Indeed, Dowriche includes the Huguenot version of Henri II's accidental death at a tournament as an example of providential punishment for his attack on the godly counselors.

Although Tymme provides only a seven-line version of Henri's reply to du Bourg, Dowriche amplifies the king's furious response into a twenty-two line invention that certainly recalls the analogy to Herod with which Dowriche begins this part of the poem. Like Elizabeth when she received a petition for free speech on religion, the king professes himself stunned at the political breach: "To speake or thinke as we have heard we deemd no subject durst" (sig. 12ʳ). His lament that the nobility have converted, that "men so grave and wise" have joined the new religion, is perhaps Dowriche's reflection on the large number of Puritan gentry and nobility in the parliaments of 1584–85 and 1586. This section of Burgeus's story ends with the king ordering his immediate arrest, after which Dowriche amplifies the chilling effect on the Senate: "Which sodaine fall did sore appall, and make the rest agast" (sig. 12ᵛ).

Dowriche wrote her poem at a time when the English nonconformist movement was in grave danger of being permanently silenced. But resisting the silence imposed on public dissent and addressing a familial, communal, and perhaps even national audience, she published a complex and allusive text. As a historical text, *The French Historie* inscribes English nonconformist opposition in the parliamentary speeches of a French Huguenot martyr and joins texts such as Peter Wentworth's and Job Throckmorton's in arguing for free speech on religion.

Some years ago, Natalie Zemon Davis asked what circumstances moved a few women in the early modern period to write history. To do so, she argued, a woman would have to overcome obstacles against obtaining "access to materials about her subject," whether printed texts or oral sources, and "access to the genres of historical writing, to the rules for ordering and expressing historical material." In addition, she would need "a sense of connection through some activity or deep concern of her own, with the areas of public life then considered suitable for historical writing—namely, the political and the religious"; and she would need an audience ("Gender and Genre," 154–55). My "hypertextual" reading of *The French Historie* has offered some evidence for Davis's premises, perhaps above all the requirement of an audience. At the beginning, Dowriche pointedly sends her poem to her brother, but she also aims at a specific readership of "godlie mindes" whom she longs to inspire. In her address to her readers, she even alludes to John Foxe's widely influential *Acts and Monuments,* which has assured that "the noble Martirs of *England* are knowen sufficientlie almost to all," and she undertakes to give a similar fame to "these excellent French Histories." So eager is Dowriche to write and to be read that as she offers her poem to her readers, she anticipates the pleasure of their approval for "this my pleasant exercise ... which, if I perceive to be accepted, thou shalt incourage mee to proceede, to make thee acquainted with more excellent actions." At present, we do not know about the reception of *The French Historie* or about the existence of any sequels. Only the author's fervent dedication to her occupation is clear.

8

Mary Wroth and the Politics of the Household in "Pamphilia to Amphilanthus"

Linda L. Dove

Beginning with Sir Philip Sidney's *Astrophil and Stella*, published posthumously in 1591, England experienced a sonnet craze. Male poets wrote sonnet sequences numbering in the dozens, using Petrarch's *Canzoniere* as a model and seemingly competing among themselves to erect an "Englished" version of the form.[1] In stark contrast to the number of men paying zealous attention to the sonnet form, however, is the relatively low number of women writers choosing to work in this genre. Only a few examples of early modern English women who composed sonnet sequences remain known to us, including Lady Mary Wroth in 1621, who addended "Pamphilia to Amphilanthus" to her larger romance, *The Countess of Montgomeries Urania*.[2] These sonnet sequences did more than reproduce the erotic valence of contemporary love lyrics. Wroth's sonnets critique the leadership of King James by envisioning the reformation of a tyrannous Cupid in the *corona* section of the sequence.[3]

---

1. Useful general studies of Petrarchism and the sonnet sequence include Spiller; Roche, *Petrarch*; and Ann Rosalind Jones, *Currency of Eros*.

2. For the purposes of this essay, I will follow Roberts's numbering of all the songs and sonnets sequentially, rather than Wroth's episodic numbering strategy. Wroth's sequence includes a total of 103 songs and sonnets, presumably divided into four unequal sections. She portrays her speaker Pamphilia's emotional progress—and regress—across these sections, which are connected by her struggle toward a definition of female subjectivity. Pamphilia's most successful moments appear to occur in the "third" section of the sequence, during the *corona*. For the argument against dividing Wroth's sequence this way, see Masten, 68–69.

3. A *corona* is a series of sonnets in which the last line of one sonnet becomes the first line of the next, and so on until the final sonnet of the series, which repeats the first line of the *corona* as its last line. Thus the poet achieves a circular form, or "crown," that turns back on itself and ends where it began.

Consequently, her speaker Pamphilia lays claim to a subject position that is both aesthetically and politically viable.

Acquiring subjectivity within the sonnet sequence was foremost on the minds of the men who chose to work with this form. As Arthur Marotti has demonstrated, "Love lyrics could express figuratively the realities of suit, service, and recompense with which ambitious men were insistently concerned as well as the frustrations and disappointments experienced in socially competitive environments . . . ambitious men could fantasize a kind of mastery they lacked in their actual experience" ("'Love Is Not Love,'" 398). Most masculine sonnet speakers assume an anticourtier posture as a rhetorical means of subverting the power of the female monarch. Sidney's Astrophil can make every decision regarding Stella, for she is his creation; he can thus imagine an aesthetic retribution for actual political woes. Shakespeare's speaker can shift praise (and dolor) onto a "master-mistress" male beloved and thus represent a network of male alliances and friendships rather than a queen and her court, as preeminent in his life.[4] As a result, Wroth must negotiate not just a genre of male erotics, but a genre of intellectual and political games as well. Her female speaker reflects Wroth's own unstable position in the political world of early modern England. Far from appearing as an autonomous individual full of purpose and action, a female subject, according to Catherine Belsey, "is linguistically and discursively constructed and displaced across the range of discourses in which the concrete individual participates" ("Constructing the Subject," 48). Although male poets were struggling with their own sense of fledgling autonomy, they were able to exploit the paradigm of Petrarchism to achieve a special status as an "anticourtier poet." Women were excluded from the role of Petrarchan courtier to begin with and were not then privy to its capacity for subversion. Thus, when Wroth—the well-connected niece of Sir Philip Sidney and of Mary Sidney, countess of Pembroke—found herself banished in 1610 from Queen Anne's court, she could not readily seize anticourtier discourse as a means of flaunting her indifference.[5] Instead, she had to manipulate other discourses against the Petrarchan conventions in order to create space for her female speaker.

In fact, much critical work on Wroth in the past two decades has focused on how she managed conventional sonnet motifs and images in

4. I am grateful to Donna Hamilton for first suggesting to me the connection between Shakespeare's speaker and his beloved boy as representative of his network of male friends and professional contacts.

5. For evidence that 1610 was the year of Wroth's banishment from court see Schleiner, *Tudor and Stuart Women Writers*, 137.

order to establish subjectivity for her female speaker and to avoid the objectified female position traditional to the sonnet sequence.[6] Not much mention has been made of the ways that she mediates the sonnet sequence's claim to political relevancy.[7] However, I argue that Wroth challenges King James's absolute authority by providing a vision of Cupid as the ruler and her female speaker as his subject joining in marriage and reigning happily together over a court of lovers like themselves. When placed in the larger political context of domestic theory, this vision of an idealized love match also works as a model of good government. Wroth's female speaker, who initially receives only contempt from both Cupid and her inconstant lover, corresponds politically to a beleaguered populace, bound to the absolute rule of an indifferent king.

This analogy between the relationship of lovers and the relationship of sovereign to subject is not purely speculative; it was commonplace in English political theory at the time. Wroth alters the analogy by imagining a reciprocal partnership in the *corona* and thus suggests a state ruled with the help of the people. In this essay, I begin by describing the contemporary debate concerning marriage and the family, which developed in early modern England as a vehicle for discussing issues of state. This general discourse was revised in the Jacobean era by James himself in order to secure a more patriarchal model of government. Early in her sequence, Wroth explores one of the analogues for the state that appeared frequently during this period—good social order exemplified by bees in their hive—but in her *corona* she relies on the domestic paradigm alone to elevate her speaker's role. In the second half of the essay, I address a specific vein of the discourse of domestic theory—that of the companionate marriage—to demonstrate how Wroth adapts the analogy between family and state for her own purposes by enlarging the role of women in the household and thus by enlarging the role of subjects in the commonwealth.

Although Protestant theology has often been identified as the source of family-state discourse, earlier Christian humanists such as Desiderius

6. Most critics identify Wroth's model of "heroic constancy" as crucial to her development of female subjectivity, although they disagree as to what that "constancy" signifies. They include, but are not limited to, most contributors to *Reading Mary Wroth*, ed. Naomi J. Miller and Gary Waller; Lamb, *Gender and Authorship*, 166–167; Krontiris, *Oppositional Voices*, 102–40; and Lewalski, *Writing Women*, 251–63.

7. Some critics have rightly suggested, albeit in passing, that Wroth's sonnet sequence is political—that is, involved in issues of nation-state management (as opposed to sexual politics, with which Wroth is also concerned). See Jones, *Currency*, 152; and Lewalski, *Writing Women*, 263.

Erasmus, Juan Luis Vives, and Sir Thomas Elyot constructed the domestic space of the household and its familial relations as the commonwealth in miniature.[8] In fact, these humanists' sources are classical: Aristotle originally discusses the state as growing directly out of the relationships in the household (*Politics*, 1.1.2), and Cicero presents the family as "the nursery . . . of the state" (*De Officiis*, 1.xvii.54). This idiom becomes pedestrian in early modern England: James even stamps his coins with part of the marriage vows—"Quae Deus Conjunxit Nemo Separet" [what God has joined together, let no man put asunder]—to reflect his position as head of Britain's household (Goldberg, *James I*, 43–46). As a result, Wroth obtains an opportunity to use the roles of wife and mother to recover a "civic" life for her sonnet speaker, although this construction would be bound necessarily to theoretical limits. Like the kingdom to which James is wed, Pamphilia represents the body politic itself to whom Cupid, the king, is wed. In the role of the body politic, however, she is able to function against the common love-lyric trope of a feminized kingdom or landscape that has been conquered, annexed, enjoyed, harvested, and generally ruled over by a "deserving" masculine leader. Petrarch's famous "Italia mia" canzone, to name but one example, functions within this tradition of female *sparagmos*, or dispersion.[9] Wroth reimagines the relationship between king and kingdom in nonabsolutist terms as a reformed alliance based on a seemingly contractual obligation between ruler and subject. Thus, she enables her speaker to critique the established order of the court, particularly a court such as James's with a ruler known for his absolutist tendencies. This ability lends her sonnet speaker entrée into the full tradition of male anticourtier poets who sought to coopt the monarch's power by creating autonomous and politically independent masculine speakers. Wroth's fantasy, however, imagines a reformed state in which man and woman, king and subject, ideally govern together.

When James ascended the throne in 1603, the central metaphor used to describe and justify the government shifted from a husband-wife paradigm to a father-child paradigm because James decided to make a strategic distinction between his commonwealth and his subjects. The commonwealth could continue to be figured as a "wife," as indeed it was on Jacobean coinage. However, this new father-child metaphor better fit

8. See Margo Todd, "Humanists," 18–34. Other overviews of the household analogy include Constance Jordan, "Household," esp. 307–26; Schochet; and Troeltsch.

9. See Brose, 1–20. This essay on the "*Italia mia*" discusses the body politic as a wounded or dismembered feminine body.

James's conception of the unconditional duty owed him by his subjects, a conception known as the patriarchal theory of obligation and eventually espoused by Stuart writers such as Sir Robert Filmer in his *Patriarcha* (1680).[10] Based on an explanation of patrilineal rule as the descent from Adam, patriarchal theory attempted to re-naturalize the hierarchical order so that it was not open to challenge, thus also securing James's divine right. What these theorists were trying to avoid in the marital theory was the assumption that wives were spiritually equal to their husbands with the ability to act conscientiously on their own, which would leave husbands open to their counsel or resistance. The possibility of petition or rebellion was unacceptable to James, so he switched the prevailing paradigm of government to one that did not sanction any form of challenge to his will. As Constance Jordan notes, "the monarch's position as husband was inherently less absolute than his position as father" ("Household and the State," 308). For Wroth, apparently, the father-child analogy simply did not work: it did not lend itself to a romantic narrative like that of husband and wife, and in fact excluded female agency altogether. More importantly, Wroth adopted the marital model of leadership that James abandoned as a way of correcting him and as a way of suggesting resistance to his theories of absolutism directly. By casting her sonnet speaker Pamphilia as wife to a king, then, Wroth secured a symbolic medium through which she can counsel and resist James's tyrannical rule.[11]

In fact, the ubiquitous association of the household and the state enabled the respective vocabularies of each to cross discourses and created a rhetorical opening for female participation in public activities. On the one hand, the terminology of state politics surfaced in descriptions of familial roles. For example, in *Of Domesticall Duties* William Gouge suggests

10. Filmer's justification of the rights of kings depended on the fatherhood analogy. See also Jenny Wormald, "James VI," 36–54, for the argument that James's absolutist views, especially in *The Trew Law*, were not genuine but in part a rhetorical exercise. Nonetheless, Wormald does acknowledge that their reception in England "went very badly awry" (52). For my study of Wroth, I am more interested in how the English received James and his "ideas," rather than whether he intended them or not.

11. See Josephine Roberts, "Critical Introduction" to Lady Mary Wroth's *Urania,* lxxiii–iv, who argues that Wroth offers "explicit defenses of absolutism" in the *Urania* (xlviii). However, all of Robert's evidence for this conservative position comes from the Newberry manuscript continuation of the *Urania*. Wroth's endorsement of monarchy in this later narrative may reflect the increasing civil unrest in England as the country edged toward civil war; she may be reacting against calls for the complete abandonment of the monarchy and its attendant aristocratic class.

the mother's role "be accounted a publike worke" so that "they shall be as well accepted of the Lord, as if they had publike offices" (sigs. C^v–C2^r). Writing nearly two decades into James's reign, Gouge has in 1622 the hindsight of more than a century of domestic conduct books and moralistic texts, the majority of which trade in like rhetorical currency. In addition to constructing the wife's role as household governance, domestic theorists allowed the companionate marriage to function as a model of dual leadership. Edmund Tilney's *A brief and pleasant discourse of duties in Mariage, called the Flower of Friendshippe* (1568) suggests that husband and wife should be partners in more than name only. He also displaces the language of the political commonwealth into the activities of the household: "the office of the husbande is, to maintayne well hys livelyhoode, and the office of the woman is, to governe well the houshold" (sig. C5^v).

On the other hand, the language of the home was sometimes located in the realm of politics. In 1559 John Aylmer, a defender of Elizabeth's right to the throne, argues that women can and should rule. His argument operates by extending a woman's role as leader in the household to a role in the public weal: "If then [women] may governe men in the house by saynt Paules commission, and an houshold is a lytle common welth . . . Then I can not see howe you can debarre them of all rule, or conclude that to be heads of men is against nature" (sig. D^r). Sir Thomas Smith's influential *De Republica Anglorum* (1583) follows the prevailing construction of women as inferior by nature and subordinate by convention; however, he too succeeds in associating the language of a larger political life with both men and women: "where their wisedome doth excell, therein it is reason that ech should governe. . . . Thus ech obeyeth and commaundeth other, and they two togeather rule the house" (sigs. C2^v–C3^r). Similarly, in 1595, the Lord Keeper recorded that Queen Elizabeth diligently chose her judges and justices of the peace " 'like a good housewife looking unto all her household stuff' " (quoted in Bassnett, 90). Therefore, as Margo Todd comments, early modern parents obtained an opportunity to become "king and queen of the little commonwealth" and "joint governors of the household," if only rhetorically ("Humanists," 23 and 25).

It is important to remember, in fact, that these designations were only rhetorical; Smith and nearly every other early modern domestic theorist ultimately insists on the subjection of the wife to the husband. However, these theorists are then forced to navigate through some difficult waters: they must rectify a wife's joint status with her husband as household manager and educator of future citizens with her ultimate subjugation to his authority. Smith accomplishes this feat by describing the society of the family not as a monarchy, but as an "*Aristocratia* where a few & the best doe governe, and where not one alwaies: but sometime and in some thing one, & sometime and in some thing another doth beare the rule" (sig. C3ʳ). In *Of Domesticall Duties*, Gouge explains the discrepancy in even more minced terms: "it might be demanded, if wives must feare and obey their husbands and be subject unto them, where is their preferment above their children and servants. But it hath beene shewed that though the same things for matter be required of wives which are required of children and servants, yet there is a great difference in manner of performing them" (302). Gouge appeals to the slippage between practice and theory in order to avoid his own contradictory message. Smith reluctantly admits that his model is finally only that—a model; it "cannot be called *Aristocratia*, but *Metaphorice*, for it is but an house, and a litle sparke resembling as it were that governement" (sig. C3ʳ). Clearly, these humanist and Protestant theorists are unable either to elevate women completely or to infantilize them completely—becoming trapped by their own terms, leaving the roles prescribed for women in flux and, by their own admission, open to interpretation.

Although James preferred the political analogy of parent and child to that of husband and wife, he was merely choosing between two classical metaphors. As early as 1516, in *The Education of a Christian Prince*, Erasmus, quoting Aristotle, implores that a "good prince ought to have the same attitude toward his subjects, as a good *paterfamilias* toward his household—for what else is a kingdom but a great family?" (170) However, after James's accession, conduct books and political treatises alike began to associate the language of fatherhood with the monarch's role more exclusively than before. For example, in *The doctrine of Subjection to God and the King* (1616) Stephen Egerton espouses obedience to James by using parental rights as his foundation. He starts with the fifth commandment to argue that parental rule is merely the private example of the same leadership found in the king. Even though James changed the analogy's focus, his representation of the state was still a domestic one— albeit one that offered a less flexible dynamic.

Such language and its implications are clearly on the mind of Wroth in her composition of "Pamphilia to Amphilanthus." Wroth's speaker Pamphilia first exploits the language of domestic theory well before the *corona*, seventy-seven poems into the sequence. In one of her apostrophic sonnets, "How fast thou fliest, O Time, on loves swift wings," Wroth attempts to reform the predatory relationship between the lover and Time into one that displays mutual consideration and profit. Pamphilia constructs an image of herself as a beehive, another common analogy used by political theorists when discussing the commonwealth.[12] "Time" appears as a tyrannous force bent on the hive's destruction, and Pamphilia's didactic voice attempts to coax him into a more leisurely, yet industrious pace. Her admonition seems to imagine the masculine "Time" (a stand-in for the male beloved) in the typical role of husband-provider:

> O! slacke thy pase, and milder passe to love;
> Bee like the Bee, whose wings she doth butt use
> To bring home profitt, masters good to prove
> Laden, and weary, yett againe pursues,
> Soe lade thy self with honnye of sweet joye,
> And doe nott mee the Hive of love destroy. (P37.9–14)[13]

In the *Politics*, Aristotle envisions the beehive as another sort of family unit and thus as a microcosm of the state. Following this classical lead, Sir Thomas Elyot refers to the ideal government of bees in *The boke named the Governour* (sigs. A7ᵛ–A8ʳ), and Gouge uses the beehive-family analogy in *Of Domesticall Duties*: "[The family] is as a Bee-hive, in which is the stocke, and out of which are sent many swarmes of Bees: for in families are all sorts of people bred and brought up: and out of families are they sent into the Church and common wealth" (sig. Cʳ).

Although the comparison between the beehive and the commonwealth was widely disseminated and reproduced, one use of it is worth particular mention because it concerns Wroth. Thomas Moffett's scientific treatise *The Theater of Insects* (1658) offers the beehive as a model of contractual monarchy:

BEES are swayed by soveraity, not tyranny, neither do they admit of a King properly so called, by succession or lot, but by due advice, and circumspect choice; and though they willingly submit to regall authority; yet so, as they retain their liberty; because they still keep their Prerogative of Election; and when their King is once made sure to them by oath, they do in a principal manner love him. (892)

Moffett was the personal physician to the Sidney family and a beneficiary of the countess of Pemboke's patronage, so he or his work may have

---

12. See J. P. Sommerville, *Politics and Ideology*, 48–49.

13. Compare Wroth's bee sonnet to the English ballad entitled "The Good Husband," recorded in *The Roxburghe Ballads*: "They, like the industrious Bee, will delight / To labour, and bring home their profit at night" (7:148).

been directly encountered by the countess's inquisitive niece. In any case, Timothy Raylor observes that Moffett's interest in contractual theories of government "was surely influenced by his own political allegiance, for he moved among members of the Sidney circle, a group which flirted with republican ideas" (111). As heir to this political heritage, Wroth may have understood her version of the apian household as a model of the ideal state, one that her speaker insists should function "mildly" and be mutually profitable for all concerned. If so, then Wroth's counsel on correct government carries a specific warning against the destruction of the feminized hive as if it were the destruction of the commonwealth itself: "doe nott mee the Hive of love destroy." The speaker's private (female) body has been refigured as the body politic, and Wroth reserves the right to challenge models of power that are hostile to it.

Although Wroth has initially cast the god of love and various other personified figures as tyrants in her sequence, even claiming that Cupid possesses a "badge, and office of his tirannies" (P64.8), she abandons that course of blame as she enters the *corona*. Instead, she constructs an idealized vision of "the court of Love, and reason" and "crowne[s]" Cupid as a noble ruler (P86.1, P76.12). To underscore the political subtext of this love narrative, she locates us within a political site—the "court." Moreover, she has reimagined the conventional "Court of Love" trope in which Cupid and Venus struggle against each other as the ruling figures of love and lust.[14] Wroth's court is one of mutual respect, where both love and reason must learn to rule together. In fact, respect replaces scorn, and reason replaces lust, just as Pamphilia replaces Venus. Yet, Wroth's *corona* is driven by constancy in love, not necessarily by chastity, so "reason" becomes a euphemism for love within marriage.[15] As a result, Wroth defines constancy as the better way to love and to rule, and her *corona* becomes a sort of miniature conductbook for lovers and rulers alike.

To achieve her contented society, Wroth borrows from the discourse of domestic theory. She develops the relationship between the king "Love" (Cupid) and his queen "reason" (Pamphilia) using the language of the companionate marriage. Speaking about the newly crowned Cupid, Pamphilia remarks that

14. For an explanation of the Court of Love tradition see Neilson.

15. For evidence that Pamphilia was in fact married to Amphilanthus in a secret ceremony, see Roberts, "Critical Introduction" to Lady Mary Wroth's *Urania*, in which she notes that in the *Urania*, Pamphilia may assume that she and Amphilanthus have a *de praesenti* marriage, "which even though unsanctified by the church, had binding legal authority" (lxxiii).

> Hee may owr profitt, and our Tuter prove,
> In whom alone wee doe this power finde,
> To joine two harts as in one frame to move;
> Two bodies, butt one soule to rule the minde;
> Eyes which must care to one deere object bind
> Eares to each others speech as if above
> All els they sweet, and learned were; this kind
> Content of lovers wittniseth true love. (P82.1–8)

In spite of the Petrarchan convention of extramarital love, the language of this sonnet is strikingly spousal ("two as one"). The lovers' mutually exchanged "speech" is both "sweet" and "learned," their eyes meet each other's, and their love enriches their "witts" as well as their senses of themselves. In keeping with a sonnet sequence predicated on the absent male beloved, Wroth's interlocutors often shift roles, which enables Amphilanthus to merge, in this case, with the god of Love. Thus, Wroth's ideological model operates to provide parity for a wife in her relationship with her husband and, by analogy, for a subject in her relationship with the monarch.

Several early humanist texts provide fodder for this scripting of a companionate marriage, which later became an ideal of Protestant wedlock as well. For example, William Harrington in his *Commendacions of Matrymony* (1528) presents the three goals of marriage that are reconstituted in numerous early modern texts: "mary pryncypally for to have chyldren or to avuoyde fornycacyon, or for to have consolacyon and helpe" (sig. A4r). Eventually, the order of these goals is rearranged to suggest a preference for companionship above all else.[16] In his epistle "To the Reader" prefacing his treatise *The Christen State of Matrimonye* (1543), Heinrich Bullinger places the social bond between husband and wife at both the beginning and the end of his matrimonial aims: "to the intent that they maye lyve honestly and frendly the one with the other, that they maye avoyde unclennesse, that they maye bring up children in the feare of god, that the one maye helpe and comforte the tother" (sig. A6v). The Elizabethan homily on matrimony of 1563 announces this goal immediately: "[Marriage] is instituted of God, to the intent that man and woman should live lawfully in a perpetuall friendship, to bring foorth fruite, and to avoide fornication" (Church of England, "An Homilie of Matrimony," 239). Vives, Erasmus, Sir Thomas Elyot, Sir Thomas More, and, later, countless Protestant theorists all allow for the preeminence of

---

16. For a summary of why and how these goals are reordered, see Todd, "Humanists," 21–22.

friendship within the marriage bond. As far as the analogy of marriage extends to the political bond between monarch and subject, then, Wroth's use of a companionate model—particularly one that occurs between this king Cupid and his subject Pamphilia—suggests her endorsement of a limited monarchy.

James, however, does not follow prevailing discourse when he records the aims of marriage for his son and heir, Prince Henry, in the *Basilikon Doron* (written in 1598 and published in 1603). After dividing these goals into two categories—"the three causes" of marriage and "the three accessories" of marriage—James exposes the little regard he has for any sort of spousal parity by altogether avoiding the idea of "friendship" between husband and wife: "The three causes [marriage] was ordeined for, are, for staying of lust, for procreation of children, and that man should by his Wife, get a helper like himselfe. . . . The three accessories, which as I have said, ought also to be respected, without derogating to the principall causes, are beautie, riches, and friendship by alliance" (quoted in *Political Works of James I*, 1:35). His reference to "friendship by alliance," which he lists as the last "accessory," does not occur between husband and wife, but between men who gain social bonds with each other via the bodies of women. Thus, he writes the companionate nature of marriage out of the discourse, substituting in its usual place a phrase that designates wives as biblical "helpmetes": "that man should by his Wife, get a helper like himselfe." What's missing from this formulation is any sense of reciprocity; James's language—"by" and "get"—suggests that his goal will be to take and not to give. Although he concludes the phrase with the tag "like himself," which might imply that he too is to be a helper in the marriage, it could also mean that she should be the helper and that she should be like him. In a text designed as a political conductbook for his young successor, James apparently refuses to accord a wife any position of mutuality. This refusal is in keeping with his political ideology to maintain absolute control over his subjects: it would be too dangerous to endorse a philosophy that allowed for marital friendship if that friendship is taken as an analogue to the state.

In her *corona*, Wroth also celebrates an expanded role for mothers, which was an integral part of the companionate marriage, according to early-modern domestic theorists. This larger maternal role in the household would also serve as a political challenge to James, who had embraced as his model of leadership the household's role of the father. As the king of hearts, Cupid teaches Pamphilia "To joine two harts as in one frame to move," playing the role of her "Tuter." However, they engage in the same activity; they both create love "in one frame"—the frame of a story. One creator uses a pen, the other an arrow. Wroth shifts the dynamic of their relationship from tutor and student to creative partners.[17] Furthermore, Pamphilia goes Cupid one step better as she reminds him that she has generative powers exclusively her own. Speaking of love, she remarks:

> Itt doth inrich the witts, and make you see
> That in your self, which you knew nott before,
> Forcing you to admire such guifts showld bee
> Hid from your knowledg, yett in you the store;
> Millions of thes adorne the throne of Love,
> How blest bee they then, who his favours prove. (P82.9–14)

Writing these love sonnets has the effect of making "you see / That in your self, which you knew nott before." Thus, Wroth invokes a metaphor of pregnancy—"such guifts showld bee / Hid from your knowledg, yett in you the store"—to emphasize her double claim to the title of creator, as both mother and writer. She is one of the "Millions" who seek to "adorne the throne of Love," both with poems and with future citizens of the kingdom of love. Not everyone succeeds, although this female subject apparently has a better chance than the men. Only "they then, who his favours prove" can be thus "blest."

Wroth's elevation of the maternal role occurs in an earlier sonnet of the *corona,* as well. Pamphilia describes love as "the shining starr" that turns into the "lasting lampe fed with the oyle of right; / Image of fayth, and wombe for joyes increase" (P78.7–8). She moves from an image of stellar love to an image of feeding, or actually of nursing (the lamp "fed with the oyle of right"), and ultimately back into the "wombe" itself. By withdrawing love from its objectified position in masculine sonnet discourse, she reclaims it for herself and internalizes it as only a woman can. Quite literally, Pamphilia yanks Sidney's star from the sky and plants it in her womb. Success on these erotic and poetic levels of creation produces

> A lyfe wherof the birth is just desire,
> Breeding sweet flame, which hearts invite to move
> In thes lov'd eyes which kindle Cupids fire,
> And nurse his longings with his thoughts intire. (P83.2–5)

---

17. See Schleiner, who reads the character Sylvesta in Wroth's play Love's Victorie as Wroth "writing herself into the position of King of Love" (*Tudor and Stuart Women Writers,* 148).

Wroth conflates her dual creative roles. Words such as "birth," "Breed-ing," and "nurse" give way to a discussion of the artist: "Love will a painter make you" (P83.9). She can "drawe" her "only deere / . . . more true / . . . and to you more neere" (P83.10–12) because her creation can also be life itself, inside her, "more neere." Male sonneteers can claim the status of creator only through their labor as an artist or, as Margaret Brose reminds us, through the theft of the feminine: "In the Petrarchan version, poetizing is a surrogate form of female creativity, a virtual theft of a distinctively female mode of creation" (14). Yet Wroth manages both to take back the role of the maternal *and* to resist conventional Petrarchan objectification of the beloved. Having recovered herself from among the stars, Pamphilia does not choose to "drawe" her "only deere" there. She sustains a focus on selfhood—a traditional concern of the sonnet se-quence speaker—but still insists on the value of a close partnership: "Hee that shunns love doth love him self the less" (P83.14). Thus, she also provides a model of government based on pregnancy that directly usurps James's patriarchal rhetoric of state. Wroth does not suggest distance from her beloved (or from the monarch) as a way of claiming more power for her speaker. The fantasy of an empowered self in this sociopolitical model derives from a "more neere" relationship, not from one invested in subject-object divisions.

Wroth's introduction of the mother's role and her representation of children in this idealized kingdom perhaps suggest that Pamphilia func-tions as more than just an analogue to James's subjects. She may repre-sent an elevated body of his subjects, such as the Parliament, which must work with the king to protect and rule the populace. In fact, Wroth does structure her "court of Love, and reason" as a household with children:

> Desert, and liking are together borne
> Children of love, and reason parents just,
> Reason adviser is, love ruler must
> Bee of the state which crowne hee long hath worne. (P86.3–6)

The parents—"love ruler" and "Reason adviser"—produce their children "Desert" (or merit) and "liking." Wroth's speaker explains this relation-ship in seemingly hierarchical terms: love "must / Bee" the ruler of this kingdom, whereas reason acts only as "adviser," apparently because that arrangement is traditional—it's the "crowne hee long hath worne." How-ever, she immediately qualifies this formulation of the court (or the house-hold) by insisting that the children will respond only to a "government" ruled equally by both parents:

> Yett soe as neither will in least mistrust
> The government wher noe feare is of scorne,
> Then reverence both theyr mights thus made of one. (P86.7–9)

In this sonnet, the analogue of the subject shifts from the wife to the child, just as the dominant analogy of Jacobean monarchy shifted from husband-wife to father-child. In Wroth's version, however, the woman is not excluded; she appears united with the man—"both theyr mights thus made of one"—in a government free of contempt for its subjects. In fact, because the wife appears in an "advisory" role, Wroth could very well imply Parliament as the other "might" of this government. As Constance Jordan comments, "the essential freedom of the wife . . . when analogized to the freedom of the subject as citizen, could be made to stand for the people's right to assemble and as a body advise the monarch" ("Household and State," 320). Thus, Wroth would be advocating a state run by the consent of the people. She does not seek to overthrow the monarch—merely to ensure against his tyranny so that the commonwealth will be a place "wher noe feare is."

Without that sense of mutual partnership between husband and wife, and analogously between king and subjects, only a bleak vision of future events is possible: "Fruit of a sowre, and unwholsome ground / Unprofitably pleasing, and unsound" (P86.13–14). If the government is "unsound," then its weakness corrupts the entire nation, causing ruin even to the land itself. This practice of linking a corrupt ruler to a bleak landscape is familiar from biblical narratives such as those of David and Hezekiah, literary plots such as Shakespeare's *Richard II*, and political texts such as the *Mirror for Magistrates*. Wroth includes a pair of sonnets that work as mirror opposites—one of a garden hidden in shade, where hemlock thrives and "unruld vapors swimm in endles rounde" (P87.8), and the other of a garden "shining faire, and cleere" (P88.14), where spring's flowers give way to autumn's harvest. These two templates showcase the consequences of good or bad leadership. Her prognostication for a land under corrupt rule includes this dark look at an anti-Eden:

> Unprofitably pleasing, and unsound
> When heaven gave liberty to frayle dull earth
> To bringe forth plenty that in ills abound
> Which ripest yett doe bring a sertaine dearth.
> A timeles, and unseasonable birth
> Planted in ill, in wurse time springing found,
> Which hemlock like might feed a sick-witts mirthe
> Wher unruld vapors swimm in endles rounde. (P87.1–8)

In this postlapsarian sonnet, Wroth's speaker alludes to the loss of paradise as the moment "When heaven gave liberty to frayle dull earth / To bringe forth plenty that in ills abound." Wroth uses this image of a corrupted garden to suggest a failed government and is helped in this comparison by the early modern identification of the Garden of Eden as an archetype for sociopolitical order. Because Adam and Eve were counted as the earth's first husband and wife and as its first rulers, their initial behavior was considered exemplary. As Ernest Troeltsch notes, "the overlordship of man was only established when the curse was pronounced and Adam and Eve were driven out of Paradise" (1:130). Wroth impugns Adam's overlordship by portraying tyranny as imperfect and fallen. In this sequence, the loss of paradise is not Eve's fault; it results from "shady pleasures" and "coole, and wann desires" (P87.10, 12), which Wroth does not make gender specific. Wantonness in both women and men gets figured as tyrannous behavior. Rather than adhering to the Edenic model of joint governance, the inconstant partner destroys the garden by generating a "hemlock like" poison, which creates a murky, anarchical swamp fit only to "feed a sick-witts mirthe."[18] Thus, Wroth proposes that although the ideal state should not be an absolutist model of patriarchy, neither should it be completely "unruld." Her preference for government remains a limited form of monarchy—a king who has consideration for and commerce with his subjects as the husband of a companionate marriage has with his wife.[19]

To remedy the miasmic landscape of her kingdom, Wroth substitutes a vision of Eden before the fall, which knew parity between man and

18. Compare this sonnet to Shakespeare's description of the garden in *Richard II*:

> Go bind thou up yon dangling apricocks,
> Which, like unruly children, make their sire
> Stoop with oppression of their prodigal weight,
> Give some supportance to the bending twigs.
> Go thou and, like an executioner,
> Cut off the heads of too-fast-growing sprays
> That look too lofty in our commonwealth.
> All must be even in our government. (3.4.29–35)

19. Compare this to James's denial in *The Trew Law of Free Monarchies* "that every man is borne to carry such a naturall zeale and duety to his commonwealth, as to his mother." Instead, he suggests the people's compliance and passivity, "For a king cannot be imagined to be so unruly and tyrannous, but the commonwealth will be kept in better order, notwithstanding thereof, by him, then it can be by his way-taking . . . better it is to live in a Common-wealth where nothing is lawfull, then where all things are lawfull to all men." Quoted in *Political Works of James I*, 66.

woman. By replacing the hemlock bush with blossoming trees that "lose theyr coulers bright / Yett dy nott, but with theyr loss repaire" (P88.3–4), Wroth reinvokes the virtues of constancy and reason. Trees that experience decline in the fall and winter are not destroyed but rewarded for their patience by the arrival of spring. As in the biblical Eden, the components of this garden "dy nott." Furthermore, Wroth replaces the image of a vaporous swamp with a place "Free from all fogs butt shining faire, and cleere" (P88.14). Her recovered landscape owes itself to her recovered vision of true love, "Wher holly friendship is esteemed deere" (P89.3). This language of "friendship" between husband and wife borrows directly from the discourse of companionate marriage, such as the Elizabethan religious practice of urging couples to live in "a perpetuall friendship." Because political theorists used "the descent from Adam's power" to justify a patriarchal monarchy, especially in the Stuart period, Wroth's rejection of it here and her formulation of a "friendship" between husband and wife, or by analogy between king and subject, may reveal her interest in the concept of government by consent.[20]

Pamphilia admits that subjects will agree to be governed if reciprocity is observed in political and personal relationships alike. The final sonnets of the *corona* emphasize this conditional—and thus negotiable—submission of the subject. Although Wroth's speaker addresses her ruler as the "Great King of Love" in whom she places her "trust," she maintains her position as his peer: "As enimies to you, my foes must bee" (P90.10). She acknowledges his rule over her but not in an absolutist form: "In love thes titles only have theyr fill / Of hapy lyfe" (P89.5–6). His "titles" of husband and king are useful and fulfilling only if they are wagered kindly, with "love." Thus, Wroth follows the constitutional ideals of Aristotle, who cast the wife "as free yet a subordinate in marriage and, correspondingly, of the people as free yet subjects in a republic."[21] Likewise, at the end of this sonnet she comments, "I offer to your trust / This crowne, my self, and all that I have more" as if demonstrating that the origin of the king's political power is in his subjects. They "offer" him the "crowne"; they "offer" him themselves to be ruled; they charge to his "trust" all their possessions. He rules over them but only with their consent. Through these potentially subversive images, Wroth participated in a political debate concerning royal prerogative that eventually led to civil war.

20. See the chapter in Schochet entitled "Sir Robert Filmer: Patriarchalism and the Descent of Adam's Power," 136–58.

21. As summarized by Jordan, "Household," 326. Elsewhere in her essay, Jordan likewise comments that the Aristotelian notion of justice "gives to the free but subject citizenry a virtual equality even while it guarantees the functional hierarchy of government" (314).

9

Elizabeth Cary's Edward II

ADVICE TO WOMEN AT THE COURT OF CHARLES I

Karen Nelson

The History of the Life, Reign, and Death of Edward II . . . written by E.F. in the year 1627, by Elizabeth Cary,[1] first published in 1680,[2] is firmly located in the events of 1626 and 1627[3] and was involved in shaping

I thank Jane Donawerth for envisioning this book and for assisting me throughout this essay's drafts and re-drafts. I could not have completed this project without the patience of my children, Adam and Susanna Maisto, or the help of my husband, John Maisto, and of the Nelson and Maisto families.

1. Like *The Tragedy of Mariam* and much sixteenth- and seventeenth-century literature, *Edward II* was originally circulated only in manuscript, if at all. The existence of a dated author's preface to the reader supports the possibility of the text's manuscript circulation; Margaret Ezell, in *The Patriarch's Wife*, makes the point that manuscripts usually have "prefaces, dedications, and are usually dated" (166); they are created not as "closet productions" but for circulation and presentation controlled by the author (68). For recent summaries of the debate over Cary's authorship of this text, see Cary, *Tragedy of Mariam*, ed. Weller and Ferguson, 12–17; Purkiss, "Introduction" to *Renaissance Women*, xxi–xxx; Schleiner, 186–91; Lewalski, *Writing Women*, 201–3 and 317–20; Kim Hall, 139; Gwynne Kennedy, 206, 219–22; Stephanie Wright, 61–62.

2. There are two related published versions of *Edward II* attributed either to Elizabeth Cary or to Henry Cary: *The History of the Life, Reign, and Death of Edward II. King of England, and Lord of Ireland. With the Rise and Fall of his great Favourites, Gaveston and the Spencers. Written by E.F. in the year 1627 and Printed verbatim from the Original* (1680), hereafter shortened to *The Reign and Death*; and *The History of the most unfortunate Prince King Edward II. With Choice Political Observations on Him and his unhappy Favourites, Gaveston and Spencer* (1680), whose publishers claimed to have found the manuscript among Henry Cary's papers. I will focus on the longer version, *The Reign and Death*, because its text includes the title page assigning it to E. F., the initials of Elizabeth Falkland, the signature Cary used at that time, and also introduces itself with a letter to the reader from E. F. Diane Purkiss includes a modern-spelling version of *The History of the Life, Reign and Death* in *Renaissance Women* (1994). Kim Hall examines the differences between the two versions and argues that the "changes in the octavo *History* suggest its return to the traditions of masculine historiography" (143).

3. We do not know whether the "1627" of the dedication is an old style or new style date. Cary, the Catholic, may have preferred the Gregorian calendar, but that is purely speculation.

behavior at the court of Charles I of England. Although Cary's text, like other Edward II narratives, can be read as a commentary on men's politics,[4] it also appropriates from the mother's or woman's advice-manual strategies of negotiation for a woman at court. Cary uses the development of her female character, Queen Isabel, as well as the general didactic tone of her history to analyze opportunities for power available to women in the public sphere.[5] Cary writes of a woman who shapes her own and her son's destiny; because this woman is queen, she maps the course the country will follow. Consequently, Cary's version of the Edward II history is no passive retelling of a chronicle. It involves itself in political commentary and religious controversy; it advocates an active role for women at court; and it serves as a handbook of behavior for a powerful and effective queen.

Cary's text differs from other versions of the Edward II story, including Christopher Marlowe's *Edward II* and Samuel Daniel's *Collection of the Historie of England*, as well as a narrative poem by Francis Hubert,[6] in its construction of this Queen Isabel, although it shares with them the basic story of Edward II's downfall. The Edward II story as told during the reign of James I usually includes a king who follows on the heels of a powerful father-ruler and whose leadership choices are manipulated by his male favorites, Gaveston and Spencer. In many of the chronicles Mortimer seduces Isabel and uses her as a way to gain access to the throne. Most narratives include Isabel's and Mortimer's flight from England to France and the Low Countries in order to enlist political and military support. On their return they imprison Edward, and both are involved in his violent end. In Cary's version, Edward's favorite, Spencer, is the villain most responsible for the destruction of England; Cary's Isabel rescues England from the political misfortunes Edward and Spencer have caused, and Isabel's usurpation of the throne for her son and the

---

4. For possible links between Cary's history and the court politics of the late 1620s, especially the relationship between Charles I and his favorite, George Villiers, Duke of Buckingham, see Lewalski, *Writing Women*, 204–7; Schleiner, 186–91; Cary, *Tragedy of Mariam*, ed. Weller and Ferguson, 15–16; Bradbrook, "Review," 93; and Nelson, 10–18. Stephanie Wright reads Cary's Edward II in the tradition of cautionary tales such as *The Mirrour for Magistrates* (62), and Gwynne Kennedy explores issues of political obedience.

5. Critics discussing the private role of women, or the lack of access to the "public voice," include Hobby, 3; Hannay, "Introduction" to *Silent but for the Word*, 7; and Travitsky, *Paradise of Women*, 4–5.

6. Lewalski offers an overview of these and other contemporary versions of Edward II in *Writing Women*, 203–11 and 392–93. See also Gwynne Kennedy, n. 3, 217–18; Kim Hall, 142–45.

murder of Edward are rationalized and foreshortened in one of the last passages in the text. After a lengthy catalogue of Edward's mistakes as a ruler, the narrator comments briefly, "yet withal observe, here was no second Pretendents, but those of his own, a Wife, and a Son, which were the greatest Traytors: had he not indeed been a Traytor to himself, they could not all have wronged him. But my weary Pen doth now desire a respite" (160). Unlike the weak or villainous queens in other Edward II narratives, this Isabel is the hero, and even her questionable behavior is excused. Cary constructs her as a model queen.

Cary may have specifically constructed her model for the young and recently married Queen Henrietta Maria, the French Catholic wife of Charles I, or she may have offered her exemplary politician to other women who were powerful at court at the time.[7] The Catholic queen could act as a useful ally to Catholics in England and to Cary specifically if she could learn to exercise her office's potential power.[8] She could act as a champion for English Catholics either by intervening with their persecutors or by convincing Charles to act in their favor; her ultimate success would be to facilitate Charles's conversion. Barring that achievement, she could bear heirs and raise England's next rulers as Catholics. Cary was at least nominally connected with the Queen at this time; according to *The Lady Falkland Her Life*,[9] Cary's daughter Victoria was "one of the first English maids that had the honor to serve her majesty" (206).[10] Cary herself made public her conversion to Catholicism in the company of the queen. A correspondent to the Reverend Joseph Mead remarks, in a letter dated 26 November 1626, "The Lady Falkland is newly banished from court, for lately going to mass with the Queen, in whose conversion the Roman church will reap no great credit, because she was called home out of Ireland for grievous extortions."[11] Henrietta Maria, married to

7. Schleiner briefly discusses some of the ways in which Isabel serves as a model for Henrietta Maria (187–91).

8. For a summary of penal laws against Catholics enacted during Elizabeth I's reign, increased during James I's tenure, and left in place during Charles I's rule, see James Fitzjames Stephen, 483–92. Stephen makes the point that "the execution of these laws under James I and Charles I was very uncertain" (488).

9. Weller and Ferguson (Cary, *Tragedy of Mariam*, 1–2) identify the author of the biography as either Anne Cary or Lucy Cary. Isobel Grundy attributes the biography to either Anne Cary or Mary Cary ("Women's History?" 126).

10. Charles I ordered Henrietta Maria's French household to leave England in late July or early August 1626. Cary's daughter, if she was one of the first English maids called to court, would have gained her position at about this time.

11. Letter quoted in Thomas Birch, 170.

Charles in 1625, was still struggling in 1626 and 1627 to gain access to the possible roles of power available to a queen.[12] In Cary's history, Edward's wife Isabel is savior of the nation because she can manipulate court politics. Indeed, as a result of her power, Isabel returns the nation to the traditions that Edward has left behind, and this construction offers an example for women with access to some measure of authority. Cary's text could also offer advice to women such as Katherine Manners Villiers and Susan Villiers Fielding, both of Buckingham's circle. Cary's text shows women at court the kinds of reform (or perhaps counters to reform) for which a woman can act as catalyst, and it offers negotiating strategies and methods of manipulation for an insider at court, working as a mother's advice text for women with access to political power.

One aspect of Cary's chronicle that links it to the mother's advice genre is the method Cary uses to authorize the queen's ability to act. Because Edward abdicates his political responsibilities and begins to lose his hold on the nation, his irresponsiblity threatens his son's inheritance. In the first half of the narrative, Cary exhaustively develops Edward's irresponsibility and negligent leadership. In the second half of the text Cary empowers Isabel to act on behalf of her son in much the same way that women, fearing death in childbirth, maneuvered for their own ability to act as authors. These women claimed to write mother's advice manuals to protect the interests of their children. Dorothy Leigh, in *The Mother's Blessing* (first published in 1616), makes explicit use of this strategy to justify the peril she faces by writing and publishing: "And will not a Mother venture to offend the world for her Childrens sake? Therefore let no man blame a Mother, though she something exceed in writing to her Children, since every man knowes, that the love of a mother to her children, is hardly contained within the bounds of reason" (11–12). Leigh claims that she is ready to offend the world to aid her children; she defends their interest with writing. Cary's Isabel takes a similar stance; she will leave behind her husband and the safety of her home so that she

12. Before James arranged Charles's match, English Protestants worried about the influence of a Catholic queen over Charles. Henrietta Maria, a fifteen-year-old woman at the time of her marriage, initially hampered any influence she might have had over Charles with her complete commitment to her mother's and the priests' instructions. Various historians and biographers of Henrietta Maria place the beginning of the queen's era of influence after the death of Buckingham and after the birth of an heir, usually between 1630 and 1632. See, for example, Quentin Bone, 55–57; Oman, 45–47; Lockyer, 335; Veevers, 82. However, in 1627 and 1628, Henrietta Maria still needed to learn her trade as queen. See Bone, 19–20; Lockyer, 190.

can appeal to her brother, to the German princes, or to anyone else who may assist her son's cause. She even risks the ire of the pope. Isabel truly takes on the world as Leigh pretends she must, and Isabel, like Leigh, excuses her authority with her concern for her child's welfare.

The text emphasizes the fact that queens gain power by bearing sons instead of making the point that bearing sons is a queen's duty. Isabel uses her concern for her son's inheritance to legitimate her struggles against Edward. In her speech to the French, she says:

> yet 'tis not I alone unjustly suffer; my tears speak those of a distressed Kingdom, which, long time glorious, now is almost ruin'd. . . . Would you dispute it, can there be a motive more weighty, than to succour these poore Ruines which else must lose their portions, being Birthright? See here, and view but with a just compassion, two Royal Plants depress'd, and like to wither. . . . Would your impartial wisdom but consider how good a work it is to help distresses, a wronged Sister cannot be forsaken, and an Heir of such a Crown be left unpitied. (96–97)

Her own cause may inspire only pity, but the usurpation or frivolous loss of her son's lands and right to rule will upset the "natural order" in England. If those whose rule nationally or locally depends on primogeniture for their positions allow the precedent she fears, they weaken their own authority. Isabel as the defender of her son's property carries more clout than she does in her own right.

Cary's text offers a reason for motherhood that benefits the mother instead of the king, the country, or the church, and she reminds a potential mother that the child she bears offers leverage that she might not otherwise have. She neglects to mention traditional reasons for childbirth: the debt women pay for Eve's mistakes, the pain and suffering that are a woman's due. The important aspect of a woman's role as mother is the power she gains from it, and this advertisement would be an especially appropriate one to direct at Henrietta Maria in 1627 or 1628. After two years as queen, Henrietta Maria was still not pregnant and needed to be aware of the power her role as mother would offer her. Antonia Fraser discusses the common assumption at this time of immediate motherhood for women: "Once the blessed knot had been tied, a married woman was expected to shoulder forthwith that special burden of motherhood bequeathed to her by Grandmother Eve. It did not need the incentive of royal succession (or a king's favour); the desire for children in marriage, as many children as possible, to be born as quickly as possible, was universal" (60).[13] Henrietta Maria surely recognized that carrying the king's seed was one of the primary aspects of her role as queen; in fact, she was pregnant nine times in fifteen years, and four of those pregnancies occurred between the spring of 1629 and the fall of 1633. In 1627 and 1628, though, she had shown no signs of fulfilling her destiny. A baby would solidify Henrietta Maria's position as queen; as she educated it and shaped its life, she could shape the future of her new nation. The text points to this potential source of power, and it shows ways in which the practices governing women's lives can be used by women for their own gain.

In addition to exploiting mother's advice strategies of authorization and advertising a source of women's power as mothers, this history of Edward II uses a tone very similar to mother's advice tracts. The reader immediately notices the didactic nature of the *Reign and Death*; throughout the history, the author offers comments and opinions on the way a king should rule and on bargaining strategies the nobles or Spencer might use to solidify their position. For example: "It is a politique part of Court-wisdome, to insinuate and lay hold of all the befitting opportunities, that may claw the Prince's humour. . . . There is not a more ready and certain way of advancement" (11). This statement clearly speaks of politic methods of advancement at any court. Similar advice appears throughout the text, much of it lecturing on the nature of leadership: Edward I tells Edward II how he should and should not rule; the narrator informs the reader of the results of kings' errors (44), describes the characteristics and training essential for effective generals (46–47), defines the reciprocal nature of the king's authority (68), notes the benefits of divided factions at court (74–75), and generally comments on many aspects of rulership throughout the text.[14]

Cary offers an example of proper court behavior with the figure of the queen, and her shaping of the character is evident when it is compared to the Isabels that Marlowe, Daniel, and Hubert create. These queens, too, were active in Edward's destruction, but they were directed by their passions for Mortimer. They act because Edward neglects them; Mortimer offers them the love they need, and they are easily seduced. In all three of these Edward II stories Mortimer uses the queen, whom Edward forgets, as a means to the throne. Cary's queen is a very different woman from these three other Isabels. Cary involves her Mortimer much

13. In "Marital Fertility" Dorothy McLaren (22) points out that fertility rates were high especially among rich women and tended to be lower in other families.

14. *The Reign and Death*, 89, 105–6, 110, etc.

less in the queen's rebellion; as a result, her queen acts for herself and her son instead of acting for the love for a usurper. In her chronicle, Cary almost erases Mortimer as the queen's consort. Her eye wanders to him (89), and they exchange love letters (90). He wants to leave the Tower to escape to France and serve her (90), but her journey is not entirely motivated by his promises to accompany her: "Love and Jealousie, that equally possess the Queen, being intermixed with a stronger desire of Revenge, spurs her on to hasten on this Journey" (89). Isabel's other concern is her son: "[t]hen, with the Prince her Son and Comfort, that must be made the Stale of this great action, she fearless ventures on this holy Journey" (91). Her son allows her a justification for the journey; Spencer is constructed as a clear threat: as usurper or squanderer of the prince's inheritance. Isabel, a good mother, protects the interests of her son and at the same time preserves her position as Queen Mother and enacts revenge upon Spencer. If Mortimer will come, too, he "make[s] the Consort perfect" (91), but his presence is not necessary for the journey to begin. Isabel boards the ship before he arrives and reveals his successful escape (91). Presumably his absence will not prevent her departure.

Cary's narrative thrusts Isabel to the foreground of Edward's history at this point. Throughout the first half of the text, the reader sees her only when she marries Edward and when Spencer begins his rise. Once Isabel plans her trip to France, Cary foregrounds her as the central figure of the text. In Hubert's, Marlowe's, and Daniel's Edward II stories, Edward sends Isabel to ease his transactions with the French. Cary modifies this journey; her Isabel chooses to go and must sneak out of the country (91). The initiative for the trip belongs to her, and she acts on her own accord instead of as an appendage to Edward. During Isabel's negotiations with her brother and with the French court, she acts with no apparent aid from any of her party, which includes the bishop of Hereford and the earl of Cane as well as Mortimer. These powerful men exist in Cary's text only to complain against the French; Isabel then shows her leadership by rationally refuting their arguments (104). She plans their next move alone, wins by herself the support of Robert of Arthois, the earl of Henault, and Henault's brother (105–6, 110–13), and returns to England with the allies she has won (115–17). Cary's Isabel is an actor in her own right, and she shapes the events that surround her.

Unlike the Isabels other authors create, Cary's Isabel displaces Edward herself instead of becoming the facilitator for Mortimer's rise. Cary relegates Mortimer to playing the heavy, especially concerning the king's fate. Mortimer convinces Isabel that the king must be killed (151). Although the queen sees that the king threatens their position, she refuses to implicate herself in his death: "'I dare not say I yield, or yet deny it; Shame stops the one, the other Fear forbiddeth: only I beg I be not made partaker, or privy to the time, the means, the manner.' With this she weeps, and fain would have recanted, but she saw in that course a double danger" (154). Mortimer helps her with political reform and regicide; he screens her from too much malevolent activity. Cary works to protect and excuse Isabel; Isabel appears evil and vengeful in her treatment of Spencer and Spencer's father (128–30), but in the more serious business of killing the king she maintains the kind of "innocence" that Elizabeth I claimed in Mary Stuart's death. Isabel, like Elizabeth, agrees with the general need for the deed, but Mortimer bears the guilt for suggesting the idea, tempting her with his talk, and carrying out the murder. Cary uses Mortimer to allow the queen to act and still keep her reputation intact.

Because throughout her text Cary asserts to rulers the importance of their images, Mortimer performs an essential function in her narrative. Her construction of Edward's fall and Isabel's rise relies on the contrast in their abilities to present themselves effectively. Edward rarely realizes that his people's impressions of him help him keep his throne, whereas Isabel masters the art of seeming to be the person her audience expects to see. Edward cannot act the part of the king: "for [Edward's] effeminate weakness had left him naked of that Royal resolution, that dares question the least disorderly moving of the greatest Subject. He was consistent in nothing but his Passions, which led him to study more the return of his left-handed Servant, than how to make it good, effected. He lays aside the Majesty of a King, and thinks his Power too slender" (24). Isabel, on the other hand, realizes how to play the part expected of her. Because Isabel consistently reads people's perceptions of her, she conforms herself to their notions. Once she convinces them to believe her character, she takes the course of actions she wants to take. The text shows Isabel using this strategy effectively on two occasions; in both instances, she needs to convince people who can potentially block her intended course of action that she plans only to do as they wish.[15]

Isabel first tests her ability to dissemble on Spencer. Spencer begins to feel threatened by her possible influence with the king when conflicts begin between England and France. Suddenly her international connections can carry more weight than the domestic ones Spencer has worked

15. Tina Krontiris, in "Style and Gender," sees these passages as evidence of Isabel's hypocrisy (143–44).

so hard to monopolize. The text tells the reader specifically what Spencer fears from her: "He knew her to be a Woman of a strong Brain, and stout Stomack, apt on all occasions to trip up his heels, if once she found him reeling; and was not without some discreet suspicion, that she was as well contriving inward practice. . . . To pare her nails before she scratcht him, he thinks occasion had presented him with a fit opportunity [to send her to France]" (86–87). Spencer at this point recognizes Isabel as a rival. Isabel forgets for a moment to act her part, and she almost gives herself away. She re-masks herself and "seem[s] as pure and clear as Crystal" (90) when his spies investigate. She then successfully lulls him and "with his own Weapons wounds his Wisdome" (91); she keeps her own counsel, deceives her watchers with a pious pilgrimage, and makes her escape before he sees the plot. Cary highlights Isabel's acting by allowing her to forget for a moment her passive compliance. Spencer suspects Isabel because she shows enthusiasm. Isabel recovers, however, and because she veils herself effectively from his scrutiny she can continue to manage her own business.

Isabel again dissembles when her brother orders her to leave France. He has the backing of the pope, the French court, and Spencer's myriad spies; fortunately, Robert of Artois offers her possible refuge in the German principalities. Isabel disguises her intentions in order to enact them:

> with a wary and secret carriage, settles herself for her intended Journey [to Henault]; yet still gives out she means to go for *England*, whither she sends a Post to treat Conditions, with Letters smoothly writ in all submission. . . . Unto her Royal Brother she discourseth, that now she understood the Peace was finisht, which made her first a stranger to her Husband, who now would hasten home to make it perfect. And to the Council, which well she knew were bribed to send her back perforce, if she deny'd it, she more and more extols and praiseth *Spencer*. . . . The *English* thus abus'd, the *French* deluded, both are secure; she was providing homewards, which made the one remiss, the other careless; else she, forestall'd, had found her Project harder. (107)

Once Isabel obtains a place of safety to which she can plan a journey, she knows exactly what steps she must take to gull all the groups with which she works. Isabel operates effectively because she can adeptly seem to be the person other people expect her to be and because she recognizes the power of the parties involved. She interprets the part she needs to play—"with a wary and secret carriage"—and she acts accordingly.

By making her hero a responsive actress, Cary sets up an example for behavior in terms that Henrietta Maria would understand. The new queen enthusiastically involved herself in play-acting as soon as she arrived in England. She arranged and acted in a masque during her first English Christmas season.[16] Henrietta Maria seems, though, to have confined her understanding of acting to the stage, neglecting to play to the English people who made up her everyday audience. She misjudged her role at the time of Charles's coronation in February 1626. At a ceremony that could have made her entry into English royalty official and should have shown her unity with Charles, she chose to make an issue of her Catholicism and her difference. Because a Catholic bishop could not crown her, she refused to participate in the Anglican ceremony. She declined to accompany her husband for the solemnities and instead watched them from a window. The censure she excited with this move was enormous; Sir Benjamin Rudyard and the Rev. Joseph Mead both remarked on her rebuff in their correspondence,[17] and Bone refers to other letters among Ellis's *Original Letters* and in the *Harlein Manuscripts* that comment negatively on her behavior. The new queen needed to develop her diplomatic skills and to understand effective ways of winning supporters as well as potential converts; she needed to learn to work the crowd that was her new nation. *The Reign and Death* repeatedly emphasizes both role-playing and the importance of understanding the people for whom the performer plays, and its successful actor is a queen operating in "the Theater of Justice" (158) that is England instead of confining her work to a limited company watching a masque. Cary attempts to correct the style of a young and ineffective queen by couching her lesson in terms that her pupil will understand.

A method of maneuvering that Cary's text particularly recommends is the advantageous use of connections; Isabel defeats her husband in this text because she realizes the importance of the people around her, whereas Edward loses power in part because he ignores this aspect of ruling. Isabel effectively takes advantage of the powerful people in her life. With the assistance of Winchelsey, who provides transport, and the attendance of the earl of Cane and the bishop of Hereford, she escapes from England to the sanctuary that her brother, the king of France, provides (91). She then has among her circle of friends Robert of Arthois, who brings her to the attention of the earl of Henault (105–6, 109–13).

---

16. See Great Britain, P.R.O., *Calendar of State Papers, Domestic Series, of the Reign of Charles I, 1627–1628* (hereafter *CSP*); David M. Bergeron, 276–77; Malcolm Smuts, 165–87.

17. Sir Benjamin Rudyard in *CSP 1625–126*, 246; Rev. Joseph Mead in Birch, 70.

Her friends in England send her letters notifying her of their support for her cause (103), and her supporters appear once she returns to England (117–18). The queen relies on a system of allies to make her cause a reality. This weapon saves her son's throne.

Although Cary genders money and arms as men's weapons and saves the virtuous ideal for women, she offers this web of friendship as something both men and women can use. Cary develops Isabel as an example of how to use patronage effectively, whereas the figures of Edward and Spencer reveal the detrimental effects of believing one can act without aid. Isabel succeeds in her bid for the throne because she effectively uses her connections with people of influence; she realizes her dependence on people with power, and she takes advantage of the ties she has to them. She achieves her political ends because she, unlike Edward, understands that their successful rule is linked to the people who allow it. Cary offers this model to Henrietta Maria, and she uses Edward and Spencer as negative examples. Their destruction warns the reader of the dangers in underestimating the value of a web of friendships. Henrietta Maria, who in 1626 and 1627 was spending too much time with the French household and ignoring the overtures of the English, could especially benefit from this warning; she needed to build a network of support in the English court. Cary offers advice to the queen while she urges against relying too heavily on a favorite at the expense of other counsel; she connects her didactic program with her analysis of the ills of court.

Because Cary makes Isabel's success result from her access to her friends' resources, the author describes a patronage system that includes powerful people's succor of men and women; women as well as men achieve their political ends by using the resources provided by their affiliates. With Isabel as a model, Cary depicts a system of patronage that can help extend our twentieth-century understanding of seventeenth-century exchanges of power beyond the two forms we tend to generate for it: the powerful male helping another male, and, less frequently, the powerful female (such as Mary Sidney, countess of Pembroke; Lucy Harrington Russell, countess of Bedford; Queen Anne; and Queen Henrietta Maria) aiding a male.[18] I do not suggest that Cary offers access to a system of patronage to all women; Isabel is, after all, a queen and the mother of a future king. She, like Henrietta Maria or Katherine Villiers or, possibly, Elizabeth Cary, "deserves" certain opportunities that might be

18. For women as patrons, see Lewalski, *Writing Women*, on Queen Anne and on Lucy Harrington Russell, and Hannay, *Philip's Phoenix*, 106–42, on Mary Sidney.

denied to a person, male or female, of a lower position. Cary's text argues only for the queen, but in her own life, she took advantage of her friendships and her understanding of court politics to attain the ends she wanted.

Cary's life, like her text, offers an example of how a woman can use her connections at court to gain the ends she desires. After her public conversion to Catholicism in late 1626, her husband and her mother cut off their economic support to her. Correspondence regarding her financial difficulties appears in the *Calender of State Papers, Domestic Series, 1627–1628*, beginning with a letter dated March 1627 and ending with letters of instruction and thanks in September 1627.[19] *The Lady Falkland Her Life* also comments upon her difficulties and the intervention she received from friends, first by noting that after her husband restricted her financial support, her maid remained faithful to her, and Lord Ormond "daily sent her dishes of meat" (206–7). It continues with a long account of her friends during this time of hardship and the services they offered her, friends among whom are priests and courtiers (210–16). Cary actively involved herself in using her own connections at court during much of 1627. Katherine Villiers, duchess of Buckingham, first solicited support for her (*CSP 1627–28*, 109); Cary wrote letters to Secretary Conway on her own behalf and eventually had the matter petitioned to King Charles. Her letters were not completely unusual for a woman; women were "principal plaintiffs" in a quarter of chancery suits during the seventeenth century, according to W. R. Prest (181–82). On a more specifically courtly level, Anne Clifford used similar methods to contest matters regarding her estates, and Katherine Manners Villiers, Susan Villiers Fielding, and Lucy Hay, countess of Carlisle, all wrote letters petitioning various members of the court on behalf of numerous people during 1627. Villiers, Fielding, and Hay, however, were all Ladies of the Queen's Bedchamber, and, unlike Cary, had rank entitling them to intervene in court politics.

Cary employed the patronage system to her full advantage by having Katherine Villiers represent her case. Villiers, as the wife of the favorite of Charles I and as Lady of the Bedchamber, possessed high standing at court, and Cary gained access to that position through her friendship with Villiers, with Villiers's mother-in-law, the countess of Buckingham, and with Villiers's sister-in-law, Susan Fielding, countess of Denbigh. Walter Montagu linked them in a letter to John Cosins in 1626: "It was my good happ to dine with his Grace [the duke of Buckingham] and my Lady Denbighs the day before, that is on Saturday, where I mett, and had

19. *CSP 1627–1628*, 109, 167, 180, 182, 237, 264, 292, 317, 325, 326, 337, 364.

much good talke with, that worshipfull the Lady Faulkland. I also became acquainted with my Lord Duke's mother, the Duchess of Buckingham. . . . Were I with you I would tell you what discourse we had" (Cosins, 101). Cary's biographer similarly connects Cary to Susan Fielding, the Lady Denbigh, when she tells the reader that Cary hoped to reconcile herself with the Catholic church in the company of Susan Fielding. Fielding evidently delayed the conversion for almost six months. When Cary resolved to carry out the move to Catholicism, Fielding detained her at court and notified Buckingham, who notified the king (*Lady Falkland her Life*, 204–5).

The biography also tells of Fielding's support of Cary once her economic difficulties began, of the intervention with the king that Katherine Villiers and the Catholic countess of Buckingham provided (211), and of the emotional support Cecily Tufton Manners, a "cousin" of Cary's, stepmother to Katherine Manners Villiers and a Catholic, gave to Cary (208). Letters of the time frequently mention Katherine Villiers and Susan Fielding together[20]; the sisters-in-law seem to have been allies. In a 1628 portrait of the Villiers family whose artist is unknown, Fielding sits apart from her brothers, who cluster around their mother. Fielding is, instead, linked to the family by Katherine. Possibly the countess, as a widow, enacts a male role and belongs with the men instead of with her daughter and daughter-in-law. Perhaps Susan, as a married daughter, leaves her place in the family behind and Katherine, as a wife, replaces her. However, neither of George's brothers' wives is figured. Instead, the family, centered around George, includes his children, his brothers, his mother, his wife, and his sister—George's "nuclear" family, a group constructed from their direct relations to George. In this grouping, George's connection to his sister is a result of his connection with his wife, not his mother. The arrangement of the portrait indicates a relation between the sisters-in-law that the mother and daughter, and the mother-in-law and daughter-in-law, do not share.

Elizabeth Cary shared a feeling of kinship with all three of the women figured in the portrait.[21] In a letter to Conway she claimed: "If [Conway] seconds [her petition] strongly he will receive extraordinary thanks from

20. According to a bibliography in *Renaissance Englishwoman in Print*, ed. Haselkorn and Travitsky, 351–52, A. Sutcliffe dedicates her *Meditacions of Mans Mortalitie . . .* (1634) to the two women.

21. Meredith Skura discusses Cary's positive relationships with father figures and complicated relationships with females, especially mother figures, in "The Reproduction of Mothering"; she speculates on the connections between Cary and female friends based on the names of Cary's daughters (45–46).

all the three great ladies of the Duke of Buckingham's family" (*CSP 1627–28*, 182). Her biography describes the support the three offered in a fight against her husband (211). Katherine Villiers claimed an affiliation with Elizabeth Cary as well; she commented in a letter to Edward Nicholas dated 20 July [?] 1627: "Lady Falkland's children are so near to the Duchess in blood, and she a lady whom the Duchess so much respects, that she requests Nicholas to show her all the lawful favour he can" (*CSP 1627–28*, 264). Even if this remark was courteous rhetoric designed to move Nicholas, and even if the "friendship" between Cary and Villiers was a tenuous or social one, Villiers felt involved enough in Cary's life to respond when Cary called upon her. Cary's letters to Conway and the letters of her friends eventually won the backing of the king for her suit for "maintenance." Cary converts her web of friendships into something tangible: economic support. Her life experience provides her with a platform of experience from which to offer advice to those who have not yet been exposed to the challenges of the cruel world; like an older woman writing to a younger one on the threats of childbirth, or a mother advising her sons on choosing names or wives or servants, she uses her expertise as a reason for writing.

Cary's text offers Isabel as an exemplary woman at court; by portraying a woman whose actions can teach other women codes of behavior, *The Reign and Death* acts as a handbook for women at court. Here, too, Cary's text takes advantage of mother's advice strategies. Wendy Wall describes the ways in which female legacy tracts by Elizabeth Grymeston, Frances Aburgavennies, and Elizabeth Brooke Joceline prescribe behavior for people other than their children and become "general guidebooks[s] for the Christian wanderer" (40). The actions of Cary's Isabel provide a similar guide, but the advice operates more to assist the wanderer at court than the Christian wanderer. The signposts that Cary offers in the didactic comments interspersed throughout the text help to convert the history into an advice manual, an example of how one should behave effectively in a courtly situation.

Cary's text offers many methods for maneuvering to the young queen and to other women with connections at court. She enables Isabel to overcome her own impotence in a man's world by relying on the succor of those with access to power. Because Cary's queen recognizes that Edward responds to his favorites more than to his wife, she knows that any minion of Edward's has more leverage with the king than she has. Therefore, when Spencer replaces Gaveston as the object of Edward's passion, Isabel must cultivate an alliance with Spencer in order to have some kind of authority within the court. She stays within the king's graces by befriending Spencer: "She seeing into the quality of time, where he was powerful, and she in name a Wife, in truth a Hand-maid, doth not oppose, but more increase [Spencer's] Greatness, by letting all men know that she receiv'd him" (52). Instead of resisting Spencer's influence and incapacitating herself, Isabel assists the new favorite and increases her own potential power.

Just as Cary's Isabel circumvents a possibly stifling situation with Spencer, she converts her lack of resources after she leaves England by mustering an army that can defeat Edward. Upon her arrival in France, the text includes the following among Isabel's "assets": her family links to her brother and to her son, whom she brings along; her image as a forlorn woman and a wronged wife; faith in her just cause; and her rhetorical skills. Edward's advisors point out how weak her position is: "'Alas, what can the Queen, a wandring Woman compass, that hath nor Arms, nor Means, nor Men, nor Money?'"(93). Isabel should not be a threat to Edward's throne because she does not have any way to endanger him, and Spencer increases the odds against her by intervening with the money that sends his spies to France and that bribes the English nobles.

With such comments by Spencer, Cary makes the reader aware of Isabel's limited opportunity, but Cary then undermines these imposed limitations by allowing the queen access to power with the resources she has. Isabel initially convinces her brother and the French court to fight on her behalf with her dramatic monologue: "The Queens discourse and tears so far prevail'd, the King and all his Peers are deeply moved; their longing hearts beat strongly for expression, which might assure her, they embrac'd her quarrel, and with their Lives would venture soon a tryal" (97–98). Isabel converts her family connections into an army to defend her interests by playing the destitute sister.

Because Isabel still carries a faith in her cause and an understanding of the hopelessness that awaits her at home (104–5), she continues to work with the means she has. The text shows her using the image of herself as a forlorn woman with the righteous goal of obtaining the support of Robert of Arthois, who "loves Goodness for her own sake" (105). He offers sanctuary in the German states; once there, she meets the Henault brothers. She especially plays here upon her portrait as "helpless maid." Sir John fashions himself a chivalrous knight, and he seizes the opportunity to defend "Beauty, Justice, Goodness" (110). Isabel provides the quest an idle knight needs to justify his martial adventures. Cary here has translated history to enhance her own construction of Isabel; in Daniel's version of Edward II, Isabel leaves France because she receives a death threat. She "withdrawes to the Earle of Haynault being then a Prince of great meanes, and likewise Earl of Holland, to whose daughter Phillipa she contracts her sonne the Prince, and gets aide and mony of him to transport her into England" (182). In Daniel's version, Isabel uses her son's worth as future husband and future king to bargain for backing for her own assault on Edward II's throne. In contrast to this construction, Cary erases the connection with Holland, a connection that almost certainly would imply alliance to Protestants in 1627, and allows Isabel to negotiate on her own terms. Isabel may not have arms or soldiers, but she offers a cause to someone eager to involve himself in battle.

Cary provides the women who read her text, especially women with court connections to the queen, a strong message about women's access to power. Although they may have no money, no political legitimacy, and no soldiers with which to fight their battles, they can take advantage of the people who possess these weapons by offering themselves as a justification for the use of the weapons. Cary constructs an Isabel whom Spencer and Edward should easily overcome; instead, Isabel becomes the flag around which the dissatisfied nobles can rally. When she arrives in England, she realizes that she needs assistance to succeed; she "receives a fair and free refreshing, and yet but a faint hope of present succour, without the which she knew her case was desperate" (117). She has the support of only three hundred men, and if the kingdom turns against her, she will lose. However, her representative army and the idea of her rebellion are enough to unify the forces of dissatisfaction in the kingdom: "But when they knew the bent of her intentions not fixt to rifle, but reform the Kingdom, they come like Pigeons by whole flocks to her assistance. Soon flew the News unto the grieved Barons, whose itching ears attentive, long'd to meet it: It doubled as it flew, and ere it toucht them, three hundred *Henaults* were ten thousand Souldiers" (117–18). Isabel centers an anger already present; she acts as catalyst because she provides the significance for a battle already wished for in the minds of the men who fight it.

Cary's construction of Isabel's return to England reveals where women's power lies. She shows a queen who wins a kingdom because she understands how to convert a woman's resources into currency valid in the world of men. Cary's queen does not attempt to act the part of a man or confront outright the power structure, as Henrietta Maria did in her early attempts to convert Charles to Catholicism. Henrietta Maria attacked directly when she was not equipped to battle Charles, as she did when she asserted her Catholicism and refused to participate in the coronation, thus injuring herself instead of changing Charles's mind. Cary suggests, with her Isabel, that women understand where their strengths lie instead of trying to fight with tools they do not have. Her "feminism" resembles the movement that Elaine Beilin describes in *Redeeming Eve*: "These [women] writers, in keeping with their era, devoted themselves to regenerating the image of women in the familiar terms of their own culture, not to imagining or advocating a different society in which all women might change their ordained feminine nature for equality with men or public power" (xvii). Cary's text fits with this model; Isabel, a queen empowered particularly by her husband the king's refusal to act, takes advantage of resources available already to her as a high-ranking, well-connected female.

Cary's text does not advertise itself as advice to a woman or a queen. But because it attempts to shape women's behavior by showing them their strengths and because it offers the mother's role as a source of that strength, it allies itself with this genre. In discussing the trends she finds among mothers' manuals and women's advice tracts, Betty Travitsky notices the importance this maternal role holds as a source of strength and as a space in which women can negotiate the chaste, silent, and obedient self proscribed for them.[22] Women's advice manuals offer the women writing them the opportunity to shape someone. Because the possibility of death in childbirth is theirs,[23] they can stretch the limitations on their writing by fulfilling their obligations as mothers to instruct their children. They write these texts because the particular position as educators, especially of infants and daughters, is theirs. The general tone of Cary's text, like that of women's advice tracts, is didactic. The mother does, after all, want to form her child; the older, more experienced woman wants to share her wisdom with the younger generation. She offers general advice that could apply to any reader but that specifically tells one how to be an effective courtier, king, queen, or favorite; these comments also criticize ineffective methods, but by couching her criticism in terms of advice and the translation of history, she defuses some of the danger of her remarks and separates them from the people to whom they might be addressed. Nevertheless, in her project of advising a queen, she is very aware of the sources of power accessible to upper-class women, just as she manipulates the genres available to them.

22. For discussions of women's prescribed role as chaste, silent, and obedient beings, see Belsey, *Subject of Tragedy*, 191; Ferguson, "A Room Not Their Own," 97–116; Hobby, *Virtue of Necessity*, 2–3; Lamb, *Gender and Authorship*, 5. For a discussion of mother's advice manuals as a way to escape these roles, see Travitsky, *Paradise of Women*, 51.

23. R. V. Schnucker claims that among titled women, 45 percent died before age fifty, with one quarter of these dying from childbirth (643). Laurel Thatcher Ulrich sets the maternal death rate before 1930 at one maternal death for every 150 births in the United States (172) and discusses the intricacies of these statistics (170–75; 393 n. 11). See also B. M. Wilmott Dobbie, who estimates that from ten to twenty-nine mothers died per thousand births, according to seventeenth- and eighteenth-century parish registers in England (79–80).

Part Four

Popular Culture and Women's Pamphlets

10

In Defense of Their Lawful Liberty

A LETTER SENT BY THE MAYDENS OF LONDON

Ilona Bell

In 1567 there appeared in print *A Letter sent by the Maydens of London, to the vertuous Matrones & Mistresses of the same, in the defense of their lawfull Libertie. Answering the Mery Meeting by us Rose, Jane, Rachell, Sara, Philumias and Dorothie.* With only one known copy of the original published text, *A Letter sent by the Maydens of London* does indeed qualify, as John Payne Collier observed in 1866, as one of the rarest books in the English language. That does not necessarily mean the text was rare in its own day, however, for controversial pamphlets were often passed about from one reader to another until they fell apart.[1]

Studies of Renaissance women have burgeoned in the last decade, yet the Maydens' *Letter* has received almost no attention since being reprinted in *English Literary Renaissance* in 1984. Renaissance feminists who concentrate on women writers have disregarded it because the modern editor argued "the author was thus likely a man."[2] I will examine the arguments for and against a female author in due course. To leave the question open, I simply refer to the author as "The Maydens," which happily calls for plural pronouns, neither masculine nor feminine.

Whether or not the Maydens were a group of women, a single woman, a man or group of men, *A Letter* is a fascinating and important document in the history and literature of early modern women. Although *A Letter* is far too deeply rooted in the conditions of London life to ignore the importance of wealth and rank, it nonetheless argues that all women, from the lowliest servants to the most powerful matrons and mistresses, face common cultural constraints solely because they are women. Most

1. See John Payne Collier, *Bibliographical and Critical Account*, 267 ff.
2. R. J. Fehrenbach, "A Letter Sent by the Maydens of London (1567)," 288.

important of all, *A Letter* contains a lot of information about the lives of sixteenth-century London women. Moreover, its bold defense of female liberty, of women's right to marry whom they please and to go freely about the city, drinking beer in a tavern or attending the theater, demonstrates that as early as 1567 women of all ranks were being exhorted to join together to fight for social change on behalf of all women.

The title page—"Answering the Mery Meeting by us Rose, Jane, Rachell, Sara, Philumias, and Dorothie"—identifies *A Letter* as the response to an earlier pamphlet. The Stationers' Company register states that Henry Denham received "his lycense for pryntinge of a boke intituled *a mery metynge of maydes in London &c*" shortly after July 1567 (Stationers' Company, *Transcript of the Register*, 162). A mere twenty-five entries later we learn that Thomas Hackett obtained "his lycense for pryntinge of *a letter sente by the maydes of London to the vertuous matrons and mistres[ses] of ye same Cetie*" (Stationers' Company, *Transcript*, 163). Based on contemporary references to *The Mery Meeting*, Collier deduced that it was written by the lawyer, Edward Hake.[3] Unfortunately, neither Collier nor any subsequent scholar has located even a single extant copy of *The Mery Meeting*; hence there is no way of corroborating or qualifying what the Maydens say about it.

The Maydens' title suggests not only that Hake's pamphlet dramatized a meeting of the six serving women, but also that the same six women subsequently joined together to write a response, *Answering the Mery Meeting by us Rose, Jane, Rachell, Sara, Philumias and Dorothie*—a claim that is reiterated by the conclusion: "Scribled in haste this xiii. of November. 1567.[4] Your handmaydens and servants Rose, Jane, Rachell, Sara, Philumias & Dorothy. FINIS."

The Maydens' explain that *The Mery Meeting* was written in the form of "three Dialogues" (299) which "recited six of us by name" (297). Neither Fehrenbach nor Collier considered the possibility that *The Mery Meeting* might have described six real women who, outraged by the attack on their character, joined together to defend themselves and "their lawfull libertie" in print. The possibility is at least worth considering, though it seems more likely that the six female authors are pseudonyms, drawn from a tract that represents a fictive, or partially fictionalized, account of

3. For the evidence pointing to Hake's authorship, see Collier, 355–57, and Fehrenbach, 286–87. In *Crooked Rib* Francis Lee Utley summarizes most of Collier's findings but adds nothing new.

4. Collier observes (270) that "the whole form of the tract is in the form of a vindicatory epistle from the Maids to their Mistresses."

the kind of meeting that was actually taking place among London serving women, out to enjoy themselves on a Sunday afternoon.

By attributing the authorship to the six women named in Hake's tract, whoever wrote the response gives the argument verisimilitude, particularity, and the strength of numbers: "He forgate certainly the Latine Proverbe, *Ne Hercules quidem contra duos* [not even Hercules could struggle against two], when he recited six of us by name, and under those six names above six thousand of us" (297). By using first names alone, the Maydens protect their character from direct attack, even as they insist that every *Rose, Jane, Rachell, Sara, Philumias and Dorothie* has a right and a responsibility to defend her lawful liberty: "We must then of necessitie addresse our selves to Replie in defense of our liberty, and eke of our honesty, least our silence yeld us gilty" (298). Indeed, given the ethics of female silence, the unconventional and mysterious signature is itself a powerfully unsettling political act. By inviting the reader to wonder whether the author could be a woman, the Maydens force us to reexamine our assumptions about what sixteenth-century women were capable of knowing and doing.

From the very first sentence, *A Letter* speaks passionately and forcefully about the ways in which *The Mery Meeting* could hurt both the maidens and the mistresses of London were it to have been believed: "We were in very evill case, and ryght good cause had we to dread and to dispaire of oure well doings, (moste woorthie Matrones & Mistresses) wer it not that we knew ye to be such as are not moved wyth every wynde, nor such as hang upon the blastes of every mans mouth: for else what great mischiefe and trouble those fonde and malicious Dialogues of *The Mery meting of Maydens in London,* might have bred us siely girles" (293–94). Although the Maydens refer to themselves as "siely girles," or simple, helpless girls, the complex sentence structure, the hypothetical logic, and the subjunctive voice contrary to fact all reveal a verbal sophistication and logical intricacy that belies their conventional feminine modesty. At the same time, their judicious observation that matrons and mistresses do not "hang upon the blastes of every mans mouth" suggests that male writers cannot expect, on the basis of their sex alone, to exercise authority over female readers.

Hake's ignorance and misunderstanding of the servant/mistress relationship is the leitmotif that motivates and energizes the Maydens' argument, punctuating one satiric thrust after another: "the Author doth so much invey against our overmuche libertie, in that he wryteth that hee knoweth not, and medleth of that he hath no skill off" (295). As the Maydens assert repeatedly, the male author of *The Mery Meeting,* being neither a preacher, a serving woman, nor the mistress served, has no business interfering, being too ignorant and uninformed to give useful advice about how women should lead their lives: "After his serious study he wold have found out some honester recreation, and medled in maters meter for his vocation, wherein also his skill and knowledge had bene greater: and in that the common law is his studie & profession, he might farre better have written of some Writte, as *Supersedeas,* or *Corpus cum causa,* or *De Idiota inquirenda"* (297–98).

The three legal terms pack a powerful punch. *Supersedeas,* meaning a writ staying a proceeding, functions almost as a metonymy inasmuch as *A Letter* is itself a writ which puts a stop to proceedings initiated by Hake's attack. *Corpus cum causa,* "a writ . . . which transferred a case from one court to another" (Fehrenbach, 297), shifts the case of the Maydens' liberty from Hake's misguided pamphlet back to the household body where it can receive a fair hearing. *De Idiota inquirenda,* "a writ, the purpose of which was to inquire whether a person be an idiot" (Fehrenbach, 298), wittily suggests that Hake is an idiot for meddling in affairs he cannot possibly understand.

Citing the opening paragraph of *A Letter,* Collier comments that it "reads like the wordy style of a lawyer, and we know that Hake was of that profession" (268); therefore, he concludes that *A Letter* might have been written by Hake himself. Fehrenbach argues astutely that Hake's authorship "is disproved by even a casual reading of the ridicule aimed at him in *A Letter"* (288). Recognizing the improbability of Hake's authorship, Fehrenbach nonetheless assumes that the author of *A Letter* must have been trained in the law. Because women were "[b]arred from the profession of law" (287) and from the Inns of Court, Fehrenbach thinks "not the slightest evidence exists to suggest that any woman was likely" to have "the range of legal knowledge revealed in *A Letter."* Indeed, according to Fehrenbach, knowledge of the law is "the matter on which the sex of the author must turn" (288). We need to take a closer look both at the Maydens' legal rhetoric and at the legal knowledge available to sixteenth-century men and women.

Significantly, the only legal terms mentioned in the Maydens' letter are the three cited above, and the paragraph ends by calling our attention to its parodic purpose: "Wherin, if according to his promise he proceede and make you laugh, we will borow a litle of the law, and laugh at him for company, we will lay apart, and part of our bashfulnesse, and deale merily with a mery man in meeter" (298). There is little more reason to conclude that the Maydens are alliterative writers than to conclude they are lawyers. Both aspects of Hake's style receive equal mockery. Rather than suggest that the author of *A Letter* was a man trained in the law, the paragraph suggests that the Maydens went out of their way to parody and puncture Hake's pretentious legal rhetoric. The point of the satire is to demonstrate that lawyers such as Hake should stick to the law and leave the regulation of serving women to those who understand their lives. The Maydens' repeated insistence that the male author of *The Mery Meeting* does not know enough about and should not interfere in women's lives—"in that he wryteth that hee knoweth not, and medleth of that he hath no skill off" (295)—argues strongly for a female writer.

If, as the scathing parody of Hake's legal rhetoric suggests, the Maydens themselves were not lawyers, they could have learned the terms from a brother, friend, or fiancé trained in the law, or they could have found the terms themselves in one of the bestselling books explaining English common law.[5] All three terms appear, for example, with concise, easily comprehensible explanations in *La Nouvelle Natura Brevium* by Sir Anthony Fitzherbert. The text was readily available: not only were five editions published in Law French between 1534 and 1567, but there was also an English translation, *The newe boke of iustices of the peas*, which was printed nine times between 1538 and 1554.[6]

In addition to the three Latin terms cited—and parodied—above, the Maydens discuss a few legal matters bearing directly on the lives of Elizabethan women: (1) the year-long term of Dorothy's service; (2) the right to refuse to marry "the partie that our parentes have provided for us," since even "the Warde for sundry lawful causes may lawfully refuse to marie, when mariage is by his Gard[ia]n tendred to him" (300); (3) customary law, which gives London widows a third of their husbands' estates, though means were often taken to convey it elsewhere.[7] Just as

5. William Holdsworth, *History of English Law*, vol. 5, observes that in "the middle of the sixteenth century a race of lay civilians was arising who did the work of their ecclesiastical predecessors." They were "mainly Englishmen who had learned their civil law at Oxford or Cambridge and had become members of the Doctors Commons." Other collections of legal terms were also available; for example, *The Exposicions of the termes of the lawes of England, with Diuers rules*, first published in 1527 in Old French and reprinted in both Old French and English in 1530, was printed solely in English in both 1563 and 1567, the year *A Letter* appeared in print. *The Institutions or principall groundes of the lawes and statutes of England, newly and very truely corrected and amended* also appeared in 1567.

6. As Martin Ingram, *Church Courts*, 135, observes, "by the early sixteenth century a powerful body of both clerical and lay commentators was urging that the existing law provided inadequate protection for family interests."

7. In *Church Courts*, which offers a detailed and illuminating study of legal cases relating to women's lives, Ingram observes (244–45), "Quite often the woman accused of incontinence was a widow holding lands by manorial customs which specified that her

servants had to know they were bound to serve for a year, London matrons surely would have known that widows customarily inherited a third of their husbands' estates. The lawful liberty of marriage for girls over the age of twelve and boys over the age of fourteen was also a matter of common knowledge; growing numbers of Elizabethan men and women were marrying without their parents' consent, while more and more wards were refusing their guardians' choice of a spouse.[8]

Any literate person, male or female, could have acquired a basic knowledge of common law from the press. A more specific knowledge could be obtained by being personally involved in a court case, or by discussing the case with someone who was.[9] The records of the ecclesiastical courts and autobiographical writings such as Anne Clifford's diary demonstrate that early modern women were regularly involved in legal disputes involving marriage contracts, wills, and terms of service. The Maydens might, for example, have worked for a widow who inherited a third of her husband's estate "upon condition not to mary againe" (300) or whose husband found means of conveying the property elsewhere. They could have been involved in, related to, employed by, or friendly with a woman who was involved in a disputed marriage contract.[10]

---

rights lasted only so long as she remained 'chaste and sole'; the accuser was usually someone who stood to benefit if the widow forfeited her holding." Barbara J. Harris, "Women and Politics," writes: "[t]he ease which upper-class women intervened for their clients and servants shows that boundaries between public and private concerns as we understand them either did not exist or were extraordinarily permeable in the early Tudor period" (268–69). In particular, Harris notes (269), that "the common law permitted both married and single women to serve as justices of the peace."

8. In "Single Women in the London Marriage Market: Age, Status and Mobility, 1598–1619," in *Marriage and Society,* ed. R. B Braithwaite, 97, Vivien Brodsky Elliott concludes, based on an examination of London marriage licenses, that "migrant servant women in particular and migrant women in general enjoyed greater freedom in the choice of a spouse, and without the control or influence of their parents, the marriage process for them was one in which they had an active role in initiating their own relationships, in finding suitable partners, and in conducting courtships." For additional information on freely chosen and clandestine marriages, see John R. Gillis, *For Better, For Worse*; on the easing of wardship, see Joel Hurstfield, *Queen's Wards.*

9. Here, too, Ingram's findings (47), are pertinent: "The old idea that the church courts conducted all their business in Latin has been exposed as a myth. As in other courts of law in this period, the formal instruments and records were at least in part *written* in Latin, but the actual conduct of cases in the presence of defendants was in English. Moreover, the complexity of procedure was no greater than in other contemporary tribunals."

10. In *Virtue of Necessity,* 8, Elaine Hobby writes: "Women's legal and economic position, and the ideological statements made justifying their subjection are the 'necessity' they lived under. In different ways, their own writings show us, they were able to 'make a virtue' of this: to turn constraints into permissions, into little pockets of liberty or autonomy."

Finally, the Maydens' legal references divide into two kinds: witty, satiric attacks on Hake's style; and serious references to basic questions of law bearing directly on the daily lives of Elizabethan women. The first suggests an ironic distance from the law rather than training in it. The second suggests a serious concern about the impact of the law on women's lives. Neither demonstrates that the author of *A Letter* had formal legal training.

Indeed, *A Letter* demonstrates much greater knowledge of and immersion in the actual daily life of London serving women than it does of the law. It derives much of its rhetorical power from personal testimony, compellingly supported by precise accounts of serving women's daily chores and weekly schedules. To cite just one example, *The Mery Meeting* apparently criticized Rose and Jane for spending their Sundays in a tavern, wasting their wages on drink. The Maydens respond by explaining how little time they have left on Sundays after going to church and preparing the Sabbath meal and by specifying just how much Rose and Jane drank: "he hath but sayd a thing that he hath not proved, and so have we the lesse to say therein. . . . For when *Rose* would have sent for wyne, *Jane* wold not suffer hir" (301).

If, on the one hand, one believes that *A Letter* was actually written "*by us Rose, Jane, Rachell, Sara, Philumias and Dorothie*," one will be all the more likely to trust its first person account of Hake's misinformation. If, on the other hand, one assumes (as Collier and Fehrenbach do) that *Rose, Jane, Rachell, Sara, Philumias and Dorothie* are pseudonyms, or personae, artfully constructed by Hake himself, one will realize that it was foolish of Hake to attack all London's serving women on the basis of what six fictional women may or may not have said and done.

The Maydens' argument not only consistently emerges out of their experiences as servants, but it is also carefully constructed to persuade, not a general reading public, but the particular women who control the Maydens' lives and supply their very livelihood. The Maydens' employers—and targeted audience—comprise some of London's most powerful women. "Matrones" are married women, usually with the accessory idea of (moral or social) rank or dignity. "Mistresses" are primarily women who rule or have control, particularly women who have the care of and authority over servants and attendants (the word also denotes female teachers, women who are courted by a man with a view to marriage).[11]

From the very outset, *A Letter* urges the Maydens' female employers to muster their greater rank and authority in "*the defense of their lawfull*

---

11. All definitions taken from the *Compact Edition of the OED.*

Libertie." At first, it may sound as if it is only their serving women's freedom that is at stake, but the maidens, matrons, and mistresses are all common antecedents of "their lawfull libertie." The opening sentence, quickly moving from the "great mischiefe and trouble those fonde and malicious Dialogues of *The Mery meting of Maydens in London,* might have bred us siely girles" to "what disquietnesse of minde and body also to you myghte therby have growne" (293–94), makes it clear that the "Matrones & Mistresses of London" are being urged to join the Maydens of London in defending their *common* liberty. Regardless of who the Maydens actually were, their defense represents itself as the voice not of a single, isolated individual, but of a group of women working together to urge their employers to resist any attempt to curtail "their lawful libertie." The elegant *double entendre* of the title, confirmed by the first paragraph, epitomizes the Maydens' most powerful rhetorical strategy: despite differences in maturity, wealth, and status, serving women, handmaidens, matrons, and mistresses are all subject to legal, social, and ethical constraints unjustly imposed on them simply because they are women.

Following the name of the printer, the bookseller, and the publication date, the Maydens' title page concludes with a dedication: "To the right wise, sober, and discrete Matrons, and Mistresses of London, the Maidens of the same Citie send greeting" (293). By praising the matrons and mistresses in these terms, the Maydens argue that early modern women should be allowed to exercise discernment in determining their own speech and actions. The very term *greeting* strikes a familiar note that, although respectful, shuns the elaborately self-effacing entreaties and aggrandizing encomiums that one generally finds in dedications of the period. Of course, there is nothing radical about the terms *wise, right, sober,* and *discrete.* In *The Womans Lesson,* published in 1549, Robert Crowley writes: "Be thou modeste, sober and wise / And learne the poyntes of houswyfry." Sixteenth- and seventeenth-century marriage manuals repeatedly advise their readers that "a wife ought to be discret" (1569), and that "wives must be modest, wise, chaste, keepers at home, lovers of their husbands, and subject unto them" (141).

The title page discreetly abstains from characterizing the Maydens themselves, but as the treatise unfolds it becomes increasingly evident that "right wise, sober, and discrete" (293) are precisely the qualities of character and mind that the Maydens strive to uphold and defend— qualities remarkable for their pointed but discreet divergence from the norm prescribed for early modern women. What is unconventional in *A Letter* is the corresponding lack of restraining terms: modest, shamefast, keepers at home, silent, and obedient. By citing only attributes that apply equally to men and women, and by scrupulously avoiding those qualities specifically used to subordinate women, the Maydens posit a code of ethics that eschews all gender-specific limitations on women's liberty.

Looking back from the perspective of the nineteenth and twentieth centuries, we might assume that serving women are by definition lower class; however, in the sixteenth century children from all social ranks were placed in service, and living-in servants were "a normal component of all but the poorest households" (Stone, 28). William Harrison's *Description of England*, for example, distinguishes gentleman servants from yeomen servants: "not idle servants as the gentlemen do, but such as get both their own and part of their master's living." The social hierarchy of early modern servants replicated the larger social order, for the quality of the servants signified the masters' and mistresses' own social standing.[12]

It was customary for the nobility and gentry to be served by their social equals.[13] Isabella Whitney, an unusually independent and well-educated gentlewomen and the author of two published books of poetry, worked in London as a serving woman, as did her unmarried younger sisters. Margaret Dakins, the daughter of a wealthy Yorkshire landowner, left her parents' home to live and study in London in the service of and under the protection of the countess of Huntington.[14] Because English houses were constructed without hallways, and "the only way of moving about was by passing through other people's chambers," sixteenth-century servants lived in close proximity and intimacy with their masters and mistresses (Stone, *Family*, 169). Gentlewomen serving women waited on their mistresses' tables and aided them in donning and doffing the elaborate dress of the day. Just as importantly, they shared and enhanced their mistresses' pleasure, joining in the festivities and social life of the household, accompanying their mistresses on walks, joining them at the theater, visiting friends and relatives.

More mature and experienced servants were expected to manage the business of the household and bring up the young folk. Lady Weston recommends to Lady Lisle a gentlewoman whom she describes as "a

12. William Harrison, *Description of England*, 117–18. For further information, see Amussen, *Ordered Society*, 95–96.

13. Amussen, *Ordered Society*, 158, notes, "Especially in the sixteenth century, children from prosperous families sent into service were the social equals of the family they worked for. In such cases, servants may well have been treated as family members." See also Barbara Harris, "Women and Politics," 262.

14. For additional information, see Samuel Rawson Gardiner, *Fortescue Papers*; and *Diary of Lady Margaret Hoby*, ed. Dorothy M. Meads.

good maid, both sad and wise, and true of hand and tongue, I dare be bound for her; and she is of xxvj year[s] age. Your gentlewoman, Mistress Green, knoweth her well. Her father is one Christopher More, a gentleman which my Lord knoweth well. This maid was brought up with my lady Bourchier, and she hath been with me upon iij or iiij year." Expert in housekeeping, she would also be a proper handmaid who can "bring [the daughters] up well and can teach them right good manners" (*Lisle Letters*, ed. Byrne, 1:330).

Sixteenth-century serving women, commonly entering service as young teenagers, contributed to the functioning of the household in exchange for an education in practical matters of domestic management as well as finer points of decorum and learning appropriate to their social standing. Women generally remained in service until they were ready to marry, on the average in their mid-twenties. Indeed, one of the principle reasons for a woman to enter service was to enhance her matrimonial prospects. Some parents from the aristocracy and upper gentry paid substantial sums to gain an advantageous position for their daughters through which they could obtain an education, social graces, household skills, and social connections. Richard Whalley, for example, paid £20 twice a year to keep a niece in Lady Barrington's household (Margaret Ezell, *Patriarch's Wife*, 19). Except in the highest social ranks, serving women received a modest wage, the savings from which constituted an important contribution to the costs of setting up an independent household upon marriage.[15] For a woman in the lower ranks with no hope of an inheritance, these earnings might be her only hope of a marriage portion.

The liberties the Maydens defend, the freedom to go to a tavern on Sunday afternoon or to attend the theater, are both pleasurable in themselves and important ways of meeting marriageable men. As the numbers of women living away from home in service increased, so too did the opportunities for courtship and freely chosen marriage: "indeed it is hardly too much to say that there existed an adolescent culture, associated above all with servants, one of the features of which was a degree

15. For a fuller discussion of women's role in courtship, see Ilona Bell, *Elizabethan Women and the Poetry of Courtship* (1998). Elliott writes (95), "Women at all levels of the social hierarchy may have found it essential to bring a dowry to marriage even if it consisted solely of household goods. Service provided the means of accumulating the necessary capital, yet it was a drawn-out process since wages were rarely more than 3£ per annum." In *Women and Gender*, 90, Merry E. Wiesner writes, "Young women generally regarded service as a time to save a dowry for later marriage."

of liberty" (Ingram, 354). As Lady Weston explains to Lady Lisle, her gentlewoman departed because "she did cast love to a young man, a servant of my husband, and he likewise to her." But the young man "had nothing," so there could be "no promise of matrimony betwixt them, for the which my husband took great displeasure with the young man and put him out of service . . . and commanded me in like wise to put the maid out of my service" (*Lisle Letters*, ed. Byrne, 1:330).

Unlike Lady Weston's maid, the Maydens "are not so wynching wood [insane] to choose boyes or lads that lacke experience and the trade to live" (301). They well know that the "good propertie" of a marriage partner depends upon "goods and money" and "qualitie" [meaning *rank or position in society, ability, mental or moral attributes* and *accomplishments*]. Yet they nonetheless defend the importance of love and sexual desire: "And sith love should be the principall cause in mariage, why shold we be blamed, for chosing wher we most love and fansie?" (300). Above all, they insist upon their lawful liberty to "refuse such olde doting fooles as sometimes ar procured by our paretes to be suters to us, & have a thousand worse impedimentes, and nothyng but their goods and money to mary them" (300).

The Maydens' "defense of their lawfull Libertie" is closely tied to the demographic conditions of mid-sixteenth-century London. During the Elizabethan period it was fashionable among the upper social ranks for families to spend as much as nine months to a year in the capital, in close proximity to the court. The London social season brought the aristocracy and "thousands of gentry families to the capital for all or part of the year." Their concomitant need for servants precipitated a large migration of unmarried women to London (Steve Rappaport, *Worlds*, 370-71). The Maydens argue that if their liberty were to be curtailed, as *The Mery Meeting* argued it should be, women would simply refuse to serve in London: "in a verie shorte time and space, ye shoulde have gotten very fewe or no servants at al, when such as are born in the countrey shoulde choose rather to tarie at home, and remaine there to take paines for a small stipend or wages with libertie: and such as are Citizens borne, should repaire also to the cou[n]try, or to other Cities where they might be free, than to abide as slaves and bondewomen in London" (294). Repeatedly complaining of the "small stipend or wages" paid women (women earned about half to two-thirds of the wages earned by their male counterparts), the Maydens argue that there would be little incentive for women to remain in service if they were not allowed to enjoy the pleasures and opportunities the city offered.

The Maydens' warning is confirmed by demographic trends of the period.[16] The social mobility so characteristic of the early modern period was greatest during the years of "young adulthood, when people moved from place to place as servants."[17] While the overall population of London increased significantly during the Elizabethan period, the proportion of young people, of apprentices, servants, and unemployed poor, grew at an even greater rate (Archer, 242). London was a city full of immigrants and transient workers. Servants were legally bound to work for a year's time; hence, as the Maydens pointedly remind their mistresses, "in a verie shorte time and space, ye shoulde have gotten very fewe or no servants at al" (294).

The Maydens return to this point later: "What a long tale told he of *Dorothy*, when she would serve no longer? how she was brought before the Alderman's Deputie, what gained hir master therby? . . . *Dorothy* might depart laufully, there was no cause to the contrary. For why? she was by the yere hired, hir time was expired, she ought no longer service, she was overcharged with worke, she had complained and found no amendment, she sought for more easement, she liked not that intertainment" (303).

There is no way of determining whether Dorothy was a representative Elizabethan serving woman, created by Hake and recreated by the Maydens, or whether she was indeed a real person who joined Rose, Jane, Rachell, Sara, and Philumias in writing *A Letter*. Regardless, by treating Hake's "long tale" as if it were a matter of fact that needs correcting, the Maydens give their answer both verisimilitude and specificity, even as they demonstrate that it was a straightforward and feasible matter for a London serving woman to defend her lawful liberty.

The Maydens' concise but witty recounting of Dorothy's story demonstrates their own superior judgment and wit. Having already described Hake as a windbag who blathers on to little purpose ("wer it not that we knew ye to be such as are not moved wyth every wynde," 293), the reference to this "long tale" is calculated to produce a derisive laugh. The initial questions encourage the reader to wonder exactly what happened and why. The ensuing answer states the facts of the case, along with the pertinent legal data.[18] By bluntly asking ("For why?") how Dorothy could

16. As Ingram writes (72), "servants were customarily hired by the year, and at the end of their term of contract often migrated to another parish: the existence of this sizable and shifting group formed one of the most prominent features of the social structure." Rappaport makes much the same point (77).

17. Amussen, *Ordered Society*, 73; see also Ingram, 72.

18. Fehrenbach's introduction (287) notes that *A Letter* includes both legal terminology and a basic "knowledge of common, statutory, and customary law."

possibly derive any satisfaction or pleasure from such a situation, the Maydens warn the matrons and mistresses of London that women will not remain in service if the workload is unreasonable and the conditions of employment unpleasant. The string of short, simple clauses, filled with pithy details, make the conclusion, "she liked not that intertainment," seem inevitable—and all the more compelling for its epigrammatic understatement. As the Maydens retell the story, Dorothy was morally and legally justified in terminating her service: though poorly treated, she had fulfilled the term of her contract.

The gist of the Maydens' argument is that the servant/mistress relationship must be mutually rewarding, answering not only the needs but also the pleasures of both parties. Even as the Maydens go out of their way to defend even the poorest female servants, their language betrays their own gentility: "First trie us, then trust us: Faire words and gentle entreating of us shal do more a gret deale with us, than a thousand of threattes & stripes, we would not wish you to kepe that servant that serveth you not in a maner as much for your love as for your money" (303-4). The repeated references to the "trifle" serving women earn argue that women should be fairly compensated for their labor, even as they imply that the Maydens themselves are not "so destitute" that they need rely solely on their wages.

As the Maydens politely but pointedly observe, the matrons' and mistresses' liberty and pleasure depends on being served. By way of illustration, the Maydens introduce an extended conceit comparing the household to a corporeal body. Just as a body depends on its organs, so too a household depends on its various members. The Maydens serve as hands, eyes, and feet for the matrons and mistresses who are unaccustomed or unable to run their own lives: "withoute your maides what coulde ye doe when now ye are paste paines taking youre selves, some by reson of age waxen unweldie, some by the grossenesse of your bodies, some by lack of bringing up in paines taking, and som for sundry and divers other reasonable respects and causes" (294).

The Maydens' conceit adapts the conventional analogy underlying a patriarchal theory of government: as the head directs the body, so too the prince governs the commonwealth, the husband rules the wife, and the husband and wife discipline the children and servants. Indeed, it was only one year before the publication of the Maydens' letter that Queen Elizabeth, having been denied the title head of church and state when she was first crowned, declared herself the head of those reckless parliamentary feet that were wandering astray: "I will deal therein for your safety, and offer it unto you as your Prince and head, without request; for it is monstrous that the feet should direct the head" (quoted in Neale, *Elizabeth I and Her Parliaments*, I:150). But monstrosity, like beauty, alters with the eyes of the perceiver and the norms of the culture. To Elizabeth, exasperated with parliament's insistence that she marry forthwith, it was not a female ruler that was monstrous but "men of wit [who] can so hardly use that gift they hold" (quoted in Neale, I:150). By refusing to submit her liberty and judgment to husband or Parliament, Elizabeth's speech challenged the traditional gender hierarchy upon which a patriarchal social order was based.

The Maydens' version of the traditional political metaphor is equally remarkable. Although Elizabethan women are subject to their husbands by both law and custom, the husband, the traditional head of the household, is strikingly absent from the Maydens' conceit. One might therefore expect the matrons and mistresses to be the head of this all female body. Not so: "we are to you very eyes, and ha[n]ds, feete & altogether" (294). The Maydens' organic, nonhierarchical household body eschews social distinctions, evaluating the lowliest servant, the most respected gentlewoman attendant, and the most powerful mistress "altogether." The Maydens are not only the feet to carry out their mistresses' requests and the hands to wait on them, but also the eyes to foresee their wants, and implicitly the brains as well, for their perspicacity foresees their mistresses' desires and sees that the body/household functions efficiently.

Fearing, at this point, that they may have overstepped their position, the Maydens pause briefly to reassure their mistresses—"And wherein from time to time we know that we may pleasure you, as redy we are to offer it, as ye are to demaund it, as redy to obey you as ye to commaund us" (294–95). They then proceed to argue that the greater a mistress's responsibility and power, the more complex and important the tasks performed by her serving woman: "The more & the greater that your businesse are (right worthie Matrones) and the lesse able that ye your selves are to accomplishe them, the more merite those your poore maidens, that take that toyle for you."

Just as the syntactical ambiguity of the title, "*in the defense of their lawfull Libertie*," embraces Maydens, matrons, and mistresses alike, so too does the extended conceit make the Maydens, matrons, and mistresses all integral and essential members of a household body that can thrive only if there is a reciprocity of need and reward: "For as ye are they that care & provide for our meat, drinke and wages, so we are they that labor and take paines for you: so that your care for us, and our labor for you is so requisite, that they cannot be separated: so needeful that they may not be severed" (295). Mistresses and serving women must understand, love, and respect each other, something the author of *The Mery Meeting* clearly does not understand, as the Maydens immediately proceed to point out: "And where the Author [of *The Mery Meeting*] doth so much invey against our overmuche libertie, in that he wryteth that hee knoweth not, and medleth of that he hath no skill off" (295).

Surveying the numerous advice books written for and about early modern Englishwomen, Suzanne Hull reaches the following conclusions.[19] Instructional manuals generally offered simple, unsophisticated, even crudely written advice, but in so doing they indirectly describe the practical, everyday lives of early modern women. Instructional manuals reinforced both the class structure and the gender hierarchy, representing women as inferior and subservient to men; however, women did not always do what the books advised. Women were supposed to take their instructions from men, but the growing numbers of printed books made it possible for women to teach themselves and each other. Printed books often attempted to control and subdue the female population, but they were also the cause of social change.

The Maydens' letter poses a direct challenge to the code of ethics that strived to control and curtail early modern women's liberty. Although the Maydens acknowledge briefly, in one sentence, that women must serve their husbands, they never mention the matter again. Instead *A Letter* speaks directly to the matrons and mistresses—the women who have power over their serving women's lives. In so doing, it constructs a household body where women serve and govern other women, making their subordination to men seem almost moot. The Maydens' letter, like late twentieth-century feminist discourse, "constitutes a discursive space which defines itself in terms of a common identity; here it is the shared experience of gender-based oppression which provides the mediating factor intended to unite all participants beyond their specific differences" (Felski, 166).

The Maydens summon their female readers to join a potential army of "above six thousand" (297) skeptical, resisting female readers who are armed and ready to defend female liberty against attacks by male-authored prescriptive texts like *The Mery Meeting*. For all these reasons, *A Letter sent by the Maydens of London, to the vertuous Matrones & Mistresses of the same* is not only a remarkable piece of writing but also a powerful political act that demonstrates that Elizabethan women were not as "chaste, silent, and obedient" as they were repeatedly told they were supposed to be.

19. Suzanne Hull, *Chaste, Silent & Obedient* (1982). The revised paperback edition of 1988 includes *A Letter Sent by the Maydens*.

At present there are no extrinsic data to decide whether the author of the Maydens' remarkable letter was a man, as Collier and Fehrenbach argue; a group of Elizabethan women, as the title page announces; or an educated gentlewoman, like Isabella Whitney and her sisters who migrated to London, as I might be inclined to infer from the richly detailed account of the needs and daily activities of Elizabethan serving women and their mistresses. If the author was a woman or a group of women, *A Letter* provides a valuable example of women writing to women, defending the common cause of all women who, regardless of class, age, or marital status, are nonetheless subject to ethical norms and social practices that strive to curtail their liberty on the basis of their sex alone. If the author was a man—like the modern-day male feminist who takes it upon himself to write a defense of women's liberation—*A Letter* demonstrates that Elizabethan men were beginning to enunciate, write, and publish defenses of women's subjectivity, liberty, and agency.

Rather than debate the author's sex or discount *A Letter* because it may have been written by a man, it seems more useful to recognize that *A Letter sent by the Maydens of London, to the vertuous Matrones & Mistresses of the same*, constitutes a bold and important female subject position.[20] By declaring that male writers such as Hake have no business using the press to manage and control the female population, the Maydens urge early modern women of all ages and ranks to join together, using their own power as writers, readers, and speaking subjects to decide what is best for themselves.

Whether the author raising these questions was male or female, *A Letter sent by the Maydens of London, to the vertuous Matrones & Mistresses of the same* nonetheless suggests that Elizabethan England provided the kind of "intellectual and political climate favorable to those raising fundamental questions about social relationships, including relationships between the sexes" (Hilda Smith, xi). Finally, however, *A Letter* is concerned less with relations between the sexes than with relations among the female sex. The Maydens' defense of early modern Englishwomen's liberty, knowledge, and power suggests that modern feminism, with its commitment to consciousness-raising among women and political action and social change on behalf of all women, has much stronger roots in the sixteenth century than most modern scholars have hitherto recognized.

20. In "Eve's Dowry" in this volume, Barbara McManus explores ways in which "a consideration of subject positions, platforms constructed by discourse from which an individual is able to speak," provide "a place from which [women] could interrogate, if not subvert, the master narrative of Adam and Eve."

11

Eve's Dowry

GENESIS AND THE PAMPHLET CONTROVERSY ABOUT WOMEN

Barbara McManus

After the fall, and after they were all arraigned and censured, and that now *Adam* saw his wives dowrie, and what blessings God hath bestowed upon her, hee being now a bondslave to death and hell, stroke dead in regard of himselfe, yet hee comforts himselfe, he taketh heart from grace, he engageth his hope upon that promise which was made to the woman.[1]

Varying interpretations of the import and value of Eve's "dowry" as presented in the Tudor-Stuart pamphlet debates about the nature of womankind[2] provide an excellent example of the complex interactions between cultural ideologies and textual representations. This topic is particularly interesting for a consideration of the cultural reproduction of gender, because writers during this period were, for the first time in the English language, attempting to create *female* subject positions as defenders of women in print. Because the biblical account of the creation and fall of human beings carried the weight of divine authority, it constituted the foundation of Renaissance discourse about the essential nature and

I thank the Faculty Resource Network of New York University for making possible the research for this article and the faculty and participants of the 1994 NEH Institute on Sappho and Lady Mary Wroth for their helpful comments and stimulating interaction.

1. Ester Sowernam, *Ester hath hang'd Haman* (1617), 10. Full titles, printers, and STC numbers for the Tudor-Stuart pamphlets mentioned in this article can be found in Katherine Usher Henderson and Barbara F. McManus, *Half Humankind*, 381–85.

2. For more detailed discussion of these debates, see Henderson and McManus; Woodbridge; Beilin, *Redeeming Eve*. Extensive selections from ten attacks and defenses can be found in Henderson and McManus, while all the defenses from this period published under female names are presented in Simon Shepherd, ed., *Women's Sharp Revenge*.

function of women[3]; Genesis therefore became an especially complex site of negotiation for writers whose explicit agenda was to challenge *from a feminine perspective* the dominant cultural attitudes toward women.

These pamphlet controversies would seem to provide an ideal locus for the "politics of complexity" advocated by Laurie Finke, which enjoins feminist critics "to proceed strategically on two opposing fronts: recognizing that 'woman' is a production of culture, feminists must simultaneously insist that women have always been producers of culture."[4] First of all, these texts give an exceptionally clear picture of the constructed nature of the concept of "woman" they present; it is easy to trace the building blocks of this construct, for they have been taken from the Bible, from earlier literary, theological, philosophical, and social writings (including those of classical antiquity), and even from previous attack and defense treatises. Linda Woodbridge has argued that both the writers and the readers of these pamphlets were aware of the culturally constructed nature of "the woman question"; she demonstrates that texts in the pamphlet debate were highly rhetorical and conventional, part of an intricate literary game.[5] But a concept that reveals its own artifice may still exert a powerful influence over people's lives, particularly when it resonates with deep structures in the culture. Certainly the commercial success of these pamphlets (especially the attacks on women), as evinced by the number that were printed and reprinted during this period, indicates that the pamphlet debates struck a sympathetic chord in the social group that frequented the stationers' shops. Ester Sowernam says that she first heard about Joseph Swetnam at a dinner party during which "as nothing is more usuall for table-talke; there fell out a discourse concerning women, some defending, others objecting against our Sex" (sig. A2^r). In fact, she cites the popularity of the pamphlet as a principal

3. For a detailed discussion of this discourse as embodied in theological, medical, philosophical, and legal scholarly texts of the period, see Ian Maclean, *Renaissance Notion of Woman*. Maclean suggests that information passed between these disciplines "in the form of commonplaces" (82); the pamphlet debates both drew on and helped to popularize and transmit many of the commonplaces about women. See also John A. Phillips, *Eve*.

4. Finke, 194–95. Finke argues that feminists not only can, but must, have it both ways; they must "develop more sophisticated theoretical models that offer a way out of the impasse" between poststructuralist questioning of categories such as "woman" or "author" and feminist insistence on the importance of the gendered subject (4). Her book suggests "a dialogical and nonauthoritarian theoretical orientation and method for feminist literary criticism" (28), which she demonstrates pragmatically through a series of detailed readings of texts by women in varying historical and social contexts.

5. Woodbridge sees this emphasis on artifice as unfortunate when regarded from the perspective of women's lives, claiming that "the formal controversy may in fact have actively prevented the development of true feminist debate" (133).

reason for her response: "seeing his booke so commonly bought up, which argueth a generall applause, we are therefore enforced to make answere in defence of our selves" (sig. A2ᵛ). In her opening poem to Joseph Swetnam, Constantia Munda also castigates the popularity of the pamphlet, which the "Truth-not-discerning rusticke multitude / ... thirsts to drinke / ... Like nibling fish they swallow bait and hooke / To their destruction."[6]

Second, the Tudor-Stuart defense pamphlets highlight women's role in producing culture, for these writings enable us to view the creation of a new subject position in the long history of the literary debate about woman's nature—that of the female defender of "our sex." Although a few women on the continent had previously written about "the women question" (notably Christine de Pizan), their works belong to a more scholarly and courtly tradition than do the five pamphlets that were printed under women's names in Tudor-Stuart England. Before this, defense pamphlets offered *male* authors a number of possible subject positions: the female character created by a male writer to defend women in a humanistic dialogue (Zenobia in Sir Thomas Elyot's *The Defense of Good Women*, 1540); the writer "atoning" for previous attacks (imitating Chaucer, Edward Gosynhill adopts this pose in the dream-vision of Venus that opens *The prayse of all women, called Mulierû Pean*, 1542); the chivalrous champion of women, outraged at the vicious nature of the attacks (Edward More, *A Lytle and Bryefe treatyse, called the defence of women*, 1560); the tongue-in-cheek writer who defends women to demonstrate his wit (Nicholas Breton, *The Praise of vertuous Ladies*, 1597). What all of these poses share is their emphasis on the authorizing presence of the male writer, so the uniqueness of an authorizing *female* presence cannot be overemphasized. The importance and efficacy of this authorizing feminine voice does not require actual female authorship of every pamphlet that adopts such a voice, however.[7]

There is a strong probability that most, if not all, of the five Tudor-Stuart pamphlets published under women's names were actually written

6. Constantia Munda, *Worming of a Mad Dogge* (1617). The pamphlets attacking women enjoyed greater commercial success than the defenses, and Swetnam's work was the most popular of all, with ten editions printed between 1615 and 1637. The defense pamphlets, whether published under male or female names, were rarely reprinted.

7. Traditional scholarship has tended to assume that all anonymous and pseudonymous authors were male unless proven otherwise, and Carol Thomas Neely is right to insist that the burden of proof should lie on the opposite side in the case of female pseudonyms: "[A feminist critique] needs to over-read, to read to excess, the possibility of human (especially female) gendered subjectivity, identity, and agency, the possibility of women's resistance or even subversion" ("Constructing the Subject," 15). Although I initially felt that it was important to determine whether the pseudonymous authors of these Tudor-Stuart

by women, thought only Rachel Speght's identity has been documented. Although "Jane Anger" may have been a pseudonym, there were a number of Jane (or Joan) Angers living near London in 1588. "Ester Sowernam" and "Constantia Munda" are clearly pseudonyms, but Rachel Speght refers to them as women in the "Dream" preface to her second work, *Mortalities Memorandum, with a Dreame Prefixed* (1621), and Munda also calls Sowernam a woman.[8] The most serious objections have been raised about "Mary Tattle-well" and "Joane Hit-him-home," the pseudonymous authors of *The womens sharpe revenge* (1640), which modern scholars frequently attribute to John Taylor, whose *Juniper Lecture* is attacked in the pamphlet. In fact, Simon Shepherd calls this pamphlet "a spoof female reply" which effects "a two-fold silencing of women: they are attacked as scolds, and their 'reply' is written by a man. The woman is effectively removed from the gender controversy altogether and the male take-over is complete."[9]

---

pamphlets were "really women," (see Henderson and McManus, 20–24), I now feel that the questions posed by Laurie Finke are more appropriate: "If instead we ask, . . . What are the modes of existence of this discourse? . . . What are the places in it where there is room for possible subjects? Who can assume these various subject-functions? then we open up our criticism to a more dialogic conception of subjectivity and gender relations, as well as to the historical and political struggles through which they are constituted and resisted" (107).

8. See Shepherd 30, 58, 86, 126. See also Maureen Bell, George Parfitt, and Simon Shepherd, *Biographical Dictionary*. Shepherd entertains the possibility that Sowernam "could be a man taking advantage of Speght's precedent" (86) and "half suspects" that Munda is a man because of the pamphlet's Juvenalian tone and quotations ("the mind seems almost too learned for a woman," 126). Rachel Speght provides evidence that this kind of doubt was also prevalent in the Renaissance, for she emphatically claims personal authorship of her second work because "criticall Readers" had been attributing *A Mouzell for Melastomus* to her father: "I am now, as by a strong motive induced (for my rights sake) to produce and divulge this of spring of my indeavor, to prove them further futurely who have formerly deprived me of my due, imposing my abortive upon the father of me, but not of it" (*Mortalities Memorandum*, sig. A2ᵛ).

9. Shepherd, 195 and 22–23. Shepherd's arguments involve the timing of the various pamphlets and "links between style, language and subject matter in WSR and Taylor's other works" (160). Although it is certainly possible that Taylor wrote *Women's sharp revenge* (attributed to Tattle-well and Hit-him-home), this is not the virtual certainty that Shepherd claims, for all of his evidence can also be explained by the hypothesis that a woman (or women) collaborated with Taylor in setting up this pamphlet war. The timing is not a problem if they had early access to his pamphlets, and the links (which are not overwhelming in number or similitude) can be explained by familiarity with his work and by the general Renaissance tendency to reiterate phrases and echo other writers (as Shepherd himself points out, *Women's sharp revenge* also has links with Sowernam and Swetnam). Although Shepherd claims that Taylor is silencing women through *Women's sharp revenge*, it is interesting to note that most of what he says about the pamphleteers who "are answering back as women" (12) is equally applicable to *Women's sharpe revenge*.

Our reading of the significance of Taylor's possible authorship of the pamphlet will be very different from Shepherd's, however, if we turn from questions about the historical identity of individual authors to a consideration of *subject positions,* platforms constructed by discourse from which an individual is able to speak. I have already noted the variety of platforms available to a man who wished to write a defense pamphlet, but the long tradition of literary defenses offered no subject position for a voice gendered as female.[10] The Tudor-Stuart defenses published under female names, therefore, give us a rare opportunity to view a subject position in the process of construction. If Taylor has indeed spoken from a female platform, this can be seen as evidence that such a platform had already been built by 1640.[11] True silencing would require a *visible* male presence behind the female voice (e.g., Elyot's creation of Zenobia, Gosynhill's reiterated name in the envoy of *Mulierû Pean*), but neither the content nor the tone of *The womens sharpe revenge* reveal a masculine authorizing presence, and there is no indication that Renaissance readers identified Taylor as the author.

Before considering how the story of Adam and Eve appeared from this female platform, I would like to examine some features of the subject position created by these early writers. After an opening epistle asking for the protection of "the Gentlewomen of England" because of her "rashnesse" and "presumption," Jane Anger addresses a second epistle in *Jane Anger her Protection for Women* (1589) "To all Women in generall." Emphatically beginning, "Fie on the falsehoode of men," she uses the previous silence of women to justify her own speech: "Shal surfeiters raile on our kindnes, you stand stil & say nought, and shall not *Anger* stretch the vaines of her braines, the stringes of her fingers, and the listes

10. What Catherine Belsey says about Renaissance drama can also be applied to defense pamphlets prior to Anger, Speght, and others: "Women were denied any single place from which to speak for themselves. A discursive instability in the texts about women has the effect of withholding from women readers any single position which they can identify as theirs" (*Subject of Tragedy,* 149).

11. I am indebted to Marilyn L. Williamson for this insight. Speaking about love poets in the latter half of the seventeenth century, Williamson maintains, "Women began to write from an acknowledged female persona, often represented to the reader by a classical female pseudonym. . . . If [Ephelia's] book was discovered isolated from its context, any reader would know that it was written by a woman or someone pretending to be a woman. . . . If a male writer can pretend to be a woman, women have developed a discourse, and this is another achievement of seventeenth-century women" (*Raising Their Voices,* 35). Even Bell, Parfitt, and Shepherd concede that "the 'faking' of a female authorial persona by Taylor and Okes suggests a new value being placed on the idea of women speaking and on the authority of what is spoken by them" (282).

of her modestie, to answere their Surfeitings?" (title pages). The vehemence of her rhetoric underlines her consciousness of the novelty of her enterprise, and she imagines male attackers assuming that women cannot or dare not reply because "not one amongst us" has ever done so: "the time wherein they have lavished out their wordes freely, hath bene so long, that they know we cannot catch hold of them to pull them out, and they think we wil not write to reproove their lying lips" (sig. B^r). The persona of anger and outrage dominates the style and content of the pamphlet, which is as much a counterattack on men as a defense of women. But the most striking feature of the new subject position presented here is Anger's repeated insistence on her shared identity and common experience with her audience, whom she defines as exclusively female ("seeing I speake to none but to you which are of mine owne Sex," sig. C2^r): "let us secretlye our selves with our selves, consider howe and in what, they that are our worst enemies, are both inferiour unto us, & most beholden unto our kindenes" (sig. C^r).

Anger's pamphlet did exert some influence in the pamphlet debates; Nicholas Breton, for example, borrowed unattributed chunks of it for his defense. However, there is no indication that Rachel Speght in *A Mouzell for Melastomus* (1617) was aware of a female predecessor when she wrote her defense nearly thirty years later. Hence she too stresses the novelty of what she is attempting ("not perceiving any of our Sex to enter the Lists of encountring with this our grand enemy among men" [sig. A4^r]), but defines her persona in terms very different from Anger's. In fact, she explicitly rejects the stance of outrage both for herself and for other women: "This I alleage as a paradigmatical patterne for all women, noble & ignoble to follow, that they be not enflamed with choler against this our enraged adversarie, but patiently consider of him according to the portraiture which he hath drawne of himselfe, his Writings being the very embleme of a monster" (sig. A4^r). Although she dedicates her first epistle to all women and refers several times to "our sex," the platform from which she speaks has been constructed by the dominant male discourse, for she presents herself as a chivalrous champion of women, whom she discusses in the third person throughout the pamphlet. The anomaly thus created must be smoothed over, and this I take to be the function of the three pseudonymous poems that use distanced and authoritative male voices to justify her writing, a function they would serve even if Speght herself actually wrote the poems. Speght also frequently apologizes for her "insufficiency in literature and tendernesse in years" (sig. A4^v) and even uses this as an excuse to curtail her invective, which is directed exclusively at Joseph Swetnam rather than at men in general

("Minority bids me keepe within my bounds," sig. B2^r). The religious discourse of the period also helps to justify her speech, and her arguments are heavily religious in emphasis[12]: though young and weak, she is "armed with the truth . . . and the Word of Gods Spirit" (Sig. A4^r)

Both Sowernam and Munda present themselves as carrying forward the work that was begun by Speght, invoking not only a sense of common experience (both use the "we woman" persona much more emphatically then Speght), but also a sense of common enterprise that is new to the defense tradition. In *The Worming of a Mad Dogge* (1617) Munda calls Speght "the first Champion of our sexe that would encounter with the barbarous bloudhound" and praises her for the modesty, gravity, learning, and prudence of her "religious confutation of [Swetnam's] undecent raylings" (15). But it is Sowernam's work, not Speght's, which she says prevented her from writing further lest she be criticized for undertaking a "worke that's done already." She distinguishes her tone from Speght's even in her title, calling it "No Confutation but a sharpe Redargution of the bayter of Women"; her persona is even more vehement than Anger's, and she employs dramatic and sometimes shocking invective.[13] The most striking aspect of Munda's self-presentation, however, is her learning, which she emphasizes throughout, even in the dedicatory poem addressed to her mother, the "Lady Prudentia Munda." Instead of conventionally thanking her mother for the difficulties of childbirth and nurture, Munda expresses gratitude for the "second birth of education" and uses an elaborate financial conceit to justify her own "writing hand" as an essential surety for her debt.

If Munda's tone and display of learning were too extreme for most Englishwomen of the period, Sowernam found a balance in *Esther hath hang'd Haman* (1617) that did constitute a viable feminine subject position in the defense tradition at that time. The enigmatic pronouncement on her title page—"Written by *Ester Sowernam*, neither Maide, Wife, or Widdowe, yet really all, and therefore experienced to defend all"—accomplishes three things at once. First, it contradicts Joseph Swetnam, who had castigated "unmarried wantons" for making themselves "neither maidens, widowes, nor wives," calling them a "foule leprosie of

---

12. Elaine Beilin characterizes Speght's approach as "quintessentially Protestant": "Rachel Speght chose to appear as an exemplary woman reasoning and arguing from Scripture for the justice of her cause" (*Redeeming Eve*, 256–57).

13. As Beilin points out, Munda's use of language that "violated the very modesty she claimed for her sex" was a paradoxical and risky strategy, but "it may well have encouraged readers to sit up and listen" (*Redeeming Eve*, 265).

nature."[14] It also creates a logical paradox where none was thought possible (in "the paradigm of marriage" that dominated theological, legal, and moralistic Renaissance discourse about women).[15] Finally, this statement, because of its logical impossibility, opens up a space in the discourse and establishes the credentials for a new subject position: only women have the experience to defend other women, only they can "really" play the roles allotted to women by society (although they are never reducible to any of those roles).[16] Her voice is engaged but confident and authoritative: "Some will perhaps say, I am a woman and therefore write more for women then they doe deserve: To whom I answere, if they misdoubt of what I speake, let them impeach my credit in any one particular" (sig. A4^r). Addressing herself both to women and to men (especially to the "young youths of *Great Brittaine*," sig. A3^v), she is equally at home with Scripture and logic, drawing examples from more recent history as well as from classical antiquity and the Bible. It is no accident, I believe, that *The womens sharpe revenge*, published twenty-three years later under the names Mary Tattle-well and Joan Hit-him-home, echoes Sowernam's pamphlet in a number of places; despite the prevalence of jest and humor in the latter work, the subject position from which its female narrators speak is essentially that of Sowernam.

Let us turn now to the topos of Adam and Eve. Without attempting to present a complete picture of the treatment of this topos, I will concentrate on a few arguments relating to the creation, the fall, and the dowry of women in order to show how defenders writing from a female subject position negotiated with the dominant discourse about women's inheritance from Eve. The arguments about the creation of woman tended to center on the place (earth for man, Paradise for woman), the original substance (dust/earth for man, a rib/living flesh for woman), or the order of creation (man first, woman second). Of all the female defenders, Rachel Speght presents the lengthiest and most traditional discussion of creation, in keeping with the religious tone of her pamphlet, organizing her discussion under the headings of efficient, material, formal, and final

---

14. In Joseph Swetnam, *Araignment of Lewde, idle, froward, and unconstant women* (1615), 27.

15. Ian Maclean describes the "belief that woman cannot be considered except in relation to the paradigm of marriage" (57) and characterizes the paradigm of "maiden/ wife/widow" as "an immovable object in the way of change, while religion maintains its authority" (26–27).

16. Part of Sowernam's objection to Rachel Speght's defense may lie in Speght's adoption of a masculine platform and her lack of challenge to such patriarchally defined roles (hence, perhaps, her insistence on terming Speght "the Maide," sigs. A2^v and 6^r).

causes. Although she mentions that woman was made of a more "refined mould" than man, she immediately adds the commonplace that she was not produced from Adam's foot to be his inferior, or from his head to be his superior, but rather "from his side, neare his heart, to be his equall" (9–11). Her emphasis throughout is on the importance of companionate marriage and the meetness of woman as helper to man. In fact, the only unusual feature of her discussion lies in her practical application of the helper motif: "if she must be an *helper*, and but an *helper*, then are those husbands to be blamed, which lay the whole burthen of domesticall affaires and maintenance on the shoulders of their wives" (12).

Contrast the effect of Speght's traditional and detached arguments with that of the following passage from Jane Anger:

> Then lacking a help for him, GOD making woman of mans fleshe, that she might bee purer then he, doth evidently showe, how far we women are more excellent then men. Our bodies are fruitefull, whereby the world encreaseth, and our care wonderful, by which man is preserved. . . . They are côforted by our means: they [are] nourished by the meats we dresse: their bodies freed from disease by our cleanlines, which otherwise would surfeit unreasonably through their own noisomnes. Without our care they lie in their beds as dogs in litter. (sigs. C–Cᵛ)

The presence of the first-person pronouns gives the passage a sharper sense of immediacy and involvement, although Anger does not scruple to take the "purer substance" argument to its logical extreme and claim feminine *superiority*, in contrast to Speght, who simply aims "to decipher the excellency of women" (9). Most significantly, Anger defines the word *helper* from a position of strength rather than of weakness, drawing concrete (if humorously exaggerated) examples from daily domestic life.

With regard to the order of creation, Adam's priority was usually interpreted as primacy (Anger herself, in another context, quotes the Latin adage "*Primû est optimû*," sig. C2ʳ). Defenders of women, however, typically stand this point on its head, arguing that Eve was God's masterpiece because she was created last. Female defenders are certainly not unique in presenting this argument, although they tend to couch it in more serious and far-reaching terms.[17] For example, Constantia Munda

17. Ian Maclean summarizes the "series of theological proofs of female excellence" based on the creation story, as presented by such humanist defenders of women as Cornelius Agrippa. However, he notes, "these 'proofs' are clearly inconsistent with the wider context of theology; Agrippa himself admits that, in declamations of the sort he wrote in favour of woman, there are many invalid arguments" (91).

uses this aspect of the creation story to posit the essential superiority of woman: "the consummation of his blessed weekes worke, the end, crowne, and perfection of the never sufficiently glorified creation, . . . the greatest part of the *lesser world*" (sig. B3ʳ). She also brings new life to the concept by changing the metaphor to a literary one (thereby considerably anticipating the contemporary feminist slogan "Adam was a rough draft"): "Woman the second edition of the Epitome of the whole world, the second Tome of that goodly volume compiled by the great God of heaven and earth is most shamefully blurd, and derogatively rased by scribling penns of savage & uncought monsters" (sig. B2ᵛ).

Although the story of creation could be turned to women's advantage, the account of the fall was more recalcitrant: Eve was tempted first and sinned first; she was the tempter of Adam and the instrument by which sin and death entered the world, and her punishment was divinely decreed subservience. The variety and ambiguous nature of the female defenders' responses to this account mark it as a particularly conflictual site for negotiations with the dominant discourse. Rachel Speght again echoes traditional methods of defense: "Sathan first assailed the woman, because where the hedge is lowest, most easie it is to get over, and she being the weaker vessell was with more facility to be seduced" (4). Munda and Tattle-well/Hit-him-home avoid the fall altogether, although the latter discuss creation several times. Sowernam, however, does grapple with the issue, even claiming the privilege of "taking all the advantages I may, to defend my sexe" (8). Her main strategies involve amplifying the sins of Adam and emphasizing the role of the "Serpent of the masculine gender" (7). She plays with these ideas by quoting Swetnam's statement that the devil appeared to Eve "in the shape of the beautifull yong man": "Men are much beholding to this author, who will seeme to insinuate, that the devil . . . might make bold of them, whom he knew in time would prove his familier friends." So the devil began his evil career in the shape of a man and has "never changed his suite sithence" (33–34). In the quotation that opens this chapter, Sowernam downplays the fall and concentrates instead on the promise of redemption; because she presents only Adam's perspective here, she emphasizes the powerlessness of the male to change the situation ("stroke dead in regard of himselfe") and by implication confers on the woman a more powerful role. Indeed, an earlier passage uses a wonderful play on the word "fruit" to stress the active part woman plays in redemption: "Woman supplanted by tasting of fruit, she is punished in bringing forth her owne fruit. Yet what by fruit she lost, by fruit she shall recover" (9).

Although Sowernam terms this promise of redemption the "dowrie" that Eve brought to Adam, most writers of the time claimed that her dowry was rather the shrewish willfulness and unchastity that women ever after inherited from Eve. As Joseph Swetnam interprets the fall, Eve "was no sooner made but straightway her minde ws set upon mischiefe, for by her aspiring minde and wanton will she quickly procured mans fall, and therefore ever since they are & have been a woe unto man, and follow the line of their first leader" (1). Hence it appeared just and fitting that God Himself should decree woman's eternal subservience to man in Genesis 3:16, "Thy desire shall be to thy husband, and he shall rule over thee." Here was a major weapon in the arsenal of antifeminine arguments, and the attackers employ it with full recognition of its power to quell feminine aspirations. For example, the anonymous pamphlet *The deceyte of women* (c. 1560) observes that women are getting ideas above their station because of defenders' arguments such as the claim that woman is superior to man because she alone was created in Paradise: "therefore som womê have an opinion and say that they be better than ŷ mê and wyll be mens maysters . . . nowe a dayes in the worlde." However, the pamphlet cautions, such women forget "the Wordes that god spake to the Woman after that the commanndement was broken . . . ye shall be under the power of your husband, and he shall be your mayster, and shal have Lordshyp over you" (sigs. A3^{r-v}).

In an age when the Bible was interpreted strictly, this commandment represented ultimate, unchallengeable authority, and the combined authority of church and state in this matter offered the female defenders little scope for negotiation. Munda and Tattle-well/Hit-him-home simply ignore it, concentrating instead on emphatically declaring woman's excellence. Rachel Speght calls male supremacy "a truth ungainesayable" but emphasizes the duties this sovereignty imposes on men (16). Esther Sowernam tries to make a virtue of necessity: "She is commanded to obey her husband; the cause is, the more to encrease her glorie. Obedience is better than Sacrifice: for nothing is more acceptable before God then to obey: women are much bound to God, to have so acceptable a vertue enjoyned them for their pennance" (9–10). The vehement Jane Anger, wielding her marvelous sarcastic wit, reinterprets the doctrine more aggressively: "The Gods knowing that the mindes of mankind would be aspiring, and having thoroughly viewed the wonderfull vertues wherewith women are inriched, least they should provoke us to pride, and so confound us with Lucifer, they bestowed the supremacy over us to man, that of that Cockscombe he might onely boast, and therefore for Gods sake let them keepe it" (sig. B2ᵛ). Her reference to "the Gods," however, avoids a direct challenge to Genesis.

In addition to willful disobedience, Eve's sin was also linked with unchastity, inasmuch as she was viewed as seducing Adam to eat the fruit, an action symbolically associated with sex through their subsequent shame at their own nakedness. In the Renaissance, as in earlier periods, it was believed that women had a capacity for sexual pleasure far exceeding that of men and that they were consequently more subject to imperious physical desires. Even male defenders of women such as Christopher Newstead describe "the natural pronenesse of their bodies" to "gape after pleasures," (in *An Apology for Women* [1620], 11) and the sexual sins of women are a prime topic for the attackers' pens. The alleged sexual insatiability of women is not only evil in itself but is also directed at the ruination of men. In the words of Joseph Swetnam, "they lay out the foldes of their hare to entangle men into their love, betwixt their breasts is the vale of destruction, & in their beds there is hell, sorrow, & repentance. Eagles eate not men till they are dead but women devour them alive" (16).

Very few people of the time, at least in print, challenged the prevalent view of females as highly sexual beings. But male apologists claimed that most women succeed in controlling their desires, rendering themselves all the more virtuous. According to Christopher Newstead, men who live chastely are merely "temperate," but chaste women, because their natures are so much more passionate, are laudably "continent": "by this they are most vertuous, that their mindes should be sober, amongst the riotous pleasures of their bodies" (12). Newstead, in fact, defends individual women while simultaneously identifying the category "woman" with sexual evil: male seducers have "metamorphosed into a woman: pleasures and delights, are the ingendring Serpents, that have womanized their affections" (3).

Female writers, however, did quarrel with the attribution of greater sexual desires to women. Esther Sowernam questions Swetnam's claim that women are seductresses, luring men to ruin through their beauty. Beauty in itself, says Sowernam, cannot be a direct cause of ruin, only what the philosophers call "an accidental cause." Men are tempted by beauty only because of their own wantonness; the beauty that women inherit from Eve is a beneficial dowry that men misappropriate in the service of their own inherent lustfulness. Thus Sowernam neatly turns Swetnam's argument back against himself: "Doe not say and rayle at women to be the cause of mens overthrow, when the originall roote and cause is in your selves" (35–39). More radically, she goes on to defend women's use of cosmetics, an almost universal subject of attack in this period. A "faire woman, which doth make the best use that she can to set out her beautie" is actually to be commended for glorifying God, because she is showing her respect for the jewel that God has given her by displaying it "as carefully and as curiously as she may" (37). Rachel Speght uses a more biblical argument to challenge the prevalent association of women and sexuality: it was not until *Adam* sinned that humans felt shame at their nakedness and first experienced "the rebellion & disobedience of their members in the disordered motions of their now corrupt nature" (6).

Thus a major characteristic of the new female subject position was its inversion of the dominant discourse's projection of sexuality onto women; the female defenders repeatedly attributed most sexual desires and sexual temptation to men. For example, Jane Anger describes men as "ravenous hawkes, who doe not onely seize upon us, but devour us" (sig. B3ʳ); note the contrast with Swetnam's characterization of seductive women as eagles who devour men. The female defenders present men as seducers who apply every possible kind of pressure to assault women's chastity; this image is rarely employed by a male defender, although Christopher Newstead does refer to men as "assailants" who "batter the walles" of women's chastity despite the fact that men are more chaste by nature than women (14–15). Both Sowernam and Tattlewell/Hit-him-home strongly protest the double standard for sexual behavior; they contrast the consequences of sexual misbehavior for men and women through a metaphor of apparel: for a man, sexual scandal is "like a suit of Tiffany, or Cobweb Lawne, soone worne out: but the faults of a weake Woman . . . are ingraven in brasse, and like a suit of Buffe, it may be turn'd, and scour'd and scrapt, and made a little cleanly, but it lasts the whole life time of the wearer" (9) *The womens sharpe revenge* even notes the influence exerted by social and economic pressures (an observation that is quite rare in this type of treatise). For example, the authors of this pamphlet maintain that prostitution is a means of survival for some women, pointing out that such women at least draw on their own resources instead of taking from others: "some through extreame want and poverty have beene forced to make more bold with that which is their owne, then to begge, steale, or borrow from others" (6–7). They argue that men call women "weaker Vessells" but deny them the "generous and liberall Educations" that would make them stronger. Instead of the classical education that would enable women "to vindicate our owne injuries," men educate women "for their own particular ends, the better to please and content their licentious appetites, when we come to our maturity and ripenesse: and thus if we be weake by Nature, they strive to makes us more weake by our Nature" (40–42).

Finally, some of the female writers, particularly Anger and Tattle-well/Hit-him-home, go so far as to claim that women, unlike men, are *inherently* chaste. According to Tattle-well and Hit-him-home, in *The womens sharpe revenge* (1640), women have little natural sexual desire and marry primarily from a desire for children, rather than from "any carnall delight or pleasure they had to accompany with men": "surely if there had beene any lawfull way for them to have had Children without Husbands, there hath beene, and are, and will bee a numberless number of Women that would or will never be troubled with wedlocke, nor the knowledge of man" (133–34). This is a vision of woman familiar to us from the Victorian era but dramatically different from the view of female sexuality prevalent in Western thought since antiquity. It is significant that it appears only when women have succeeded in creating a public platform from which to speak.

According to Marilyn Williamson, "representations within the text perform complex social work as they endorse, interrogate, or subvert the cultural ideologies that produce them and are produced by them" (9). In the process of creating a female subject position within the masculine discourse of the defense tradition, women writers found a place from which they could interrogate, if not subvert, the master narrative of Adam and Eve.

12

Eleanor Davies and the Prophetic Office

Esther S. Cope

Eleanor Davies became a prophet in 1625 after she heard the biblical prophet, Daniel, tell her that the Day of Judgment would come in nineteen and one-half years.[1] Before she died in 1652, she had published more than sixty prophetic writings.[2] In these prophecies she reflected on the tension and incongruities that affected her as a woman and as a prophet. She drew upon the language and concepts of her own culture and its Judeo-Christian heritage to create a prophetic idiom that allowed her to condemn the sorrows and limitations of her own experience and to escape from them. Prophecy enabled her to be the "Messenger of Life" and to write critically about the woman she was struggling not to be, the "Mother not of the Living Child, but of Divisions and Massacres," the Old Testament woman of 1 Kings 3:16–28 (Davies, *From the Lady Eleanor*, 11 and 35). This chapter explores the vision of the woman prophet that emerges in Lady Eleanor's writings and in her daughter Lucy's defense of her.

In her preface to the first of her prophecies, *A Warning to the Dragon and All His Angels* (1625), Lady Eleanor described her work as an "office not a trade." Throughout her career she assumed a professionalism about

The opportunity to reflect again on Eleanor Davies and her writings came as a consequence of a research leave from the University of Nebraska—Lincoln and a Fellowship from the Henry E. Huntington Library in San Marino, California. In addition to the many debts I incurred in the course of my previously published work about Eleanor Davies, I owe particular thanks to the staff of both libraries.

1. She described this experience many times in her writings. See, for example, Davies, *Lady Eleanor Her Appeal*, 10. Born Eleanor Touchet, she was the fifth daughter of George, baron Audeley and first earl of Castlehaven. She married Sir John Davies (d. 1626) in 1609 and Sir Archibald Douglas (d.1644) in 1627. Concerning Davies's life, see Cope, *Handmaid*.

2. Her writings are entered under "Audeley" in Pollard and Redgrave, *Short-Title Catalogue*, 2d ed., and under "Douglas" in Wing, *A Short-Title Catalogue*, 2d ed. Thirty-eight of these tracts are printed in Cope, ed., *Prophetic Writings of Lady Eleanor Davies*.

prophecy that was not unlike the attitude that holders of public offices in church and state were expected to have in early-modern England. Although the terms *Writer* and, especially, *Secretary*, which she used to refer to herself in a later tract introduce a slight ambiguity into her claim because they suggest a kind of subordination, the most prominent secretary, the monarch's secretary, was a person of considerable importance.[3] Had Lady Eleanor not been a woman, her noble birth and her education in the classics, which could have rivaled that of many of her male contemporaries, would have meant that she probably would have held some office, but for a woman to have an office contravened the notions of gender that were then current.[4] Women in her day did not ordinarily have the education or professional training associated with such a position. Neither were they, regardless of social status, thought able to assume the authority and responsibility of office. Women did practice at least some trades, the skilled or semiskilled occupations of the lower middle classes, but these would have been beneath Lady Eleanor.[5]

By designating her call to prophesy an office, Lady Eleanor exhibited a concern with reputation that was common among her contemporaries. "Estimation and Reputation" were, according to Sir William Cornwallis, "the most deare and most precious commodities of man" ("Of Estimation and Reputation," in *Essayes*, no. 29). Both women and men were with increasing frequency resorting to litigation to defend themselves against slander and defamation.[6] Women's suits usually attacked those who had called them whores. For a woman, a good reputation required first and foremost sexual probity. Being a prophet placed this in jeopardy. The public role of a prophet left a woman without the protection of her husband or father who would shield her and society from the consequences of unchaste conduct or inappropriate speaking and writing. Neither the knowledge that God sometimes chose women as prophets nor the belief that prophets lost their own identity to become divine instruments allayed the discomfort of the seventeenth-century British in seeing women as prophets.[7]

---

3. Davies, *From the Lady Eleanor*, 7. See Beale, "Treatise of the office of a councillor and secretary," in Elton, 124–27.

4. Concerning her education, see Cope, *Handmaid*, 10–11.

5. See Prior, "Women and the Urban Economy," 93–117.

6. John March commented about this increase in litigation in his treatise, *Actions for Slaunder*.

7. See Mack, "Women as Prophets," 19–45; Purkiss, "Producing the Voice," 139–58; Hobby "'Discourse so unsavoury,'" 16–32.

Lady Eleanor was particularly susceptible to charges of impropriety because, as a prophet, she never lost touch with her body and her personal history.[8] Instead of becoming an androgynous empty vessel for a divine message, she had incorporated her personal identity in her prophetic persona. She demonstrated this with the anagram, "Reveale O Daniel," that she made from her own name, Eleanor Audeley (Davies, *Warning to the Dragon*, 1). By showing that the instruction to prophesy was embodied in her name ("Eleanor Audeley," because her father was Baron Audeley), that anagram also confirmed that she was indeed meant to prophesy. The justification of her otherwise unacceptable conduct depended on her authenticity as a prophet. Prophecy, in turn, because its essence was truth-telling, gave her a means of rectifying the wrongs she had endured in marriage, motherhood, and in her birth-family.

Insisting that her prophetic message was the truth that had been concealed, Lady Eleanor emphasized openness. In her prologue to *Great Britains Visitation* (1645), she described the manner of Christ's birth, which had occurred in an "open Stable . . . like the truth which no Corners or Curtaines requires" and noted how the Second Coming would also be "revealed." Through prophecy, "whatsoever spoken in darkenesse or in the Eare assur'd [was] to be made cleare as the light," although, she recognized, not all would hear and heed it (Davies, *Great Brittains Visitation*, prologue, 10). Her claim to tell the truth acknowledged the values that her society in its law and religion placed on truth and, because she was a woman, a daughter of Eve, that very claim also violated those values.[9]

Lady Eleanor addressed contemporaries who believed that she was not God's prophet, but a woman led astray by the devil, by telling and retelling the story of the moment in 1625 when Daniel spoke to her (Davies, *Lady Eleanor Her Appeal*, 14; *Star to the Wise*, 18; *Her Appeal from the Court*, 10; *Everlasting Gospel*, 3–4). She also repeatedly pointed out occasions when her predictions had been accurate. In *Lady Eleanor Her Appeal* she offered a "list of some" of the "judgments" that had occurred "since prophesies Thundring Reign began" (14 ff).[10] With biblical exegesis she showed how Britain's history corresponded to events that the Bible said would precede Judgment. Particularly important to her was the fact that, because she had been called before the High Commission

8. Roy Porter speaks to this point in "The Prophetic Body," 51–64.
9. See Gilmore, *Autobiographics*, chap. 3.
10. See also the marginalia in Davies, *Strange and Wonderfull Prophesies*.

and because Archbishop Laud had burned her books, her prophecies were "Extant on Records." They had achieved official recognition, and so had she. The court's sentence against her was also on record.[11] Thus, through her prophetic office, she had broken through her society's constraints on women and linked her history with Britain's.

The very evidence that Lady Eleanor believed would confirm her credibility as a prophet also testified to the professionalism with which she approached prophecy. Whether correcting previous errors of translation in the biblical texts from which she worked, arguing about the theology of redemption, calculating when Judgment would occur, responding to objections against the Book of Revelations, or arranging to be present at "the Prophetical Tragedy" of the king's execution, she showed that she was not merely conscientious about fulfilling her professional responsibilities but committed to excellence in performing them. She was proud of the important role that prophecy bestowed upon her.[12] As prophet, she dealt with matters far more important than those that occupied either the monarch or the greatest of public officials. Accordingly, she could approach them with a demand to be heard. Although she signed herself "The humble Servant of your Excellence, Eleanor," when she wrote Lord General Fairfax in January 1649, she described her message as "The Word of the Most High" and minced few words in informing the general what prophecy required of him (Davies, *Her Appeal from the Court*). In 1633 she had delivered Archbishop Laud his fate.[13] In the same year she had told King Charles that Laud was the Beast from the Bottomless Pit of the Book of Revelations (in *Given to the Elector*), and in 1649 she had written the imprisoned king, "you are hereby required to make a publique acknowledgement of such your capital Trespass and high Offence; and first to Ask me foregiveness, if so be you expect to finde Mercy in this world or the other" (*Blasphemous Charge Against her*, 2).

Lady Eleanor saw in the moment of the king's trial an opportunity to rectify the wrongs done to her in 1633. She prefaced her 1649 letter to the king with one of her many accounts of her hearing before the High Commission in 1633 where she had been sentenced to be fined, make a "publique submission . . . so many times; that Jerico forever cursed, and farther a close prisoner to continue at your pleasure" (*Blasphemous Charge*

11. Davies, *Apocalypsis*, prologue. See also Davies, *Lady Eleanor Her Appeal*, 34; *Everlasting Gospel*, 12; *As Not Unknowne*.

12. See, for example, Davies, *Je Le Tien*, 3 and 34–36; *Mystery*; and *Given to the Elector*.

13. Her prophecy for Laud appears among the Domestic State Papers in the Public Record Office in London (Great Britain, P.R.O., SP 16/248/93). See her comments about that in *As Not Unknowne*.

against her, 2). Prophecy allowed her to reinterpret that event and her several subsequent imprisonments which, because they were public, were more humiliating than the scenes of judgment and virtual imprisonment familiar to women in their domestic life.[14] She concluded *The Gatehouse Salutation* (1646) with these lines, which, she said, should be sung "To the Tune of *Magnificat*," the Virgin Mary's song of praise to God (Luke 1: 46–55): "So Gates and Prison Doors be no more shut, / The King of Glory comes, your souls lift up" (7).

As a prophet, Lady Eleanor even ventured to write about her own married life and thus to magnify the gossip that circulated about her defiance of her husbands' opposition to her prophesying. To Sir John Davies who, upon discovering that she had become a prophet, had "thrown" her prophecies "into the fire," she had given his "Doom . . . in letters of his own Name," an anagram, *"John Daves, Ioves Hand."* She told him he would die within three years (*Lady Eleanor Her Appeal*, 15). His death within that period became one of the examples she cited to show the verity of her prophecies. Unlike the women concerned about their reputations, who regarded comments about wifely insubordination or marital discord as anathema, she reported that the king himself had mentioned her prediction of Davies's death (*Lady Eleanor Her Appeal*, 18–19). Her accounts of the seizure and subsequent mental dysfunction suffered by her second husband, Sir Archibald Douglas, who had also burned her prophetic writings, were similarly forthright. She had predicted that he too would suffer as a consequence of his act (*Lady Eleanor Her Appeal*, 15–16, 20–21, 27).

Prophecy provided Lady Eleanor a way of telling the truth about her experiences and, by reinterpreting them, of transforming suffering and injustice into power and redemption. She had no doubt that her work, "what she hath been a sufferer so many years for," was of greater significance than that which she had done before she had become a prophet or that which most men did (*Her Appeal from the Court*, 2). Weighing upon her was the stigma of having been confined in Bedlam, London's mental hospital, in 1636, after she had vandalized the altar hanging at the cathedral of Lichfield. She complained in a petition to the House of

14. In addition to being imprisoned in the Gatehouse from 1633–35, Lady Eleanor was confined to the Tower of London from 1638 to 1640 (Cope, *Handmaid*, 95–96; London's Wood Street Compter in 1646 (Davies, *Hells Destruction*, 11); the Gatehouse again in 1646 (Davies, *Gatehouse Salutation*); the Upper Branch (she refers to it as the Queen's Bench) in 1650 (Davies, *Before the Lords Second Coming*, 16); and the Fleet in 1651 (Davies, *Restitution of Prophecy*, epistle to the reader).

Commons in 1647 that those who had committed her to the hospital had presumed to "make her ever incapable of anie Complaint but ever held or taken to bee a person non Compos mentis to the perpetuall blott and infamie of her familie and posteritie" (House of Lords Record Office, Main Papers, 22 September 1647). In *Bethlehem, Signifying The House of Bread: or War* (1652) she described Bedlam as a "loathsome Prison, infected with those *foul Spirits* day and night *Blaspheming*" (6), but she told those who had committed her to the hospital that they would be punished. By virtue of Bedlam's name (it was formally the hospital of St. Mary of Bethlehem), she claimed that she was the Virgin who would be the bearer of new life just as Mary had given birth to Jesus Christ (*Everlasting Gospel*, 8–11).

Through Mary's role as mother, Lady Eleanor evoked a central aspect of her prophetic self. The words that she had heard calling her to prophesy in 1625 and informing her that she was to be "the meek Virgin" (Davies, *Lady Eleanor Her Appeal*, 10) offered her a persona that stressed the qualities that contemporaries valued in women but at the same time entitled her to a public role of a significance that no man could challenge. Citing a multitude of parallels between her own experiences and Mary's, Lady Eleanor, in her books, which she regarded as her "babes," brought the promise of redemption to Britain, whose ravishment through the wars had grieved her.[15] Her prophetic maternity gave her a voice and allowed her to move beyond disappointment and death that had characterized her own experiences of motherhood. She never mentioned that her son Jack, who had had some disability, had drowned at an early age, and his brother had also died young, but when Archbishop Laud burned her prophetic books before her eyes in October 1633, she publicly mourned the death of these "babes." She declared Laud's act murder, pronounced judgment, and rejoiced when he was executed in 1645.[16] She indicted her prosecutors for interfering with God's message.

Through the new motherhood of prophecy Lady Eleanor subverted gender order to give her daughter the priority and place that a son would have had. She concluded the tract she dedicated to Lucy, *From the Lady Eleanor, Her Blessing to Her Beloved Daughter* (1644), by acknowledging

15. For parallels between her experience and those of Mary, see, for example, Davies, *The Everlasting Gospel*, 3–6; also see the conclusion of *Samsons Legacie*, 24, where she presented herself as "the Blessed Ladie, her Day in Lent, &c," that is the Virgin Mary, whose "Day in Lent" was the Feast of the Annunciation. Although she signed *Restitution of Prophecy*, as "Ele[anor] Da[vies] & Do[uglas]," she dated it, "Her Purification" (51). She spoke of having "her childe [her prophecy] ravished" in 1625 in *Everlasting Gospel*, 9–10.

16. Davies, *As Not Unknowne*, 9–10. Concerning her sons, see Cope, *Handmaid*, 21–22.

that Lucy had been more than a daughter in the traditional sense. Lucy had, in fact, done what a husband was supposed to. "You," she told Lucy, "that so punctually have discharged that duty of the first commandement with promise, in so much and such dishonour endured, have bene your mothers Copartner, even You, her alone and sole support under the Almighty" (Davies, *From the Lady Eleanor, her blessing*, 38). In the body of the tract she discussed, from the standpoint of maternity, inheritance and the coats of arms, which were so important in the patriarchal world in which she lived, and pointed out the signs of impending Judgment in the arms that showed Britain's lineage.

Although Lady Eleanor's father had been the eleventh Baron Audeley and first earl of Castlehaven, he was not a particularly wealthy lord who, after about 1600, lived in relative obscurity in Ireland.[17] In *Her Appeal* (1641) she described him as "NO inferior PEERE" (11), and in *Star to the Wise* (1643) as "the *first* Peer or Baron" (18).[18] By the time she wrote those tracts, the family's reputation had become a subject of considerable gossip, if not infamy. In 1631 her brother, Mervin, who had inherited his father's titles, was tried and executed for sodomy and for being an accessory to rape.[19] At the time, she herself joined in neither her three sisters' petition in Castlehaven's behalf nor that from Sir Archibald Douglas, but, later, in her prophecies she denounced those who had had a hand in her brother's execution.[20] Rather than make a detailed reexamination of evidence in the case, she condemned Castlehaven's prosecutors and offered a kind of prophetic vindication and promise of redemption for him. Like her, he attained through prophecy a respectability that in his own life he had been denied.

For herself Lady Eleanor claimed through prophecy a new lineage that rivaled that of the monarchs whose title declared that they ruled England, Scotland, France, and Ireland. By virtue of her ancestry and marriages, she asserted that she was connected with the same territories. Heaven was her "Joynture place," the property that was to support her

17. See Cope, *Handmaid*, 15–16.

18. See also her comment about the antiquity of his title (Davies, *The Appearance or Presence of the Son of Man*, 8–9).

19. Whether or not the issue that most offended contemporaries was, as Cynthia Herrup argues, his violation of patriarchy in bestowing his estate upon servants rather than his son, Castlehaven's offences were widely seen as "fowle and horrible." See Great Britain, Public Record Office, C.115/M30/8074, newsletter written to Lord Scudamore; also Cope, *Handmaid*, 53–54.

20. Her prophetic words about Castlehaven were *Word of God* (1644) and *Crying Charge* (1649); she also discusses the case in *Restitution of Prophecy* (1651). Concerning the petitions, see Cope, *Handmaid*, 54.

in her widowhood.[21] She knew only too well the trials and tribulations of a widow whose husbands had not provided for what she needed, and the biblical injunctions to care for the poor widow gave her a basis for condemning those who took the widows' estates. Envisioning herself as Britain, she expounded upon the fate of women, ravished, divorced, or widowed, and looked for a better future (Davies, *Appearance*, 16; *Elijah the Tishbite's Supplication*, 6; *A Prayer or Petition for Peace*, 5–6). Here was no submissive woman, but a prophet who assumed preeminence upon earth and looked forward to life in heaven.

Lady Eleanor was at her most eloquent about the inheritance she believed she was entitled to in *The Appearance or Presence of the Son of Man* (1650). She identified herself with the "Spirit" and employed language that those who ruled themselves might use in official documents. "Proclaiming no other than the Supreme Order or Authority, their unlimited Commission" which, she said was greater "then the Conqueror, Parliaments Prerogative not exempted," she proceeded to declare the truth about Britain's future (3–4). Later, she referred to herself in almost blasphemous terms: "She whose Throne heaven, earth her footstool" and declared in an echo of Revelations 1:8, "I am A. and O. *alias*, Da: and Do."[22]

No one reading her prophecies could escape knowing that Lady Eleanor had violated the rules concerning gender. For a woman, even a woman of the upper classes such as she was, a commitment to truth-telling dramatically altered her way of being in the world. In her prophetic preoccupation with publishing God's truth, she told the truth about her own experiences. Sometimes she spoke directly about events in her life. When she submitted to God's authority and became a prophet, helpless to stave off the imprisonment and other awesome consequences of her obedience, she mirrored her own life as a woman, but, as a prophet, she also challenged the patriarchal society in which she lived, not only by claiming to be exempt from the boundaries it imposed upon women, but also by pronouncing Judgment upon it. In her prophetic office, she had work that she knew was both radical and important. As she told the court of High Commission when they sentenced her in 1633, "the Gates of Hell shall not prevail against her."[23]

21. Davies, *Appearance*, 9–10. See also Davies, *Bethlehem*, 10–11.

22. Davies, *Appearance*, 7–8. Cf. Isa. 66:1 and Rev. 1:8. Alpha and omega were the first and last letters of the Greek alphabet; Davies and Douglas were Lady Eleanor's husbands.

23. She wrote these words on a transcript of the Commission's proceedings (HEH, Hastings MSS, Legal Papers, Box 6, folder 1. See Cope, *Handmaid*, 75.

Lady Eleanor's daughter, Lucy, countess of Huntingdon, never claimed to be a prophet, but, in writing about her mother, she too assumed a stance of authority that departed from her society's norms. Almost a decade after Davies's death, Lucy wrote historian William Sanderson, who had just published a history of the reign of Charles I, to demand that he revise his harsh treatment of her mother. She explained her intervention on two grounds: the first was public, the desire to amend his "blott and wound" to "ye name & fame of a person of <ye most> auncient nobility <of this nation> of <religious> and virtuous conversation"; the second was personal, her interest in avenging the injury she herself had incurred. Although "deceased," Lady Eleanor was "not without posterity <deeply> participating in ye wrong" that Sanderson had perpetrated.[24]

Sanderson, who presented his history of Charles's reign as a commentary on Hamon L'Estrange's work on the same topic, had followed L'Estrange's ("our Author's") organization and had, accordingly, mentioned Lady Eleanor's prediction of the death of the duke of Buckingham in the course of reporting that event.[25] L'Estrange had commented that her prophecy concerning Buckingham "added to her former prediction concerning this parliament, and both verifi'd in the event, rear'd the Lady up the fame of a great Prophetesse." Although he had then made a peroration about prophecy and the devil, he had abstained from any judgment about the source of Lady Eleanor's predictions and resumed, instead, his discussion of the topic that preceded his reference to Lady Eleanor, the fate of "the duke's devil," London astrologer John Lambe, who had been attacked and killed by a mob in the city in the aftermath of Buckingham's death (L'Estrange, 88–89).

Sanderson, however, had declared that Lady Eleanor's "Predictions were sundry, concerning this *Parliament*, and her other mad-brains Prophecies, never seriously observed by any so remarkable as our *Authour*."[26] In his subsequent digression, which was much longer than L'Estrange's, he had discussed the way that God and the devil used prophets. Focusing on

24. Two versions of her protest survive among the Hastings MSS at the Huntington Library. The second of these is signed with initials, L. H. [Lucy, countess of Huntingdon]. All quotations come from that second version. Words in pointed brackets <> have been inserted in the manuscript. Sanderson's book was *A Compleat History of the Life and Raigne of King Charles* (1658).

25. L'Estrange is identified only by his initials (see the letter to the author from James Howell that precedes Sanderson's history).

26. Sanderson, 124. Lucy's letter includes the page reference to Sanderson's work, and in the marginalia in Sanderson's text are references to the relevant pages of L'Estrange's.

women and, particularly, the sybils whose "Prophecies," he said, "were most famous among the ancient *Pagans* and *Christians*," he concluded that "the words and writings" of "the Lady *Davies* and Mistris *Carew*, [another woman prophet] . . . [were] always vain, full of whimsies, uncertain, full of mysterious expressions, they knew not what, and so assuredly were from and by the Devil, knowing by several designs of wicked men, what the Event was likely to be, but not certainly what to be" (Sanderson, 124–26).

In her letter of protest, Lucy responded point by point to Sanderson and at the same time offered an alternative view of Lady Eleanor's prophetic office, a view based on Lady Eleanor's own premises about her career. For Lucy as for her mother, the personal and the prophetic were intertwined. Each gave significance and meaning to the other.

The style Lucy employed was common in polemics of her day. Going through Sanderson's work, she analyzed his statements and responded to them. Like her mother, who, the High Commission claimed, had taken "upon her (which much unbeseemed her Sex) not only to interpret the Scriptures, and withal the most intricate and hard places of the Prophet *Daniel*," Lucy had a classical education that enabled her to enter into areas of discourse that were reserved for men in that era (Huntingdon, *Blasphemous Charge*, 9–10). Neither the topic nor the formal argumentative manner of addressing it daunted her. Her evaluation of the evidence in various biblical texts and translations about the relationship between God and Jesus Christ had formed the basis of a tract that Lady Eleanor had published in 1649.[27]

To combat Sanderson's charge that Lady Eleanor was inspired by the Devil, not the Holy Spirit, Lucy drew upon her studies of the Bible and theology.[28] Citing "those arguments wch have bin used in vindication of Moses from ye like calumny and by our blessed savior against his blasphemers," she maintained that Lady Eleanor's "utter detestation" of "all such unlawfull curious arts" should clear her. With examples that her mother had used in her prophetic writings, she also pointed out that God had previously "reveale[d] his councell by unlikely meanes. . . . Ordinary shepheards, were ye first Heraclds of Christ birth and women of his resurection."[29]

27. Huntingdon, *New Proclamation*. "Lu: H.," Lucy, countess of Huntingdon, appears on 8 at the end of the tract.

28. Among the Hastings manuscripts are books and papers that testify to Lucy's religious interests and studies, for example, HEH, Hastings MSS, Personal Papers, HAP, Box 18, folder 1, Memoranda Book of Lucy Hastings, countess of Huntingdon; and another similar book, HEH, Hastings MSS, Religious, Box 3, folder 16.

29. Cf. Lady Eleanor's defence of her claim to prophesy in *Star to the Wise*, 11–12.

Lucy saved copies of her mother's works and was clearly familiar with them even if she did not have them beside her as she was writing to Sanderson.[30] To demonstrate the accuracy of her mother's prophecies, she mentioned, in addition to Sanderson's example of Buckingham's death, Laud's execution nineteen and a half years after July 1625. In the latter instance, Lucy related the tale much as Lady Eleanor told it. She included not only her mother's initial message from Daniel, but also the events in 1633, when Laud had responded to the prophecy of doom for him by burning her books.[31] The prediction of Buckingham's death, Lucy insisted, illustrated the error of Sanderson's complaint that Lady Eleanor's prophecies were "vaine" and "mysterious" although she admitted that mystery was appropriate in prophecy, and that "since Majesty was concerned, it was less safe and more harsh to have bin too plaine" (Huntingdon, Letter to Sanderson).

Lucy was no political neophyte. She had negotiated her mother's release from imprisonment in 1635 and again in 1640, and during the civil war, she had dealt with the military forces who threatened and ultimately attacked her home.[32] Taking advantage of the fact that by the time she was writing to Sanderson monarchy had been restored in England, she pointed out that in a prophecy of July 1651, Lady Eleanor had "foretold <and published in print our> pardon, peace, release, and returne to rest with ye suppression of ye <or continued upon distemper to be accomplished>."[33] In the years following 1644 her mother had indeed written frequently about her belief in general redemption, "That after the last Period expird, ther is a Release out of HELL, Redemption for all the DAMNED," but nowhere had she been very specific about what this involved.[34]

Politics, theology, and the details of prophecy were only one facet of Lucy's address to Sanderson. She was also writing as a daughter to defend

30. A volume of Lady Eleanor's tracts that was probably Lucy's is preserved in the Folger Shakespeare Library.

31. Cf. Davies, *Appearance*, 13–14; *Everlasting Gospel*, 10–13; *Lady Eleanor Her Appeal*, 33–34.

32. See Cope, *Handmaid*, 77, 96–97; also her correspondence, e.g., her letter to her husband reproving him for lack of political wisdom in January 1650 (HEH, Hastings MSS, Correspondence, HA 5744) and another concerning her efforts to save the house (HEH, Hastings MSS, Correspondence, HA 5745).

33. Davies, *Serpents Excommunication*. The tract is in the form of a poem. It is not one of those included in the volume now in the Folger Library that probably belonged to Lucy.

34. Davies, *For Whitsontyds*, 13. Lady Eleanor called that tract "Her Creed or Confession," 5; see also *Mystery of General Redemption* and *Restitution of Reprobates*.

her mother's reputation. To do that, she also invoked personal knowledge. Lady Eleanor had taken "diligent care to advance ye honor of God and his kingdom, both by her own exemplary virtue and by her christian instruction of her neere relations and others in her family." How could she have been inspired by the devil? Although neither Lucy nor Lady Eleanor provide any details about the nature of "christian instruction" that may have occurred, Lucy's papers verify that she took religion seriously.

In conclusion, Lucy challenged Sanderson's research. "It seems," she alleged, that he had "never consulted" the records which, "notwithstanding ye potency" of Lady Eleanor's "enemys and ye iniquity of theire proceedings," contained "no such censure" as he had made.[35] What was worse, Lucy declared, was that Sanderson had violated his own precept, "That in uncertaine relations it becoms a historian to admitt ye most christian and charitable." His offense was particularly odious because he was injuring someone who was not alive and therefore could vindicate herself. "To create and cronicle a fatall scandall upon ye soule of a noble person dying and that irrecoverably beyond all reach of repair is noe doubt unbeseeming a historian or a good Christian. How most inexcusable then is hee who thus judging an other condemnes himselfe."

Like her mother, Lucy both avowed and challenged contemporary standards and images of women. She presented herself as the dutiful daughter and good Christian who is defending a mother who is equally virtuous. At the same time she employed subjects and techniques of discourse reserved to men in order to tell the truth about her mother's career as a prophet, about the content of those prophecies, and about the public consequences of prophesying. That truth was potentially shaming, but Lucy stated it to vindicate her mother and herself. Her efforts evoked an apology from Sanderson. Expressing himself in terms that were conventional in court-ordered or private submissions, he professed to be convinced by the "clear information, and ample testimony" that he had received. He asked "pardon withall from such who are concernd for what I have offensively written to the sayd Lady deceased her disreputation or to any of her noble Relations dissatisfaction."[36]

35. Lady Eleanor herself talked about her enemies. In the letter to the reader with which she prefaced *Restitution of Prophecy* she declared, "This Babe, object to their scorn, for speaking the truth." See also *Apocalypsis*, 1.

36. There is no threat of litigation in Lucy's letter. Sanderson's apology appears along with her request for it in HEH, Hastings MSS, Misc. Box 1, folder 17.

Sanderson, who was also engaged in a series of polemical exchanges with Peter Heylyn about the contents of his history, never published a second edition and, consequently, never had to make good his promise to Lucy.[37] Her letter to him and a later letter that Roger L'Estrange wrote her suggests that she may also have had a hand in altering the treatment of her mother in Baker's *Chronicle of the Kings of England*. Although the third (1660) and the fourth (1665) editions of Baker refer to Lady Eleanor only briefly in connection with Buckingham's death, the fifth edition (1670) mentions her in connection with her own death and prints a tribute to her written by Peter DuMoulin, to which Sanderson refers in his apology (Baker, *Chronicle*, 3d ed. [1660] 494; 4th ed. [1665] 494; [1670] 635). Apparently not satisfied with this, Lucy wrote Roger L'Estrange (son of Hamon, to whom Sanderson was responding) to ask his help in procuring an even more favorable assessment. His reply indicated that he had pursued the matter but, he explained, the book had "allmost past ye Presse with some few alterations" about other points.[38]

The reputation which both Eleanor Davies and her daughter Lucy sought to defend in their writings was one that was consciously feminine. It was both based in their culture and in conflict with that culture. The two images that Lady Eleanor had invoked in 1644 illustrate the tension that she and Lucy expressed between what was and what they sought. Although prophetic office opened the possibility of being the woman who was the "Messenger of Life," the reality of life (and of prophecy) involved being the woman who was the "Mother not of the Living Child, but of Divisions and Massacres" (Davies, *Lady Eleanor, Her Blessing*, 11 and 35).

37. See *Dictionary of National Biography*, s.v. "Sanderson, William." Also see Sanderson, *Post-Haste: A Reply to Peter*; *Peter pursued, or Dr. Heylin Overtaken, Arrested, and Arraigned*.

38. HEH, Hastings MSS, Correspondence, HA 8258. I am grateful to Mary Robertson for making a photocopy of this letter available to me. The text about Lady Eleanor in the sixth (1674) and seventh (1679) editions of Baker's *Chronicle* is the same as that in the fifth edition (1670). Lucy died in 1679.

Part Five

Embodying Culture

13

St. Frideswide and St. Uncumber

CHANGING IMAGES OF FEMALE SAINTS IN RENAISSANCE ENGLAND

Carole Levin

In the later Middle Ages in England a number of female saints were powerful images and examples for women. Stories of these saints' lives, and the shrines to them, gave many women comfort and succor. Shrines to the Virgin Mary were plentiful, but there were other, less well remembered virgin female saints who were also significant. Their virginity proved to be a powerful resource in giving them strength in the various accounts of their lives; for their followers, the image of these virgin saints was also empowering. One was St. Uncumber, a bearded woman saint who gave special comfort to unhappy, ill-used wives, many of whom prayed to her for aid and assistance. Another was St. Frideswide, a patron saint of Oxford who was widely known as a healer, especially of women. Both of these virgin saints were especially appealing to women supplicants, and both had shrines that were destroyed during the Reformation. This destruction of shrines potentially meant less comfort for sixteenth-century women who needed spiritual aid. Some of these saints' aspects were taken over by Elizabeth I during her forty-five year reign. A number of scholars have noted how Elizabeth deliberately appropriated some of the imagery and symbolism of the Virgin Mary as she ruled as Virgin Queen.[1]

Earlier versions of this paper were read at the Patristic, Medieval, and Renaissance Conference at Villanova University and at the Medieval Congress at Kalamazoo. I would like to thank Al Geritz, Karen Robertson, Martha Skeeters, and especially Georgianna Ziegler for their helpful suggestions and the editors of this collection for their careful reading. I am also grateful to the New Paltz Medieval and Renaissance group, Karin Andriolo, Kit French, Dan Kempton, Yu Jin Ko, Todd Quinlan, Pat Sullivan, and Michael Willis, for reading and offering such useful critiques.

1. Particularly useful on this subject are Elkin Calhoun Wilson; Wells; Yates; Roy Strong; and John N. King, *Tudor Royal Iconography*.

S. WILGEFORTIS, *alias* LIBERATA, *quam Belgæ à depellen curis, ONTCOMMERAM nominant, Regis Portug.ª Filia: postq̃ à Xp̃o sponso suo, deformari rogasset, ne ab Amasio ad nuptias expeterẽtur; atq̃ ita subito promissa illi barba excreuisset: pro Xpriana Relig: ac pudicitiæ defensione, Cruci affixa fuit: miraculis hodieq̃ clarissima, Aq̃ hoc inter cætera; quod simulachrum Ipsius Cytharoedi cuiusdam ad mortem damnati, atq̃ ad patrocinium Eius confugientis, Inno: centiam vnius ocreæ argenteæ excussione, declararit. Vide Martyrolog: Rom. et Molan: ad Vsuard.*

P. B. Bouttats. Sculp

S. Wilgefortis or Saint Uncumber. From Rev. S. Baring-Gould, *The Lives of the Saints*. New and revised edition. Edingburgh: John Grant, 1914. Vol. 8, opp. p. 488.

I would argue, however, that in a less conscious and deliberate manner, Elizabeth also represented some of the attributes of other virgin saints, and that during her reign there was a synthesis of medieval and Protestant beliefs that can be examined through a discussion of St. Uncumber and St. Frideswide, two saints who strenuously avoided marriage.[2] Early modern Englishwomen's spirituality in certain respects shifted from medieval models as some aspects of the power of these female saints became associated with Elizabeth, a Protestant female ruler.

A bearded female saint who was worshipped throughout areas of Europe was Wilgeforte, also known in some versions as Kummerniss, Liberata, Livrade, Liberatrix, Ontkommer, or, particularly in England, Uncumber. The legend appears to have had its earliest roots in a story told by Pope Gregory the Great. Scholars agree that her "legends [are] a labyrinth from which there is no exit."[3] Uncumber was the daughter of a pagan king, perhaps of Portugal; her mother was a Christian. Some traditions say she was one of septuplets or even nontuplets—quite a miraculous exploit for her mother, even if she was a Christian. We do not know what happened to the rest of Uncumber's siblings, but very early she decided to dedicate her life to Christianity and vowed to remain a virgin. Her father refused to accept this idea and ordered Uncumber to marry his enemy, the king of Sicily, as part of a peace negotiation.

Desperately Uncumber prayed to Christ for some way to avoid this marriage and keep her vow. Her prayer was answered in a rather bizarre fashion: she immediately grew a long and curly beard. Her father was as stubborn as she was and insisted that the marriage proceed. But when the king of Sicily saw his intended bride at the altar without her veil he not unnaturally refused to go ahead with the ceremony. Uncumber's

2. In some medieval legends, virgin saints avoided unwanted attentions of men by becoming visibly like a male through the miraculous growth of a beard. Rudolf Dekker and Lotte van de Pol say of these women, "These female saints may all be viewed within a single pattern. They broke with their female past; they quarreled with their families; they refused to obey their parents; and they rejected their sexuality" (45). Marie Delcourt also argues that the beard, like wearing men's clothing, suggests renunciation of sex (92).

3. The statement is made by Cuper in the *Acta Sanctorum* and quoted by Agnes Dunbar, II, 303; and Lina Eckenstein, 35. For more on Uncumber, see also Schulenburg, 152–53; Farmer, 437–38; Bullough, 1387; Delcourt, 92; Edwards, 75–82; Brown, 279; Sir Thomas More, *Dialogue*, 667; Dunbar, 302–3; Eckenstein, 35–38; and Baring-Gould, 8 and 488–89. Baring-Gould says of Wilgefortis, "The story of this saint is almost too absurd to be given" (488). See also Dekker and van de Pol, 45, who suggest that the cult was especially popular from the eleventh century onward. For simplicity's sake, I will refer to the saint in the text only as Uncumber, her English name.

father was so furious that his daughter was resisting his will—and in such a grotesque fashion—that he ordered her crucifixion. The date of her death is variously given as July 12, July 20, and October 2 (Baring-Gould, VIII, 488). We might consider the incredible hostility of the father to his daughter. Would he have responded in such a violent manner had the form of her resistance been otherwise? We cannot know, and certainly other pagan parents also treated their Christian daughters dreadfully. One might think of St. Barbara, who was locked in a tower and later martyred by her pagan father for her refusal to give up her faith, as well as Thecla, whose own mother asked that she be burned to death (Farmer, 31 and 399). But the beard does seem to have elicited a particularly brutal response. The subsequent cult of the bearded woman saint that spread through Western Europe is at least suggestive of the female response to the potential power of male anger at a woman's wish for autonomy. Perhaps connected with this concept, in at least some of the legends of Uncumber, she grew the beard not only to avoid her unwanted suitor but also to ward off the incestuous love of her father, a theme that is often mentioned in the legends of early women saints (Eckenstein, 36). Was the choice for some women expressed as either unnatural, coercive sex or no sexual relations at all?

Some historians suggest that the image of the bearded female saint developed from misreadings in the later Middle Ages of images of a bearded, robed Christ, possibly the celebrated crucifix of Lucca, which showed a completely dressed and crowned Christ, the devotion to which was widely extended in the twelfth century (Delehaye, 87–88; Edwards, 77–78; Baring-Gould, VIII, 488; Butler, III, 151). Perhaps, yet this does not explain the tenacity of the image.

One wonders as well if the stories of Uncumber also gave comfort to women in the Middle Ages who had excessive facial hair. Then as now, cultural norms have told women this is unattractive, unnatural, even grotesque. This sense of grotesqueness and gender discomfort echoes through Montaigne's travel journal. In September 1580 he passed through the small town of Vitry-le-François. There he heard three memorable stories. One was about a man, still alive at the time, named Germain. Until the age of twenty-two Germain was a girl named Mary. As a girl she was "noticed because she had a little more hair about her chin than the other girls; and they called her bearded Mary" (Montaigne, 6). One day while Mary was jumping over a stream, male genitalia dropped down, thus making it clear that Mary was actually a man and confirming the belief that women were but men turned outside in. Thereafter, Mary was called Germain. Montaigne reports that he did not actually meet

Germain but heard of a song girls of the town sang, warning one another that they better not stretch their legs too wide apart, or they too might become a "Marie Germain," suddenly, fearfully a male.[4] Marie Germain is so different from a bearded woman saint and so much more immediate. How comforting for a woman with facial hair not only to confront the image of a Marie Germain but also know of the stories of women whose blessing from God was a full beard. Yet to add further to the confusion—to the multiplicity of perspectives—there were not only bearded female saints but also bearded female witches. In *Macbeth* Banquo says of the three weird sisters, "You should be women, / And yet your beards forbid me to interpret / That you are so" (I.iii.45–47). As James Schiffer notes, "the bearded women are *the* emblems of the drama, the play's essence distilled" (206). And transvestitism was one sign of witchcraft, while another was sexual insatiability. This doubling of meaning, of holiness and sin, of sacredness and sexuality, echoes throughout these stories of bearded women. These women are somewhere on the margins, at risk, and a lesson to other women to take care. Lina Eckenstein suggests this as well, "for in Tyrol Kummerniss [one of the names of Uncumber] is venerated as a saint, but the word Kummerniss in ordinary parlance is applied to immoral women" (37).

In some of the visual representations of Uncumber she is seen fully clothed as she is hanging on the cross but with only one shoe on, a golden slipper. Occasionally she is wearing two golden slippers, and below the cross is a young man playing a fiddle. The reason for this representation is that it has also been told of Uncumber that a destitute musician prayed to her statue for aid and she stretched out her foot and threw him one of her golden boots. When it was found on him no one believed his story and he was condemned to be hanged. He begged that once before he died he might be allowed to play in church before the holy statue. As he did so, in the presence of the king and all the people, the saint threw him her other boot and his life was saved (Eckenstein, 36; Dunbar, II, 302–3; Baring-Gould, VIII, 488). One wonders if Uncumber could comfortably relate to a man only when she was a symbol. How generous, and derisive, to toss a man one's shoe, an ironic twist of the old Cinderella story, and one where the woman, as opposed to the prince, is the powerful one.[5]

4. The medical belief held by many in the Renaissance that women were incomplete men and thus could move from less complete to more would have made this story appear much more believable.

5. The story of Cinderella was already well known by the sixteenth century and, in some versions, it was a "poor cinder boy" who was the protagonist of the story (Spence, 207).

The cult of Uncumber was well developed by the fourteenth century, especially in Flanders, France, Bavaria, and England, where there were a number of images of her. These included ones in the church of St. Peter de Parmentegate, Norwich, in the church of St. Mary-le-Port in Bristol, in churches in Norfolk, Worstead, and Boxford, and a statue of her in the Henry VII chapel in Westminster (Farmer, 404; Edwards, 75; Brown, 279; Simpson, 248; *Notes and Queries,* series i, iii, 250; *Notes and Queries,* series iv, vi, 559). Originally people saw Uncumber as a saint who would give people a good death, with no prolonged suffering. In England, however, the death prayed for was someone else's. Women prayed to Uncumber, and brought her wild oats as an offering, if they wished to be rid of their husbands—disencumbered, as it were—and perhaps be able to sow a few wild oats of their own.[6] The pun is actually that of Thomas More. He suggested that "Women hath therfore chaunged her name and in stede of saynt wylgeforte call her saynt Uncumber bycause they reken that for a pecke of otys she wyll not fayle to uncumber theym of theyr housbondys" (227). More added rather scornfully that the oats were to provide evil husbands with horses so that they might ride to the devil. And More had little sympathy for these "pevyshe" women who would pray to St. Uncumber. He argued that their positions would be improved instead "yf them selfe peradventure chaunge theyr comberous toungues" (232). If that does not aid them, "yf they can not be uncombred but by deth," he hoped "yet it may be by theyr owne and so theyr housbondys saufe ynough" (235). Michael Woddes's *Dialogue,* published in 1554, listed a number of saints he considered fraudulent, concluding with "If a wife were weary of her husband, she offred otes at Poules, at London, to St. Uncumber." Woddes adds, "Thus we have been deluded with their images" (cited in Brand, I, 359). And a poem by the Protestant John Bale, probably ironically, offered the advice:

> If ye cannot slepe, [nor] slumber,
> Geve Otes unto Saynt Uncumber. (Bale, 342)

Some scholars suggest that the oats came from a coalescing of the Uncumber legends with that of St. Radegund, the wife of a sixth century French king, Clothaire IV (or Clothacar), who left her husband to live in

6. The concept of a saint to whom one prayed to be rid of one's husband seemed to be so incomprehensible to historian Basil Clarke that he reworked the concept to suggest it was a sort of informal divorce rather than the prayer that a husband would die opportunely (212). The sources he cites, however, do not support his theory.

a cloister. According to legend, once when she was being closely pursued by her husband, a crop of oats sprang up miraculously and concealed her from her followers (Clarke, 212). Adds a Victorian correspondent of *Notes and Queries*, "Besides . . . it is recorded that, as part of her monastic mortifications, she ate barley-bread, some say rye. . . . Hence, also, it may have been presumed that she would not view with disfavour an offering of oats."[7]

During the Reformation the shrines to St. Uncumber were despoiled with many others. In August 1538 Thomas Cromwell sent a message to Lord Mayor of London, Sir Richard Gresham, through Robert Barnes about destroying the images in St. Paul's. Gresham wrote to Cromwell that he had had this undertaken immediately. "In the mornyge I went to Powlles, and ther I dyd see that alle thinges was doon accordyngly" (Great Britain, P.R.O., Gairdner and Brodic, eds., 13, Pt. 2, 81). According to Charles Writothesley's *Chronicle* for 24 August 1538, part of what Gresham had accomplished was "the roode of the north doore in Paules was taken downe . . . and the image of Saint Uncomber also in the same church" (84).

Uncumber was the patron saint of unhappy wives. We might wonder if the despoiling of Uncumber's shrines took away one comfort from abused married women. Did their lives become that much more difficult after the Reformation in England? Both Catholic and Protestant religious writers of the sixteenth century told women to submit patiently to battering. The official homily on marriage, produced by Elizabeth's bishops, argued, for example, that a cruel husband was no excuse for lack of obedience and honor. "If thou lovest him only because he is gentle . . . what reward will God give thee therefor?" asked the homily, and added, "I will exhort the women, that they would patiently bear the sharpness of their husbands. . . . For if we be bound to hold out our left cheek to strangers, which will smite us on the right cheek; how much more ought we to suffer an extreme and unkind husband!" (Griffiths, 431 and 433). One wonders how much more despair these women might have felt once they no longer had Uncumber to give them comfort.[8]

---

7. "St. Uncumber," *Notes and Queries*, series i, iii (1851): 404; "St. Uncumber," *Notes and Queries*, series 2, ix (1860): 164. In today's culture one might almost see Saint Radegund and Saint Uncumber being used as spokeswomen for oat bran! For more on Radegund, see Eckenstein, 51–65.

8. In a private communication Terence Murphy suggested this, arguing that perhaps suicides for unhappily married women increased in England after the Reformation. I am grateful for his helpful comments on Uncumber. On the continent, images of the saint continued to be valued into the nineteenth century. Writing in 1896, Eckenstein comments,

We can get another echo of Uncumber and the beard as a sign of female independence and possible escape from marriage in the interpretation of dreams of the Elizabethan period. A 1576 book, *The moste pleasaunte arte of the interpretacion of dreames,* assured readers that for a married woman to dream that she had a beard meant that she would part from her husband either through separation or death: "And if a woman thinketh in her dreame to have a bearde . . . if she shalbe maryed she shal then lose her husbande, or shall departe from hym and shall governe her huse, lyke as shee were husbande and wyfe." The author also gives a specific example of a woman, "the wyfe of Diognosta," who dreamed that she had half of a beard. After this dream she "lyved seperate from her husband." But if she had dreamed that she had a whole beard, the author insists, she would have "after to be a wydowe" (Hill, n. p.).

The woman in the dream was both "husbande and wyfe." Elizabeth, unmarried ruler, was both "king and queen." Perhaps the example of Elizabeth, who like Uncumber refused to take a husband, was in some ways a replacement for the discredited saint. Elizabeth, despite her many courtships, never married. She never publicly proclaimed her choice as an appropriate one for other women; indeed, the homily on marriage was added to the homilies in 1563 when she had them reestablished. Yet the queen's very example as a woman who refused to marry despite great pressure by her Council and Parliament could well serve as an example to other women whether she intended or not, and may have been the substitute for St. Uncumber, the saint who provided such comfort for women who either did not want to marry, or wanted to end an unhappy marriage. It was Elizabeth, after all, who said, "There is a strong idea in the world that a woman cannot live unless she is married, or at all events that if she refrains from marriage she does so for some bad reason" (Great Britain, P.R.O., *CSP Spain,* I, 409). Elizabeth must have been convinced that she could refrain from marriage for the best of reasons, since she also proclaimed: "I would rather be a beggar and single than a queen and married" (Chamberlain, 61). Thus with the Reformation the lives of these virgin saints were no longer presented as models as before, but with a powerful, unmarried woman ruling, Elizabeth could in some sense replace their need with her own image.

"Images of the saint are preserved and venerated in a great number of churches in Bavaria and the Tyrol, but the ideas popularly associated with them have raised feelings in the Church against their cult. We hear that a Franciscan friar in the beginning of this century destroyed one of the images, and that the bishop of Augsburg in 1833 attempted in one instance to do away with the image and veneration of the saint, but refrained from carrying out his intention, being afraid of the anger of the people" (37).

Certainly with the despoiling of these saints' shrines under Henry VIII there was also in the sixteenth century a Protestant emphasis away from female virginity and an encouraging of marriage. Some of these shrines, or at least the worship, were restored under Mary I. And with the succession of Elizabeth in 1558 there were yet more modifications to the Anglican Settlement and the attitude toward virginity and female sanctity.

But though Elizabeth, Supreme Governor of the Church of England, was Protestant, throughout her reign also echo reverberations of the lives of women's saints, and the fact of the unmarried Elizabeth ruling as Virgin Queen added another level of ambiguity to the dominant ideologies about women promulgated during the latter part of the sixteenth century. Elizabeth continued a number of practices from medieval Catholic tradition, such as washing the feet of the poor on Maundy Thursday, begun by Edward II. Elizabeth, however, washed the feet of poor women; previously, kings had performed this ritual on their male subjects. Elizabeth also continued the royal practice of touching to cure the disease of scrofula, known as the king's evil. But as a queen instead of a king, she invoked comparisons not only to earlier monarchs but also to female virgin-saints whose purity allowed them to cure by touch.[9]

We can ascertain some of the ambivalence toward religious practice and women's roles in sixteenth century England in examining the case of what happened to the shrine—and the bones—of another female saint, Frideswide. Whereas Uncumber, with a beard, parallels the male, kingly side of Elizabeth, and the queen's aversion to marriage, Frideswide, patron saint of Oxford, is an interesting comparison to Elizabeth as a healer.[10]

Frideswide supposedly lived in the late seventh and early eighth centuries.[11] The daughter of Didanus, an underking, she was piously

9. For more on this subject, see Levin, 10–38.

10. For more on Frideswide, see Blair, "Saint Frideswide Reconsidered," 71–101, and *Saint Frideswide*; Butler, IV, 150–51; James Parker, 95–101; Horstmann, 80–82; Stanton, 503–4; Wall, 63–71; Dunbar, I, 327–28; and Christina Hole, 48–49, and 150–51. *Carr's Dictionary of English Queens* is dedicated "to the beautiful Frideswide (c. 755), that young lady, wise beyond her years, who anticipating marriage to a savage bore, similar to many littering these 16 pages, refused queenship, preferring a life of contemplative virginity in a pigsty at Binsey Abbey" (R. D. and J. M. Carr, n. p.).

11. Though H. H. Salter says of her, "When we examine the records about St. Frideswide we find that she certainly existed, which is more than can be said of some saints, for her bones were in one of the parish churches of Oxford, but we have nothing historical to show who she was, when she lived, or what she did. . . . In volumes containing lives of saints we have lives of St. Frideswide, which follow somewhat different patterns, but none of the manuscripts are earlier than the first half of the twelfth century" (4–5). Stenton concurs: "St.

educated and early had a calling for a religious life. Despite her vows King Algar wished to make her his wife because of her beauty and wealth. He threatened to burn down Oxford if Frideswide was not delivered up to him. Frideswide managed to escape, but when he caught her she prayed to St. Catherine and St. Cecilia for aid, and Algar was immediately struck blind. It was Frideswide's own prayerful intervention, once he repented, that restored his sight.

Frideswide founded a monastery and was known for her healing, possibly learned from her abbess/aunt. Her shrine was decorated with delicately carved plants, all of which were known for their healing properties, to demonstrate Frideswide's great gift as a healer. Her most remarkable healing was when a leper conjured her in the name of Christ to kiss him. Despite what was described as his "loathsome condition" and her "fear of infection," Frideswide made the sign of the cross and gave the leper a kiss. "Immediately the scales fell from him, and his flesh came again like that of a child" (Dunbar, I, 328). She was able to cure a fisherman, who was subject to violent fits, perhaps by casting the devils out of him. In some versions she also healed a blind girl, perhaps echoing the blindness and recovery of sight of Algar.

The relics of St. Frideswide, if so indeed they were, were preserved in a beautiful shrine at Oxford in a chapel dedicated to her. During Lent and again on Ascension Day, the chancellor of Oxford and principal members of the University, along with the scholars, came to the shrine in solemn procession proffering gifts. Especially during the twelfth century there were numerous instances of the faithful being miraculously cured after a pilgrimage to her shrine. Of those who came to be cured, women outnumbered men two to one, and many of these diseases had to do with specifically female maladies, including severe pain caused by intercourse or female madness. To give one example: in the late twelfth century a young girl, Emelina of Eddington, sneaked out of her parents' house one night and attempted to drown herself. Rescued, she was brought back home where she then slipped into a state of hysterical numbness. Eventually, at their wits' end, her mother and brother brought her to St. Frideswide's shrine, where, after several days, she was dramatically cured. Emelina decided to stay at the shrine and dedicate her

---

Frideswide is little more than a name . . . unaccompanied by any genuine tradition of incident or personal relationships" (4). The stories that developed about her three or four centuries after her death are "an attempt to give some appearance of substance to one of the most nebulous of English monastic legends" (5). This does not mean, however, that it was not widely believed in in the sixteenth century.

life to the saint rather than to return home. Prayers at St. Frideswide's shrine also cured one knight's daughter of scrofula, which makes the identity of Frideswide with Elizabeth even more powerful. St. Frideswide must have been a well-known saint in medieval England. In "The Miller's Tale" Chaucer has the carpenter call out "Help us, seinte Frydeswyde!" Ruth Cline suggests the choice of this saint was especially appropriate because not only was she a familiar saint, but she was also "a healing saint."[12]

In the later Middle Ages St. Frideswide's shrine was Oxford's richest church, and St. Frideswide's fair, sanctioned by a charter from Henry I, was the most important one in Oxford. The fair received particular attention in 1382 and 1384 because of a dispute between the university and St. Frideswide's priory over jurisdiction. Henry Mayr-Harting argues that Frideswide's shrine enlarged areas of freedom, especially for women, in the later Middle Ages, providing an alternative authority and possibilities for autonomy (202–3).

We find references to the shrine and the saint in the early sixteenth century as well. In 1518 Katherine of Aragon made a pilgrimage to St. Frideswide's shrine, probably to ask for intercession so that she might achieve another successful pregnancy. One can imagine the popularity of St. Frideswide from the fact that some girls were named for her. For example, one of Mary I's ladies of the Privy Chamber was Frideswide Sturley.[13] Pope Clement VII allowed Cardinal Wolsey to dissolve the priory of St. Frideswide in 1525 and Cardinal College was established on its site. In 1546 Henry VIII reestablished the college as Christ Church, and St. Frideswide's church became the college chapel, as well as the cathedral of the new diocese of Oxford. The shrine, however, was destroyed with many others in 1538, though the faithful rescued some of the saint's relics (Dunbar, I, 328; Parker, 99–100; Leyland, 126; Hardy, I, Pt. 1, 462; Stanton, 504; Mayr-Harting, 193–206).

The history of Frideswide's relics becomes more ambiguous in the mid-sixteenth century, and, getting to the heart of this essay, I would suggest, more indicative of the confusion over women's power and na-

12. Cline, "Four Chaucer Saints," 480–82; "The Miller's Tale," ll. 3448–49, in *The Works of Geoffrey Chaucer*. For more on Chaucer's use of Frideswide, see also Cline, "Three Notes on The Miller's Tale," 131–45.

13. Frideswide Sturley was the only one of all Mary's ladies who was honest enough not to pretend that Mary was pregnant when she could tell the queen was not. Mary told her sadly, "I see they all be flatterers, and none true to me but thou" (Anne Somerset, 51, and 57).

ture. The Italian reformer, Peter Martyr Vermigli, who had fled to Zurich and Basel after being accused of heresy, was invited by Archbishop Cranmer to come to England. In 1548 he was appointed to the chair of Regius Professor of Theology at Oxford. He lived in college with his wife Catherine Dummartin (also referred to in some records as Catherine Cathie), a former nun. Catherine was one of the first two women to reside at college, and Peter and Catherine's windows were often broken by papists indignant at a woman's presence, as well as those upset by Peter's views of the Eucharist (*DNB*, XX, 253–55). Early in 1553, Catherine died and was buried in the church near where the shrine had been.

A few months later Edward VI was also dead, and Mary's ascension meant the restoration of Catholicism in England. In January 1556 a commission was given authority by Mary I to hunt out "pestilent heresies" at Cambridge and Oxford. The jurisdiction of the commissioners extended not only over the living but also over the dead. At Cambridge the bodies of Martin Bucer and Paul Fagius were burned posthumously as heretics. At the same time papal legate Cardinal Reginald Pole wrote to the dean of Christ's Church, Oxford, Dr. Marshall, to ask him to restore the devotion to St. Frideswide and punish reformers at Oxford, both living and dead. As part of this restoration, investigation, and punishment, Marshall had the bones of Catherine Martyr exhumed. At first there was some suggestion of having Catherine Martyr tried posthumously, as Bucer and Fagius had been the month before. Then, if found guilty, her bones too would have been burned, a fierce act of purification (Froude, VI, 465–68). The posthumous trial and subsequent destruction of the bones of the heretic was so common in medieval England that bone fires became known as bonfires.[14] Burning was the preferred method for dealing with heretics, whether posthumously or not. As an excruciatingly painful death, it would cause onlookers to reconsider their own actions and beliefs. The fire was also thought to purify the contamination of the heretic in the body politic. Moreover, it also suggested the fate of the heretic soul, condemned to burn in hell fire everlastingly. One could also see the burning of the body as the most extreme punishment possible. Cremation was not allowed, for the faithful believed that with the second coming the bones of the dead would rise again and be made flesh. Thus to

14. *Oxford English Dictionary*, II, 386–87. There are references to the posthumous disgracing of heretic bones as early as about the year 1000 (Wakefield and Evans, 75). One of the most famous people to have his bones exhumed after his death and burned was John Wycliffe. Though Wycliffe died in 1384, it was not until 1428 that this order was carried out (Kenny, 149).

destroy someone's very bones in a sense condemned them for all eternity
(*New Catholic Encyclopedia*, IV, 440; VI, 512; XII, 419).

But the authorities came to believe that they did not have enough
evidence for a trial because Catherine had not herself written about
doctrine, and because witnesses affirmed they could not say what were
her religious views "by reason they understood not her language," as
John Foxe tells us (VIII, 296). Cardinal Pole then suggested that "as
Catherine Cathie, of detestable memory, had called herself the wife of
Peter Martyr, a heretic, although both he and she had before taken vows
of religion; forasmuch as she had lived with him in Oxford in fornication,
and after her death was buried near the sepulchre of the Holy Virgin St.
Frideswide . . . the Dean of the Cathedral [should] cast out the carcase
from holy ground, and deal with it according to his discretion" (Froude,
VI, 468). Marshall decided to have her reburied in the dunghill next to
his stable, as fitting punishment for a nun who had violated her vows to
marry. The bones of Frideswide, if indeed they were hers, were disin-
terred and placed in two silk bags and placed back in the church. The
relics of St. Frideswide were again exalted, though it does not appear
that there was any attempt to rebuild her shrine. With the accession of
Elizabeth and the Anglican Settlement, there were further questions over
what to do about the bones of St. Frideswide and Catherine Martyr. In
1561, as part of the Ecclesiastical Commission, Matthew Parker and
Edmund Grindal inquired into the matter and issued instructions to the
authorities of Christ Church to remedy the scandal done to Catherine's
body: "For though the body being once dead, no great estimation were
to be had, how or where the bones were laid; yet was some reverence to
be used toward her for sex and womanhood sake" (Foxe, VIII, 297).

The subdean, James Calfhill,[15] had his servants again dig up Catherine
Martyr's bones, which were by this time, he stated, quite disjointed. The
bones were brought into the church, and on 11 January 1561/2 there was
a solemn ceremony, and Calfhill preached an oration praising Catherine
for her modesty and good works. Calfhill was known for the breadth of
his scholarship as well as his eloquent and forceful sermons. He described Catherine as "an honest, grave, sober matron, who was a great
helper of the poor," and referred to those who worshipped Frideswide as
"crazy old men." But Calfhill did not want to show disrespect to the

15. For more on Calfhill, see the introduction to James Calfhill, ed. Gibbings, vii–viii;
and *Dictionary of National Biography*, III, 704. Thurston and Attwater argue of Calfhill, "It
would seem he must have been insane with fanaticism," but this hardly seems like an
accurate or unbiased view (Butler, IV, 151).

bones he found in the bags: "Since I hold that nothing less becomes a good man than to copy hateful Popish sacrilege and barbarous cruelty, I was determined on no account to let anything unseemly or insulting be done with them. So I hit upon a scheme by which the bones could be dealt with decently, while at the same time all foolish superstition could be suppressed" (Blair, *Saint Frideswide,* 22). The relics of Frideswide and the bones of Catherine were then commingled.

This strange story is little known today, but it was certainly discussed at the time. Writing later in the century in Paris about the progress and decadence of heretics, Catholic Florimond de Rémond wrote of the indignity done to this celebrated and revered saint (297).[16] Protestants had, obviously, a rather different perspective, and one that demonstrates the fragility of the Anglican Settlement and fears about the future of Protestantism in England. John Foxe was convinced that the procedure was done "that in case any cardinal will be so made hereafter to remove this woman's bones again, it shall be hard for them to discern the bones of her, from the other" (VIII, 297). Writing more than a hundred years later, John Strype's version is more respectful to Frideswide: "For the preventing of any future superstitions with those relics, (and yet that no indecency might be used towards the said saint and foundress's bones,) and withall, for the better securing of this late buried holy woman's bones from being disturbed any more, by the advice of Mr. Calfhill, the bones of both were mixed and put together" (Strype, I, 199). Calfhill informed Grindal that now no one could distinguish the bones of one from the other, and so they were placed in the same coffin (Blair, *Saint Frideswide,* 22).[17] One wonders, despite the supposed honor due to Catherine Martyr, if there might have been an underlying element of contempt in the attitude toward all women—in mixing up her bones with that of a discredited saint. Or, despite some reformers' gibes at saints, it may be a reluctance to let go totally of such a comforting and healing presence that her bones too must be protected by being placed with the good Protestant woman. By mixing the bones, the individuality of each woman is lost. The woman is indistinct as an individual, and the men who control the ceremony are free to generalize about all women. Indeed, what was said about Catherine Martyr is the typical panegyric for the Protestant "good woman." It had little to do with her specifically.

16. A common Catholic perspective on the ceremony was, "Here lies Religion with Superstition." Alban Butler glossed this statement with the comment, "The obvious meaning . . . would lead us to think these men [Calfhill and Grindal] endeavoured to extinguish and bury all religion" (IV, 151).

17. The story also appears in Anthony Wood, I, 329.

And one wonders, too, what these men who commingled these bones thought would happen to either Frideswide or Catherine Martyr at the time of the resurrection, when all would be risen, when the promise is that all who are just will one day be fully redeemed not only in soul but also in body. Would God sort out and separate their bones then, or did it not matter? Had each woman, so different from the other, instead become every woman? In the ceremony run by Calfhill, it is men who are in control, and it is they who are packaging and manipulating the women's bones. But women have been eliminated from direct participation. And shrines of female saints to which women had flocked were now despoiled. In the reign of Elizabeth, it was only one female body, that of the queen herself, that could so directly participate. We have no direct evidence that Elizabeth saw herself as a continuation of such saints as Uncumber and Frideswide, nor that those who thronged for her touch, or who watched her maneuver herself out of being pressured into marriage, were consciously making such a connection. But surely the tradition of the virgin saint as healer would resonate as well for a Virgin Queen who refused to marry and who healed by touch.

The ceremony at the shrine of Frideswide also demonstrates the fragility of the Anglican Settlement in the minds of its leading exponents in the early Elizabethan period. At Elizabeth's coronation only a few years before there had been great uncertainty over what would be the exact nature of the religious settlement of the new reign, and many feared her reign would be brief and further trouble would come to England. Foxe himself foresaw that there might be another time coming when cardinals again would rule England to the cost of the true believers. But perhaps the metaphor of the mixed bones could be read yet another way: that the Anglican Settlement was a mixture of traditions just as Elizabeth herself mixed traditions as the religious leader of her people. The bones of the female saint and the Protestant good woman together became an amalgam and symbol for the mix of rituals and beliefs represented in Elizabethan religion and the way its culture was reproduced.

14

The Reproduction of Culture and the Culture of Reproduction in Elizabeth Clinton's The Countesse of Lincolnes Nurserie

Marilyn Luecke

The *Countesse of Lincolnes Nurserie* (1628) is one of the few written remnants of seventeenth-century women's experience of the female culture of childbirth. It was originally written in 1622 as personal correspondence between female family members; the countess dowager Elizabeth Knevet Clinton addressed it to her daughter-in-law Briget, the countess of Lincoln referred to in the title. Clinton urges maternal breastfeeding in the context of her own history as a mother, claiming that because of her own lack of conscientious consideration, her husband's authority and the social pressures of the Stuart court prevented her from breastfeeding her children. Her urgent plea that her daughter-in-law not capitulate to similar pressures soon extended beyond intimate correspondence. When published in 1628, *The Nurserie* was intended to encourage a larger audience of noblewomen in the Stuart court to put aside the custom of hiring wetnurses in favor of nursing their own children.

If we read *The Countesse of Lincolnes Nurserie* as merely one of numerous defenses of maternal breastfeeding printed in the early seventeenth century, its near reproduction of elements of popular conduct books would lead us to conclude that its only distinction is its female author and its female audience. This, in fact, has been the history of its reception. "T. L.," who wrote the introductory comments for the publication of the text in 1628, positioned it as little more than a celebrity endorsement, featuring Elizabeth Clinton's beauty, nobility, and "ancient honour" as an inspira-

I have greatly benefited from the knowledge and support of Frances E. Dolan, Miami University, Oxford, Ohio.

tion to the rest of society (and praising her brevity). Assumptions about Clinton's aristocratic background still influence our readings of her text. As Margaret Ezell has discussed, there is a certain hesitancy in women's studies about constructing women's history from texts penned by privileged women, especially those who seem to participate intellectually in or benefit economically from patriarchal hierarchies.[1] For this reason, perhaps, *The Nurserie* has received little critical attention; what attention it has received, for the most part, has failed to consider Clinton's more radical notions of women's freedom of conscience.[2]

In response to these assumptions, I will argue that Elizabeth Clinton was one of the most outspoken female proponents of the validity of women's experience in the Stuart period. Although Clinton does borrow both argumentative strategies and "medical knowledge" from male-authored sources, the focus of my analysis will be to consider what happens to discourses of cultural authority when Elizabeth Clinton, motivated to exercise her conscience, speaks them.

The distinctiveness of the *The Nurserie* becomes apparent when it is compared to other seventeenth-century women's texts. Unlike mothers who wrote privately to their children, Clinton is a mother writing for publication to an audience of other women. She neither anticipates her death, seeking to leave a written legacy to her children as Elizabeth Joceline did; nor does she excuse her limitations as a woman, as Dorothy Leigh did.[3] *The Nurserie* differs from controversial texts written by other women as well. Unlike the authors who defended women under female pseudonyms in the pamphlet controversy that raged around the same time, Clinton sought neither to return criticism nor to display her wit by beating men at their rhetorical games.[4] Without this perspective, we can easily misread Clinton when she says she chose to "leave the larger, and

1. For a discussion of the critical response to seventeenth-century aristocratic women authors, see Margaret Ezell, *Writing Women's Literary History,* chap. 1.

2. For example, Travitsky, *Paradise of Women,* 57. Only Charlotte F. Otten, in brief introductory comments in *English Women's Voices,* 181–82, notes Clinton's resistance to her husband's authority.

3. See Elizabeth Joceline, *The Mothers Legacie to Her Unborn Childe* (1624); and Dorothy Leigh, *The Mother's Blessing* (1616). See also, Patricia Crawford, "The Construction and Experience of Maternity," in *Women as Mothers,* edited by Valerie Fildes, 28–29. Mary Beth Rose, in "Where Are the Mothers," 219–314, discusses how other mothers authorize their writing on the condition of their immanent deaths, often limited to audiences of family members. In contrast, Clinton takes a much less costly and more public approach to self-authorization that suggests to me that she has greater confidence in her argument and her right to speak it.

4. See Henderson and McManus, *Half Humankind.*

learneder discourse here . . . unto men of art, and learning" (11–12). There is no contextual indication that she understands herself to be inadequate to the task. Rather, in order to create a rhetorical space for women, she banishes men from *The Nurserie*; she alters the cultural "wisdom" and biblical references she borrows from male-authored texts in light of women's interests. Finally, unlike other devoutly religious women writers, she does not claim her authority to be divine inspiration;[5] her purpose is to assert the authority of her own experience as a wife and mother. In the very first sentence of her text she explains her qualifications: "Because it hath pleased God to blesse me with many children, and so caused me to observe many things falling out to mothers, . . . I thought good to open my minde concerning a speciall matter belonging to all childebearing women."[6]

Clinton's narration of her own history makes *The Nurserie* unique among defenses of maternal breastfeeding. That narrative subordinates her husband's authority, as well as social custom, to her own conscience, reversing the hierarchies that once shaped her decisions. Explaining her failure to breastfeed her own children, she writes:

> it was not for want of will in my selfe, but *partly I was overruled by anothers authority*, and *partly deceived by somes ill counsell, & partly I had not so well considered of my duty in this motherly office*, as since I did, whe[n] it was too late for me to put it in execution. (15–16)

Without discounting her husband's heavy-handed influence in the past, Clinton claims personal responsibility for not having "well considered her duty." Furthermore, she anticipates that her writing will, to some extent, remedy her past mistakes by enabling other women to enter into these considerations on their own terms, as women, wives, and mothers. Elizabeth Clinton's ability to bring her own experience to bear on the collective experience of women—not only aristocratic women like herself, but also middle-class women who aspired to imitate aristocrats and lower-class women who labored as wetnurses—challenged constructions of women in her own century, yet also earns the interest of those of us in women's studies today.

As postmodern readers, our challenge is to read *The Countesse of Lincolnes Nurserie* in the context of seventeenth-century English society in which, contrary to our expectations, the concept of "motherhood" had

---

5. See Mack, "Teaching About Gender," 223–37.
6. Clinton, 1. Clinton gave birth to eighteen babies; nine lived to adulthood.

yet to be defined as an ongoing, "nurturing" relationship with one's own child. Clinton's depiction of motherhood shifts our attention away from pregnancy and childbirth, that is, the womb, to the breast as the site of ideological conflict around contending notions of motherhood in early modern England. Despite recent scholarship aimed at describing a humanist-Protestant "consensus" about the merits of maternal breastfeeding in Stuart England,[7] the very existence of *The Countesse of Lincolnes Nurserie* reveals that women of the Stuart court were no more in agreement about the practice of "motherhood" than their male counterparts. Contradictory views of the female body, condensed and focused in the function of the female breast, constructed conflicting models of maternity that Clinton exposes and subverts. She positions a woman's authority to decide for herself to "nurture" her child by breastfeeding as having significant ramifications for her authority to influence broader issues of "nurture" as childrearing, or, in Clinton's terms, "bringing up" her child.

As Elizabeth Clinton entered young adulthood, wetnursing had become so entrenched in the social customs of the nobility that many women did not consider it a matter of choice.[8] Misogynist medieval theology had idealized women who were dissociated from reproductive activity, often through literal or figurative separation from the breast. The symbolic heroines of this ideal were virgin martyrs, venerated for having transcended their bodies, which were often depicted as mutilated or dismembered.[9] A favorite icon was St. Agatha displaying her breasts, which had been brutally severed from her body. They were later miraculously restored, but only after her virginity was preserved in death.[10] Popular pre-Reformation representations of motherhood as a blessed, nurturing activity also utilized the strategy of separating the spiritualized breast from the material female body. Thus, in the midst of medieval anxiety about women's

7. Margo Todd, *Christian Humanism*, 97 ff.; Kathleen Davies, "Continuity and Change," 58–80; and Crawford, *Women and Religion*, 40–43. Jean Marie Lutes, in "Negotiating Theology and Gynecology," writes, "While Puritan patriarchs exerted tremendous influence on their communities, their authority was not perfectly seamless nor even perfectly unified. Nevertheless, pronouncements from such socially authorized sources set the stage for particular acts of interpretation. They created the shifting ground on which women like Bradstreet slipped and slid their efforts" (311).

8. See Fildes, *Breasts, Bottles, and Babies*, 48. For a fuller discussion of what is known and understood about breastfeeding in the period, see R. V. Schnucker, "The English Puritans and Pregnancy," 637–58; Hilda Smith, "Gynecology and Ideology in Seventeenth-Century England," 97–114; and Adrian Wilson, "Participant or Patient?" 129–44.

9. See Ruether, 159.

10. See Schulenberg, 61. There are other positive associations of the breast with sanctity which I did not have space to consider in this article. Elaine Hobby writes in *Virtue of*

bodies, we find numerous icons of the "new Eve," the Virgin Mary, breast exposed, positioned to nourish her son and, symbolically, the faithful as well. Yet as a model of motherhood, Mary presents women with an impossible ideal; she represents all that woman cannot physically achieve (Warner, 193).

These attitudes supported entrenched "knowledges" about the female breast that were only beginning to be challenged in the seventeenth century.[11] Although Protestant doctrine enthusiastically heralded motherhood as the sole redemptive vocation for women,[12] Eve's curse remained a lingering taint on attitudes toward the fluids associated with reproduction, including breast milk. Menstruation was understood to be the passing of unclean blood, a voiding like other excremental functions. The filthy waste products of menstruation nourished the fetus *in utero* and after birth were transformed into "whitened blood," as seventeenth-century physician James Guillimeau calls breast milk. He counsels that a mother should not breastfeed for at least eight days after birth "because she is not as yet well cleans'd and purified of her afterpurgings" which might contaminate the milk (10). As a result, nurture, whether in the womb or through mother's milk, was conflated with pollution and carried with it the possibility of infecting both body and character.[13]

Belonging to a family of the "stricter sort" of Protestantism,[14] Clinton adopts humanist arguments that privileged nature as a reflection of God's

---

Necessity (42) that references to God as nursing mother are "commonplaces" in religious writings of the period. Furthermore, men of Clinton's acquaintance assume the divine image of nurturer for themselves. King James I refers to himself as the "nursing father" of his kingdom as noted by Debora Shuger in *Habits of Thought in the English Renaissance* (228), while John Cotton, minister of the Lincolnshire parish before migrating to New England, figures the act of preaching as "nursing" the congregation with the Word of God (Edward Davidson, 131). The fact that men would co-opt this feminine function suggests that breastfeeding was a powerful image, but Clinton refrains from associating herself with divine or masculine images of authority, perhaps in order to better establish women's experiential authority.

11. Laurent Joubert, *Popular Errors* (1579), is a notable example of the effort to popularize new knowledges in medicine.

12. Crawford, *Women and Religion*, 38 ff.; Margaret Olofson Thickstun, in *Fictions of the Feminine*, exposes the contradictions in this construction of the "new mother."

13. My understanding of the "ideology" of the breast is informed by Gail Kern Paster, *The Body Embarrassed*.

14. Although I must be cautious in assigning the term *Puritan* to Elizabeth Clinton's arguments (see note 8), it is much more clearly appropriate to Clinton family members who were among those Puritan "pilgrims" who founded the Massachusetts colony as a refuge for the "godly." Daughter Arabella and her husband sailed with John Winthrop to the Massachusetts Bay in 1629. Also aboard ship were John Cotton, the Clinton family pastor; Thomas Dudley, the Clinton's steward; and Dudley's daughter, poet Anne Bradsteet, who

original plan over the corruption exhibited in human society. This recourse to nature enables Clinton to expose and subvert the intensely artificial "customs" of the Stuart court. Her concept of motherhood depends on the reassertion of the "natural" continuity of the processes of conception, childbirth, and lactation: that is, in the midst of strategies that severed the breast from the female body, she figuratively reconnects the breast to the female reproductive body, its functions and fluids. She challenged the assumption that breast milk was polluted or polluting, emphasizing instead the continuity of nurture of the child from womb to breast, and by extension, the wholesome nature of mother's milk. Depicting babies as women's "own natural fruit, borne so neare their breasts, and fed in their owne wombes" (11), Clinton rhetorically reverses the sites of bearing and feeding, conflating their functions. Even if the quality of the milk of a wetnurse could be guaranteed, it was foreign to the newborn. The baby's health is secured by the continuous availability of the mother's fluids. By overturning centuries of cultural discourse separating the nurturing breast from the childbearing female body, these arguments establish motherhood within an optimistic view of the redemption of women.

Clinton points to the female body for evidence of "natural" processes. She positions the mother's desire to breastfeed as a natural instinct, instilled by divine providence, which "*so worketh in the very nature of mothers* . . . by his secret operation . . . [that] the mothers affection is so knit by natures law to her tender babe, as she findes no power to deny to suckle it, no not when shee is in hazard to lose her owne life" (8). Clinton may well be thinking of the lactating mother's physiological reaction to the cry of a child; her milk "lets down," or flows automatically, anticipating the sucking of the baby. The sensation of the milk being drawn from the inner breast to the nipple may also be what Dorothy Leigh is thinking of when she describes feeling blood coming from her heart to nourish her baby (Leigh, 10). Such powerful experiences of the authority of the woman's body, the demand to nurse, conflate the physical and affective and can make both seem equally "natural."

---

with her husband Simon was raised in the Clinton household. See Anne Bradstreet, *Works,* ed. Jeannine Hensley, 244 ff. In "The *Countesse of Lincolne's Nurseries* as Inspiration for Anne Bradstreet," 364–65, Virginia Brackett more fully suggests the influence of Elizabeth Clinton on Anne Bradstreet. Jean Marie Lutes also notes the relationship in note 18 of "Negotiating Theology and Gynecology." A second Clinton daughter, Susan Humphrey, immigrated to Massachusetts in 1635. For biographical notes, see also Fildes, 99; and Mahl and Koon, eds., *Female Spectator,* 88–89.

Clinton's arguments return again and again to the "natural" experience of maternal affection. Although Clinton, like her male counterparts, regularly refers to maternal breastfeeding as a duty, she also defends it as a right and a privilege. In claiming that Eve nursed "not only of meere necessitie, because yet no other woman was created; but especially because shee was their mother, and so sawe it was her duty: and because shee had a true naturall affection, which moved her to doe it gladly" (3), Clinton privileges affection over duty, the nurturing relationship over the "necessitie" of nourishment. To this end, she warns women about being mere "step-mothers" (3), sharing the affections of their children with the wetnurse who forms the nursing bond.

Her conflation of the natural, the physical, and the affective into the primacy of the mother-child bond is compelling. On the basis of these arguments, Clinton constructs an alternate narrative of women's bodies: God wills "younger women to marry, and to *Beare* children, that is, not only to *Beare* them in the wombe, and to bring the[m] forth, but also to *Beare* them on their knee, in their armes, and at their breasts: for this *Bearing* a little before is called nourishing, and bringing up" (6). The rhetorical play on the word *bearing* connects marriage and conjugal relations to conception and childbirth, and then conflates the various parts of the body—knee, arm, breast—in the continuing natural process of reproduction that is "bringing up" or nurturing children. Thus, the new mother is not only redeemed by breastfeeding; she is also empowered.

In this way, although Clinton shares many arguments with her male peers, the impact is significantly different. Valerie Fildes, in her overview of conduct books on maternal breastfeeding, notes that seventeenth-century authors focused on the benefits of nursing for the child, whereas eighteenth-century authors focused on the health of the mother (114). Clinton develops her own position, stressing the satisfaction of the mother in the appropriate care of her child—satisfaction in both the preservation of her child from the dangers inherent in the practice of wetnursing and satisfaction in the mother-child bond itself. This bond empowers women to extend the "nurture" of their children beyond providing nourishment through breastmilk into an ongoing relationship of childrearing, authorized by maternal affection. In this narrative, the husband is not the arbiter of value; indeed, he is absent altogether.

However a woman might understand the duties and privileges of motherhood, as Clinton herself had experienced, her choice to breastfeed could ultimately be superceded by her husband's authority. In the emerging capitalist mindset, the breast itself figures as part of the family capital, "common goods," controlled by the male head of the household.

According to Robert Cleaver's 1598 treatise, a woman is given breasts "to be of help to her husband" (sig. [P5ʳ]). Because they are his possession, he determines their use. As William Gouge and other advocates of maternal breastfeeding admitted, "Husbands for the most part are the cause that their wives nurse not their own children" (Gouge, 87).

Clinton criticizes those fathers who place "conjugal duty" over their wives' duties as nurturing mothers. Early-modern physician Laurent Joubert, in his widely circulated text *Popular Errors*, locates the problem in domestic conflicts such as household conditions where nursing children shared bedrooms with their mothers: "some husbands do not want to put up with the noise and racket the children often make." Other husbands, according to Joubert, "hate the smell of milk on their wives' bosoms" (200–201). Whatever the excuse, the lactating breast physically interrupts erotic relations with evidence of woman as mother. This could prove distasteful for the husband, especially if he subscribed to the courtly privileging of the erotic and aesthetic over the maternal and nurturing, which insisted that he should have freest access to his wife's breasts. Joubert notes: "There are also some husbands who do not wish to allow their wives to nurse so that their breasts will not sag but stay prettier, the way they want them for caressing" (200)—and presumably for whatever degree of exposure fashion dictated in the court.

For this reason, male-authored seventeenth-century advice books, while speaking to, and often scolding, the wife are in fact directed at convincing the husband to allow his wife to nurse their children. Arguments that were originally aimed at convincing women were rhetorically refigured to appeal to men. For example, the argument that continuing the process of childbirth through lactation was good for the mother's health or the child's well-being is reformulated to appeal to the father. A promise to the Old Testament patriarch Joseph that his wives will nurse his children—"as it is a blessing to have children of a true lawfull wife; so to have those children nursed of the same wife their mother"—settles the argument for continuity of the maternal relationship in favor of a seventeenth-century husband's sense of authority.[15]

This privileging of paternal authority contradicted the notions of "motherhood" Clinton espoused. Although humanist theories successfully recombined the womb and the breast as part of the same natural

---

15. Gouge, 508. Clinton engages in this rhetorical contest as well. In *The Nurserie*, the traditional references to biblical characters Sarah, Hannah, and Mary as women whose sons were indebted to their mothers for nursing them become models for women's character and agency.

process of reproduction that authorized a "nurturing" motherhood, they were less successful in forming a consensus around the notion of "nurture" itself. Humanist theories that the child is a *tabula rasa*, unspoiled at birth and easily molded by the appropriate influence, collided with anxieties about "spoiling" children prevalent in English culture even before the Renaissance.[16] This anxiety about childrearing permeates advice books, which seek to formulate a balance between extreme affection—"The extreme in the excess is too much *doting* upon children: as they doe who unmeasurably love them, as they make reckoning of nothing in comparison of children"—and harsh discipline that would "provoke . . . children to wrath" (Gouge, 500).

Theoretically, the affection of either parent was feared to so soften the child that he/she would not adapt successfully to adulthood. Maternal affection was especially feared as intemperate and potentially overwhelming. Many women internalized this anxiety about unbounded maternal affection. Dorothy Leigh admitted: "every man knows that the love of a mother to her children is hardly contained within the bounds of reason" (11). Cultural fears that maternal affection threatened social order came to fruition in Anne Hutchinson's heresy trial. Hutchinson was accused of having so bound her children to her through affection that they were misled into defending her against the church court.[17]

Patriarchy characteristically asserted its control of maternal affection in the name of both love and reason. Familial hierarchies, authorized by biblical precedents and custom, as well as notions of the more rational nature of men, privileged the father as parent. For example, Gouge enumerates his "duties of parents" in ways that invite the gendering of various aspects of childrearing:

1. To *nourish* children, namely with food, apparrell, and other like necessaries. . . .
2. To *nurture* them, namely with good discipline. (Gouge, 497)

So dividing the function of "nourishing" (as the provision of necessary food) from the fuller act of "nurturing" (as childrearing) marginalizes the nursing bond and limits maternal authority. This formulation of "nurture" as the father's responsibility and prerogative is consistent thoughout the male-authored advice books of the period. Although it was deemed

16. See Schucking, 72.
17. For Anne Hutchinson's story, see David D. Hall, 369. See also Mary Beth Rose, "Where Are the Mothers," 291–314, for further discussion of the fear of maternal influence.

appropriate for mothers to interact with small children of nursery age, fathers were warned to counter the influence of a mother's "indulgence" as the child grew older.[18] The patriarchal ideal held that just as the wife functioned as "helpmeet," so too should the mother: "she holds not his hand from due strokes, but bares their skins with delight, to his fatherly stripes"—so urged Daniel Rogers in his 1642 treatise (299). This vivid picture depicts not only the proper nurture/discipline of the child, but perhaps even more vividly, subordination of the mother to paternal authority, and her complicity in it.

In this context, Clinton's privileging of maternal affection is an unusual and potentially radical claim for women's authority and responsibility. Clinton qualifies the value of obedience to one's husband through reference to her own experience. After confessing her fear that two of her children died because of the poor care of a wetnurse, Clinton questions her own and other mothers' responsibility for such deaths: "divers [mothers] have had their children miscarry in the nurses hands, and are such mothers (if it were by the nurses carelessnesse) guiltless?" (18)

There were counterindications in the culture that pricked a woman's uneasy conscience. Oft-repeated humanist theory suggested models for maternity in the providential instincts of animals, which were assumed to preserve and nourish offspring even at the jeopardy of mothers' lives. By comparison, mothers who deserted their children by not breastfeeding them were described in terms of seventeenth-century monsters: "more savage than the Dragons, and as cruell to their little ones as the Ostriches."[19] Like other humanists, Guillimeau dramatizes the plight of the newborn who "cries and moanes, thereby to shew, in what need he stands of helpe. He craves and demands the secour of his owne Mother to be nourisht and fed, otherwise hee would dye in a short space" ("To the Reader," n.p.). Failure to nurse was equated with abandonment of the child.

To further complicate the situation for women, advice books insisted that it was a wife's duty to convince her husband to allow her to breastfeed: "Because it is a bounden duty, wives must use all the meanes they can by themselves or others to persuade their husbands to let them perform it" (Gouge, 516). We can only speculate what kind of influence a wife might legitimately exercise. It was generally agreed that it was better for a wife to be less capable than her husband, so that her knowledge might

18. See Koehler, 123.

19. Clinton, 8. See Dolan, 149–50, for discussion of this image in other texts about motherhood.

not be a burden. On the other hand, because her talents and insights were God-given, they must be used to assist her husband.[20]

At the same time, there was very real anxiety about how a wife might choose to influence her husband, given the chance. Gouge abruptly interrupts his encouragement to warn: "[wives] must take heede that they make this not a pretext to cover their own sloth" (517). But finally, unable to settle the contradiction between judicious counsel and submission, Gouge privileges the husband's authority: "if their husbands will stand upon their authority, and be perswaded by no means to the contrary, they must be meere patients in suffering the childe to be taken away" (516). Patriarchal reassurance addressed questions of women's conscience by locating the ultimate authority of husbands in hierarchy or status, rather than righteousness or reason. Gouge writes: "Tho an husband in regard of evil qualities may carry the image of the devil, yet in regard of his place and office, he beareth the image of God" (275). Historian John Morgan explains the ramifications of this contradiction: "Thus William Gouge could emphasize the primacy of a woman's obligation to obey God, but imply that in practice her duty was first to her husband, regardless of his religious state" (*Godly Learning*, 144). In theory, despite her own moral preference, a woman could—and should—rest easy in her conscience if she had conformed in obedience to her husband's will. Although Clinton submitted to the conventional wisdom of obeying her husband's wishes, conventional reassurances did not afford her peace of mind. She describes her regret at failing to resist her husband's will: "whe[n] it was too late for me to put it in execution . . . [I was] priced in hart for my undutifullnesse, this way I studie to redeeme my peace, first by *repentance* towards God, humbly and often craving his pardon for this my offence" (16). In Clinton's conscience, the obligations of duty have shifted from husband to child.

Clinton contests the husband's role as final arbiter because of her own experience. The deaths of her two babies weighed heavily on her, and she felt her relationships with her surviving children had been damaged by the lack of the nursing bond (Clinton, 16). She cuts to the heart of the contradictions: "Oh, what peace can there be to these women's consciences, unlesse through the darknes of their understanding they judge it as no disobedience" (2). Clinton argues that women find "peace" when they can understand their own choices, their own actions, as obedience to a righteousness greater than their husbands' authority. Thus maternal nursing becomes an urgent occasion for the independent exer-

20. See Todd, *Christian Humanism*, 105.

cise of women's conscience, however improbable that might seem. Her call to women—"Wee have followed *Eve* in transgression, let us follow her in obedience" (19)—is, paradoxically, nothing less than a radical call for wifely disobedience.

This remarkable move, privileging obedience to personal conscience over obedience to husband's authority, leaves us wondering whether Clinton believed that she could have changed her husband's mind with the right arguments and persistance, or that she should simply have chosen to disobey him. She assumes responsibility for her own earlier misjudgments, attributing them to her failure to consider her decision seriously. To redress her wrongs, she arms other women with the arguments that might inform their consciences and convince their husbands; and as Gouge had encouraged, she urges them to argue persuasively. She hopes to educate women to view this choice as an act of obedience, even if their husbands oppose them: If women face a choice between "divided duties," Clinton reorders those duties, placing "motherhood," that is, duty to nature, to children, to personal conscience, first.

The relationship of Elizabeth Clinton to the marginalization of "motherhood" that accompanied the rise of the market economy is complex, as is our relationship to her. The postmodern reader is understandably uncomfortable with her privileging of motherhood over other occupations, as well as her dependence on arguments from nature. Postmodern readers have the benefit of hindsight—sentimentality about the mother-child bond and arguments from biological necessity supported by humanist theories eventually contained women within constructions of motherhood. On the other hand, as Clinton argues, the nurturing activities of motherhood are not valueless in themselves; it was, in part, by degrading the nurturing activities of mothers that the new economy confined women.[21]

Asserting the need for women to take responsibility for themselves, Clinton implicates women's choices in what she sees as a deterioration of their status. She seems to have grasped the consequences of both the removal of aristocratic women from participation in productive activity and its parallel, the privatization of the domestic.[22] She depicts her world, the Stuart court, as one in which the maternal or lactating breast was at odds with the sexualized breast, in which the court had considerably more interest. An example is her condemnation of women's acquiescence to the standards of "fashion" that compromised the female breast. For a

21. My understanding is indebted to Susan Cahn, *Industry of Devotion*.
22. See Crawford, "Construction," in *Women as Mothers*, ed. Fildes, 14.

short time around 1610, it became fashionable to expose the breasts completely, using rouges to set off the nipples against artificially whitened skin (Paster, 205). Less shocking styles such as the closely fitted Stuart gown simultanously displayed and constricted the breast. Such fashions symbolically reproduced conflicts regarding the availability of the breast, conflicts Clinton construes as between the husband and the infant. These garments display the breast for men's erotic pleasure, yet, given aristocratic preference for hired wetnurses, withhold the breast from the sucking infant, who is also banished to a wetnurse's home.

Fashion impinged on breastfeeding in more practical ways. Closely fitted gowns may have been the cause of many reported cases of inverted nipples which inhibited breastfeeding (Fildes, *Breasts*, 102). Clinton scolds women for worrying about "spoiling" their gowns with leaking breast milk. She also notes that women avoid breastfeeding because it "makes one look old." She disparages such concerns as "idleness," "foolish finenesse," and "pride" (13). Historian Valerie Fildes corraborates Clinton's insights with evidence of a fashionable "snobbishness" on the part of wealthy women excusing themselves from the labor of childrearing (203).

It is difficult to assess the personal freedom hiring a wetnurse might afford a woman. Should we sympathize with those women whom Clinton scolds for choosing "idleness" and the freedom to "gad about?" It seems that for women who complained that they did not have freedom of choice in marriage (Clinton, 14), the choice not to nurse might be an exercise of some agency. Furthermore, nursing is a demanding activity, or in Clinton's terms has always been "hard" and inspired "many doubts" (15).[23] Even in a household with servants to care for the baby, the nursing mother must be available to the child at all times. In contrast, the hired wetnurse took over all the duties of raising the child, in many cases even removing the child from the family home into her own, thus according mothers freedom. Nevertheless, Clinton invites her readers to consider the costs of this freedom in terms of authority, influence, and pleasure.

Clinton's assertion of class responsibility leads her toward a materialist analysis of the impact of the emergent market economy on both women and children. What I find so interesting about Clinton is that although she offers herself and her daughter-in-law as members of the "higher sort," she does so in full awareness of both the opportunities and

---

23. An example of women's consciousness of the "pain" of breastfeeding can be found in Anne Bradstreet's poetry in which she honors her mother's as well as her own "sacrifices" in nurturing their children. See Lutes, 325, and Ross W. Beales' "Anne Bradstreet and Her Children," n. 13.

the complexities class brings to the situation. She knowingly trades on her celebrity status in order to have her message heard; but she also confesses her own failings, focusing honor and attention on her daughter-in-law, who finally succeeded in nursing her own children, as an "example" to others. She upbraids the conventionality and privilege on the basis of which her peers excuse themselves from the physical labor of breastfeeding, insisting instead that "wee have more helpes to performe it, and have fewer probable reasons to alleage against it, then women that live by hard labour, & painfull toile" (11).

Wetnursing was becoming an industry, a situation that caused Clinton to distrust those who would sell breast milk. She warns other mothers: "trust not other women, whom *wages hyres* to doe it ... [because] I have found by grievous experience, such dissembling in nurses" (17–18). On the other hand, she speaks to the disruption of families, of both the wealthy and the poor: "bee not accessary to that disorder of causing a poorer woman to banish her owne infant, for the entertaining of a richer womans child, as it were, bidding her unlove her owne to love yours" (19). She argues that "nursing for pay" potentially alienates both women and children from the nurturing aspects of the nursing bond. She is consistently concerned for the welfare of all the children involved.

Moreover, Clinton is concerned about the example that the nobility is setting for the growing middle class: "some nice and prowd idle dames, who will imitate their betters, till they make their own poor husbands beggars. And this is one hurt which the better rank doe by their ill example; egge, and imbolden the lower ones to follow them to their losse" (11). In the medieval economy, middle-class women justified hiring wetnurses in order to free themselves to continue their essential work in family businesses (Fildes, *Breasts*, 98). In a very different context, the middle class of the seventeenth century hired a wetnurse so the mother could be idle as a display of the family's wealth (Cahn, 176–77). Clinton, who consistently deplored idleness in the rich, resists its adoption by the middle class.

Clinton intervened in the definition of motherhood by reconnecting nourishing and nurturing, the breast to the reproductive female body, in order to create a space for women to exercise their consciences and influence the upbringing of their children. Ultimately, she finds her own peace and agency in writing this text, rhetorically creating the possibility of the resistance to her husband's will that she did not enact. She redeems her past through an imagined future in which Briget will nurse her children, Clinton's grandchildren, and Clinton will "prevent many christian mothers from sining in the same kinde" (16). Her model, Briget the early modern "supermom," remained in her position at court, demonstrating that breastfeeding was not necessarily a "private" function, nor one that inevitably withdrew women from public life. As a noblewoman publicly performing "domestic labor," Briget subverted notions of nursing as a poor women's industry, valuing nurture as an exercise of agency in the household and influence within larger society. Clinton urged mothers to seek dignity and autonomy in their own lives by becoming "natural" advocates of justice for children in a period that had not yet defined the mother or child as a separate legal entity, let alone protected by law. Clinton's own authorial agency anticipates the possibility of a woman's public voice that is powerful enough to recast wifely disobedience as maternal authority by articulating women's ways of knowing.

Works Cited

Index

Works Cited

Agrippa, Heinrich Cornelius. *De nobilitate et praecellentia foeminei sexus*. Antwerp, 1529.

Akrigg, G. P. V. *Jacobean Pageant or the Court of King James I*. Cambridge, Mass.: Harvard Univ. Press, 1962.

Amussen, Susan Dwyer. "Elizabeth I and Alice Balstone: Gender, Class, and the Exceptional Woman in Early Modern England." In *Attending to Women in Early Modern England*, edited by Betty S. Travitsky and Adele F. Seeff, 219–40. Newark: Univ. of Delaware Press, 1994.

——. *An Ordered Society: Gender and Class in Early Modern England*. Oxford: Basil Blackwell, 1988.

Anderson, Bonnie S., and Judith P. Zinsser. *A History of Their Own: Women in Europe from Prehistory to the Present*. Vol. 1. New York: Harper and Row, 1989.

Anger, Jane. *Iane Anger her Protection for VVomen*. London, 1589.

Archer, Ian W. *The Pursuit of Stability: Social Relations in Elizabethan London*. Cambridge: Cambridge Univ. Press, 1991.

Aristotle. *The Politics*. Vol. 1, edited and translated by Sir Ernest Barker. Oxford: Oxford Univ. Press, 1948.

Armstrong, M. H. *The Casket Letters: A Solution to the Mystery of Mary Queen of Scots and the Murder of Darnley*. Washington, D.C.: Univ. Press and the Community College Press, 1965.

Ascham, Roger. "The Scholemaster (1570)." In *English Works: Toxophilus, Report of the Affaires and State of Germany, The Scholemaster*, edited by William Aldis Wright. Cambridge: Cambridge Univ. Press, 1904.

Askew, Anne. *Examinations*, edited by Elaine Beilin. Women Writers in English 1350–1850. New York: Oxford Univ. Press, 1997.

Audeley, Eleanor Davies. See Davies, Eleanor.

Aylmer, John. *An Harborowe for Faithfull and Trewe Subjectes, Agaynst the Late Blowne Blaste, Concerning the Government of Women, Wherein be Confuted All Such Reasons as a Straunger of Late Made in that Behalfe with a Breife Exhortation to Obedience*. Strasborowe, 1559.

Babington, Gervase. *A Profitable Exposition of the Lords Prayer*. London, 1588.

——. "To the Right Honorable, and vertuous Ladie, the Ladie, Marie, countesse of Penbrooke." *A Brief Conference betwixt mans Frailtie and Faith*. London, 1584.

Bainton, Roland. *Women of the Reformation in France and England.* 1973. Reprint. Boston: Beacon, 1975.

Baker, Richard. *Chronicle of the Kings of England.* 3d ed. London, 1660.

———. *Chronicle of the Kings of England.* 4th ed. London, 1665.

———. *Chronicle of the Kings of England.* 5th ed. London, 1670.

———. *Chronicle of the Kings of England.* 6th ed. London, 1674.

———. *Chronicle of the Kings of England.* 7th ed. London, 1679.

Baldwin, T. W. *William Shakspere's small Latine and lesse Greeke.* 2 vols. Urbana: Univ. of Illinois Press, 1944.

Barash, Carol. *English Women's Poetry, 1649–1714: Politics, Community, and Linguistic Authority.* Oxford: Clarendon, 1996.

Barbaro, Francesco. "On Wifely Duties." Translated by Benjamin G. Kohl. In *The Earthly Republic: Italian Humanists on Government and Society,* edited by B. G. Kohl and R. E. Witt, with E. B. Welles, 189–228. Philadelphia: Univ. of Pennsylvania Press, 1978.

Baring-Gould, S. *The Lives of the Saints.* New and revised edition. Vol. 8. Edinburgh: John Grant, 1914.

Barrell, John. *Poetry, Language, and Politics.* Manchester: Manchester Univ. Press, 1988.

Barroll, Leeds. "Looking for Patrons." In *Aemilia Lanyer: Gender, Genre, and the Canon,* edited by Marshall Grossman, 29–48. Lexington: Univ. of Kentucky Press, 1998.

Bassnett, Susan. *Elizabeth I: A Feminist Perspective.* New York: St. Martin's, 1988.

Beal, Peter. *In Praise of Scribes: Manuscripts and Their Makers in Seventeenth-Century England.* Oxford: Clarendon Press, 1998.

Beales, Ross W. "Anne Bradstreet and Her Children." In *Regulated Children/Liberated Children: Education in Psychohistorical Perspective,* edited by Barbara Finkelstein, 10–23. New York: Psychohistory Press, 1979.

———. Private correspondence, 20 Dec. 1998.

Beilin, Elaine V. "Anne Dowriche." In *Sixteenth-Century British Non-Dramatic Writers,* fourth series, edited by David A. Richardson, 79–95. Dictionary of Literary Biography, vol. 172. Detroit: Bruccoli Clark Layman, 1996.

———. *Redeeming Eve: Women Writers of the English Renaissance.* Princeton: Princeton Univ. Press, 1987.

———. "Writing Public Poetry: Humanism and the Woman Writer." *Modern Language Quarterly* 51, no. 2 (1990): 249–71.

Bell, Ilona. *Elizabethan Women and the Poetry of Courtship.* Cambridge: Cambridge Univ. Press, 1998.

Bell, Maureen, George Parfitt, and Simon Shepherd. *A Biographical Dictionary of English Women Writers 1580–1720.* Boston: G. K. Hall, 1990.

Belsey, Catherine. "Constructing the Subject: Deconstructing the Text." In *Feminist Criticism and Social Change: Sex, Class, and Race in Literature and Culture,* edited by Judith Newton and Deborah Rosenfelt, 45–64. New York: Methuen, 1985.

———. *The Subject of Tragedy: Identity and Difference in Renaissance Drama.* London: Methuen, 1985.

Benson, Pamela Joseph. *The Invention of the Renaissance Woman: The Challenge of Female Independence in the Literature and Thought of Italy and England.* University Park: Pennsylvania State University Press, 1992.

Bergeron, David. "Women as Patrons of English Renaissance Drama." In *Patronage in the Renaissance,* edited by Guy Fitch Lytle and Stephen Orgel, 274–90. Princeton, N.J.: Princeton Univ. Press, 1981.

Bernard-Cheyre, Catherine. *La Femme au Temps de Shakespeare.* Paris: Stock/ Laurence Pernoud, 1988.

Berry, Boyd. " 'Pardon . . . though I have digrest': Digression as Style in 'Salve Deus Rex Judaeorum.' " In *Aemilia Lanyer: Gender, Genre, and the Canon,* edited by Marshall Grossman, 212–33. Lexington: Univ. of Kentucky Press, 1998.

Bèze, Théodore de. *The Psalmes of David, truly opened and explaned by paraphrasis, according to the right sense of everie Psalme.* Translated by Anthony Gilby. London, 1581.

Birch, Thomas. *The Court and Times of Charles the First; Illustrated by Authentic and Confidential Letters, from Various Public and Private Collections. . . .* London, 1848.

Blain, Virginia, Isobel Grundy, and Patricia Clements, eds. *The Feminist Companion to English Literature: Women Writers from the Middle Ages to the Present.* New Haven: Yale Univ. Press, 1990.

Blair, John. *Saint Frideswide: Patron Saint of Oxford.* Oxford: Perpetua, 1988.
———. "Saint Frideswide Reconsidered." *Oxoniensia* 52 (1987): 71–101.

Blayney, Peter W. M. "The Numbers Game: Appraising the Revised *STC.*" *Papers of the Bibliographical Society of America* 88, no. 3 (1994): 353–407.

Blissett, William. "Caves, Labyrinths, and *The Faerie Queene.*" In *Unfolded Tales: Essays on Renaissance Romance,* edited by George M. Logan and Gordon Teskey, 281–311. Ithaca, N.Y.: Cornell Univ. Press, 1989.

Bone, Quentin. *Henrietta Maria: Queen of the Cavaliers.* Urbana: Univ. of Illinois Press, 1972.

Borstein, Diane, ed. *Distaves and Dames: Renaissance Treatises for and about Women.* Delmar, N.Y.: Scholars' Facsimiles and Reprints, 1978.

Borzello, Frances. *Seeing Ourselves: Women's Self-Portraits.* New York: Harry N. Abrams, 1998.

Brackett, Virginia. "The *Countesse of Lincolne's Nurserie* as an Inspiration for Anne Bradstreet." *Notes and Queries* 42, no. 3 (1995): 364–65.

Bradbrook, Muriel. Review of Betty Travitsky, ed., *The Paradise of Women. Tulsa Studies in Women's Literature* 1 (1982): 89–93.

Bradstreet, Anne. *Works,* edited by Jeannine Hensley. Cambridge, Mass.: Belknap, 1967.

Brand, John. *Observations on the Popular Antiquities of Great Britain.* Arranged, revised, and enlarged by Henry Ellis. 3 vols. London: George Bell and Sons, 1908.

Brant, Clare, and Diane Purkiss, eds. *Women, Texts, and Histories 1575–1760.* New York: Routledge, 1992.

Brennan, Michael. *Literary Patronage in the English Renaissance: The Pembroke Family.* London: Routledge, 1988.

Breton, Nicholas. *The Praise of Vertuous Ladies.* Published in *The Will of Wit.* London, 1597.

———. *The Works in Verse and Prose of Nicholas Breton,* edited by Alexander Grosart. 2 vols. 1879. Reprint. New York: AMS, 1966.

Brose, Margaret. "Petrarch's Beloved Body: 'Italia mia.' " In *Feminist Approaches to the Body in Medieval Literature,* edited by Linda Lomperis and Sarah Stanbury, 1–20. Philadelphia: Univ. of Pennsylvania Press, 1993.

Brown, Ivor. *Chosen Words.* Westport, Conn.: Greenwood, 1979.

Bullinger, Heinrich. *The Christien State of Matrimonye.* Translated by Miles Coverdale. London, 1528.

Bullough, Vern L. "Transvestites in the Middle Ages." *American Journal of Sociology* 79, no. 6 (1974): 1381–94.

Burke, Kenneth. "Literature as Equipment for Living." In *The Philosophy of Literary Form: Studies in Symbolic Action,* 293–304. 2d ed. Baton Rouge: Louisana State Univ. Press, 1967.

Burnett, Mark Thornton. "Giving and Receiving: *Love's Labour's Lost* and the Politics of Exchange." *English Literary Renaissance* 23.2 (1993): 287–313.

Burton, John Hill, ed. *Register of the Privy Council of Scotland.* Edinburgh, 1877.

Butler, Alban. *Lives of the Saints,* edited, revised, and supplemented by Herbert Thurston, S. J. Attwater, and Donald Attwater. Vol. 3. London: Burns, Oates and Washbourne, 1956.

Byrne, Muriel St. Clare, ed. *The Lisle Letters.* 6 vols. Chicago: Univ. of Chicago Press, 1981.

———. *The Lisle Letters: An Abridgement.* Selected and arranged by Bridget Boland. Chicago: Univ. of Chicago Press, 1983.

Cahn, Susan. *Industry of Devotion: The Transformation of Women's Work in England, 1500–1660.* New York: Columbia Univ. Press, 1987.

Calderwood, David. *History of the Kirk of Scotland.* 2 vols. Edinburgh: Wodrow Society, 1842–49.

Calfhill, James. *An Answer to John Martiall's Treatise of the Cross,* edited by Richard Gibbings. Cambridge: Cambridge Univ. Press, 1846.

Calvin, John. *The Psalms of David and others. With M. John Calvins Commentaries.* Translated by Arthur Golding. London, 1571.

Camden, Carroll. *The Elizabethan Woman.* New York: Elsevier, 1952.

Carew, Richard. *The Survey of Cornwall,* London, 1602.

Carr, R. D., and J. M. Carr. *Carr's Dictionary of English Queens, Kings' Wives, Celebrated Paramours, Handfast Spouses, and Royal Changelings.* Bury St. Edmunds, Suffolk: R. D. Carr and J. M. Carr, 1977.

[Cary, Elizabeth, the Lady Falkland]. *The History of the Life, Reign, and Death of Edward II, King of England, and Lord of Ireland with the Rise and Fall of his Great Favourites, Gavestone and the Spensers, written by E. F. in the Year 1627, and printed verbatim from the original.* London, 1680.

———. "The History of the most unfortunate Prince, King Edward the Second. With Choice Political Observations on Him and his unhappy Favourites, Gaveston and Spencer. . . ." In *The Harleian Miscellany: A Collection of Scarce, Curious and Entertaining Tracts, As Well as Manuscripts as in Print. . . .* Vol. 1, edited by William Odys, 67–95. London, 1808.

———. "The Life, Reign, and Death of Edward II." In *Renaissance Women: The Plays of Elizabeth Cary, the Poems of Aemilia Lanyer*, edited by Diane Purkiss, 79–237. London: William Pickering, 1994.

Cary, Elizabeth, the Lady Falkland. *The Tragedy of Mariam, the Fair Queen of Jewry. With The Lady Falkland: Her Life, by one of her daughters*, edited by Barry Weller and Margaret W. Ferguson. Berkeley: Univ. of California Press, 1994.

Cerasano, S. P., and Marion Wynne-Davies, eds. *Gloriana's Face: Women, Public and Private, in the English Renaissance*. Detroit: Wayne State Univ. Press, 1992.

Chamberlain, Frederick. *The Sayings of Queen Elizabeth*. London: John Lane, 1923.

Chartier, Roger. *The Order of Books: Readers, Authors, and Libraries in Europe between the Fourteenth and Eighteenth Centuries*. Translated by Lydia G. Cochrane. Stanford: Stanford Univ. Press, 1994.

Chaucer, Geoffrey. *The Riverside Chaucer*, edited by F. N. Robinson and Larry Benson. Boston: Houghton Mifflin, 1987.

Church of England. "An Homilie of the State of Matrimonie." In *Certain Sermons or Homilies*, 255^v-6^r. London, 1563.

Cicero, Marcus Tullius. *De Officiis*, vol. 1. Translated by Walter Miller. London: Loeb Classic Library, 1913.

Clarke, Basil. *Mental Disorder in Earlier Britain: Exploratory Studies*. Cardiff: Univ. of Wales Press, 1975.

Cleaver, Robert. *A godly Forme of Houshold Government*. London, 1598.

Cliffe, J. T. *The Puritan Gentry: The Great Puritan Families of Early Stuart England*. London: Routledge, 1984.

Clifford, Anne. *The Diary of Anne Clifford 1616–1619*, edited by Katherine O. Acheson. New York: Garland, 1995.

———. *The Diary of Lady Anne Clifford*, edited by V. Sackville-West. London: Heineman, 1923.

Cline, Ruth Huff. "Four Chaucer Saints." *Modern Language Notes* 60 (1945): 480–82.

———. "Three Notes on the Miller's Tale." *Huntington Library Quarterly* 26 (1962–63): 131–45.

Clinton, Elizabeth Knevet. *The Countesse of Lincolnes Nurserie*. Oxford, 1628.

Coiro, Ann Baynes. "Writing in Service: Sexual Politics and Class Position in the Poetry of Aemelia Lanyer and Ben Jonson." *Criticism* 35, no. 3 (1993): 357–76.

Collier, John Payne. *A Bibliographical and Critical Account of the Rarest Books in the English Language*. New York, 1866.

Collins, A. Jeffries, ed. *Jewels and Plate of Queen Elizabeth I: The Inventory of 1574*. London: Cambridge Univ. Press for Trustees of the British Museum, 1955.

Collins, An. *An Collins: Divine Songs and Meditacions*, edited by Sidney Gottlieb. Binghamton, N.Y.: Medieval and Renaissance Text Society, 1996.

Collins, Arthur, ed. *Letters and Memorials of State.* London, 1746.

Collinson, Patrick. *The Elizabethan Puritan Movement,* 1967. Reprint. Oxford: Oxford Univ. Press, 1991.

———. "The Foreign Reformed Churches of London." 1964. Reprinted in *Godly People: Essays on English Protestantism and Puritanism,* edited by Patrick Collinson, 245–72. London: Hambledon Press, 1983.

———. "The Role of Women in the English Reformation Illustrated by the Life and Friendships of Anne Locke." *Studies in Church History* 2 (1965): 258–72.

The Compact Edition of the Oxford English Dictionary. Oxford: Clarendon, 1971.

Cook, Ann Jennalie. *Making a Match: Courtship in Shakespeare and His Society.* Princeton: Princeton Univ. Press, 1991.

Cope, Esther S. *Handmaid of the Holy Spirit: Dame Eleanor Davies, Never Soe Mad a Ladie.* Ann Arbor: Univ. of Michigan Press, 1992.

———, ed. *Prophetic Writings of Lady Eleanor Davies.* Women Writers in English. New York: Oxford Univ. Press, 1995.

Cornwallis, Sir William. *Essayes,* edited by Don Cameron Allen. Baltimore: Johns Hopkins Press, 1946.

———. "Of Estimation and Reputation." In *Essayes,* edited by Don Cameron Allen. Baltimore: Johns Hopkins Press, 1946.

Cosin, John. *The Correspondence of John Cosin, D.D., . . . Together with Other Papers Illustrative of His Life and Times, Part One,* edited and compiled by George Ornsby for the Suretees Society. London, 1869.

Cotgrave, Randle, comp. *Dictionarie of the French and English Tongues.* 1611. Reprint.

———. "Vertue." In *Dictionarie of the French and English Tongues,* sig. Lllliv. 1611. Reprint. Columbia: Univ. of South Carolina Press, 1968.

Coxhead, J. R. W. *The Romance of the Wool, Lace, and Pottery Trades in Honiton.* 6th ed. Honiton: P. H. Thrower, 1968.

Cowan, Ian B., ed. and comp. *The Enigma of Mary Stuart.* New York: St. Martin's, 1971.

Crawford, Patricia. "The Construction and Experience of Maternity." In *Women as Mothers in Pre-Industrial England: Essays in Memory of Dorothy McLaren,* edited by Valerie A. Fildes, 3–38. London: Routledge, 1990.

———. *Women and Religion in England, 1500–1720.* London: Routledge, 1993.

———. "Women's Published Writings 1600–1700." In *Women in English Society 1500–1800,* edited by Mary Prior, 211–82. London: Methuen, 1985.

Croiset van Uchelen, Anthony R. A. "Dutch Writing-Masters and the 'Prix de la Plume Couronnée.' " *Quarendo* 6 (1976): 319–46.

Crowley, Robert. *The Woman's Lesson.* London, 1541.

Daniel, Samuel. *The Collection of the Historie of England (1618): A Facsimile Reproduction with an Introduction by D. R. Woolf.* Delmar, N.Y.: Scholars' Facsimiles and Reprints, 1986.

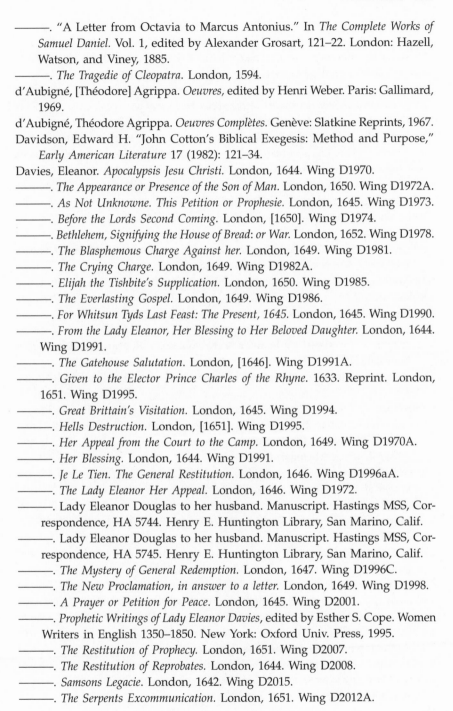

————. "A Letter from Octavia to Marcus Antonius." In *The Complete Works of Samuel Daniel*. Vol. 1, edited by Alexander Grosart, 121–22. London: Hazell, Watson, and Viney, 1885.

————. *The Tragedie of Cleopatra*. London, 1594.

d'Aubigné, [Théodore] Agrippa. *Oeuvres*, edited by Henri Weber. Paris: Gallimard, 1969.

d'Aubigné, Théodore Agrippa. *Oeuvres Complètes*. Genève: Slatkine Reprints, 1967.

Davidson, Edward H. "John Cotton's Biblical Exegesis: Method and Purpose," *Early American Literature* 17 (1982): 121–34.

Davies, Eleanor. *Apocalypsis Jesu Christi*. London, 1644. Wing D1970.

————. *The Appearance or Presence of the Son of Man*. London, 1650. Wing D1972A.

————. *As Not Unknowne. This Petition or Prophesie*. London, 1645. Wing D1973.

————. *Before the Lords Second Coming*. London, [1650]. Wing D1974.

————. *Bethlehem, Signifying the House of Bread: or War*. London, 1652. Wing D1978.

————. *The Blasphemous Charge Against her*. London, 1649. Wing D1981.

————. *The Crying Charge*. London, 1649. Wing D1982A.

————. *Elijah the Tishbite's Supplication*. London, 1650. Wing D1985.

————. *The Everlasting Gospel*. London, 1649. Wing D1986.

————. *For Whitsun Tyds Last Feast: The Present, 1645*. London, 1645. Wing D1990.

————. *From the Lady Eleanor, Her Blessing to Her Beloved Daughter*. London, 1644. Wing D1991.

————. *The Gatehouse Salutation*. London, [1646]. Wing D1991A.

————. *Given to the Elector Prince Charles of the Rhyne*. 1633. Reprint. London, 1651. Wing D1995.

————. *Great Brittain's Visitation*. London, 1645. Wing D1994.

————. *Hells Destruction*. London, [1651]. Wing D1995.

————. *Her Appeal from the Court to the Camp*. London, 1649. Wing D1970A.

————. *Her Blessing*. London, 1644. Wing D1991.

————. *Je Le Tien. The General Restitution*. London, 1646. Wing D1996aA.

————. *The Lady Eleanor Her Appeal*. London, 1646. Wing D1972.

————. Lady Eleanor Douglas to her husband. Manuscript. Hastings MSS, Correspondence, HA 5744. Henry E. Huntington Library, San Marino, Calif.

————. Lady Eleanor Douglas to her husband. Manuscript. Hastings MSS, Correspondence, HA 5745. Henry E. Huntington Library, San Marino, Calif.

————. *The Mystery of General Redemption*. London, 1647. Wing D1996C.

————. *The New Proclamation, in answer to a letter*. London, 1649. Wing D1998.

————. *A Prayer or Petition for Peace*. London, 1645. Wing D2001.

————. *Prophetic Writings of Lady Eleanor Davies*, edited by Esther S. Cope. Women Writers in English 1350–1850. New York: Oxford Univ. Press, 1995.

————. *The Restitution of Prophecy*. London, 1651. Wing D2007.

————. *The Restitution of Reprobates*. London, 1644. Wing D2008.

————. *Samsons Legacie*. London, 1642. Wing D2015.

————. *The Serpents Excommunication*. London, 1651. Wing D2012A.

————. *The Star to the Wise*. London, 1643. Wing D2013.

————. *Strange and Wonderfull Prophesies*. London, 1649. Wing D2014.

————. *A Warning to the Dragon and All His Angels*. London, 1625. Wing D904.

————. *The Word of God to the Citie of London*. London, 1644. Wing D2018.

Davies, Kathleen. "Continuity and Change in Literary Advice on Marriage." In *Marriage and Society: Studies in the Social History of Marriage*, edited by R. B. Outhwaite, 58–80. London: Europa, 1981.

Davis, Natalie Zemon. "Beyond the Market: Books as Gifts in Sixteenth-Century France." *Transactions of the Royal Historical Society*, 5th ser., 33 (1983): 69–88.

————. "Gender and Genre: Women as Historical Writers, 1400–1820." In *Beyond Their Sex: Learned Women of the European Past*, edited by Patricia H. Labalme, 153–82. New York: New York Univ. Press, 1984.

Davis, Norman, ed. *Paston Letters and Papers of the Fifteenth Century*. 2 vols. Oxford: Clarendon, 1971.

de Bruyn, Jan. "The Ideal Lady and the Rise of Feminism in Seventeenth-Century England." *Mosaic* 17, no. 1 (1984): 19–28.

The deceyte of women, to the instruction and ensample of all men. London, [c. 1560].

Dekker, Rudolf M., and Lotte C. van de Pol. *The Tradition of Female Transvestism*. New York: St. Martin's, 1989.

Delcourt, Marie. *Hermaphrodite: Myths and Rites of the Bisexual Figure in Classical Antiquity*. Translated by Jennifer Nicholson. 1956. Reprint. London: Studio Books, 1961.

Delehaye, Hippolyte. *The Legends of the Saints*. New York: Fordham Univ. Press, 1962.

Diefendorf, Barbara B. "The Huguenot Psalter and the Faith of French Protestants in the Sixteenth Century." In *Culture and Identity in Early Modern Europe (1500–1800)*, edited by Barbara B. Diefendorf and Carla Hesse, 41–63. Ann Arbor: Univ. of Michigan Press, 1993.

Diefendorf, Barbara B., and Carla Hesse, eds. *Culture and Identity in Early Modern Europe (1500–1800)*. Ann Arbor: Univ. of Michigan Press, 1993.

Dobbie, B. M. Willmott. "An Attempt to Estimate the True Rate of Maternal Mortality, Sixteenth to Eighteenth Centuries." *Medical History* 26 (1982): 79–90.

Dolan, Frances E. *Dangerous Familiars: Representations of Domestic Crime in England, 1550–1700*. Ithaca: Cornell Univ. Press, 1994.

Dolce, Lodovico. *Dialogo della alogo della institutione delle donne*. Venice, 1545.

Dollimore, Jonathan, and Alan Sinfield. Forward to *Political Shakespeare: New Essays in Cultural Materialism*. Manchester: Manchester Univ. Press, 1985.

Donaldson, Gordon. *All the Queen's Men: Power and Politics in Mary Stewart's Scotland*. New York: St. Martin's, 1983.

————. *The First Trial of Mary Queen of Scots*. New York: Stein and Day, 1969.

————. *Mary Queen of Scots*. London: English Universities Press, 1974.

Douglas, Eleanor Davies. See Davies, Eleanor.

Dowriche, Anne. *The French Historie*. London, 1589.

Dowriche, Hugh. *The Jaylors Conversion.* London, 1596.

Dunbar, Agnes B. C. *A Dictionary of Saintly Women.* 2 vols. London: George Bell and Sons, 1904–5.

Duncan-Jones, Katherine. *Sir Philip Sidney: Courtier Poet.* New Haven: Yale Univ. Press, 1991.

Dunn, Kevin. *Pretexts of Authority: The Rhetoric of Authorship in the Renaissance Preface.* Stanford: Stanford Univ. Press, 1994.

Durkan, John. "The Library of Mary, Queen of Scots." In *Mary Stewart: Queen in Three Kingdoms,* edited by Michael Lynch, 71–101. Oxford: Basil Blackwell, 1988.

Eckenstein, Lina. *Women under Monasticism: Chapters on Saint-Lore and Convent Life between 500–1500.* Cambridge: Cambridge Univ. Press, 1896.

Edgcumbe, W. H. *Records of the Edgcumbe Family.* Plymouth: W. Brednon and Son, 1888.

Edwards, Gillian Mary. *Uncumber and Pantaloon: Some Words with Stories.* New York: E. P. Dutton, 1969.

Egerton, Stephen. *The doctrine of the Subjection to God and the King.* London, 1616.

Eisenstadt, S. N., and Louis Roniger. "Patron-Client Relations as a Model of Structuring Social Exchange." *Comparative Studies in Society and History* 22, no. 1 (1980): 42–77.

Eisenstein, Elizabeth L. *The Printing Revolution in Early Modern Europe.* Cambridge: Cambridge Univ. Press, 1983.

Elias, Norbert. *The Court Society.* Translated by Edmund Jephcott. New York: Pantheon, 1983.

Elizabeth I of England. *The Letters of Queen Elizabeth,* edited by G. B. Harrison. London: Cassell and Co., 1935.

———. "Speeches." In *The Public Speaking of Queen Elizabeth,* edited by George P. Rice Jr., 77–81, 114–18, 88–97, 106–9. New York: Columbia Univ. Press, 1951.

———. "Speech to the Troops at Tilbury," edited by Frances Teague. In *Women Writers of the Renaissance and Reformation,* edited by Katherina M. Wilson, 542–43. Athens and London: Univ. of Georgia Press, 1987.

Elliott, Vivien Brodsky. "Single Women in the London Marriage Market: Age, Status and Mobility, 1598–1619." In *Marriage and Society: Studies in the Social History of Marriage,* edited by R. B. Outhwaite, 81–100. London: Europa, 1981.

Elsky, Martin. *Authorizing Words: Speech, Writing, and Print in the English Renaissance.* Ithaca: Cornell Univ. Press, 1989.

Elton, G. R., ed. *The Tudor Constitution: Documents and Commentary.* Cambridge: Cambridge Univ. Press, 1960.

Elyot, Thomas. *The boke named the Governour.* London, 1531. Facsimile reprint edited by R. C. Alston. English Linguistics 1500–1800, no. 246. Menston, England: Scolar, 1970.

———. *The Defence of Good Women.* London, 1540.

———. *The Defence of Good Women.* London, 1545.

Emerson, Kathy Lynn. *Wives and Daughters: The Women of Sixteenth Century England.* Troy, N.Y.: Whitson, 1984.

Erasmus, Desiderius. *The Education of a Christian Prince.* Translated by Lester K. Born. New York: Columbia Univ. Press, 1936.

———. "Paraphrase of the Gospel of St. John." In *The first tome or volume of the Paraphrase of Erasmus vpon the new testamente.* Translated by Mary Tudor, edited by Nicholas Udall. London, 1548.

Evans, Robert C. *Ben Jonson and the Poetics of Patronage.* Lewisburg, Pa.: Bucknell Univ. Press, 1989.

Ezell, Margaret. *The Patriarch's Wife: Literary Evidence and the History of the Family.* Chapel Hill: Univ. of North Carolina Press, 1987.

———. *Writing Women's Literary History.* Baltimore: Johns Hopkins Univ. Press, 1993.

Farmer, David Hugh. *The Oxford Dictionary of Saints.* 2d ed. New York: Oxford Univ. Press, 1987.

Farrell, Kirby, Elizabeth H. Hageman, and Arthur F. Kinney, eds. *Women in the Renaissance: Selections from English Literary Renaissance.* Amherst: Univ. of Massachusetts Press, 1990.

Fehrenbach, R. J. "A Letter Sent by the Maydens of London (1567)." *English Literary Renaissance* 14, no. 3 (1984): 285–304.

Felch, Susan. Introduction to *The Collected Works of Anne Vaughan Lock.* Binghamton, N.Y.: Medieval and Renaissance Text Society, 1999.

Felski, Rita. *Beyond Feminist Aesthetics: Feminist Literature and Social Change.* Cambridge, Mass.: Harvard Univ. Press, 1989.

Ferguson, Margaret W. "A Room Not Their Own: Renaissance Women as Readers and Writers." In *The Comparative Perspective on Literature: Approaches to Theory and Practice,* edited by Clayton Koelb and Susan Noakes, 93–116. Ithaca: Cornell Univ. Press, 1988.

Ferguson, Margaret W., Maureen Quilligan, and Nancy J. Vickers, eds. *Rewriting the Renaissance: The Discourses of Sexual Difference in Early Modern Europe.* Chicago: Univ. of Chicago Press, 1986.

Ferguson, Moira, ed. *First Feminists: British Women Writers 1578–1799.* Bloomington: Indiana Univ. Press, 1985.

Fields, Barbara Jeanne. "Slavery, Race, and Ideology in the United States of America." *New Left Review* 181 (1991): 95–118.

Fildes, Valerie A. *Breasts, Bottles, and Babies: A History of Infant Feeding.* Edinburgh: Edinburgh Univ. Press, 1986.

———, ed. *Women as Mothers in Pre-Industrial England: Essays in Memory of Dorothy McLaren.* London: Routledge, 1990.

Filmer, Sir Robert. *Patriarcha,* edited by Peter Laslett. Oxford: Oxford University Press, 1949.

Finke, Laurie A. *Feminist Theory, Women's Writing.* Ithaca: Cornell Univ. Press, 1992.

Fisken, Beth Wynne. " 'The Art of Sacred Parody' in Mary Sidney's *Psalmes.*" *Tulsa Studies in Women's Literature* 8.2 (1989): 233–39.

————. "Mary Sidney's *Psalmes:* Education and Wisdom." In *Silent But for the Word: Tudor Women as Patrons, Translators, and Writers of Religious Works,* edited by Margaret Hannay, 166–83. Kent, Ohio: Kent State Univ. Press, 1985.

Foxe, John. *Acts and Monuments.* 8 vols. Edited by Stephen Reed Cattley. London: R. B. Seeley and W. Burnside, 1838.

Fraser, Antonia. *Mary, Queen of Scots.* New York: Delacorte, 1969.

————. *The Weaker Vessel: Woman's Sexual Lot in Seventeenth Century England.* 1984. Reprint. New York: Vintage Books, 1985.

Freer, Coburn. *Music for a King: George Herbert's Style and the Metrical Psalms.* Baltimore: Johns Hopkins Univ. Press, 1972.

Froude, James Anthony. *History of England from the Fall of Wolsey to the Death of Queen Elizabeth.* 3d ed. 12 vols. London: Longmans, Green, 1867.

Frye, Susan. *Elizabeth I: The Competition for Representation.* New York: Oxford Univ. Press, 1993.

————. "Esther Inglis and Early Seventeenth-Century Print Conventions of Authorship." Unpublished manuscript, March 1994.

Fugger, Wolfgang. *Handwriting Manual, entitled, A practical and wellgrounded formulary for divers fair hands (1553).* Translated by Frederick Plaat. London: Oxford Univ. Press, 1960.

Fumerton, Patricia. *Cultural Aesthetics: Renaissance Literature and the Practice of Social Ornament.* Chicago: Univ. of Chicago Press, 1991.

Gallagher, Catherine. "Embracing the Absolute: The Politics of the Female Subject in Seventeenth-Century England." *Genders* 1 (Mar. 1988): 24–39.

Garber, Marjorie B. *Vested Interests: Cross-Dressing and Cultural Anxiety.* New York: Routledge, 1992.

Gardiner, Samuel Rawson, ed. *The Fortescue Papers: Consisting Chiefly of Letters Relating to State Affairs, Collected by John Packer, Secretary to George Villiers, Duke of Buckingham.* Westminster, England, 1871.

Geneva Bible. 1560. Facsimile reprint. Madison: Univ. of Wisconsin Press, 1969.

Geneva Bible: The Annotated New Testament, 1602 Edition, edited by Gerald T. Sheppard. Cleveland, Ohio: Pilgrim, 1989.

Gibson, Wendy. *Women in Seventeenth-Century France.* New York: St. Martin's, 1989.

Gillis, John R. *For Better, for Worse: British Marriage 1600 to the Present.* Oxford: Oxford Univ. Press, 1985.

Gilmore, Leigh. *Autobiographics: A Feminist Theory of Women's Self-Representation.* Ithaca: Cornell Univ. Press, 1994.

Gledhill, Christine. "Pleasurable Negotiations." 1988. Reprinted in *Cultural Theory and Popular Culture,* edited by John Storey, 241–54. New York: Harvester-Wheatsheaf, 1994.

Goldberg, Jonathan. *James I and the Politics of Literature.* Baltimore: Johns Hopkins Univ. Press, 1983.

————. *Writing Matter: From the Hands of the English Renaissance.* Stanford: Stanford Univ. Press, 1990.

Goodare, Julian. "Queen Mary's Catholic Interlude." In *Mary Stewart: Queen in Three Kingdoms*, edited by Michael Lynch, 154–70. Oxford: Basil Blackwell, 1988.

Goreau, Angeline, ed. *The Whole Duty of a Woman: Female Writers in Seventeenth Century England*. Garden City, N.Y.: Dial, 1985.

Gosynhill, Edward. *The Prayse of All women, Called Mulierû Pean*. London, [c. 1542].

Gouge, William. *Of Domesticall Duties: Eight Treatises*. London, 1622.

Great Britain. House of Lords Record Office. *Main Papers*. 22 September 1647.

Great Britain. Public Records Office. *Calendar of State Papers, Domestic Series, of the Reign of Charles I, 1625–1626*, edited by John Bruce. 1858. Reprint. Nendeln, Liechtenstein: Kraus Reprint, 1967.

———. *Calendar of State Papers, Domestic Series, of the Reign of Charles I, 1627–1628*, edited by John Bruce. 1858. Reprint. Nendeln, Liechtenstein: Kraus Reprint, 1967.

———. *Calendar of the Letters and State Papers Relating to English Affairs, Preserved in the Archives of Simancas*, edited by Martin Hume. 4 vols. London: printed for H. M. Stationery Office by Eyre and Spottiswoode, 1896–99.

———. *Calendar of State Papers Relating to Scotland and Mary, Queen of Scots, 1547–1603*, edited by Joseph Bain, W. K. Boyd, H. W. Meikle, A. I. Cameron, M. S. Guiseppi, and J. D. Mackie. 13 vols. Edinburgh: H. M. General Register House, 1898.

———. *Domestic State Papers*. Manuscript. PRO SP 16/248/93.

———. *Letters and Papers, Foreign and Domestic, of the Reign of Henry VIII*, edited by James Gairdner and R. H. Brodie. London: Her Majesty's Stationery Office, 1864–1932.

———. *Privy Purse Records for Henry, Prince of Wales*, by David Murray. PRO SP 14/57/89.

———. Sidney, Sir Henry, to Sir Francis Walsingham. 1 March 1583. PRO SP 12/159.

Great Britain, sovereigns (Elizabeth). *Lists of New Year Gifts Given and Received by the King, Elizabeth*. Manuscript 1584. Z.d.16. Folger Shakespeare Library, Washington, D.C.

———. *List of New Year Gifts Given and Received by the King, Elizabeth*. Manuscript 1598/9. Z.d.17. Folger Shakespeare Library, Washington, D.C.

Greenblatt, Stephen. *Shakespearean Negotiations: The Circulation of Social Energy in Renaissance England*. Berkeley: Univ. of California Press, 1988.

Greengrass, M. "Mary, Dowager Queen of France." In *Mary Stewart: Queen in Three Kingdoms*, edited by Michael Lynch, 171–94. Oxford: Basil Blackwell, 1988.

Greer, Germaine, Susan Hastings, Jeslyn Medoff, and Melinda Sansone, eds. *Kissing the Rod: An Anthology of Seventeenth-Century Women's Verse*. New York: Farrar, Straus, and Giroux, 1988.

Gregory, C. A. *Gifts and Commodities*. London: Academic, 1982.

Greville, Fulke. *The Prose Works of Fulke Greville, Lord Brooke*, edited by John Gouws. Oxford: Clarendon, 1986.

Griffiths, John, ed. *The Two Books of Homilies to be read on Churches*. Oxford: Oxford Univ. Press, 1859.

Grossberg, Lawrence, Cary Nelson, and Paula A. Treichler, eds. *Cultural Studies*. New York: Routledge, 1992.

Grossman, Marshall, ed. *Aemilia Lanyer: Gender, Genre, and the Canon*. Lexington: Univ. Press of Kentucky, 1998.

Grundy, Isobel. "Falkland's *History of . . . King Edward II*." *Bodleian Library Record* 13, no. 1 (1988): 82–83.

———. "Women's History? Writings by English Nuns." In *Women, Writing, History 1640–1740*, edited by Isobel Grundy and Susan Wiseman, 126–38. Athens: Univ. of Georgia Press, 1992.

Grundy, Isobel, and Susan Wiseman, eds. *Women, Writing, History 1640–1740*. Athens: Univ. of Georgia Press, 1992.

Guillimeau, James. *Child-birth or, the Happy Deliverie of Women*. London, 1612.

Gundersheimer, Werner. "Patronage in the Renaissance: An Exploratory Approach." In *Patronage in the Renaissance*, edited by Guy Fitch Lytle and Stephen Orgel, 3–23. Princeton: Princeton Univ. Press, 1981.

Guy, John. *Tudor England*. Reprint. Oxford: Oxford Univ. Press, 1990.

Hall, David D. *The Antinomian Controversy, 1636–1638: A Documentary History*. 2d ed. Durham, N.C.: Duke Univ. Press, 1990.

Hall, Kim F. *Things of Darkness: Economies of Race and Gender in Early Modern England*. Ithaca, N.Y.: Cornell Univ. Press, 1995.

Hamilton, Donna B. *Virgil and the Tempest: The Politics of Imitation*. Columbus: Ohio State Univ. Press, 1990.

Hampton, Timothy. *Writing from History: The Rhetoric of Exemplarity in Renaissance Literature*. Ithaca, N.Y.: Cornell Univ. Press, 1990.

Hannay, Margaret. " 'House-confined maids': The Presentation of Woman's Role in the *Psalmes* of the Countess of Pembroke." *English Literary Renaissance* 24, no. 1 (1994): 44–71.

———. Introduction to *Silent But for the Word: Tudor Women as Patrons, Translators, and Writers of Religious Works*, edited by Margaret Hannay, 1–14. Kent, Ohio: Kent State Univ. Press, 1985.

———. *Philip's Phoenix: Mary Sidney, Countess of Pembroke*. New York: Oxford Univ. Press, 1990.

———. " 'Princes you as men must dy': Genevan Advice to Monarchs in the *Psalmes* of Mary Sidney." *English Literary Renaissance* 19, no. 1 (Dec. 1989): 22–41.

———. " 'This Moses and This Miriam': The Countess of Pembroke's Role in the Legend of Sir Philip Sidney." In *Sir Philip Sidney's Achievements*, edited by M. J. B. Allen, Dominic Baker-Smith, and Arthur F. Kinney, with Margaret M. Sullivan, 217–26. New York: AMS, 1990.

———. " 'When riches growes': Class Perspective in Pembroke's Psalms." *Sidney Newsletter* 13 (1994–95): 9–19.

———. " 'Wisdome the Wordes': Psalm Translation and Elizabethan Women's Spirituality." *Religion and Literature* 23, no. 3 (1991): 65–82.

———, ed. *Silent But for the Word: Tudor Women as Patrons, Translators, and Writers of Religious Works*. Kent, Ohio: Kent State Univ. Press, 1985.

Hardy, Thomas Duffus. *Descriptive Catalogue of Material Relating to the History of Great Britain and Ireland, to the end of the Reign of Henry VII*. 1862. Reprint. New York: Burt Franklin, [1964].

Harrington, William. *Commendacions of Matrymony*. London, 1528.

Harris, Barbara J. "Women and Politics in Early Tudor England." *Historical Journal* 33, no. 2 (1990): 259–82.

Harrison, William. *The Description of England*, edited by Georges Edelen for the Folger Shakespeare Library. Ithaca: Cornell Univ. Press, 1968.

Hartley, T. E. *Elizabeth's Parliaments: Queen, Lords, and Commons, 1559–1601*. Manchester: Manchester Univ. Press, 1992.

Haselkorn, Anne M., and Betty S. Travitsky, eds. *The Renaissance Englishwoman in Print: Counterbalancing the Canon*. Amherst: Univ. of Massachusetts Press, 1990.

Heilbrun, Carolyn G. "How Girls Become Wimps." Review of *Meetings at the Crossroads: Women's Psychology and Girls' Development*, by Lyn Mikel Brown and Carol Gilligan. *New York Times Book Review*, 4 Oct. 1992, 13–14.

Henderson, Katherine Usher and Barbara F. McManus. *Half Humankind: Contexts and Texts of the Controversy about Women in England, 1540–1640*. Urbana: Univ. of Illinois Press, 1985.

Hendricks, Margo, and Patricia Parker, eds. *Women, "Race," and Writing in the Early Modern Period*. London: Routledge, 1994.

Herz, Judith Scherer. "Aemilia Lanyer and the Pathos of Literary History." In *Representing Women in Renaissance England*, edited by Claude J. Summers and Ted-Larry Pebworth, 121–35. Columbia: Univ. of Missouri Press, 1997.

Hibbert, Christopher. *The Virgin Queen: Elizabeth I, Genius of the Golden Age*. Reading, Mass.: Addison-Wesley, 1991.

Hill, Thomas. *The moste pleasaunte arte of the interpretacion of dreames*. London, 1576.

Hindley, Charles, ed. *The Roxburghe Ballads*. London: Reeves and Turner, 1873–74.

Hobby, Elaine. " 'Discourse so unsavoury': Women's Published Writings in the 1650s." In *Women, Writing, History 1640–1740*, edited by Isobel Grundy and Susan Wiseman, 16–32. Athens: Univ. of Georgia Press, 1992.

———. *Virtue of Necessity: English Women's Writing 1649–1688*. London: Virago, 1988.

Hoby, Margaret Dakins. *Diary of Lady Margaret Hoby*, edited by Dorothy M. Meads. Boston: Houghton, 1930.

Hogrefe, Pearl. *Tudor Women: Commoners and Queens*. Ames: Iowa State Univ. Press, 1975.

————. *Women of Action in Tudor England.* Ames: Iowa State Univ. Press, 1977.

Holdsworth, William. *A History of English Law.* 2d ed. 17 vols. London: Methuen, 1937.

Hole, Christina. *English Shrines and Sanctuaries.* London: Batsford, 1954.

Holmes, Michael Morgan. "The Love of Other Women: Rich Chains and Sweet Kisses." In *Aemilia Lanyer: Gender, Genre, and the Canon.* edited by Marshall Grossman, 167–90. Lexington: Univ. Press of Kentucky, 1998.

Holzknecht, Karl Julius. *Literary Patronage in the Middle Ages.* Menasha, Wis.: George Banta, 1923.

Horstmann, Carl. *The Lives of Women Saints of Our Contrie of England.* London: Early English Text Society, 1886.

Hotson, Leslie. "The Library of Elizabeth's Embezzling Teller." *Studies in Bibliography* 2 (1949–50): 49–61.

Hubert, Francis. *The Deplorable Life and Death of Edward the Second, King of England, Together with the Downefall of the two Vnforvnate Fauorites, Gauestone and Spencer. Storied in an Excellent Poem.* London, 1628.

Hughes, Paul L., and James F. Larkin, eds. *Tudor Royal Proclamations.* 3 vols. New Haven: Yale Univ. Press, 1964–69.

Hughey, Ruth, ed. *The Arundel Harington Manuscript of Tudor Poetry.* Columbus: Ohio State Univ. Press, 1960.

Hull, Suzanne W. *Chaste, Silent, and Obedient: English Books for Women 1475–1640.* San Marino, Calif.: Huntington Library, 1982.

————. *Women According to Men: The World of Tudor-Stuart Women.* Walnut Creek, Calif.: Altamira, 1996.

Humphrey, Caroline, and Stephen Hugh-Jones, eds. *Barter, Exchange and Value: An Anthropological Approach.* Cambridge: Cambridge Univ. Press, 1992.

Hungerford, John, ed. *Papal Negotiations with Mary, Queen of Scots, during Her Reign in Scotland, 1561–67.* Edinburgh: Scottish Historical Society, 1901.

Huntington, Lucy Hastings, Countess of. HEH, Hastings MSS, Correspondence, HA 5744; HA 5745; HA 8258. Huntington Library, San Marino, Calif.

————. HEH, Hastings MSS, Legal Papers, box 6, folder 1. Huntington Library, San Marino, Calif.

————. "Letter to William Sanderson, protest in defense of her mother." HEH, Hastings MSS, Manuscript. 2 versions. Includes William Sanderson's apology in reply. Hastings MSS, Misc., box 1, folder 17. Huntington Library, San Marino, Calif.

————. "Memoranda Book of Lucy Hastings, Countess of Huntingdon." Manuscript. HEH, Hastings MSS, Personal Papers, HAP, box 18, folder 1. Huntington Library, San Marino, Calif.

————. "Memoranda Book of Lucy Hastings, Countess of Huntingdon." HEH, Hastings MSS, Religious, box 3, folder 16. Huntington Library, San Marino, Calif.

Hurstfield, Joel. *The Queen's Wards: Wardship and Marriage under Elizabeth I.* Cambridge, Mass.: Harvard Univ. Press, 1958.

270 Works Cited

Inglis, Esther. "Album Amicorum" by George Craig, 1602–5, with inscriptions by Esther Inglis and Bernard Kello. MS LA.III.525. Univ. of Edinburgh Library.
———. "Argumenta in Librum Psalmorum Davidis . . . 1606." MS Typ.212. Houghton Library, Harvard Univ., Cambridge, Mass.
———. "Argumenta Psalmorum Davidis per tetraticha . . . 1608." MS V.a.94. Folger Library, Washington, D.C.
———. "Argumenta Singulorum Capitum Ebangelii Matthaei Apostoli . . . 1607." MS 361. Private collection. Microfilm on deposit. National Library of Scot-land, Edinburgh.
———. "Argumenta singulorum capitum Geneseos per Tetraticha . . . 1608." MS Typ.428. Houghton Library, Harvard Univ., Cambridge, Mass.
———. "Ce Livre contenant cinquante Emblemes Chrestiens premierement inventez par ala noble damoiselle Georgette de Montenay en France . . . 1624." Royal MS 17.D.XVI. British Library, London.
———. "Cinquant Octonaires sur la vanite et inconstance du monde . . . 1586." MS 25240. National Library of Scotland, Edinburgh.
———. "Dedication to William Jeffrey." MS V.a.92. *Octonaires of Antoine de la Roche Chandieu.* Folger Library, Washington, D.C.
———. "Dedication to Prince Maurice of Nassau." MS Folger V.a.93. *Psalms.* 1599. Folger Library, Washington, D.C.
———. "Dedication to Antony Bacon." Add. MS 27927. *Ecclesiastes.* 1599. British Library, London.
———. *Discours de la Foy.* HM 26068, Huntington Library, San Marino, Calif.
———. "Le Livre de l'Ecclesisaste, ensemble le Cantique de Salomon . . . 1599." Add. MS 27927. British Library, London.
———. "Le Livre de l'Ecclesiaste ensemble les Lamentations de Ieremie . . . 1602." MS 20498. National Library of Scotland, Edinburgh.
———. "Les C. L. Pseumes de David . . . 1599." MS V.a.93. Folger Libary, Wash-ington, D.C.
———. "Les Pseaumes de David . . . 1615." MS 8874. National Library of Scot-land, Edinburgh.
———. "Les Quatraines de Guy de Faur, Sire de Pybrac, Ensebles Les cinquante octonaires . . . 1614." Harleian MS 4324, British Library, London.
———. "Les Qutraines de Guy de Faur Sier de Pybrac . . . 1615." Add. MS 19633. British Library, London.
———. "Les Quatraines du Sieur de Pybrac . . . 1607." MS La.III.439. Univ. of Edinburgh Library.
———. "Les six vingts et six quatrains de Guy de Faur Sieeur de Pybrac . . . 1615." MS Typ.347. Houghton Library, Harvard Univ., Cambridge, Mass.
———. "Les six vingts et six quatrains de Guy de Faur, Sier de Pybrac. . . 1617." Add. MS 22606. British Library, London.
———. "Livret contenat diverses sortes de lettres. . . 1586." [Psalms 2 and 94.] Sloane MS 987. British Library, London.

———. "Livret traittant de la Grandeur de Dieu . . M.D.XCII." MS La.III.440. Univ. of Edinburgh Library.

———. "Octonaries upon the Vanitie and Inconstancie of the World . . . 1600." MS V.a.91. Folger Library, Washington, D.C.

———. "Octonaries upon the Vanitie and Inconstancie of the World . . . 1607." MS V.a.92. Folger Library, Washington, D.C.

———. [Quotations from Psalms and Proverbs.] MS Typ.428.1. Houghton Library, Harvard Univ., Cambridge, Mass.

———. [Specimens of various styles of writing.] MS 2197. National Library of Scotland, Edinburgh.

———. [Specimens of various styles of writing.] MS La.III.522. Univ. of Edinburgh Library.

———. "A Treatise of preparation to the Holy Supper of our only Saviour. . . [1608]." MS La.III.75. Univ. of Edinburgh Library.

———. "Une Estreine pour tresillustre et vertueuse Dame la Contesse de Bedford . . . 1606." Rome MS Private Collection, Philadelphia.

———. "Verbum Sempiternum . . . 1615." MS Typ.49. Houghton Library, Harvard Univ., Cambridge, Mass.

———. "Vincula Unionis sive scita Britannicae . . . Per Davidem Humium . . . [1605]." MS La.III.249. Univ. of Edinburgh Library.

Ingram, Martin. *Church Courts, Sex, and Marriage in England, 1570–1640.* Past and Present Publications. Cambridge: Cambridge Univ. Press, 1987.

Iragaray, Luce. "When the Goods Get Together." In *New French Feminisms: An Anthology,* edited by Elaine Marks and Isabelle de Courtivron, 107–10. New York: Schocken, 1981.

Jackson, Dorothy Judd. *Esther Inglis Calligrapher 1571–1624.* New York: Spiral, 1937.

James I of England. *The Political Works of James I,* edited by Charles Howard McIlwain. Cambridge, Mass.: Harvard Univ. Press, 1918.

Jardine, Lisa. *Still Harping on Daughters: Women and Drama in the Age of Shakespeare.* Totowa, N.J.: Barnes and Noble Books, 1983.

Jardine, M. D. "New Historicism for Old: New Conservatism for Old?: The Politics of Patronage in the Renaissance." *Yearbook of English Studies,* special no.: Politics, Patronage and Literature in England 1558–1658, 21 (1991): 286–304.

Jeanneret, Michel. *Poésie et tradition biblique au XVIe siècle.* Paris: J. Corti, 1969.

Joceline, Elizabeth. *The Mothers Legacie to Her Unborn Childe.* London, 1624.

Johnson, Paul. *Elizabeth I: A Biography.* London: Futura, 1976.

Jones, Ann Rosalind. *The Currency of Eros: Women's Love Lyric in Europe, 1540–1620.* Bloomington: Indiana Univ. Press, 1990.

———. "Nets and Bridles: Early Modern Conduct Books and Sixteenth-Century Women's Lyrics." In *The Ideology of Conduct: Essays on Literature and the History of Sexuality,* edited by Nancy Armstrong and Leonard Tennenhouse, 39–72. New York: Methuen, 1987.

———. "Surprising Frame: Renaissance Gender Ideologies and Women's Lyric." In *The Poetics of Gender*, edited by Nancy K. Miller, 74–95. New York: Columbia Univ. Press, 1986.

Jones, Norman L. "Elizabeth's First Year: The Conception and Birth of the Elizabethan Political World." In *Reign of Elizabeth I*, edited by Christopher Haigh, 27–53. New York: Macmillan, 1984.

Jordan, Constance. "The Household and the State: Transformations in the Representation of an Analogy from Aristotle to James I." *Modern Language Quarterly* 54 (1993): 307–26.

———. *Renaissance Feminism: Literary Texts and Political Models*. Ithaca, N.Y.: Cornell Univ. Press, 1990.

———. "Renaissance Women and the Question of Class." In *Sexuality and Gender in Early Modern Europe: Institutions, Texts, Images*, edited by James Grantham Turner, 90–106. Cambridge: Cambridge Univ. Press, 1993.

———. "Woman's Rule in Sixteenth-Century British Political Thought." *Renaissance Quarterly* 40, no. 3 (1987): 421–51.

Joubert, Laurent. *Popular Errors (1579)*. Translated and edited by Gregory David de Rocher. Tuscaloosa: Univ. of Alabama Press, 1989.

Kahn, Coppélia. " 'Magic of Bounty': *Timon of Athens*, Jacobean Patronage, and Maternal Power." *Shakespeare Quarterly* 38, no. 1 (1987): 34–57.

Kaminsky, Howard. "Estate, Nobility, and the Exhibition of Estate in the Later Middle Ages." *Speculum* 68, no. 3 (1993): 684–709.

Kaufman, Gloria. "Juan Luis Vives on the Education of Women." *Signs* 3, no. 4 (1978): 891–96.

Kelly, Joan. "Did Women Have a Renaissance?" In *Becoming Visible: Women in European History*, edited by Renate Bridenthal and Claudia Koonz, 138–63. Boston: Houghton Mifflin, 1977. Reprinted in *Women, History, and Theory: The Essays of Joan Kelly*, 19–50. Chicago: Univ. of Chicago Press, 1984.

Kempe, Alfred John, ed. *The Loseley Manuscripts*. London: John Murray, 1836.

Kendall, Ritchie D. *The Drama of Dissent: The Radical Politics of Nonconformity, 1380–1590*. Chapel Hill: Univ. of North Carolina Press, 1986.

Kennedy, Gwynne. "Reform or Rebellion?: The Limits of Female Authority in Elizabeth Cary's *The History of the Life, Reign, and Death of Edward II*." In *Political Rhetoric, Power, and Renaissance Women*, edited by Carole Levin and Patricia A. Sullivan, 204–22. Albany, State Univ. of New York Press, 1995.

Kenny, Anthony. "The Accursed Memory: The Counter-Reformation Reputation of John Wyclif." In *Wyclif in His Times*, edited by Anthony Kenny, 147–68. Oxford: Clarendon, 1986.

Kesler, R. L. "The Idealization of Women: Morphology and Change in Three Renaissance Texts." *Mosaic* 25, no. 2 (1990): 107–26.

King, John N. *English Reformation Literature: The Tudor Origins of the Protestant Tradition*. Princeton: Princeton Univ. Press, 1982.

———. *Tudor Royal Iconography: Literature and Art in an Age of Religious Crisis*. Princeton: Princeton Univ. Press, 1989.

King, Margaret L. *Women of the Renaissance.* Chicago: Univ. of Chicago Press, 1991.

Kinnamon, Noel J. "Notes on the Psalms in Herbert's *The Temple.*" *George Herbert Journal* 4, no. 2 (1981): 10–29.

———. "The Sidney Psalms: The Penshurst and Tixall Manuscripts." *Journal of Education Media Science* 2 (1990): 130–61.

Klein, Joan Larsen, ed. *Daughters, Wives, and Widows: Writings by Men about Women and Marriage in England, 1540–1640.* Chicago: Univ. of Illinois Press, 1992.

Klein, Lisa M. "Your Humble Handmaid: Elizabethan Gifts of Needlework." *Renaissance Quarterly* 50 (1997): 459–93.

Knox, John. *First Blast of the Trumpet Against the Monstrous Regiment of Women.* Geneva, 1558.

———. *The Political Writings of John Knox: The First Blast of the Trumpet Against the Monstrous Regiment of Women and Other Selected Works,* edited by Marvin A. Breslow. Washington, D.C.: Folger Shakespeare Library, 1985.

———. "To His Loving Sister, Mistres Anne Locke." In *The Works of John Knox.* Vol. 4, edited by David Laing, 237–41. Edinburgh: James Thin, 1895.

———. *The Works of John Knox,* edited by David Laing. 6 vols. Edinburgh: James Thin, 1895.

Koehler, Lyle. *A Search for Power: "The Weaker Sex" in Seventeenth Century New England.* Urbana: Univ. of Illinois Press, 1980.

Kohl, B. G., R. E. Witt, with E. B. Welles, eds. *The Earthly Republic: Italian Humanists on Government and Society.* Philadelphia: Univ. of Pennsylvania Press, 1978.

Krontiris, Tina. *Oppositional Voices: Women as Writers and Translators of Literature in the English Renaissance.* London and New York: Routledge, 1992.

———. "Style and Gender in Elizabeth Cary's *Edward II.*" In *The Renaissance Englishwoman in Print: Counterbalancing the Canon,* edited by Anne M. Haselkorn and Betty S. Travitsky, 137–53. Amherst: Univ. of Massachusetts Press, 1990.

Labalme, Patricia H., ed. *Beyond Their Sex: Learned Women of the European Past.* New York: New York Univ. Press, 1984.

Laing, David. "Notes Relating to Mrs. Esther Inglis." *Proceedings of the Society of Antiquaries of Scotland* 6 (1865): 284–309.

Lamb, Mary Ellen. "The Agency of the Split Subject: Lady Anne Clifford and the Uses of Agency." *English Literary Renaissance* 22, no. 3 (1992): 347–68.

———. "The Countess of Pembroke's Patronage." *English Literary Renaissance* 12, no. 2 (1982): 162–79.

———. *Gender and Authorship in the Sidney Circle.* Madison: Univ. of Wisconsin Press, 1990.

Lange, Thomas. "A Rediscovered Esther Inglis Calligraphic Manuscript in the Huntington Library." *PBSA: Papers of the Bibliographical Society of America* 89 (1995): 339–42.

Lanyer, Aemilia. *The Poems of Aemilia Lanyer: Salve Deus Rex Judaeorum,* edited by Susanne Woods. Women Writers in English 1350–1850. Oxford: Oxford Univ. Press, 1993.

Lee, Maurice. *Great Britain's Solomon: James VI and I in His Three Kingdoms.* Urbana: Univ. of Illinois Press, 1990.

Lefevre, Raoul. *The auncient Historie, of the destruction of Troy.* Translated by William Caxton. London, 1596.

Leigh, Dorothy. *The Mother's Blessing.* London, 1616.

———. *The Mother's Blessing.* 1616. Reprint. London, 1640.

L'Estrange, Hamon. *The Reign of King Charles: An History.* London, 1655.

Levin, Carole. *The Heart and Stomach of a King: Elizabeth I and the Politics of Sex and Power.* Philadelphia: Univ. of Pennsylvania Press, 1994.

Levin, Carole, and Patricia A. Sullivan, eds. *Political Rhetoric, Power, and Renaissance Women.* Albany, N.Y.: State Univ. of New York Press, 1995.

Lewalski, Barbara. *Protestant Poetics and the Seventeenth-Century Religious Lyric.* Princeton: Princeton Univ. Press, 1979.

———. *Writing Women in Jacobean England.* Cambridge, Mass.: Harvard Univ. Press, 1993.

Leyland, A. " 'Miller's Tale' [I(A) 3449]." *Notes and Queries* 219, no. 21 (1974): 126–27.

Loach, Jennifer. *Parliament and the Crown in the Reign of Mary Tudor.* Oxford: Clarendon, 1986.

Loades, David M. *Mary Tudor: A Life.* Oxford: Blackwell, 1989.

Lock, Anne. *The Works of Anne Vaughan Lock,* edited by Susan Felch. Binghamton, N.Y.: Medieval and Renaissance Text Society, 1999.

Lockyer, Roger. *Buckingham: The Life and Political Career of George Villiers, First Duke of Buckingham, 1592–1628.* London: Longman, 1981.

Logan, Marie-Rose and Peter L. Rudnytsky, eds. *Contending Kingdoms: Historical, Psychological, and Feminist Approaches to the Literature of Sixteenth-Century England and France.* Detroit: Wayne State Univ. Press, 1991.

L[ok], A[nne]. "A Meditation of a Penitent Sinner: Written in a Maner of a Paraphrase upon the 51 Psalme of David." In *Sermons of John Calvin, Vpon the Songe that Esechias made after he had bene sicke, and afflicted by the hand of God, conteyned in the 38. chapter of esay.* Translated from the French. London, 1560.

Lok, Anne. *Of the Markes of the children of God, and of their Comforts.* 1590. London, 1609.

Love, Harold. *Scribal Publication in Seventeenth-Century England.* Oxford: Clarendon, 1993.

Lutes, Jean Marie. "Negotiating Theology and Gynecology: Anne Bradstreet's Representations of the Female Body." *Signs* 22.2 (1997): 309–31.

Lynch, Michael. "Queen Mary's Triumph: The Baptismal Celebrations at Stirling in December 1566." *The Scottish Historical Review* 69, no. 187 (1990): 3–21.

———, ed. *Mary Stewart, Queen in Three Kingdoms.* Oxford: Blackwell, 1988.

Mack, Phyllis. *A Fire in the Bosom: Gender and Spirituality in Seventeenth-Century England.* Berkeley: Univ. of California Press, 1991.

———. "Teaching about Gender and Spirituality in Early English Quakerism." *Women's Studies* 19 (1991): 223–37.

————. *Visionary Women: Ecstatic Prophecy in Seventeenth-Century England.* Berkeley: Univ. of California Press, 1992.

————. "Women as Prophets during the English Civil War." *Feminist Studies* 8 (1982): 19–45.

Maclean, Ian. *The Renaissance Notion of Woman: A Study in the Fortunes of Scholasticism and Medical Science in European Intellectual Life.* Cambridge: Cambridge Univ. Press, 1980.

Mahl, Mary R., and Helene Koon. *The Female Spectator: English Women Writers Before 1800.* Bloomington: Indiana Univ. Press, 1977.

March, John. *Actions for Slaunder, or, a Methodicall Collection under certain Grounds and Heads, of what words are actionable in the Law, and what not?* London, 1648.

Marcus, Leah. "Shakespeare's Comic Heroines, Elizabeth I, and the Political Uses of Androgyny." In *Women in the Middle Ages and Renaissance: Literary and Historical Perspectives,* edited by Mary Beth Rose, 135–53. Syracuse: Syracuse Univ. Press, 1986.

Marlowe, Christopher. *The Troublesome Raigne and Lamentable Death of Edward the Second, King of England: With the Tragicall Fall of Proud Mortimer.* London, 1594.

Marotti, Arthur. " 'Love Is Not Love': Elizabethan Sonnet Sequences and the Social Order." *English Literary History* 49, no. 2 (1982): 396–428.

————. "Patronage, Poetry, and Print." *Yearbook of English Studies* 21 (1991): 1–26.

————. "The Transmission of Lyric Poetry and the Institutionalizing of Literature in the English Renaissance." In *Contending Kingdoms: Historical, Psychological, and Feminist Approaches to the Literature of Sixteenth-Century England and France,* edited by Marie-Rose Logan and Peter L. Rudnytsky, 21–41. Detroit: Wayne State Univ. Press, 1991.

Martin, Randall. "Anne Dowriche's *The French History,* Christopher Marlowe, and Machiavellian Agency." *Studies in English Literature* 39 (1999): 69–88.

————. "The Autobiography of Grace, Lady Mildmay." *Renaissance and Reformation* 18, no. 1 (1994): 33–81.

Martz, Louis Lohr. *The Poetry of Meditation: A Study in English Religious Literature of the Seventeenth Century.* New Haven: Yale Univ. Press, 1954.

Mary I of England, trans. *Paraphrase of the Gospel of St. John. The first tome or volume of the Paraphrase of Erasmus vpon the new testamente,* edited by Nicholas Udall. London: Edwarde Whitechurch, the last daie of Januarie, 1548.

Mary, Queen of Scots. "Sonnets to Bothwell." In *"Bittersweet within my heart": The Love Poems of Mary Queen of Scots,* edited and translated by Robin Bell, 31–57. San Francisco: Chronicle, 1992.

————. "Sonnets to Bothwell." Translated by Clifford Bax. In *Paradise of Women: Writings of Englishwomen of the Renaissance,* edited by Betty S. Travitsky, 193–98. Westport, Conn.: Greenwood, 1981.

Mason, Roger A., ed. *Scots and Britons: Scottish Political Thought and the Union of 1603.* Cambridge: Cambridge Univ. Press, 1994.

Masten, Jeff. " 'Shall I turne blabb?': Circulation, Gender, and Subjectivity in Mary Wroth's Sonnets." In *Reading Mary Wroth: Representing Alternatives in Early Modern England,* edited by Naomi J. Miller and Gary Waller, 67–87. Knoxville: Univ. of Tennessee Press, 1991.

Matthew, Tobie. *A Collection of Letters made by Sir Tobie Matthew, Knight.* London, 1660.

Matthews, John Hobson, ed. *Cardiff Records: Being Materials for a History of the County Borough from the Earliest Times.* Cardiff: published by order of the corporation, 1901.

Mattingly, Garrett. *Catherine of Aragon.* 1941. Reprint. New York: Quality Paperback, 1990.

Mauss, Marcel. *The Gift: Form and Reason for Exchange in Archaic Societes.* Translated by W. D. Halls. 1950. Reprint. London: Routledge, 1990.

May, Stephen W. *The Elizabethan Courtier Poets: The Poems and Their Contexts.* Columbia: Univ. of Missouri Press, 1991.

Maydens of London. *A Letter Sent by the Maydens of London, to the vertuous Matrones & Mistresses of the same, in the defense of their lawfull Libertie* (1567), edited by R. J. Fehrenbach. *English Literary Renaissance* 14 (1984): 285–304. Reprinted in *Women in the Renaissance: Selections from English Literary Renaissance,* edited by Kirby Farrell, Elizabeth H. Hageman, and Arthur F. Kinney, 28–47. Amherst: Univ. of Massachusetts Press, 1990.

Mayr-Harting, H. M. "Functions of a Twelfth-Century Shrine: The Miracles of St. Fridewide." In *Studies in Medieval History Presented to R. H. C. Davis,* edited by Henry Mayr-Harting and R. J. Moore, 193–206. London: Hambledon, 1985.

McBride, Kari Boyd. "Sacred Celebration: The Patronage Poems of Aemilia Lanyer." In *Gender, Genre, and the Canon,* edited by Marshall Grossman. Lexington: Univ. of Kentucky Press, forthcoming.

McEachern, Claire. "Fathering Herself: A Source Study of Shakespeare's Feminism." *Shakespeare Quarterly* 39, no. 3 (1988): 269–90.

McGrath, Lynette. "Metaphoric Subversions: Feasts and Mirrors in Aemilia Lanier's *Salve Deus Rex Judaeorum.*" *Literature Interpretation Theory* 3 (1991): 101–13.

McLaren, Dorothy. "Marital Fertility and Lactation 1570–1720." In *Women in English Society, 1500–1800,* edited by Mary Prior, 22–53. London: Methuen, 1985.

McManus, Barbara F. *Classics and Feminism: Gendering the Classics.* New York: Twayne, 1997.

Mendelson, Sara Heller. *The Mental World of Stuart Women: Three Studies.* Amherst: Univ. of Massachusetts Press, 1987.

Merriman, M. H. "Mary, Queen of France." In *Mary Stewart: Queen in Three Kingdoms,* edited by Michael Lynch, 30–52. Oxford: Basil Blackwell, 1988.

Michaud, M. M. *Biographie Universelle.* 2d ed. Vol. 7, 214. Paris: Vives, 1880.

Mildmay, Grace. *With Faith and Physics: The Life of a Tudor Gentlewoman, Lady Grace Mildmay 1552–1620,* edited by Linda Pollock. New York: St. Martin's, 1995.

Miller, Edwin Haviland. *The Professional Writer in Elizabethan England: A Study of Nondramatic Literature.* Cambridge, Mass.: Harvard Univ. Press, 1959.

Miller, Naomi J. *Changing the Subject: Mary Wroth and Figurations of Gender in Early Modern Europe.* Lexington: Univ. Press of Kentucky, 1996.

———. (M)Other Tongues: Maternity and Subjectivity." In *Aemilia Lanyer: Gender, Genre, and the Canon,* edited by Marshall Grossman, 148–66. Lexington: Univ. Press of Kentucky, 1998.

Miller, Naomi J., and Gary Waller, eds. *Reading Mary Wroth: Representing Alternatives in Early Modern England.* Knoxville: Univ. of Tennessee Press, 1991.

Moffett, Thomas. *Nobilis: or, a view of the Life and Death of a Sidney, and Lessus Lugubris,* edited by Virgil B. Heltzel and Hoyt H. Hudson. San Marino, Calif.: Huntington Library, 1940.

———. *The Silkwormes and their Flies.* London, 1599. Facsimile reprint edited by Victor Houliston. Binghamton, N.Y.: Medieval and Renaissance Texts and Studies, 1989.

———. *The Theater of Insects.* London, 1658.

Montaigne, Michel de. *Montaigne's Travel Journal.* Translated by Donald M. Frame. San Francisco: North Point, 1983.

More, Edward. *A Lytle and Bryefe Treatyse, Called the Defense of Women.* London, 1560.

More, Thomas. *A Dialogue Concerning Heresies,* edited by Thomas M. C. Lawler, Germain Marc'Hadour, and Richard C. Marius. 2 parts. *Complete Works of St. Thomas More.* Vol. 6. New Haven: Yale Univ. Press, 1981.

Morgan, John. *Godly Learning: Puritan Attitudes toward Reason, Learning, and Education, 1560–1640.* Cambridge: Cambridge Univ. Press, 1986.

Morris, J. P. "Saint Uncumber." *Notes and Queries,* ser. 4, no. 6 (1870): 559.

Munda, Constantia. *The Worming of a Mad Dogge: or, a Soppe for Cerberus the Jaylor of Hell.* London, 1617.

Mueller, Janel. "The Feminist Poetics of 'Salve Deus Rex Judaeorum.' " In *Aemilia Lanyer: Gender, Genre, and the Canon,* edited by Marshall Grossman, 99–127. Lexington: Univ. Press of Kentucky, 1998.

Nashe, Thomas. *Have with you to Saffron Walden, or Gabrielle Harveys Hunt is Up.* London, 1596.

Neale, J. E. *Elizabeth I and Her Parliaments, 1559–1581.* 2 vols. London: Jonathan Cape, 1953.

Neely, Carol Thomas. "Constructing the Subject: Feminist Practice and the New Renaissance Discourses." *English Literary Renaissance* 18, no. 1 (1988): 5–18.

Neill, Michael. " 'Amphitheaters in the Body': Playing with Hands on the Shakespearian Stage." *Shakespeare Survey* 48 (1995): 23–50.

Neilson, William Allan. *The Origins and Sources of the Court of Love.* New York: Russell and Russell, 1899.

Nelson, Karen L. "Elizabeth Cary's *Edward II* and the Court of Charles I." Master's thesis, Univ. of Maryland, 1992.

New Catholic Encyclopedia. New York: McGraw Hill, 1967.

Newcomb, Lori Humphrey. " 'Social Things': The Production of Popular Culture in the Reception of Robert Greene's *Pandosto.*" *English Literary History* 61 (1994): 753–81.

Newman, Karen. *Fashioning Femininity and English Renaissance Drama.* Chicago: Univ. of Chicago Press, 1991.

Newstead, Christopher. *An Apology for Women: or, Womens Defence.* London, 1620.

Newton, Judith, and Deborah Rosenfelt, eds. *Feminist Criticism and Social Change: Sex, Class, and Race in Literature and Culture.* New York: Methuen, 1985.

Nichols, John. *Illustrations of the Manners and Expences of Antient Times in England, in the Fifteenth, Sixteenth, and Seventeenth Centuries, Deduced from the Accompts of Churchwardens, and Other Authentic Documents.* London, 1797.

——. *The Progresses and Public Processions of Queen Elizabeth.* 3 vols. London, 1823.

Nightlinger, Elizabeth. "The Female *Imitatio Christi* and Medieval Popular Religion: The Case of St. Wigefortis." *Feminea Medievalia* 1 (1993): 291–328.

Oman, Carola. *Henrietta Maria.* London: Hodder and Stoughton, 1936.

Ong, Walter J. *Orality and Literacy: The Technologizing of the Word.* 1982. Reprint. London: Routledge, 1991.

——. *Rhetoric, Romance, and Technology: Studies in the Interaction of Expression and Culture.* Ithaca: Cornell Univ. Press, 1971.

Otten, Charlotte F. *English Women's Voices 1540–1700.* Miami: Florida International Univ. Press, 1992.

Outhwaite, R. B., ed. *Marriage and Society: Studies in the Social History of Marriage.* London: Europa, 1981.

Oxford English Dictionary. Prepared by J. A. Simpson and E. S. C. Weiner. 2d ed. Oxford: Clarendon, 1989.

Parker, James. *The Early History of Oxford, 727–1100.* Oxford: Clarendon, 1885.

Parker, Matthew. *The Whole Psalter translated into English metre.* Setting by T. Tallis. London, 1567.

Parr, Catherine. "1544 Letter to Mary." In *The Paradise of Women: Writings of Englishwomen of the Renaissance,* edited by Betty Travitsky, 78. New York: Columbia Univ. Press, 1989.

Paster, Gail Kern. *The Body Embarrassed: Drama and the Disciplines of Shame in Early Modern England.* Ithaca, N.Y.: Cornell Univ. Press, 1993.

——. "Leaky Vessels: The Incontinent Women of City Comedy." *Renaissance Drama* 18 (1987): 43–65.

Patterson, Annabel M. *Censorship and Interpretation: The Conditions of Writing and Reading in Early Modern England.* 1984. Madison: Univ. of Wisconsin Press, 1990.

——. *Reading Holinshed's Chronicles.* Chicago: Univ. of Chicago Press, 1994.

——. "The Small Cat Massacre: Popular Culture in the 1587 'Holinshed.' " In *Reading Between the Lines,* by Annabel M. Patterson, 117–59. Madison: Univ. of Wisconsin Press, 1993.

Pembroke, Mary Sidney [Herbert], Countess of. *The Collected Works of Mary Sidney Herbert, Countess of Pembroke,* edited by Margaret P. Hannay, Noel J. Kinnamon, and Michael G. Brennan. 2 vols. Oxford: Clarendon, 1998.

——. *The Psalms of Sir Philip Sidney and the Countess of Pembroke,* edited by J. C. A. Rathmell. New York: New York Univ. Press, 1963.

―――. *The Triumph of Death and Other Unpublished and Uncollected Poems by Mary Sidney, Countess of Pembroke (1561–1621)*, edited by Gary F. Waller. Salzburg, Austria: Institut für Englische Sprache und Literatur, Univ. of Salzburg, 1977.

―――, trans. *Discourse of Life and Death. Written in French by Ph. Mornay. Antonius, a Tragedie Written also in French by Ro. Garnier. Both done in English by the Countesse of Pembroke*. London: William Ponsonby, 1592.

Phillips, James Emerson. *Images of a Queen: Mary Stuart in Sixteenth Century Literature*. Berkeley: Univ. of California Press, 1964.

Phillips, John A. *Eve: The History of an Idea*. San Francisco: Harper and Row, 1984.

Pistoia, Domenico Bruni de. *Difese delle donne*. Milan, 1559.

Pliny. *Plinies Naturall Historie*. Translated by Philemon Holland. London, 1601.

Plowden, Alison. *Two Queens in One Isle: The Deadly Relationship of Elizabeth I and Mary Queen of Scots*. Brighton: Harvester, 1984.

Pocock, J. G. A. "Postscript: Two Kingdoms and Three Histories? Political Thought in British Context." In *Scots and Britons: Scottish Political Thought and the Union of 1603*, edited by Roger A. Mason. Cambridge: Cambridge Univ. Press, 1994.

Pollard, A. W., and G. R. Redgrave. *Short-Title Catalogue of Books Printed in England, Scotland and Ireland and of English Books Printed Abroad, 1475–1640*. 2d ed. London: Bibliographical Society, 1976.

Porter, Roy. "The Prophetic Body: Lady Eleanor Davies and the Meanings of Madness." *Women's Writing: the Elizabethan to the Victorian Period* 1, no. 1 (1994): 51–64.

Powell, Chilton Latham. *English Domestic Relations, 1487–1653*. New York: Columbia Univ. Press, 1917.

Prescott, Anne Lake. "Evil Tongues at the Court of Saul: the Renaissance David as a Slandered Courtier." *Journal of Medieval and Renaissance Studies* 21, no. 2 (1991): 163–86.

Prescott, H. F. M. *A Spanish Tudor: The Life of Bloody Mary*. 1940. Reprint. New York: AMS, 1970.

Prest, W. R. "Law and Women's Rights in Early Modern England." *The Seventeenth Century* 6, no. 2 (1991): 169–87.

Prior, Mary. "Women and the Urban Economy: Oxford 1500–1800." In *Women in English Society 1500–1800*, edited by Mary Prior, 93–117. London: Methuen, 1985.

Prior, Mary, ed. *Women in English Society 1500–1800*. London: Methuen, 1985.

Pugh, T. B. "A Portrait of Queen Anne of Denmark at Parham Park, Sussex." *Seventeenth Century* 8, no. 2 (1993): 167–80.

Purkiss, Diane. Introduction to *Renaissance Women: The Plays of Elizabeth Cary, the Poems of Aemilia Lanyer*, edited by Diane Purkiss, vii–xlvii. London: Pickering and Chatto, 1994.

―――. "Producing the Voice, Consuming the Body: Women Prophets of the Seventeenth Century." In *Women, Writing, History 1640–1740*, edited by Isobel Grundy and Susan Wiseman, 139–58. Athens, Ga.: Univ. of Georgia Press, 1992.

———, ed. *Renaissance Women: The Plays of Elizabeth Cary, the Poems of Aemilia Lanyer*. London: Pickering and Chatto, 1994.

Rader, Rosemary. "Reassessing the Legend of St. Frideswide, Monastic Foundress of Oxford." Unpublished manuscript.

Rappaport, Steve. *Worlds within Worlds: Structures of Life in Sixteenth-Century London*. Cambridge: Cambridge Univ. Press, 1989.

Rathmell, J. C. A. Introduction to *The Psalms of Sir Philip Sidney and the Countess of Pembroke*, edited by J. C. A. Rathmell, xi–xxxii. New York: New York Univ. Press, 1963.

Raylor, Timothy. "Samuel Hartlib and the Commonwealth of Bees." In *Culture and Cultivation in Early Modern England: Writing and the Land*, edited by Michael Leslie and Timothy Raylor, 91–129. Leicester Univ. Press, 1992.

Rémond, Flormond de. *L'Histoire de la naissance, pogrez et decadence de l'heresie de ce siecle*. Paris: Charles Chastellain, 1610.

Rienstra, Debra. "Aspiring to Praise: The Sidney-Pembroke Psalter and the English Religious Lyric." Ph.D. diss., Rutgers Univ., 1995.

Roberts, Josephine A. Critical Introduction to *The First Part of the Countess of Montgomery's Urania* by Mary Wroth, xv–cxx. Binghamton, N.Y.: Center for Medieval and Early Renaissance Texts and Studies, 1995.

Robertson, Karen, and Susan Frye, eds. *Maids and Mistresses, Cousins and Queens: Women's Alliances in Early Modern England*. New York: Oxford Univ. Press, 1998.

Roche, Thomas P. *Petrarch and the English Sonnet Sequences*. New York: AMS, 1989.

Rogers, Daniel. *Matrimonial Honor*. London, 1642.

Rogers, Katharine M. *The Troublesome Helpmate: A History of Misogyny in Literature*. Seattle: Univ. of Washington Press, 1966.

Rose, Mary Beth. *The Expense of Spirit: Love and Sexuality in English Renaissance Drama*. Ithaca: Cornell Univ. Press, 1988.

———. "Where Are the Mothers in Shakespeare? Options for Gender Representation in the English Renaissance." *Shakespeare Quarterly* 42, no. 3 (1991): 291–314.

———, ed. *Women in the Middle Ages and the Renaissance: Literary and Historical Perspectives*. Syracuse: Syracuse Univ. Press, 1986.

Rowse, A. L. Introduction to *Poems of Shakespeare's Dark Lady: Salve Deus Rex Judaeorum by Aemilia Lanier*, 7–37. London: Cape, 1978.

Ruether, Rosemary Radford. "Misogynism and Virginal Feminism in the Fathers of the Church." In *Religion and Sexism: Images of Women in the Jewish and Christian Traditions*, edited by Rosemary Radford Ruether, 150–83. New York: Simon and Schuster, 1974.

———, ed. *Religion and Sexism: Images of Women in the Jewish and Christian Traditions*. New York: Simon and Schuster, 1974.

"St. Uncumber." *Notes and Queries* 1st ser., no. 3 (1851): 404–5.

"St. Uncumber." *Notes and Queries*, 2d ser., no. 9 (1860): 164.

"St. Uncumber and St. Wylgeforte." *Notes and Queries* series 1, no. 2 (1850): 381–2.

Salter, H. E. *Medieval Oxford*. Oxford: Clarendon, 1936.

Salter, Thomas. *A mirrhor mete for all mothers, matrones, and maidens, intituled the mirrhor of modestie.* London, 1579.

Sanderson, William. *A Compleat History of the Life and Raigne of King Charles.* London, 1658.

———. *Peter pursued, or Dr. Heylin overtaken, Arrested, and Arraigned upon his three Appendixes.* London, 1658.

———. *Post-Haste: A Reply to Peter.* London, 1658.

Sankovitch, Tilde A. *French Women Writers and the Book: Myths of Access and Desire.* Syracuse: Syracuse Univ. Press, 1988.

———. "Inventing the Authority of Origin: The Difficult Enterprise." In *Women in the Middle Ages and Renaissance: Literary and Historical Perspectives,* edited by Mary Beth Rose, 227–243. Syracuse: Syracuse Univ. Press, 1986.

Sartori, Eva Martin, and Dorothy Wynne Zimmerman, eds. *French Women Writers: A Bio-Bibliographical Source Book.* New York: Greenwood, 1991.

Schiffer, James. "Macbeth and the Beareded Woman." In *Another Country: Feminist Perspectives on Renaissance Drama,* edited by Dorothea Kehler and Susan Baker, 205–17. Metuchen, N.J.: Scarecrow, 1991.

Schleiner, Louise. *Tudor and Stuart Women Writers.* Bloomington: Indiana Univ. Press, 1994.

Schnell, Lisa. " 'So Great a Diffrence Is There in Degree': Aemilia Lanyer and the Aims of Feminist Criticism." *Modern Language Quarterly* 57.1 (1996): 23–35.

Schnucker, R. V. "The English Puritans and Pregnancy, Delivery, and Breastfeeding." *History of Childhood Quarterly* 1, no. 4 (1974): 637–58.

Schochet, Gordon J. *Patriarchalism in Political Thought: The Authoritarian Family and Political Speculation and Attitudes Especially in Seventeenth-Century England.* Oxford: Blackwell, 1975.

Schrift, Alan D., ed. *The Logic of the Gift: Toward an Ethic of Generosity.* New York: Routledge, 1997.

Schucking, Levin L. *The Puritan Family: A Social Study from the Literary Sources.* Translated by Brian Battershaw. New York: Schocken, 1970.

Schulenburg, Jane Tibbetts. *Forgetful of Their Sex: Female Sanctity and Society, ca. 500–1100.* Chicago: Univ. of Chicago Press, 1998.

———. "The Heroics of Virginity: Brides of Christ and Sacrificial Mutilation." In *Women in the Middle Ages and the Renaissance: Literary and Historical Perspectives,* edited by Mary Beth Rose, 29–72. Syracuse: Syracuse Univ. Press, 1986.

Scott-Elliot, A. H., and Elspeth Yeo. "Calligraphic Manuscripts of Esther Inglis (1571–1624): A Catalogue." *Papers of the Bibliographical Society of America* 84, no.4 (1990): 11–86.

Seneca. *The Woorke of the Excellent Philosopher Lucius Annaeus Seneca Concerning Benefyting (De beneficiis).* Translated by Arthur Golding. London, 1578.

Shakespeare, William. "Henry VIII." In *The Riverside Shakespeare,* edited by G. Blakemore Evans, 976–1018. Geneva: Houghton Mifflin, 1974.

———. "The Tragedy of King Richard II." In *William Shakespeare: The Complete Works,* edited by Alfred Harbage, 633–67. New York: Viking, 1969.

Sharp, Ronald A. "Gift Exchange and the Economics of Spirit in *The Merchant of Venice.*" *Modern Philology* 83, no. 3 (1986): 250–65.

Shepherd, Simon, ed. *The Women's Sharp Revenge: Five Women's Pamphlets from the Renaissance.* New York: St. Martin's, 1985.

Shuger, Debora. *Habits of Thought in the English Renaissance: Religion, Politics, and the Dominant Culture.* Berkeley: Univ. of California Press, 1997.

Sidney, Mary. See Pembroke, Mary Sidney, Countess of.

Sidney, Philip. *The Countess of Pembrokes Arcadia* [*The Old Arcadia*], edited by Jean Robertson. Oxford: Clarendon Press, 1973.

———. *Miscellaneous Prose of Sir Philip Sidney,* edited by Katherine Duncan-Jones and Jan van Dorsten. Oxford: Clarendon, 1973.

———. *The Poems of Sir Philip Sidney,* edited by William A. Ringler Jr. Oxford: Clarendon, 1962.

Sidney, Philip, and Mary Sidney. *The Psalms of Sir Philip Sidney and the Countess of Pembroke,* edited by J. C. A. Rathmell. New York: New York Univ. Press, 1963.

Simpson, W. Sparrow. *St. Paul's Cathedral and Old City Life.* London: Elliot Stock, 1894.

Sinfield, Alan. *Faultlines: Cultural Materialism and the Politics of Dissident Reading.* Berkeley: Univ. of California Press, 1992.

Skura, Meredith. "The Reproduction of Mothering in *Mariam, Queen of Jewry*: A Defense of "Biographical" Criticism." *Tulsa Studies in Women's Literature* 16, no. 1 (1998): 27–56.

Smith, Hilda. "Gynecology and Ideology in Seventeenth-Century England." In *Liberating Women's History: Theoretical and Critical Essays,* edited by Berenice A. Carroll, 97–114. Chicago: Univ. of Illinois Press, 1976.

———. *Reason's Disciples: Seventeenth-Century English Feminists.* Urbana: Univ. of Illinois Press, 1982.

Smith, Paul. *Discerning the Subject.* Theory and History of Literature, no. 55. Minneapolis: Univ. of Minnesota Press, 1988.

Smith, Sir Thomas. *De Republica Anglorum.* London, 1583. Facsimile reprint in the English Experience Series, no. 219. New York: De Capo, 1970.

Smuts, Malcolm. "The Political Failure of Stuart Cultural Patronage." In *Patronage in the Renaissance,* edited by Guy Fitch Lytle and Stephen Orgel, 165–87. Princeton: Princeton Univ. Press, 1981.

Somerset, Anne. *Elizabeth I.* New York: Alfred A. Knopf, 1991.

———. *Ladies-in-Waiting: From the Tudors to the Present Day.* New York: Alfred A. Knopf, 1984.

Sommerville, J. P. *Politics and Ideology in England, 1603–1640.* New York: Longman, 1986.

Sowernam, Ester. *Ester hath hang'd Haman: or An Answere To a Lewd Pamphlet, entituled, The Arraignment of Women.* London, 1617.

Speght, Rachel. *Mortalities Memorandum, with a Dreame Prefixed, imaginarie in manner: reall in matter.* London, 1621.

———. *A Mouzell for Melastomus, The Cynical Bayter of, and foule mouthed Barker against Evahs Sex.* London, 1617.

Spence, Lewis. *The Fairy Tradition in Britain.* New York: Rider, 1948.

Spiller, Michael. *The Development of the Sonnet.* London: Routledge, 1992.

Stallybrass, Peter. "Patriarchal Territories: The Body Enclosed." In *Rewriting the Renaissance: The Discourses of Sexual Difference in Early Modern Europe,* edited by Margaret W. Ferguson, Maureen Quilligan, and Nancy J. Vickers, 123–42. Chicago: Univ. of Chicago Press, 1986.

Stanton, Richard. *A Menology of England and Wales.* London: Burnes and Oates; New York: Catholic Publication Society, 1887.

Stationers' Company. *Transcript of the Register of the Company of Stationers of London, 1554–1640,* edited by Edward Arber. London, 1875. Reprint. [New York: P. Smith, 1950.]

Stauffer, Donald. "A Deep and Sad Passion." In *Essays in Dramatic Literature: The Parrott Presentation Volume,* edited by Hardin Craig, 289–314. Princeton: Princeton Univ. Press, 1967.

Steinberg, Theodore L. "The Sidneys and the Psalms." *Studies in Philology* 92 (1995): 1–17.

Stenton, F. M. "St. Frideswide and Her Times." *Oxoniensia* 1 (1936): 103–12.

Stephen, James Fitzjames. *A History of the Criminal Law of England,* 3 vols. 1883. Reprint. New York: Burt Franklin, 1973.

Stephen, Leslie, and Sidney Lee, eds. *Dictionary of National Biography.* London: Smith, Elder and Co., 1885–1901.

Sternhold, Thomas, J. Hopkins and others. *The whole booke of psalmes collected into English meter by Thomas Sternhold, J. Hopkins and others.* Geneva, 1569.

Stewart, Mary. See Mary, Queen of Scots.

Stone, Lawrence. *The Family, Sex, and Marriage in England 1500–1800.* Abridged. New York: Harper and Row, 1979.

Storey, John, ed. *Cultural Theory and Popular Culture.* New York: Harvester-Wheatsheaf, 1994.

Strong, Roy. *Cult of Elizabeth: Elizabethan Portraiture and Pageantry.* Wallop, Hampshire: Thames and Hudson, 1977.

———. *Henry, Prince of Wales, and England's Lost Renaissance.* London: Thames and Hudson, 1986.

Strype, John. *The Life and Acts of Matthew Parker.* Oxford: Clarendon, 1821.

Stuart, Arbella. *The Letters of Lady Arbella Stuart,* edited by Sara Jayne Steen. New York: Oxford Univ. Press, 1994.

Stuart, James I. See James I of England.

Stuart, Mary. See Mary, Queen of Scots.

Swetnam, Joseph. *The Araignment of Lewde, idle, froward, and unconstant women.* London, 1615.

Taffin, Jean. *Of the Markes of the Children of God, and of Their Comforts.* Translated by Anne Lok. London, 1609.

Tattle-well, Mary, and Joane Hit-him-home. *The Womens Sharpe Revenge: Or an answer to Sir Seldome Sober that writ those railing Pamphlets called the Juniper and Crabtree Lectures.* London, 1640.

Taylor, John. *A Juniper Lecture.* London, 1939.

Teague, Frances. "Elizabeth I: Queen of England." In *Women Writers of the Renaissance and Reformation,* edited by Katharina M. Wilson, 522–47. Athens: Univ. of Georgia Press, 1987.

———. "Queen Elizabeth in Her Speeches." *Gloriana's Face: Women, Public and Private, in the English Renaissance,* edited by S. P. Cerasano and Marion Wynne-Davies, 63–78. Detroit: Wayne State Univ. Press, 1992.

Thickstun, Margaret Olofson. *Fictions of the Feminine: Puritan Doctrine and the Representation of Women.* Ithaca: Cornell Univ. Press, 1988.

Thomas, William J. "St. Uncumber." *Notes and Queries,* ser. 1, no. 2 (1850): 342.

Thomson, Patricia. "The Literature of Patronage, 1580–1630." *Essays in Criticism* 2, no. 3 (1952): 267–84.

Thomson, T., ed. *Diurnel of Occurents.* Edinburg: Bannatyne Club, 1833.

Tilney, Edmund. *A briefe and pleasant discourse of duties in Mariage, called the Flower of Friendshippe.* London, 1568.

———. *The Flower of Friendship: A Renaissance Dialogue Contesting Marriage,* edited by Valerie Wayne. Ithaca, N.Y.: Cornell Univ. Press, 1992.

Todd, Margo. *Christian Humanism and the Puritan Social Order.* Cambridge: Cambridge Univ. Press, 1987.

———. "Humanists, Puritans, and the Spiritualized Household." *Church History* 49 (1980): 18–34.

Todd, Richard. " 'So Well Atyr'd Abroad': A Background to the Sidney-Pembroke Psalter and Its Implications for the Seventeenth-Century Religous Lyric." *Texas Studies in Literature and Language* 29 (Mar. 1987): 74–93.

Travitsky, Betty S. "Placing Women in the English Renaissance." Introduction to *The Renaissance Englishwoman in Print: Counterbalancing the Canon,* edited by Betty S. Travitsky and Anne M. Haselkorn, 3–41. Amherst: Univ. of Massachusetts Press, 1990.

———, ed. *The Paradise of Women: Writings of Englishwomen of the Renaissance.* Westport, Conn.: Greenwood, 1981. Reprinted New York: Columbia Univ. Press, 1989.

Travitsky, Betty S., and Anne M. Haselkorn, eds. *The Renaissance Englishwoman in Print: Counterbalancing the Canon.* Amherst: Univ. of Massachusetts Press, 1990.

Travitsky, Betty S., and Adele F. Seeff, eds. *Attending to Women in Early Modern England.* Newark: Univ. of Delaware Press, 1994.

Trease, G. E. "Dowrich and the Dowrich Family of Sandford." *Devon and Cornwall Notes and Queries* 33 (1974): 208–11.

Trinterud, Leonard J., ed. *Elizabethan Puritanism.* New York: Oxford Univ. Press, 1971.

Troeltsch, Ernst. *The Social Teaching of the Christian Churches.* Translated by Olive Wyon. 2 vols. Oxford: Oxford Univ. Press, 1960.

Tudor, Elizabeth. See Elizabeth I of England.

Tudor, Mary. See Mary I of England.

Turner, James Grantham, ed. *Sexuality and Gender in Early Modern Europe: Institutions, Texts, Images.* Cambridge: Cambridge Univ. Press, 1993.

Ulrich, Laurel Thatcher. *A Midwife's Tale: The Life of Martha Ballard, Based on Her Diary 1785–1812.* New York: Knopf, 1990.

Utley, Francis Lee. *The Crooked Rib: An Analytical Index to the Argument about Women in English and Scots Literature to the End of the Year 1568.* Contributions in Language and Literature, no. 10. English Series, no. 3. Columbus: Ohio State Univ. Press, 1944.

van Dorsten, Jan. *Poets, Patrons, and Professors: Sir Philip Sidney, Daniel Rogers, and the Leiden Humanists.* Leiden: Leiden Univ. Press, 1962.

Veevers, Erica. *Images of Love and Religion: Queen Henrietta Maria and Court Entertainments.* Cambridge: Cambridge Univ. Press, 1989.

Vickers, Nancy. "Diana Described: Scattered Women and Scattered Rhyme." *Critical Inquiry* 8 (1981): 265–79.

Vives, Juan Luis. "The Duty of Husbands [*De Officio Mariti*]." In *Vives and the Renascence Education of Women,* edited by Foster Watson, 195–210. Translated by Thomas Paynell. New York: Longmans, Green, 1912.

———. "The Instruction of a Christian Woman [*De Institutione Feminae Christianae*]." In *Vives and the Renascence Education of Women,* edited and translated by Foster Watson, 29–136. New York: Longmans, Green, 1912.

———. "Plan of Studies for a Boy [*De Ratione Studii Puerilis ad Carolum Montjoium Guilielmi filium*]." In *Vives and the Renascence Education of Women,* edited and translated by Foster Watson, 245–50. New York: Longmans, Green & Co., 1912.

———. "Plan of Study for Girls [*De Ratione Studii Puerilis*]." In *Vives and the Renascence Education of Women,* edited and translated by Foster Watson, 137–50. New York: Longmans, Green, 1912.

———. "Satellitium." In *Vives and the Renascence Education of Women,* edited and translated by Foster Watson, 241–45. New York: Longmans, Green, 1912.

Wakefield, Walter L., and Austin P. Evans. *Heresies of the High Middle Ages: Selected Sources Translated and Annotated.* New York and London: Columbia Univ. Press, 1969.

Waldman, Milton. *The Lady Mary: A Biography of Mary Tudor.* New York: Scribner, 1972.

Walker, Julia M. *Dissing Elizabeth: Negative Representations of Gloriana.* Durham: Duke Univ. Press, 1998.

Walker, Kim. *Women Writers of the English Renaissance.* Twayne's English Authors Series 521. New York: Twayne Publishers, 1996.

Wall, J. Charles. *Shrines of British Saints.* London: Methuen, 1905.

Wall, Wendy. *The Imprint of Gender: Authorship and Publication in the English Renaissance.* Ithaca: Cornell Univ. Press, 1993.

———. "Isabella Whitney and the Female Legacy." *ELH: English Literary History* 58, no. 1 (1991): 35–62.

———. "Our Bodies / Our Texts?: Renaissance Women and the Trials of Authorship." In *Anxious Power: Reading, Writing, and Ambivalence in Narrative by Women,* edited by Carol J. Singley and Susan Elizabeth Sweeney, 51–70. Albany: State Univ. of New York Press, 1993.

Waller, Gary F. *Mary Sidney, Countess of Pembroke: A Critical Study of Her Writings and Literary Milieu.* Salzburg Studies in English Literature: English and Renaissance Studies, no. 87. Salzburg: Institute for English and American Studies, Univ. of Salzburg, 1979.

———. "Struggling into Discourse: The Emergence of Renaissance Women's Writing." In *Silent But for the Word: Tudor Women as Patrons, Translators, and Writers of Religious Works,* edited by Margaret P. Hannay, 238–56. Kent, Ohio: Kent State Univ. Press, 1985.

———. " 'This Matching of Contraries': Calvinism and Courtly Philosphy in the Sidney Psalms." *English Studies* 55 (1974): 22–31.

Warner, Marina. *Alone of All Her Sex: The Myth and Cult of the Virgin Mary.* New York: Alfred A. Knopf, 1976.

Warnicke, Retha M. *Women of the English Renaissance and Reformation.* Westport, Conn.: Greenwood, 1983.

Watson, Foster, ed. *Vives and the Renascence Education of Women.* New York: Longmans, Green, 1912.

Wayne, Valerie, ed. *The Matter of Difference: Materialist Feminist Criticism of Shakespeare.* Ithaca: Cornell Univ. Press, 1991.

Weiner, Seth. "Sidney and the Rabbis: A Note on the Psalms of David and Renaissance Hebraica." In *Sir Philip Sidney's Achievements,* edited by M. J. B. Allen, Dominic Baker-Smith, and Arthur F. Kinney, with Margaret M. Sullivan, 157–62. New York: AMS, 1990.

Weir, Alison. *The Life of Elizabeth I.* New York: Ballantine Books, 1998.

Wells, Robin Headlam. *Spenser's Faerie Queen and the Cult of Elizabeth.* Totowa, N.J.: Barnes and Noble, 1983.

Whateley, William. *The Bride-Bush.* London, 1619.

Whigham, Frank. *Ambition and Privilege.* Berkeley: Univ. of California Press, 1984.

———. "The Rhetoric of Elizabethan Suitors' Letters." *PMLA* 96, no. 5 (1981): 864–82.

White, Allan. "Queen Mary's Northern Province." In *Mary Stewart: Queen in Three Kingdoms,* edited by Michael Lynch, 53–70. Oxford: Basil Blackwell, 1988.

White, Micheline. "Cunning in Controversies: Puritan Women and Religious and Literary Debates 1580–1615." Ph.D. diss., Loyola Univ. of Chicago, 1998.

Whitney, Isabella. *The Copy of a Letter, Lately Written in Meeter, by a yonge Gentilwoman: to her unconstant Louer. With an Admonition to al yong Gentilwomen, and to all other Mayds in general to beware of mennes flattery.* London, 1567.

———. *The Floures of Philosphie (1572) by Hugh Plat and a Sweet Nosgay (1573) and The Copy of a Letter (1567) by Isabella Whitney.* Introduction by Richard J. Panofsky. Delmar, N.Y.: Scholars' Facsimiles and Reprints, 1982.

———. *A sweet Nosgay, or pleasant posye, contayning a hundred and ten Phylosophicall Flowers.* London, 1573.

The Whole Booke of Psalmes, collected into Englysh metre by T. Sternhold J. Hopkins and others: conferred with the Ebrue, with apt Notes to synge them with al. London, 1562.

Wiesner, Merry E. *Women and Gender in Early Modern Europe.* Cambridge: Cambridge Univ. Press, 1993.

Williams, Franklin. *Index of Dedications and Commendatory Verses in English Books Before 1641.* London: Bibliographic Society, 1962.

Williams, Raymond. *Culture and Society 1780–1950.* New York: Columbia Univ. Press, 1958.

———. *Keywords: A Vocabulary of Culture and Society.* 1976. Rev. ed. New York: Oxford Univ. Press, 1985.

———. *Marxism and Literature.* Oxford: Oxford Univ. Press, 1977.

Williams, Robert. "A Moon to Their Sun: Writing Mistresses of the Sixteenth and Seventeenth Centuries." *Fine Print* 11 (1985): 88–98.

Williamson, Marilyn L. *Raising Their Voices: British Women Writers, 1650–1750.* Detroit: Wayne State Univ. Press, 1990.

Wilson, Adrian. "Participant or Patient? Seventeenth-Century Childbirth from the Mother's Point of View." In *Patients and Practitioners: Lay Perceptions of Medicine in Pre-Industrial Society,* edited by Roy Porter, 129–44. Cambridge: Cambridge Univ. Press, 1985.

Wilson, Elkin Calhoun. *England's Eliza.* Cambridge, Mass.: Harvard Univ. Press, 1939.

Wilson, Katherina M., ed. *Women Writers of the Renaissance and Reformation.* Athens: Univ. of Georgia Press, 1987.

Wing, Donald Goddard. *A Short-Title Catalogue of Books Printed in England, Scotland, Ireland, Wales and British America and of English Books Printed in Other Countries, 1641–1700.* 2d ed. 3 vols. New York: Modern Language Association, 1972.

Wood, Anthony A. *Athenae Oxonienses,* edited by Philip Bliss. 1813. Reprint. Hildesheim: George Olms Verlagsbuchhandlung, 1969.

Woodbridge, Linda. *Women and the English Renaissance: Literature and the Nature of Womankind, 1540–1620.* Urbana: Univ. of Illinois Press, 1984.

Woodforde, Samuel. MS B. MS Rawl. poet. 25. Bodleian Library, Oxford.

Woods, Susanne. "Aemilia Lanyer and Ben Jonson: Patronage, Authority, and Gender." *Ben Jonson Journal* 1 (1994): 15–30.

———. "The Body Pentitent: A 1560 Calvinist Sonnet Sequence." *ANQ: American Notes and Queries* 5, nos. 2–3 (1992): 137–40.

———. *Natural Emphasis: English Versification from Chaucer to Dryden.* San Marino, Calif.: Huntington Library, 1984.

———. "Vocation and Authority: Born to Write." In *Aemilia Lanyer: Gender, Genre and the Canon,* edited by Marshall Grossman, 83–98. Lexington: Univ. Press of Kentucky, 1998.

Wormald, Jenny. "James VI and I, *Basilikon Doron* and *The Trew Law of Free Mon-archies:* The Scottish Context and the English Translation." In *The Mental World of the Jacobean Court,* edited by Linda Levy Peck, 36–54. New York: Cambridge Univ. Press, 1991.

―――. *Mary Stewart: A Study in Failure.* London: George Philip, 1988.

Woudhuysen, Henry R. *Sir Philip Sidney and the Circulation of Manuscripts 1558–1640.* Oxford: Clarendon, 1996.

Wright, Stephanie. "The Canonization of Elizabeth Cary." In *Voicing Women: Gender and Sexuality in Early Modern Writing,* edited by Kate Chedgzoy, Melanie Hansen, and Suzanne Trill, 55–68. Pittsburgh: Duquesne Univ. Press, 1997.

Wriothesley, Charles. *A Chronicle of England During the Reign of the Tudors, from 1485 to 1559,* edited by William Douglas Hamilton. N.P.: Camden Society, 1875.

Wroth, Mary. *The Countess of Montgomeries Urania.* London, 1621.

―――. *The First Part of the Countess of Montgomery's Urania,* edited by Josephine A. Roberts. Binghamton, N.Y.: Center for Medieval and Renaissance Texts and Studies, 1995.

―――. *Love's Victory: The Penshurst Manuscript,* edited by Michael G. Brennan. London: The Roxburghe Club, 1988.

―――. *The Poems of Lady Mary Wroth,* edited by Josephine A. Roberts. Baton Rouge: Louisiana State Univ. Press, 1983.

Yates, Frances. *Astraea: The Imperial Theme in the Sixteenth Century.* London: Routledge and Kegan Paul, 1975.

Yciar, Juan de. *A facsimilie of the 1550 edition of Arte Subtilissima.* Translated by Evelyn Shuckburgh. London: Oxford Univ. Press, 1960.

Ziegler, Georgianna. "Hand-Ma[i]de Books: The Manuscripts of Esther Inglis, Early-Modern Precursors of the Artists' Book." *English Manuscript Studies* (forthcoming).

Zim, Rivkah. *English Metrical Psalms: Poetry as Praise and Prayer, 1535–1601.* Cambridge: Cambridge Univ. Press, 1987.

Index

abbess, 232
Abraham, 95–96
absolutism, xxvi, 125–26, 144–47, 151, 155
Aburgavennies, Frances, 170
Acheson, Katherine, xxn. 2
acrostic, 122
Adam, xxviii, 46, 63, 145, 155–56, 193, 197, 200–206
Adams, Robert, 130n. 22
Aeschines, 70, 72n. 34
aesthetics, xvii, 32–33, 142, 245
Agatha, Saint, 241
agency, women's, xviii–xix, 250, 252. See also subjectivity
Agrippa, Heinrich Cornelius, 201
Akrigg, G. P. V., 24–25
Alcides, 32
Alençon, Francis, Duc de la, 139n. 22
Alexander, 36, 73
Algar, King, 232
allegory, 96, 135
alliteration, 180
ambition, 83, 102, 110
amplification, 133
Amussen, Susan, 78, 185n. 13, 188n. 17
anagram, 209, 211
Andriolo, Karin, 223
androgyny, xxi, xxvi, 61, 74, 111, 209
Anger, Jane, xxviii, 196–98, 201–6
Anglican Settlement, 231, 235–37
Anguissola, Sofonisba, 36n. 36
Anne (queen of England) (wife to James I), 5, 24–25, 27, 38n. 1, 41–46, 142, 167
anti-Catholic propaganda, 122

anticourtier poets, 141–56
Antony, 51, 83n. 18
apocalypse, 120, 125
apprentices, 188
Aquinas, Saint Thomas. See Thomas Aquinas, Saint
Archer, Ian, 188
aristocracy, 77–80, 83–89, 93–97, 116–17, 145–47, 173, 186–87, 239–40, 249–50
Aristotle, 144, 147–48, 156
Armada, Spanish, 74, 122n. 7, 133
Armstrong, M. H., 102
ars moriendi, 15–16
Ars Poetica (Horace), 71
Arthois, Robert of. See Robert of Arthois
Ascham, Roger, xxiv, 61, 68–76
Askew, Anne, xxn. 2
Asshur, 136–37
astrology, 40n. 6
Athanasius, 90n. 30
Aubigné, Agrippa de, 30
Audeley, Baron. See Castlehaven, George Touchet, Baron Audeley and Earl of
audience, 198; female, xxvii, 41, 44, 49, 179, 191–92, 238–39
authorship, female, xvii, xx, xxiii–xxiv, 23, 105, 117, 157, 177–81, 195–97, 238
autobiography, 182
Aylmer, John (bishop), 69n. 29, 78, 107, 146

Babington, Gervase, 93, 96
Bacon, Sir Anthony, 23–24, 32–34
Bacon, Sir Francis, Lord Keeper, 73, 146

Baker, Richard, 219
Baldwin, T. W., 72n. 33
Bale, John, 121n. 5, 228
Bales, Peter, 23n. 6, 26
Balstone, Alice, 78n. 3
Barash, Carol, xxin. 5
Barbara, Saint, 226
Barbaro, Francesco, 63n. 8
Baring-Gould, S., 224–27
Barnes, Robert, 229
Barrell, John, 39n. 5, 52, 56
Barroll, Leeds, 38n. 2
barter, 4
Bassnett, Susan, 76n. 41, 146
Bax, Clifford, 104n. 4
Beal, Peter, 21n. 3, 28
Beales, Ross, 250n. 23
Beauchamp, Virginia, 10n. 17
Bedford, Lucy Harrington Russell,
    Countess of, 24–25, 27n. 19, 34, 44,
    167
Bedlam, 211–12
Beilin, Elaine, xviii, xx, xxv–xxvi, 14n.
    27, 39, 51n. 22, 83n. 18, 172, 193n. 2,
    199
Bell, Ilona, xxvii
Bell, Maureen, 196–97
Bell, Robin, 104–5
Belsey, Catherine, 3n. 1, 39n. 5, 103n. 3,
    142, 173n. 22, 197n. 10
Benson, Pamela, 78n. 3
Bergeron, David, 166n. 16
Berry, Boyd, 56n. 56
Bèze, Theodore de, 30, 89n. 28
Bible, 11–13, 17, 27–30, 33–36, 48–49,
    63, 72, 77, 85, 92, 199–200, 216, 240,
    245–46; as authority for women's
    inferiority, 193–94, 203–7. See also
    Old Testament
Binns, James, 35n. 34
Birch, Thomas, 159n. 11, 166n. 17
bishops, 6n. 10, 166, 229
Blair, John, 231n. 10, 236
Blayney, Peter W. M., 30n. 24
blazon, 109
Bodley, John, 131n. 24
Bodley, William, 131n. 24

body, female, xxviii–xxix, 109, 115, 189–90,
    204, 209, 237, 243, 251; mutilated, 241
body politic, 74, 144, 149, 234
Boleyn, Anne, 69n. 30
Bone, Quentin, 160n. 12, 166
bonfires (bone fires), 234
book, as cure for soul, 11
book burning, 210, 217
books (owned by women), 7–8
Borzello, Frances, 21n. 3, 36n. 36
Bothwell, James Hepburn, Earl of, 102n.
    2, 105n. 4, 114, 116n. 14
Bothwell, Jean Gordon, Countess of,
    102n. 2, 116n. 14
Bourchier, Lady, 186
Bourdieu, Pierre, 4
Bourg, Anne du. See Burgeus, Annas
Brackett, Virginia, 243n. 14
Bradbrook, Muriel, 38n. 2, 158n. 4
Bradstreet, Anne, 242–43, 250n. 23
Bradstreet, Simon, 243n. 14
Braithwaite, R. B., 182n. 8
Brantôme, Pierre de, 101n. 2
breast, 241–43, 249, 251
breastfeeding, xxix, 238–52
Brennan, Michael, 39n. 4, 79n. 6
Breton, Nicholas, 93, 195, 198
Brews, Margery, 9
Brose, Margaret, 144, 153
Brown, Ivor, 225n. 3, 228
Brown, Lyn, 65n. 14
Bruto, Giovanni Michele, 77
Bucer, Martin, 13, 89, 234
Buckingham, George Villiers, Duke of,
    158n. 4, 160n. 12, 169–70, 215–19
Buckingham, Katherine Manners Villiers,
    Duchess of, 160, 167–70
Bullinger, Heinrich, 150
Bullough, Vern, 225n. 3
Burgeus, Annas, 119–22, 126, 131–32,
    134–39
Burghley, William Cecil, Lord, 93n. 32
Burke, Kenneth, 51n. 22
Burke, Mary, xxi, xxv–xxvi, 14n. 26
Burnett, Mark, 3n. 2
Butler, Alban, 226, 231n. 10, 235–36
Byrne, Muriel St. Clare, 4, 186–87

Caesar. *See* Julius Caesar
Caesar, Sir Julius, 82n. 14
Cahn, Susan, 249n. 21, 251
Caiphas, 49
Calderwood, David, 107, 114n. 12
Calfhill, James, 235–37
calligraphy, 19–37
Calvin, John, 10–12, 69n. 28, 86, 88–91, 94, 96, 131n. 25
Calvinism, 24
Cambridge, 234
Cane, Earl of, 163, 166
canon, xvii, xxii, 120n. 3
capitalism, xxiii, 40, 43–44, 53, 57, 244
cardinal, 236–37
Cardinal College, 233
Carew, Mistress, prophet, 216
Carew, Richard, of Antony, 123
Carlisle, Lucy Hay, Countess of, 168
Carr, M. J., 231n. 10
Carr, R. D., 231n. 10
Cary, Anne, 159
Cary, Elizabeth, Lady Falkland, xixn. 2, xxii; *Edward II*, xxvi–xxvii, 157–73; *Tragedy of Mariam*, 9
Cary, Sir Henry, Lord Falkland, 157n. 2, 168
Cary, Lucy, 159
Cary, Mary, 159
Cary, Victoria, 159
Castlehaven, George Touchet, Baron Audeley and Earl of, 207–9, 213
Castlehaven, Mervin Touchet, Baron Audeley and Earl of, 213
Catherine, Saint, 232
Catherine de Bourbon, 23–24
Catherine de Medici (queen of France), 121n. 4, 129
Catherine de Navarre. *See* Catherine de Bourbon
Catherine of Aragon. *See* Katherine of Aragon
Catholic conspiracy, English fear of, 127, 129
Catholicism, 11n. 22, 24, 27n. 19, 30, 107, 110–11, 114, 157–59, 168–69, 172, 229, 231, 234–36; negative view of, 119–20, 127, 133–37

Catholic League, 22
Catholic mass, 13
Caxton, William, 45n. 14
Cecil, Sir Robert, 5, 23–24, 82n. 16
Cecil, William. *See* Burghley, William Cecil, Lord
Cecilia, Saint, 232
censorship, xxvi, 126
Chamberlain, Frederick, 230
Champernowne, Katherine, 61n. 3
Charles I (king of England), xxvi, 27, 34, 73n. 36, 158–60, 166, 168, 172, 210, 215n. 24
Charles II (king of England), 163, 210
Charles IX (king of France), 129
Chartellat, 113–14
Chartier, Roger, 36
chastity, 149, 205–6
Chaucer, Geoffrey, 195, 233
Cheke, Sir John, 61n. 3
childbirth, xxix, 4, 161, 170, 173, 238, 241–45
childrearing, 246, 250
chivalry, 103, 195, 198
choler, 82, 198
Christ, Jesus, 12–13, 44, 48–51, 133, 209, 212, 216, 226, 232
Christ Church College, 233–35
christening, 4
Christine de Pizan, 195
chronicle history, 157–73
Church of England, xxix, 22, 123–25, 166, 231; *Homilies*, 78, 150, 229–30
Cicero, Marcus Tullius, 25n. 13, 69, 72, 144
Cinderella, 46, 227n. 5
ciphers, 23
citizens, 187
Civil War, English, xxi, 52–53, 145n. 11, 156, 217
Clarke, Basil, 228–29
class, xviii–xix, xxi, xxiv–xxv, xxvii, 3n. 2, 6–8, 10, 13, 20, 108, 145, 173, 177–78, 182, 186–87, 191–92, 208, 214, 240, 251; women's, and patronage, 38–57; women's, and translation, 77–97
classics, 62, 64, 144, 147, 194
Cleaver, Robert, 245

Cleopatra, 51, 83n. 18
Clement VII (pope), 233
Cliffe, J. T., 123–24
Clifford, Anne. *See* Dorset, Anne
   Clifford, Countess of
Cline, Ruth, 233
Clinton, Arabella, 242n. 14
Clinton, Briget. *See* Lincoln, Briget Clinton,
   Countess of
Clinton, Elizabeth. *See* Lincoln, Elizabeth
   Knevet Clinton, Countess of
cloister, 229
Clothaire IV (king of France), 228
coat of arms, 213
Coiro, Ann Baynes, 38–39, 56n. 26
collaboration (by women), xxi
Collier, John Payne, 177–80, 183, 192
Collins, A. Jefferies, 6n. 9
Collins, An, xxn. 2
Collins, Arthur, 98n. 32
Collinson, Patrick, 10n. 17, 122n. 7, 124, 131
colonialism, xxii
commonplace book, 9, 25n. 13
commonplaces, 194n. 3, 201, 242n. 10
conduct books, 147–51, 191, 238, 245–47
conscience, 89, 116, 134, 240, 247–48
constitution, 128n. 21
constitutional theory, 122
controversy about women. *See* women,
   pamphlet controversy about
conversion, 125, 159, 169
cooking, xxiv
Cope, Anthony, 129
Cope, Esther, xx–xxi, xxvii–xxviii
copyright, 40
Cordell, Sir William, 80n. 9
Cornwallis, Sir William, 208
corona, 141–43, 147–49, 151–54, 156
coronation, 166, 172, 237
Cosins, John, 168
cosmetics, 65, 205
Cotgrave, Randle, 110
Cotton, John, 242
Counter Reformation, 110
country estate, 54
court, 187; Elizabeth's, 77, 81–83, 88;
   English, 27; factions, 90, 142–44, 149,

153, 157–73; Scottish, 103; Stuart, 238,
   241–45, 249
court entertainment, 25. *See also* masque
courtier, 77, 83–84, 87–89, 103, 142–44, 168
Court of Love tradition, 149
court poetry, 21, 103
courtship, 182n. 8, 186, 230
Coverdale, Miles, 13
Cowen, I. B., 105n. 4
Coxe, Dr. Richard, 61n. 3, 68
Coxhead, J. R. W., 131
Cranmer, Thomas (archbishop of
   Canterbury), 234
Crawford, Patricia, xviin. 1, 239n. 3,
   241n. 7 242n. 12, 249n. 22
Croiset van Uchelen, Anthony R. A., 34
Cromwell, Thomas, 229
cross-dressing, xxv–xxvi, 112, 118
Crowley, Robert, 184
crucifix, 226
crucifixion, 49–50, 226. *See also* passion
cultural studies, xvii–xx, xxiv, xxvii,
   xxix–xxx
culture (definition), xix, xxi; negotiation
   with, xvii, xix–xxi, xxiii–xxvii, 202;
   women producers of, 195
Cumberland, Margaret Cliford, Countess
   of, 38, 41–42, 50–56
Cupid, 143, 149–52
Cyprian, Saint, 72

Dakins, Margaret, 185
Daniel, 207–9, 216–17
Daniel, Samuel, 40, 83n. 18, 158, 162–63,
   171–72, 207–8, 216
Dante Alighieri, 85n. 25
Danville, M., 113
Darnley, Henry Stuart, Lord, 103, 107–8,
   112
David, 12–13, 17, 32, 36, 87n. 27, 89, 94,
   136, 154
Davidson, Edward, 242n. 10
Davies, Lady Eleanor, xx–xxii, xxviii; as
   prophet, 207–19
Davies, John, of Hereford, 25–26
Davies, Sir John, 207n. 1, 211, 214

Davies, Kathleen, 241n. 7

Davies, Lucy. *See* Huntington, Lucy Hastings, Countess of

Davis, Natalie Zemon, 3n. 2, 6, 10n. 20, 33, 139

Davis, Norman, 9

Deborah, 44, 51

declamation, 71

Dekker, Rudolf, 225

Delcourt, Marie, 225n. 2

Delehaye, Hippolyte, 226

Demosthenes, 69–72

Denbigh, Susan Villiers Fielding, Countess of, 160, 168–69

Denham, Henry, 178

Despenser, Hugh. *See* Spenser, Hugh de, and son

Devon, 121, 123–24, 127n. 18, 131

devotional treatises, 29, 45–46, 49–50

Dia, Countess of, 102

Diagnosta, 230

dialogue, 184, 195

diaries, 47, 182

Didanus, 231

Diefendorf, Barbara B., 29

discipline, 246–47

dissenters, 121, 126–29, 131–33, 139

divine right, 145. *See also* absolutism

divorce, 228n. 6

Dobbie, B. M. Wilmott, 173n. 23

Dolan, Frances, 238, 247n. 19

Dolce, Lodovico, 77

Dollimore, Jonathan, 39n. 5

Donaldson, Gordon, 102n. 2, 105n. 4

Donawerth, Jane, xxii–xxiii, 157

Donne, John, 82

Dorsannus, Jacob, 25n. 13

Dorset, Anne Clifford, Countess of, xxn. 2, 41–42, 44–48, 52–56, 168; diary of, 182

Dorset, Richard Sackville, Earl of, 42

Douglas, Sir Archibald, 207n. 2, 211, 213–14

Douglas, Lady Eleanor. *See* Davies, Lady Eleanor

Dove, Linda, xxv, xxvi, 10n. 18, 12n. 23, 115n. 13

Dowriche, Anne Edgcumbe, xx, xxii; *The French Historie*, xxvi, 119–40

Dowriche, Hugh, 122–25, 131n. 24

dowry, 9, 106, 186n. 15, 193, 200, 203–4

drama, Renaissance, 197n. 10, 227

dreams, 230

dream vision, 195

Du Bellay, Joachim, 102–3

Dudley, Guilford, 79

Dudley, John. *See* Northumberland, John Dudley, Duke of

Dudley, Robert. *See* Leicester, Robert Dudley, Earl of

Dudley, Thomas, 242n. 14

DuMoulin, Peter, 219

Dunbar, Alice, 225n. 3, 227, 231–33

Duncan-Jones, Katherine, 82n. 16

Dunn, Kevin, 36n. 37

Durkan, John, 103

ecclesiastical courts, 182

Eckenstein, Lina, 225n. 3, 227, 229

economics, xix, xxiv, xxix, 110, 116–17; and women, 40, 46, 48, 170, 182n. 10

Eden, 155–56

Edgcumbe, Honor, 123

Edgcumbe, Piers, 119–20, 122–23, 127

Edgcumbe, Richard, 122–23

Edgcumbe, W. H., 122n. 8

education, domestic, 186; for women, xxiv, 61–76, 123; in classics, 205, 208, 216

Edward I (king of England), 162

Edward II (king of England), xxvi–xxvii, 157–73, 231

Edward VI (king of England), 19, 65n. 12, 68, 79, 132n. 26, 234

Edwards, Gillian, 225–26, 228

Egerton, Stephen, 147

Egerton, Sir Thomas, 34

Eisenstadt, S. N., 8n. 14

Eisenstein, Elizabeth, 40

elect, 92

elegies, 89, 103

Elias, Norbert, 46n. 16

Elizabeth (daughter of James I), 43, 45

Elizabeth I (queen of England), xxii,
xxiv–xxvi, xxix, 5–6, 13, 16–17, 24–25,
38, 54, 61–62, 65–81, 101n. 1, 107, 113,
120, 125, 127–33, 137–39, 146, 150,
156, 159, 164, 181–83, 187–92, 229–37;
"The Mirror or Glass of a Sinful
Soul," 8n. 12; as potential patron, 19–
23, 34, 37; and Sidney *Psalmes*, 77–89,
92, 95; "To the Troops at Tilbury," 67,
74, 111–12; transfer of saint's qualities
to her, 223–25, 229–31, 233–37; as
Virgin Queen, xxvii, 78, 231, 237
Ellesmere, Sir Thomas Egerton, Lord, 25
Elliott, Vivien Brodsky, 182n. 8, 186n. 15
eloquence, 105, 214
Elsky, Martin, 29
Elton, G. R., 128n. 21, 208n. 3
Elyot, Sir Thomas, 144, 148, 150, 195–97
embroidery, xxiii–xxiv, 85, 88. *See also*
needlework
Emelina of Eddington, 232
Emerson, Ralph Waldo, 9n. 15
encomium, 93
English language, 17
Ephelia (pseud.), 197n. 11
epistle, 14–15, 20, 35, 43, 48, 120, 131n.
25, 150, 177–92, 197–98. *See also*
letters
epithalamion, 88
Erasmus, Desiderius, 62, 65, 143–44, 150;
Education of a Christian Prince, 147
erotics, 245, 250
Erskine, Elizabeth Norris, Lady, 25, 36
Essex, Robert Devereux, Earl of, 23–24,
27n. 19, 36, 80
Essex–Sidney faction, 27n. 19
Esther, 44
ethics, 69, 76, 179, 184–85, 191
Eucharist, 234
Evans, Austin, 234n. 14
Evans, Robert, 8n. 14, 38, 52
Eve, xxvii–xviii, 44, 46, 49–50, 63, 155, 161,
192n. 20, 209, 242, 244, 249; revisions of
by women writers, 193–206
examples, scriptural, 125, 132
exegesis, biblical, 209
Exeter, 130

Ezell, Margaret, xviin. 1, 3n. 1, 9n. 16,
103n. 3, 120–21, 157n. 1, 186, 239

Fage, Mary, 37n. 39
Fagius, Paul, 234
Fairfax, Thomas, Baron Fairfax of
Cameron, General, 210
faith, 12, 20–22, 93, 124, 226
Falkland, Lady Elizabeth. *See* Cary,
Elizabeth, Lady Falkland
family, 78; analogy to state, 143–49, 154
Farmer, David, 225n. 3, 228
Felch, Susan, xxn. 2, 10n. 18
Felski, Rita, 191
Fehrenbach, R. J., 177–80, 183, 188n. 18,
192
female legacy tracts. *See* mother's advice
manuals
feminism, 39, 43–44, 172, 177, 191–92, 202
feminist criticism, 194
feminist studies, xviii–xx
feminist theory, French, 121
Ferguson, Margaret, xxn. 2, 3n. 1, 103n.
3, 157–59, 173n. 22
Ferguson, Moira, xixn. 2
fetus, 242
feudalism, role of poet under, 40–42, 51,
54, 56
Fielding, Susan Villiers. *See* Denbigh,
Susan Villiers Fielding, Countess of
Fields, Barbara Jeanne, xxix
Fildes, Valerie, 239n. 3, 241n. 8, 243–44,
249–51
Filmer, Sir Robert, 145, 156
Finke, Laurie, 102, 194, 196n. 7
Fisken, Beth, 79n. 6, 88–89
Fitzherbert, Sir Anthony, 181
Flodden, Battle of, 62
food: circulation of as gift, 3–5, 7
Forman, Simon, 40n. 6
Fowler, Constance Aston, 9
Foxe, John, 13, 140, 235–37
France, 19–22, 24, 103, 119–40
Franco-Habsburg War, 67n. 21
Fraser, Antonia, 101n. 2, 103, 105n. 4,
112n. 10, 161

freedom of conscience, xxix, 239, 249

Freer, Coburn, 79n. 6

free speech movement, xxvi, 119–20, 126–28, 134–39

French, Kit, 223

friars, Franciscan, 230n. 8

Frideswide, St., xxix, 223–37

Friis, Christian (chancellor of Denmark), 25

Froude, James, 234–35

Frye, Susan, xxn. 2, 21n. 3, 23n. 6, 28n. 21, 73, 78n. 3

Fugger, Wolfgang, of Nuremberg, 29, 35

Fumerton, Patricia, 4, 8, 32n. 29

gambling, 4

Gardiner, Samuel Rawson, 185n. 14

Gaveston, Piers, 157–58, 170

Garber, Marjorie, 112

gender, xvii–xviii, xx–xxi, xxv–xxviii, 6, 20–21, 36–37, 40, 44, 49–50, 61–62, 64–67, 74–75, 78, 87n. 27, 102–3, 108–11, 114, 190–93, 196, 202, 208, 214, 226; as socially constructed, 194

Geneva, 10, 13, 22n. 5

Geneva Bible, 12, 22, 48, 83–87, 90–97, 135–38

genre, xvii, xxi, 48, 120, 122, 139, 173

gentry, 186–87, 190, 192

Geritz, Al, 223

Gethsemane, 49

Gideon, 136

gift-exchange, xx, xxii–xxiii, 3–18; on New Year's Day, 5–6, 8, 10–11, 13, 16, 19

Gilligan, Carol, 65n. 14

Gillis, John R., 182n. 8

Gilmore, Leigh, 209n. 9

Gledhill, Christine, xx

Goldberg, Jonathan, 23n. 6, 35–37, 144

Golding, Arthur, 8

"Good Husband, The" (ballad), 148n. 13

Goodare, Julian, 112

gossip, 211, 213

Gosynhill, Edward, 195–97

Gottlieb, Sidney, xxn. 2

Gouge, William, 145–48, 245–49

government (by consent), 126, 156, 162, 167; constitutional, 156; contract-based, 144, 148–49; ideal, 143–51, 154–56; ideal (compared to bees), 148–49

grace, 12–13

Grant, John, 224

Greek language, 61n. 3, 69–72

Greer, Germaine, xixn. 2

Gregorian calendar, 157n. 3

Gregory the Great (pope), 225

Gregory, C. A., 4

Gresham, Sir Richard, 229

Greville, Fulke, 80, 95n. 35

Grey, Lady Jane, 70, 76, 79, 90

Griffiths, John, 229, 267

Grindal, Edmund (bishop), 131n. 25, 235–36

Grindal, William, 61n. 3

Grossberg, Lawrence, xviii

Grossman, Marshall, 38n. 1.

Grundy, 159n. 9

Grymeston, Elizabeth, 170

Guillimeau, James, 242, 247

Gundersheimer, Werner, 45n. 14, 52n. 23

Guy, John, 130n. 23

gynecology, 241n. 8, 243n. 14

Hackett, Thomas, 178

Hake, Edward, 178–83, 188, 192

Hall, David, 246n. 17

Hall, Joseph, 27

Hall, Kim, xxiin. 6, 77n. 1, 157–58

Hamilton, Donna, 126n. 17, 142n. 4

Hampton, Timothy, 132

Hannah, 245

Hannay, Margaret, xxn. 2, xxiv–xxv, 12n. 24, 16n. 29, 17, 25, 56n. 26, 103n. 3, 158n. 5, 167n. 18; Silent But for the Word, 3n. 1

Hardy, Thomas Duffus, 233

Harrington, William, 150

Harris, Barbara, 8n. 13, 182n. 7, 185n. 13

Harrison, William, 185

Hartley, T. E., 128

Harvey, Gabriel, 84–85

Haselkorn, Anne, 103n. 3, 169n. 20
Hastings, Lucy. *See* Huntington, Lucy
    Hastings, Countess of
Hebrew, 90, 94, 96
Heiborne, Captain, 113
Heilbrun, Carolyn, 65n. 14
Henault, John, Earl of, 163–66, 171
Henderson, Katherine Usher, xixn. 2,
    72n. 34, 193n. 1, 196n. 7, 239n. 4
Hendricks, Margo, xxii, 77n. 1
Henri II (king of France), 29, 120, 133–34,
    137–39
Henri III (king of France), 5, 22, 29
Henri IV (king of France), 22, 24
Henri de Navarre. *See* Henri IV
Henrietta Maria (queen of England),
    xxvi–xxvii, 159–62, 166–67, 172
Henry I (king of England), 233
Henry VI (king of England), 73n. 36
Henry VII (king of England), 228
Henry VIII (king of England), 19, 61–62,
    65, 69n. 30, 231–33
Henry, Prince of Wales (son of James I),
    24–28, 151
Hensley, Jeannine, 243n. 14
Herbert, George, 84n. 19
Herbert, Mary Sidney. *See* Pembroke,
    Mary Sidney, Countess of
Herbert, Philip. *See* Montgomery, Philip
    Herbert, Earl of
Herbert, Susan de Vere, Lady, 25
Herbert, William. *See* Pembroke, William
    Herbert, Earl of
Hercules, 179
heresy, 131–34, 234–36
hermaphrodite, 226–27
hermeneutics, 132
hero (female), 51, 143n. 6, 159, 166;
    godly, 131; Protestant, 137
Herod, 133, 139
Herrup, Cynthia, 213n. 19
Herz, Judith Scherer, 39n. 5
Hester. *See* Esther
Heylyn, Peter, 219
Hezekiah, 12–13, 154
Hibbert, Christopher, 61n. 3, 70
High Commission, 209, 216
Hilkiah, 135–36

history (as example), 132; by women,
    119–40; writing, xxvi, 158
Hit-him-home, Joan (pseud.), 196, 200–206
Hobby, Elaine, xxin. 5, 3n. 1, 158n. 5,
    173n. 22, 182n. 10, 208n. 7, 241n. 10
Hoby, Lady Margaret, 185n. 14
Hogrefe, Pearl, 3n. 1, 10n. 19, 16n. 29,
    103n. 3
Holdsworth, William, 181n. 5
Hole, Christina, 231n. 10
Holinshed, Raphael, 62n. 5, 126
Holmes, Michael Morgan, 56n. 26
Holtzknecht, Karl, 42n. 9
Homer. *See Iliad*
Horace. *See Ars Poetica*
horsemanship, 26
Horstmann, Carl, 231n. 10
Hosea, 136
Houthusius, Jacobus, 34n. 32
Howard, Charles (lord high admiral),
    82n. 16
Howell, James, 215n. 25
Hubert, Francis, 158, 162–63
Hughes, Paul, 66–67, 70
Hughey, Ruth, 90n. 29
Hugh-Jones, Stephen, 4
Huguenots, 21–22, 25, 29, 125, 130–33, 139
Huldah, 136
Hull, Suzanne W., xviin. 1, 3n. 1, 103n.
    3, 191
humanism, xxiv, 4, 14–16, 29, 37–39, 62,
    71, 75, 103, 110, 132, 143–44, 147, 150,
    195, 241–42, 246–49
Hume, David, 37
Humphrey, Caroline, 4
Humphrey, Susan, 243n. 14
Hungerford, John, 110, 112, 114
Hunsdon, Henry Carey, Baron, and Lord
    Chamberlain, 40n. 6, 47
Huntington, Lucy Hastings, Countess of,
    xx, xxviii, 185, 212–13, 215–19
Huntly, George Gordon, Earl of, 111, 116
Hurstfield, Joel, 182n. 8
Hutchinson, Anne, 246
Hyde, Lewis, 8n. 14
hypertext, xviii, 121, 139
Hyrde, Richard, 63–64
hyssop, 12

identity, performance and, 164, 166, 171
ideology, 40–41, 48, 52–53, 57, 125–26,
    182n. 10, 193, 206, 231, 241–42; con-
    straining women, xvii, xx, xxiv–xxv,
    xxviii–xxx; reformation, 119, 124, 135
Iliad (Homer), 36
illegitimacy, 47, 52, 61
illuminated manuscript, xxiii, 21, 33
imagery, courtly, 86; maternal, 66–67;
    nature, 86; tongue, 91
imitation, 71
imperialism, xxii
Inglis, Esther, xxii, 8n. 12, 19–37
Ingram, Martin, 181–82, 187–88
Inns of Court, 180
invective, 199
Iragaray, Luce, 18
Ireland, 213
Irish, 92–93
Isabel (queen of England), xxvi, 157–73
Isabella (queen of Spain), 62, 64n. 10
Isocrates, 71–73

Jael, 44
James I (king of England), xxvi, 5, 21–27,
    72–73, 82, 158–60, 242n. 10; and
    absolutist politics, 141–47, 151–55
James VI (king of Scotland). *See* James I
Jardine, Lisa, 3n. 1, 72n. 33, 84–85, 103n. 3
Jardine, M. D., 40, 52–53
Jaster, Margaret Rose, 6n. 9
Jeanneret, Michel, 22n. 5, 29–30
Jeffrey, William, 32
Joceline, Elizabeth Brooke, 170, 239
Johnston, John, 34, 37
Jones, Ann Rosalind, xxn. 2, 3n. 1, 14,
    103–4, 115, 141n. 1, 143n. 7
Jonson, Ben, 8n. 14, 38n. 2; *Masque of
    Blackness*, 25
Jordan, Constance, 76n. 42, 77–78, 103n.
    3, 105, 110, 144–45, 154, 156
Joseph, 245
Josiah, King, 136
Joubert, Laurent, 242n. 11, 245
Juan (king of Spain), 62n. 4
Judeo-Christian tradition, 207
Judgment Day, 207, 209

Judith, 44, 51
Julius Caesar, 71
Justice of the Peace, 182n. 7
Juvenal, 196n. 8

Kahn, Coppélia, 52
Kaminsky, Howard, 46
Katherine of Aragon (queen of England),
    62–63, 66, 233
Kaufman, Gloria, 67
Kelley, Donald, 132n. 26
Kellie, Thomas Erskine, Earl of, 25
Kello, Bernard, 23–24
Kelly, Joan, xxi
Kempton, Dan, 223
Kendall, Ritchie, 121n. 5
Kenilworth, 80
Kennedy, Gwynne, 157–58
Kenny, Anthony, 234n. 14
Kent, Susan, Countess of, 42, 45
King, John, 90n. 29, 223n. 1
King, Margaret, 78n. 5
King's Evil. *See* scrofula
king's favorites: dangers of, 158, 167,
    170–71
Kinnamon, Noel, 25n. 13, 79n. 6, 84n. 19
Klein, Joan Larsen, 78n. 4
Klein, Lisa, 3n. 2, 6, 18, 21n. 3, 33n. 31,
    37n. 39
Knightley, Sir Richard, 124
Knightley, Valentine, 124, 127
Knox, John, 10, 63n. 8, 78n. 5, 101, 111–12,
    114n. 12
Ko, Yu Jin, 223
Koehler, Lyle, 247n. 18
Kohl, B. G., 63n. 8
Koon, Helene, 243n. 14
Krontiris, Tina, xxn. 2, 3n. 1, 8n. 14, 44,
    48, 50n. 20, 103n. 3, 143n. 6, 164n. 15;
    on Aemilia Lanyer, 38–39
Kummerniss, Saint. *See* Uncumber, Saint

ladies-in-waiting, 8n. 14, 16, 88–89, 168,
    233
Lamb, Mary Ellen, xxii–xxiv, 3n. 1, 103n.
    3, 143n. 6, 173n. 22

Lambe, John, 215
Lange, Thomas, 22n. 5
Langlois, Nicholas, 21–22
Languet, Hubert, 96
Lanyer, Aemilia, xixn. 2, xxii–xxiv; *Salve Deus Rex Judaeorum*, 38–57
Lanyer, Alphonso, 47
Lanyer, Henry, 47
Larkin, James F., 66–67, 70
Latimer, Hugh, 13
Latin language, xxii, 34–35, 61–62, 65, 69–72, 125–31, 179, 181–82
Laud, William (archbishop), 210, 212, 217
Law French, 181
Lee, Maurice, 24n. 11
Leicester, Robert Dudley, Earl of, 79–81, 90, 124
Leigh, Dorothy, 160–61, 239, 243, 246
leprosy, 12n. 24, 232
L'Estrange, Hamon, 215, 219
L'Estrange, Roger, 219
letters, 3–4, 9–10, 14–15, 80–82, 126, 166–69, 238. *See also* epistle
Letter Sent by the Maydens of London, A xxii, xxvii, 177–92
Levin, Carole, xxn. 2, xxi, xxviii–xxix, 6n. 9, 10n. 17, 78n. 3, 107n. 5
Lewalski, Barbara, xxn. 2, 25, 27n. 19, 46–47, 50n. 21, 79n. 6, 143, 157–58, 167n. 18; on influence of Bible, 29–30; on Aemilia Lanyer, 39–40
Lewis, C. S., 123n. 10
Leyland, A., 233
Libanus Gallus, 123
Liberata, Saint. *See* Uncumber, Saint
Liberatrix, Saint. *See* Uncumber, Saint
liberty, women's, 177–92
Lincoln, Briget Clinton, Countess of, xxix, 238–52
Lincoln, Elizabeth Knevet Clinton, Countess of, xxix, 238–52
Lisle, Robert Sidney, Viscount, 16, 26, 82n. 16
Lisle Letters, 4, 18, 185–87
literacy, xxviii, 182
literary communities, xxiii
literary tradition, xix
livery, 86

Livius, Titus, 72
Livrade, Saint. *See* Uncumber, Saint
Loach, Jennifer, 73n. 36
Loades, David M., 67–68
Lock, Anne Vaughan. *See* Lok, Anne
Lockyer, Roger, 160n. 12
Lok, Anne, xxn. 2, xxii–xxiii, 10–13
London, 13, 16, 21, 23, 130, 177–79, 182–89, 192, 228–29
love (as disease), 15
Love, Harold, 27–28
lower class, 240; definition, 185
Luecke, Marilyn, xxviii–xxix
lute, 25n. 12
Lutes, Jean Marie, 241n. 7, 243n. 14, 250n. 23
Lutherans, 133–35
Lynch, Michael, 103, 105n. 4

Machiavelli, Nicolo, 72n. 35, 121n. 4
Mack, Phyllis, xxin. 5, 208n. 7, 240n. 5
Maclean, Ian, 194n. 3, 200–201
magistrates, 93–95
magnificat, 211
Mahl, Mary, 243n. 14
Mainwaring, George, 14
Maisto, Adam, 157
Maisto, John, 157
Maisto, Susanna, 157
male gaze, 109
Manaton, Ambrose, 122n. 8
Manaton, Anne Edgcumbe Trefusis, 122n. 8
Manners, Cecily Tufton, 169
manuscript publication by women, xviin. 1, xxiii, 3, 9, 16, 19–37
March, John, 208n. 6
Marcus, Leah, 66n. 14, 69, 111
Marguerite de Navarre, 8
Marian exiles, xxii
market economy, 249–50
Marlowe, Christopher, 158, 162–63
Marot, Clément, 30
Marotti, Arthur, 8, 40n. 7. 43n. 12, 102, 142
marriage, 4, 9, 25, 62, 67–68, 74, 78, 80, 102n. 2, 114, 106–8, 117, 123n. 9,

160n. 12, 187, 200, 209–11, 225, 230–31, 237, 244, 250; as analogy to state, 145–47, 150–56; age of, 186; arranged, 79; arranged (critique of), 103, 116, 118; companionate, 143, 146, 149–56, 201; forced, 114; politics of, xxvi; theory of, 143–51; women's right to choose, 178, 181–82
marriage contract, 182
marriage license, 182n. 8
marriage manual, 184
Marshall, Dr. (dean of Christ's Church), 234–35
Martin, Randall, xixn. 2, 121n. 4
Martin Marprelate tracts, 121n. 5, 124
Martyr, Catherine Dummartin, xxix, 234–37
Martyr, Peter, 234, 237
martyrs, xxix, 13, 50–51, 126, 139–40, 226, 241
Martz, Louis, 48–49
Mary I (queen of England), xxii, xxiv–xxvi, 6–7, 10, 17, 79, 110, 132n. 26, 231, 233–34; rhetoric of, 61–71, 73–76
Mary (queen of Scots), xxi, xxv, 5, 12n. 25, 22n. 5, 128–30, 164; Sonnets, 101–18
Mason, Roger, xxii
masque, 85, 112, 166. See also court entertainment
Massachusetts Bay Colony, 242–43
Masten, Jeff, 141n. 2
materialism, xviii–xix, xxii, xxviii–xxix, 250
Matthew, Sir Toby, 82n. 16
Matthews, John Hobson, 82n. 15
Mattingly, Garrett, 62n. 6
Maundy Thursday, 231
Maurice of Nassau (prince), 23–24, 30, 32–36
Mauss, Marcel, 4–6, 9, 33n. 31
May, Stephen, 83n. 17
Maydens of London. See Letter Sent by the Maydens of London, A
Mayr-Harting, Henry, 233
maxims, 14–15. See also proverbs
McBride, Kari Boyd, 38n. 2, 44–45
McCutcheon, Elizabeth, 5n. 6

McGrath, Lynette, 45n. 15
McLaren, Dorothy, 162n. 13
McManus, Barbara, xixn. 2, xxvii–xxviii, 64n. 11, 72n. 34, 239n. 4
Mead, Rev. Joseph, 159, 166
Meads, Dorothy M., 185n. 14
medicine, 3–5, 11–15, 17–18, 239; herbal, xxiii
Melanchthon, Philip, 72
Melville, Andrew, 34–35
men's roles: civic, 64n. 11
menstruation, 242
merchant class, 10
metaphor, 87, 91–93, 147, 202, 205, 237
meter, 180
Michaud, M. M., 24n. 11
Michieli, Giovanni, 67
Middle Ages, 223, 226, 231, 233
middle class, 240, 251
migration to London, 187–88
Mildmay, Lady Grace, xixn. 2
Miller, Edwin Haviland, 39–43
Miller, Naomi, xxn. 2, 50n. 20, 143n. 6
minions. See King's favorites
Mirror for Magistrates, The, 154, 158n. 4
miscarriage, 112
miscellanies, 14
misogyny, 241
Moffet, Thomas, 93, 148–49
monarchy (limited), 126, 151, 155
monastery, 232
monopolies, 75
Montagu, Walter, 168
Montaigne, Michel de, 226
Montenay, Georgette de, 27
Montgomery, Philip Herbert, Earl of, 25
Montgomery, Susan de Vere, Countess of, 36
More, Christopher, 186
More, Edward, 195
More, Elizabeth, Lady Wolley, 5
More, Sir Thomas, 150, 225n. 3, 228
Morgan, John, 248
Mornay, Philippe de, Discours de la Vie et de la Mort, 25, 83–84, 90
Mortimer, 158, 163–64
motherhood, xxvi, xxviii–xix, 64, 161–63, 207–9, 212–13, 219, 238–52

mother's advice manuals, xxvi, 14n. 27, 157–73, 238–52
mother's role, 146, 151–55, 160–61, 173
Mountjoy, Charles, 64–65
Mountjoy, William, 65
Mueller, Janel, 50n. 20
Munda, Constantia, xxviii, 195–96, 199, 201–3
Murphy, Terence, 229n. 8
Murray, Sir David, 26, 28n. 20

narrative, 50
narrative poem, 119
Nashe, Thomas, 84–85
Neale, J. E., 73n. 37, 128–30, 190
Nebuchadnezzar, 137n. 33
needlework, 5–7, 17–18, 28, 33n. 31, 37n. 39, 62, 64, 111
Neely, Carol Thomas, 195n. 7
Neill, Michael, 35
Neilson, William, 149n. 14
Nelson, Cary, xviii
Nelson, Karen, xxv–xxvii, 14n. 26
Netherlands, 22, 129
Newcomb, Lori Humphrey, xxviin. 7, 6n. 9
New Historicism, xviii, 40
New Jerusalem, 13
Newstead, Christopher, 204–5
Newton, Judith, xviii, 39n. 5
Nicholas, Edward, 170
Nichols, John, 6–7
nightingale: as symbol of poet, 53
nobility, 241
noblesse oblige, 92
nonconformist. See dissenters
Northumberland, Henry Percy, Earl of, 6
Northumberland, John Dudley, Duke of, 79, 90
nuns, 4, 234–35

Old Testament, 133, 136, 207, 245
Olivétan, Robert, 33
Oman, Carola, 160n. 12
Ong, Walter, 29, 70
Ontkommer, Saint. See Uncumber, Saint

oration, 134–35, 137, 235
oratory, 62, 65, 69, 126. See also declamation
Ormonde, Earl of, 93, 168
Otten Charlotte, 239n. 2
Oxford, 13, 223, 231–35

painting, 62n. 4
pamphlet controversy. See women, pamphlet controversy about
Parfitt, George, 196–97
Parker, James, 231n. 10, 233
Parker, Matthew, 87, 235
Parker, Patricia, xxii, 77n. 1
Parliament, 67, 73, 119–29, 133–39, 190, 211–15, 230; role of in ideal government, 153–54
parody, 180–81
Parr, Catherine (queen of England), 8, 65
passion, Christ's, 48–51
Paster, Gail, 242n. 13, 250
Paston, John, III, 9
patriarchy, 39, 66, 106, 120–21, 143–45, 153–56, 189, 200n. 16, 213–14, 239–41, 245–48
patronage, xxii–xxiv, 8, 10, 14n. 26, 16, 22, 25–28, 33–57, 82, 103, 108–9, 167–68
patron saint, 223, 229
Patterson, Annabel, 126
Paul, Saint, 63, 107, 109, 125, 131n. 25, 146
Paynell, Thomas, 68n. 26
pedagogy, 61–76
Pelagius, 123
Pembroke, Henry Herbert, Earl of, 80–82, 96–97
Pembroke, Mary Sidney, Countess of, xxn. 2, xxii–xxv, 7, 10, 18, 39n. 4, 41–42, 45, 56n. 26, 142, 148, 167; "Even now that Care," 16–17; Psalmes, 12, 30, 77–97
Pembroke, William Herbert, Earl of, 10, 81
Penshurst, 79
Perkins, William, 124
persona, 199

personification, 54
Petrarch, xxv, 104, 144, 150
Petrarchism, 141–42, 153
Philip II (king of Spain), 17, 67–68, 74, 76, 133
Philip of Macedon, 70
Phillips, James, 105n. 4
Phillips, John, 194n. 3
pilgrimage, 232–33
piracy, 70
Philomela, 53
Pilate, 133
Pistoia, Domenico Bruni da, 78
Pizan, Christine de. See Christine de Pizan
Place, Pierre de la, 126n. 15
plague, 15
Plat, Hugh, 14
Plato, 70–71
Platonic love, 56n. 26
Pléiade, 103
Plowden, Alison, 105n. 4
Pocock, J. G. A., xxii
poems: as gifts, 3–18
poet: as servant, 55; as spiritual guide, 51
Pole, Cardinal Reginald, 234–35
political advancement, 162
political influence, through network, 167–70
political theory (Tudor and Stuart), xxvi
politics (men's), 158; religious, xxiii, xxvi–xxvii. See also women, and politics
Pollard, A. W., 207
Pollock, Linda, xixn. 2
popular culture, xviii, xxvii
Porter, Roy, 209n. 8
portraits, 21n. 2, 31, 35–36, 169; self, xxiii
postmodernism, 240, 249
poststructuralism, 194n. 4
poulter's measure, 120, 123
Powell, C. L., 161
prayer, 13, 82, 90, 138, 233
preaching, 123–24, 180, 242n. 10
pregnancy, 4, 112, 161–62, 233, 241
Presbyterianism, 129
Prescott, Anne, 89
Prescott, H. F. M., 66–68
Presot, Marie, 21

Price, Daniel, 26
primogeniture, 161
print culture, xxiii–xxiv, 3, 10, 29, 33, 40–44, 57, 194; women published in, xvii, xxiii–xxiv, 178, 191
printing press, 124
Prior, Mary, 208n. 5
Prometheus, 72n. 35
prophecy, 136–37, 207–19; female, xxi, xxviii
Protestant Alliance, 80
Protestantism, xxiii, xxvi, xxix, 10, 13, 17, 22–26, 29–30, 35, 69n. 28, 91, 110–11, 114, 122–25, 130–32, 143, 147, 150, 160n. 12, 172, 199n. 12, 225, 228–31, 236, 241–42; militant, 17, 95, 129
Protestants, persecution of, 120; England as sanctuary for, 19, 21; use of psalms with theme of justice, 90
proverbs, 72. See also maxims
providence, 125, 132, 139, 243
Psalms, 10–13, 16–17, 21, 26–30, 36, 56n. 26, 77–97, 123
psalter, 7, 95. See also Sternhold-Hopkins Psalter
pseudonyms, 178, 183, 195–96, 198, 239
Puckering, Thomas, 25–26
pun, 13
Puritans, xxvi, 27, 119–31, 135–36, 139, 241–42
Purkiss, Diane, 157n. 1, 208n. 7
Pybrac, Guy du Faur de, 22, 24n. 9, 26, 30

Quaker women, 121
queens, xxi, xxiv–xxv, xxvii, 45–46, 66–67, 88–89, 101–18, 157–73, 231n. 10; and self-fashioning, 164; source of power through sons, 160–62
querelle des femmes. See women, pamphlet controversy about
Quinlan, Todd, 223

race, xviii, xxii, 77n. 2
Radegund, Saint, 228–29
Raleigh, Sir Walter, 54
Ramus, Peter, 125n. 15

Randolphe, Thomas, 108, 111, 114
rape, 114–16, 213–14
Rappaport, Steve, 187
Raylor, Timothy, 149
readers, female. *See* audience, female
reading practice, 45, 47–50, 72, 132
real presence (debate on), 13
recovery of texts (by women writers),
     xix, xxi
Redgrave, G. R., 207n. 2
Reformation, xxix, 119, 122–25, 129–31,
     223, 229–30
reformed Christians, 19–21, 73, 234–36.
     See also dissenters
regicide, 164
relics, 3–4, 18, 232–36
religion: and social distinctions, 44
religious controversy, 158
religious discourse, 199–200, 240
religious meditation, 17, 29–30, 48–52
religious politics, 13, 17, 120, 124
Rémond, Florimond de, 236
reproduction, 238, 242–43; as role of
     queen, 162
republican government (theory), 149
resistance, 119–40
rhetoric, xxvii, 21, 41, 47, 54, 62n. 5, 69,
     73–75, 81, 103–4, 132, 142, 145–46,
     153, 170–71, 183–84, 194, 198, 239–40,
     244–45; legal, 180–81; scriptural, 122
Rienstra, Debra, 79n. 6
Riou, Mme. de, 4
Robert of Arthois, 163–66, 171
Roberts, Josephine, xixn. 2, 141n. 2,
     145n. 11, 149n. 15
Robertson, Karen, xxn. 2, 6n. 9, 223
Robertson, Mary, 219n. 38
Robinson, Richard, 42n. 11
Roche, Thomas, 10, 141n. 1
Roche Chandieu, Antoine de la, 22, 26
Rogers, Daniel, 247
Rohan, Catherine de Parthenay,
     Vicomtesse de, 23–24
Rohan, Henri, Duc de, 23–24
Rollock, Robert, 34
romance, 68
romantic heroine, 105n. 4

Roniger, Louis, 8n. 14
Ronsard, Pierre de, 102–3
Roper, Margaret More, 76
Rose, Mary Beth, 239n. 3, 246n. 17
Rosenfelt, Deborah, xviii, 39n. 5
Rowse, A. L., 38n. 2, 47n. 18, 51n. 22
ruler, female, 101, 225
Rudyard, Sir Benjamin, 166
Ruether, Rosemary, 241n. 9
rumor, 81–82, 127

Sackville, Sir Richard, 70.
Saint Bartholomew's Day Massacre, 29,
     120n. 2, 126, 129, 131
Saint Paul's Church, 228–29
saints, female, xxi, xxix, 223–37
saints' lives, 223, 225–26, 229
Salter, H. H., 231n. 11
salvation, 13, 202
Samyn, Peter, 82
Sanderson, William, 215–19
Sankovitch, Tilde, 103n. 3
Sappho, 193
Sarah, 245
sarcasm, 203
satire, 14n. 27, 84, 179, 181–83
Saul, 89
Saveuses, Anthoinette de, 4
Schiffer, James, 227
Schleiner, Louise, xxn. 2, 84n. 19, 142n.
     5, 152n. 17, 157–59
Schnell, Lisa, 39n. 43
Schnucker, R. V., 173n. 23, 241n. 8
Schochet, Gordon, 144, 156
Schrift, Alan, 9n. 26
Schucking, Levin, 246n. 16
Schulenberg, Jane, 225n. 3, 241n. 10
scold. *See* shrew
Scotland, xxii, xxvi, 19–24, 101–18, 213
Scott-Elliot, A. H., 21n. 3, 27, 35
scribes. *See* calligraphy
scrofula, 231, 233
Scudamore, Lord, 213
Scylla and Charybdis, 72n. 35
sedition, 124
Seeff, Adele, 5n. 8

self-fashioning, 69, 75, 199

Seneca, 4, 8, 14n. 27

sermons, 12–13, 21, 26, 93, 124–25, 235

Serres, Jean De, 125n. 15

servants, 5, 13

service, ideal of, 52–56; language of, 109–10; contract, 189

serving women, xxii, xxvii, 42, 177–92

sexual orientation, xviii

Seymour, Jane (queen of England), 4, 61n. 1

Shakespeare, William: *Hamlet*, 126; *Henry VIII*, 62n. 5; *Macbeth*, 227; *Richard II*, 154–55; *Sonnets*, 142

Sharp, Ronald, 3n. 2

Shepherd, Simon, 193n. 2, 196–97

shrew, 196, 203

Shrewsbury, George Talbot, Earl of, 22n. 5

Shrewsbury, Mary Talbot, Countess of, 5, 9

shrines, 223, 231–37

Shuger, Debora, 242n. 10

Sidney, Sir Henry, 79–80, 85n. 23, 92–93, 113

Sidney, Mary. *See* Pembroke, Mary Sidney, Countess of

Sidney, Lady Mary Dudley, 16, 79–80, 85n. 23, 89

Sidney, Sir Philip, 16–17, 102, 149; *Astrophil and Stella*, 141–42, 152; *Psalmes*, 25–27, 30, 80–83, 86, 89–97

Sidney, Robert. *See* Lisle, Robert Sidney, Viscount

Sidney-Herbert alliance, 10n. 21, 17, 25, 90

silver plate (as currency), 8, 16, 33n. 31

Simpson, W. Sparrow, 228

sin, 202

Sinfield, Alan, 39n. 5

Skeeters, Martha, 223

Skura, Meredith, 169n. 21

slander, 208

Smith, Hilda, 192, 241n. 8

Smith, Paul, 40

Smith, Sir Thomas, 29, 146–47

smock, 8

Smuts, Malcom, 166n. 16

social change, xx, 178, 191–92

social mobility, 188

Socrates, 68, 71

sodomy, 213

Solomon, 88–89, 94

Somerset, Anne, 22, 61n. 3, 67, 69n. 28, 74, 233n. 13

Somerset, Robert Carr, Earl of, 27

Sommerville, J. P., 148n. 12

sonnets, xxi, xxvi, 9–13, 32n. 29, 101–18, 141–56

Sophocles, 72

Sowernam, Esther, xxviii, 193–96, 199–205

Spain, 129

Speght, Rachel, xxviii, 196–205

Spence, Lewis, 227n. 5

Spenser, Edmund, 89

Spenser, Hugh de, and son, 157–58, 163–67, 170–72

Spiller, Michael, 141n. 1

spiritual bouquet, 14n. 26

spy, 89, 165; network (Robert Cecil's), 23–24

Stallybrass, Peter, 3n. 1, 5n. 7, 103n. 3, 115

Stanton, Richard, 231, 233

stationers, 194

Stationers Company, 178

Steen, Sara Jayne, xxn. 2, 5n. 8

Steinberg, Theodore, 94

Stenton, F. M., 231n. 11

Stephen, James Fitzjames, 159n. 8

Sternhold-Hopkins Psalter, 30, 84, 123

Stewart-MacKenzie-Arbuthnot, Mrs. P., 102n. 2

Stewart, Mary. *See* Mary, Queen of Scots

Stone, Lawrence, 40, 185

Strong, Roy, 24n. 8, 26, 223n. 1

Strype, John, 236

Stuart, Lady Arbella, xxn. 2, 5, 9, 44

Stuart, Mary. *See* Mary, Queen of Scots

Stubbes, Philip, 85

Stubbs, John, 130n. 22

Sturley, Frideswide, 233

Sturm, Johann, 72

style, 72, 102n. 2, 134, 183, 196n. 9, 198
subjectivity, xxvii–xxviii, 52, 78, 104,
    109, 118, 141–43, 192–206, 245n. 15,
    250–52
subjects (duties of), 125
succession, royal, 119, 161
Suffolk, Catherine Knyvett, Countess of,
    42
Suffolk, Catherine Willoughby Bertie,
    Duchess of, 10–11, 13
Sullivan, Patricia, xxn. 2, 223
sumptuary law, 84n. 20
Susanna, 44
Sussex, Thomas Radcliffe, Earl of, 80
Sutcliffe, A., 169n. 20
Swetnam, Joseph, 194–96, 199–205
Sylvester, Joshua, 25n. 14
Syon, Mount, 83

table talk, 194
tabula rasa, 246
Taffin, Jean, 10n. 21
Talbot, Mary. See Shrewsbury, Mary
    Talbot, Countess of
Tattle-well, Mary (pseud.), 196, 200–206
Taylor, John, 196–97
Teague, Frances, 74–75, 111
theater, 185–86
Thecla, Saint, 226
theology, 194, 200, 216–17, 234, 243n. 14;
    medieval, 241
theory, political, 143–51
Thickstun, Margaret, 242n. 12
Thomas Aquinas, Saint, 69n. 28
Thomson, Patricia, 43n. 12
Thomson, T., 112
Throkmorton, Job, 119, 121, 124, 127,
    129–30, 134, 139
Tilney, Edmund, 78, 146
Todd, Margo, 144n. 8, 146, 150n. 16,
    241n. 7, 248n. 20
Todd, Richard, 79n. 6
topos, 200
Toste, R., 115
Touchet, Eleanor. See Davies, Lady
    Eleanor

translation, 17, 33, 42, 71, 77, 83, 92–96,
    126, 131n. 25, 181, 210, 216
transvestism, 227
Travitsky, Betty, xixn. 2, 3n. 1, 5, 8n. 12,
    12n. 25, 65n. 16, 102–4, 158n. 5,
    169n. 20, 173, 239n. 2; on Aemilia
    Lanyer, 38n. 2; on Isabella Whitney,
    14n. 26;
Trease, G. E., 123n. 11
treason, 159
Tregian, Elizabeth, 122
Treichler, Paula, xviii
Trinterud, Leonard, 127–28
Troeltsch, Ernst, 144, 155
troubador, 102
Tudor, Edward. See Edward VI
Tudor, Elizabeth. See Elizabeth I
Tudor, Henry. See Henry VIII
Tudor, Mary. See Mary I
Tullie. See Cicero, Marcus Tullius
Tyler, Margaret, 37
Tymme, Thomas, 125–26, 131–37, 139
tyranny, 90, 130–33, 136, 145, 148–49,
    154–55; domestic, 50

Udall, Nicholas, 65n. 15
Ulrich, Laurel Thatcher, 173n. 23
Ulysses, 72n. 35
Uncumber, St., xxix, 223–37
upper class, 208, 214. See also nobility
usurper, 163
Utley, Francis Lee, 178n. 3
utopia, 102

Valentine's Day, 9
van de Passe, Simon, 85
van de Pol, Lotte, 225
van Dorsten, Jan, 80n. 10
Vatablus, Franciscus, 89
Veevers, Erica, 160n. 12
Venus, 149
Vermigli, Peter Martyr, 234
Vickers, Nancy, 109n. 7
virginity, xxvii–xxviii, 223, 225, 231, 241
Virgin Mary, 49, 211–12, 223, 242, 245n. 15

Virgin Queen. *See* Elizabeth, as Virgin Queen
Vives, Juan Luis, xxiv, 37n. 39, 76, 105, 110, 112, 144, 150; as tutor of Mary Tudor, 61–69, 71–73
voice, public (for women), xxiv, 252
Vosevich, Kathi, xxi, xxiv–xxv

Wakefield, Walter, 234n. 15
Waldman, Milton, 61n. 1, 63n. 8
Walker, Julia M., 76n. 40
Walker, Kim, 21n. 3, 37n. 39
Wall, J. Charles, 231n. 10
Wall, Wendy, xxn. 2, 3n. 1, 14n. 27, 16n. 28, 37n. 39, 44, 50n. 20, 170
Waller, Gary, 16–17, 143n. 6
Walsingham, Sir Francis, 93n. 32
wards, 182n. 8
Warner, Marina, 242
Watson, Foster, 62–65, 68
Wayne, Valerie, 39n. 5, 78n. 5
Weiner, Seth, 94n. 34
Weir, Alison, 65n. 12, 76n. 42
Weller, Barry, xxn. 2, 157–59
Welles, E. B., 63n. 8
Wells, Robin, 223n. 1
Wentworth, Peter, xxvi, 119, 121, 127–28, 130, 134, 139
wetnurses, xxix, 64, 238, 240–44, 247, 250–51
Whalley, Richard, 186
Whateley, William: *Bride-Bush*, 50
Whigham, Frank, 46, 52n. 23, 54
White, Allan, 116n. 14
White, Micheline, 120n. 2, 123n. 12
Whitney, Isabella, xxii–xxiii, xxx, 10, 13, 37n. 39, 185, 192; *A Sweet Nosgay*, xvii, 14–16
widows, 181–82, 214, 230
Wiesner, Merry E., 186n. 15
wife abuse, 223, 229
Wilgeforte, Saint. *See* Uncumber, Saint
Williams, Franklin B., 25n. 14, 39n. 4
Williams, Raymond, xix, xxi, xxiii
Williams, Robert, 21n. 3, 23n. 6
Williamson, Marilyn, xxin. 5, 197n. 11, 206

Willis, Michael, 223
Willoughby, Catherine, Duchess of Suffolk. *See* Suffolk, Catherine Willoughby Bertie, Duchess of
Wilson, Adrian, 241n. 8
Wilson, Elkin Calhoun, 223n. 1
Wilson, Katharina, 74–75
Wilton House, 82, 93
Wing, Donald, 207n. 2
Winter, Sir Edward, 82n. 16
Winthrop, John, 242n. 14
wit, 195, 203, 239
witches, 227
Witt, R. E., 63n. 8
Woddes, Michael, 228
Wolley, Lady Elizabeth. *See* More, Elizabeth, Lady Wolley
Wolsey, Thomas (cardinal), 233
woman, ideal: chaste-silent-obedient, xxiv, xxvii–xxviii, 3, 61–65, 69, 76–78, 103, 113–18, 173, 179, 191, 212; *not* chaste-silent-obedient, 184–85
woman question, 195. *See also* women, pamphlet controversy about
women: as commodities, 117; creating culture, xviii; defined by sexuality, 105n. 4, 113; as educators, 173; have greater capacity for sexual pleasure, 204; have sexual insatiability, 227; and law, 177–92, 209, 252; pamphlet controversy about, xxi, xxvii–xxviii, 177–206, 239; and politics, xxii, xxv–xxvii, 94, 104, 110, 116, 120, 127, 132, 146, 157–73, 217; in print, 193; as victims, 117
women's rights, 177–92
women's studies, 240
Wood, Anthony, 236n. 17
Woodbridge, Linda, 103n. 3, 193–94
Woodforde, Samuel, 86
Woods, Susanne, xixn. 2, 12n. 24, 46, 56, 79n. 6; on Aemilia Lanyer, 38–39
working class, 13
Wormald, Jenny, 105n. 4, 145n. 10
Wotton, Thomas, 25–26
Woudhuysen, Henry R., 21n. 3, 23n. 6, 25–26

Wright, Stephanie, 157–58
Wright, William Aldis, 68n. 27
Wriothesley, Charles, 229
writing: social prohibitions against, xxiii, 3
Wroth, Lady Mary, xixn. 2, xxii, 37, 193;
    "Pamphilia to Amphilanthus," xxvi,
    141–56; *Urania*, 9, 141; *Love's Victorie*,
    152n. 17
Wyatt's Rebellion, 66, 74
Wycliffe, John, 19, 234n. 14

Xenophon, 72n. 34

Yates, Frances, 223n. 1
Yciar, Juan de, 29
Yeo, Elspeth, 21n. 3, 27, 35

zeal, 91, 120, 125, 127; inseparable from
    politics, 124
Zenobia, 195–97
Ziegler, Georgianna, xxii–xxiii, 8n. 12,
    223
Zim, Rivkah, 79n. 6
Zion, Mount. *See* Syon, Mount